Intercultural
Communication

Intercultural Communication
Globalization and Social Justice

KATHRYN SORRELLS

California State University, Northridge

Los Angeles | London | New Delhi
Singapore | Washington DC

Los Angeles | London | New Delhi
Singapore | Washington DC

FOR INFORMATION:

SAGE Publications, Inc.
2455 Teller Road
Thousand Oaks, California 91320
E-mail: order@sagepub.com

SAGE Publications Ltd.
1 Oliver's Yard
55 City Road
London EC1Y 1SP
United Kingdom

SAGE Publications India Pvt. Ltd.
B 1/I 1 Mohan Cooperative Industrial Area
Mathura Road, New Delhi 110 044
India

SAGE Publications Asia-Pacific Pte. Ltd.
33 Pekin Street #02-01
Far East Square
Singapore 048763

Acquisitions Editor: Matthew Byrnie
Editorial Assistant: Stephanie Palermini
Production Editor: Brittany Bauhaus
Copy Editor: Megan Markanich
Typesetter: C&M Digitals (P) Ltd.
Proofreader: Gail Fay
Indexer: Rick Hurd
Cover Designer: Bryan Fishman
Marketing Manager: Liz Thornton
Permissions Editor: Adele Hutchinson

Printed in the United States of America

Library of Congress Cataloging-in-Publication Data

Sorrells, Kathryn.
Intercultural communication: globalization and social justice/Kathryn Sorrells.

p. cm.
Includes bibliographical references and index.

ISBN 978-1-4129-2744-4 (pbk.)

1. Intercultural communication. 2. Globalization—Social aspects. 3. Social justice. I. Title.

HM1211.S65 2013
303.48'2—dc23   2011039058

This book is printed on acid-free paper.

11 12 13 14 15 10 9 8 7 6 5 4 3 2 1

Brief Contents

Detailed Contents

3 Globalizing Body Politics: Embodied Verbal and Nonverbal Communication
51

4 (Dis)Placing Culture and Cultural Space: Locations of Nonverbal and Verbal Communication
75

5 Crossing Borders: Migration and Intercultural Adaptation 99

6 Jamming Media and Popular Culture: Analyzing Messages About Diverse Cultures 125

7 Privileging Relationships: Intercultural Communication in Interpersonal Contexts   149

8 The Culture of Capitalism and the Business of Intercultural Communication   175

9 Negotiating Intercultural Conflict and Social Justice: Strategies for Intercultural Relations   201

10 Engaging Intercultural Communication for Social Justice: Challenges and Possibilities for Global Citizenship   227

Glossary   251

Index   263

About the Author   289

Preface

Purpose of the Text

I wrote *Intercultural Communication: Globalization and Social Justice* with the goal of creating a new kind of introductory text for the undergraduate intercultural communication course that would provide students with critical and social justice perspectives on the dynamics of globalization that have brought so many people and cultures into contact and conversation. I want to help students understand and grapple with the interconnected and complex nature of intercultural communication in the world today. Students in my intercultural communication courses are clearly affected in direct and indirect ways on a daily basis by the forces of globalization. Their lives, livelihoods, and lifestyles are influenced in both challenging and beneficial ways by the forces of globalization—through rapid advances in communication and transportation technologies as well as changes in economic and political policies locally and globally. Globalization has catapulted people from different cultures into shared physical and virtual spaces in homes, in relationships, in schools, in neighborhoods, in the workplace, and in political alliances in unprecedented ways.

CULTURE IS DYNAMIC AND MULTIFACETED

Central to this text is the idea that our understanding of culture must be dynamic and multifaceted to address the fast-paced, complex, and often contradictory influences that shape intercultural communication today. The advantage of this approach is that it reflects a world that students will recognize as their own: a world in which notions of culture are fluid, not static. Therefore, this text aims to move beyond the basic distinctions between international and domestic U.S. communication issues to also highlight the many connections between local and global issues. To help students better understand the challenges and complexities of intercultural communication in the global context, I have also drawn attention to histories of intercultural conflict and the role power plays on macro- and micro-levels in intercultural relations. Thus, my aim in writing was to produce a text as vibrant, multifaceted, conflicting, and creative as intercultural communication itself!

Intercultural Communication: Globalization and Social Justice is built around these key concepts:

- A globalization framework
- A critical, social justice approach
- An emphasis on connections between the local/global and micro-, meso-, and macro-levels
- An emphasis on *intercultural praxis*

A Globalization Framework

Globalization provides a ubiquitous and complex context for studying intercultural communication. The context of globalization is characterized by an increasingly dynamic, mobile world and an intensification of interaction and exchange among people, cultures, and cultural forms; a rapidly growing global interdependence leading to shared interests and resources as well as greater intercultural tensions and conflicts; a magnification of inequities both within and across nations and cultural groups with significant impact on intercultural communication; and a historical legacy of colonization, Western domination, and U.S. hegemony that continues to shape intercultural relations today. Studying intercultural communication in the context of globalization allows us to highlight the following:

- Definitions of culture that address cultural continuity, contestation, and commodification
- Intercultural dimensions of economic, political, and cultural globalization
- Role of power and the impact of asymmetrical power relations on intercultural communication
- Rapid movement of people, cultures, verbal and nonverbal languages, and rhetoric through interpersonal and mediated communication
- Multifaceted, hybrid, and negotiated cultural identities
- Resignification of identity categories such as race, culture, and gender today
- Changing nature of intercultural relationships and intercultural alliances
- Culture of capitalism and the commodification of culture
- Intercultural conflict through a multidimensional framework
- Dynamic intercultural alliances and movements for social justice

A Critical Social Justice Approach

This text takes a critical social justice approach that provides a framework to create a more equitable and socially just world through communication. In the context of globalization, finding solutions to local and global challenges inevitably requires intercultural communication. Today, some of the most innovative answers to difficult social, political, and economic problems develop through intercultural alliances. And, regrettably, some of the most egregious injustices—exploitation of workers in homes, fields, and factories and violence perpetrated through racial profiling and ethnic cleansing—are performed within intercultural contexts and are enabled by intercultural communication. Today, we face many intercultural challenges—for example, wealth disparity in the United States and globally and the percentage of people in the world living under the poverty line have become steadily worse in the new millennium. It is my hope that this text will not only help students develop a deeper understanding of the opportunities and challenges of intercultural communication today but also empower students to use their knowledge and skills to confront discrimination and challenge inequities.

Over the past year, I have had the honor and privilege of working directly with Reverend James M. Lawson Jr., a close associate of Dr. Martin Luther King Jr. and leading architect of the civil rights movement, on the Civil Discourse and Social Change Initiative at California State University, Northridge (CSUN). Reverend Lawson's deep regard for all humanity, his appreciation of cultural differences, and his unwavering respect for the power of intercultural alliances stem from and are informed by his years of work in India in the 1950s, his leadership in the civil rights movement, his efforts to dismantle racism and sexism, and his efforts to gain living wages for workers and equal rights for lesbian, gay, bisexual, and transgender (LGBT) communities. We all have the opportunity to use the knowledge, attitudes, and skills gained by studying and practicing intercultural communication to build relationships, imagine possibilities, and develop alliances to create a more equitable and socially just world.

Local/Global Connection and Multilevel Framework of Analysis

Life in the globalized 21st century is characterized by a complex web of linkages between the local and the global as well as the past and present. People—and their languages, identities, cultural practices and ideas—are based in particular geographic locations, but they are also simultaneously connected—whether through communications technology (e.g., phone, e-mail, social media), interpersonal networks (e.g., friends, family), and memories with different locations around the globe.

Studying intercultural communication in the context of globalization requires us to pay attention to continuities and fragmentations of global communities over time and place.

For example, globalization links the distant towns of Villachuato, Mexico, and Marshalltown, Iowa, though global flows of capital, goods, and labor. A meatpacking plant in Marshalltown employs many Mexican workers, who return regularly to Villachuato for annual religious events, weddings, and funerals. Like many towns across the United States and Mexico, the lives of people from Villachuato and Marshalltown are intertwined and interdependent in the global context. Intercultural connections do not necessarily require travel to forge links across the globe. For example, diasporic Indian communities in the United States and around the world enjoy watching Hindi films and keeping up on the latest popular culture from India. Much more than entertainment, these experiences of cultural consumption educate younger generations born outside of India about their culture, serve as cultural bridges across time and place, and play a role in developing their bicultural identities. Of course, global intercultural links are not solely positive. The roots of many intercultural conflicts happening today can be linked to historic transgressions and involve communities that are interconnected around the globe.

In this text, key concepts in intercultural communication—identity construction; the use of verbal and nonverbal communication; the creation and re-creation of cultural spaces; interpersonal relationships; as well as migration, adaptation, and intercultural conflict—are addressed in ways that underscore the connections and disjuncture between the local and the global and the relationships between the past and the present. A multilevel framework that focuses attention on three interrelated levels—(1) the micro (individual level), (2) the meso (intermediate, group-based level), and (3) the macro (broad economic–political level)—is introduced and applied to various case studies throughout the text to examine the complexities of intercultural communication in the context of globalization.

Intercultural Praxis

This text engages students in a process of critical, reflective thinking and acting—what I call intercultural praxis—that enables them to navigate the complex, contradictory, and challenging intercultural spaces they inhabit interpersonally, communally, and globally. At all moments in our day—when we interact with friends, coworkers, teachers, bosses, and strangers; when we consume pop culture and other entertainment; when we hear and read news and information from the media outlets; and in our daily routines and travel—we have the opportunity to engage in intercultural praxis. The purpose of engaging in intercultural praxis is to raise our awareness, increase our critical analysis, and develop our socially responsible action in regard to intercultural interactions in the context of globalization.

Through six interrelated points of entry—(1) inquiry, (2) framing, (3) positioning, (4) dialogue, (5) reflection, and (6) action—intercultural praxis uses our multifaceted identity positions and shifting access to privilege and power to develop our consciousness, imagine alternatives, and build alliances in our struggles for social responsibility and social justice. The focus on intercultural praxis is intertwined with the content of the text from initial discussions of culture in the global context to explorations of our identities and finally in our roles as global citizens.

ORGANIZATION OF THE TEXT

This book offers an innovative approach to address the rapid, complex, and often contradictory forces that propel and constrain intercultural communication in the context of globalization.

A fundamental goal of the book is to understand and analyze intercultural communication on three interlocking and interrelated levels: (1) the micro, individual level; (2) the meso, cultural group level; and (3) the macro, geopolitical level. I think of it as breathing in and breathing out. As we breathe in, we focus our attention on individual levels of communication and then, breathing out, we expand to the broader levels of cultural group and macro-level intercultural communication issues. This metaphor helps my students understand the movement between levels from chapter to chapter as well as the connections that are made throughout the text between the past and the present. My goal is to encourage and support a way of thinking and being in the world that accounts for multiple frames of reference—like zooming in and zooming out on a Google map—across place and time.

Given that certain topics—language use, nonverbal communication, and cultural identity, for example—are so central to and interconnected with all facets of intercultural communication, these areas are addressed throughout the text in all chapters rather than isolated within stand-alone chapters. The organization of this text, therefore, highlights the many interconnections that define intercultural communication while also offering complete coverage of all topics commonly addressed in an introductory intercultural communication text.

PEDAGOGICAL FEATURES OF THE TEXT

A number of special features appear in each chapter of this text to encourage reflection and to move theory into practice for teachers and students of intercultural communication.

Engaging Textbox Features Highlight the Challenges and Rewards of Intercultural Communication

- **Communicative Dimensions Boxes** allow students to explore vivid examples of intercultural communication in action to see how different facets of communication—language use, nonverbal communication, rhetoric, and symbolic representation—play out in the global intercultural context.
- **Cultural Identity Boxes** help students understand how communication and culture shape and reflect identity and in turn how identity plays a role in communicating within and across cultures.
- **Intercultural Praxis Boxes** emphasize ways of developing our awareness and using our power to enable more equitable and socially just relationships across different cultures by engaging in dialogue, reflecting, and taking informed action.

ANCILLARY MATERIAL

In addition to the text, a full array of ancillary website materials for instructors and students is available at **www.sagepub.com/sorrells**. The password-protected site contains a test bank, PowerPoint presentations, sample syllabi, lecture notes, course projects, video links, and web resources. These ancillaries further support the goals of critical reflection, engaged learning, and informed action for social change presented in *Intercultural Communication: Globalization and Social Justice*.

Acknowledgments

A book like this, while written by one person, could not have been imagined or completed without the critical and creative contributions of many. I particularly want to thank my colleagues Sheena Malhotra and Bill Kelly for their careful reading and rereading of each chapter. Sheena's insightful comments and encouragement, her examples that illustrate subtlety and ambiguity, and her feedback from using chapters in her classes all enriched the text tremendously. Bill's breadth of knowledge of literature in the field and his search for a balanced middle ground were very helpful. I benefited greatly from hours of conversation with Gordon Nakagawa and Breny Mendoza who, each in their own way, had a hand in guiding the critical theoretical approach of the book. Much gratitude goes to my former undergraduate and graduate student and now Assistant Professor Sachi Sekimoto, who provided invaluable research and editorial assistance and developed the discussion questions and activities at the end of the chapters. Hengameh Rabizadeh, also a former graduate student, carefully edited every word and provided research assistance for the text. I also want to acknowledge both of my parents, Daniel Jackson Sorrells and Eleanor Kathryn Sorrells, whose love for learning and cultures continues to inspire me. Their memory is inextricably bound to this book as they both passed away during the research and writing of the text.

The team at SAGE deserves many thanks for all their support, patience, and sustained effort. Todd Armstrong, my editor throughout much of the project, and Matthew Byrnie, who brought it to fruition, each believed in the importance of the project and offered valuable guidance. The thoughtful assistance of Aja Baker, Nathan Davidson, and Elizabeth Borders made this project possible. I want to thank Megan Markanich for her careful editing of the book. Finally, I am grateful to Brittany Bauhaus and Liz Thornton for bringing the book into the world!

The book was much improved by the encouragement, insights, critical comments, and suggestions offered by the reviewers. I would like to thank Andy O. Alali (California State University, Bakersfield), Nilanjana Bardhan (Southern Illinois University, Carbondale), Devika Chawla (Ohio University), Daniel Chornet Roses (Saint Louis University, Madrid Campus), Robbin D. Crabtree (Fairfield University), Melissa L. Curtin (Southern Illinois University, Carbondale), Alexa Dare (The University of Montana), Sara DeTurk (University of Texas at San Antonio), Jane Elvins (University of Colorado, Boulder), Gloria J. Galanes (Missouri State University), Rebecca S. Imes (Carroll College), Peter Oehlkers (Salem State College), Ruma Sen (Ramapo College of New Jersey), and Curtis L. VanGeison (St. Charles Community College).

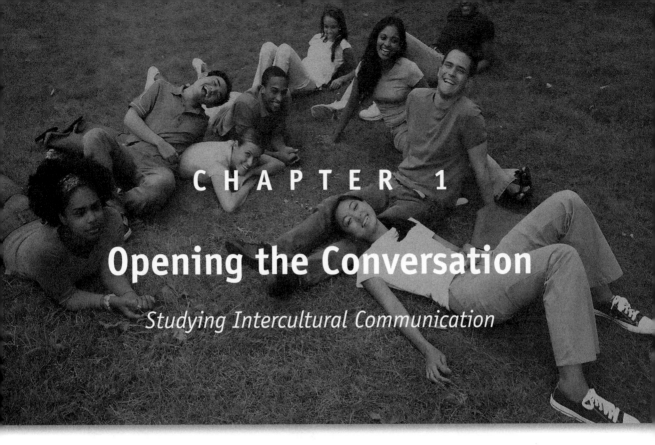

CHAPTER 1

Opening the Conversation

Studying Intercultural Communication

What creates positive intercultural interactions?

We, the people of the world—nearly 7 billion of us from different cultures—find our lives, our livelihoods, and our lifestyles increasingly interconnected and interdependent due to the forces of globalization. Changes in economic and political policies, governance, and institutions since the early 1990s have combined with advances in communication and transportation technology to dramatically accelerate interaction and interrelationship among people from different cultures around the globe. Deeply rooted in European colonization and Western imperialism, the forces of this current wave of globalization have catapulted people from different cultures into shared physical and virtual spaces in the home, in relationships, in schools, in neighborhoods, in the workplace, and in political alliance and activism in unprecedented ways.

Today, advances in communication technology allow some of us to connect with the world on wireless laptops sitting in the backyard or in our favorite café. While about 30% of the world's people wake up each morning assured of instant communication with others around the globe (Internet World Stats, 2011), about 50% of the world's population live below the internationally defined poverty line, starting their day without the basic necessities

Source: Chapter-opening photo © Comstock Imagesg/Comstock/Thinkstock.

of food, clean water, and shelter (Global Issues, 2010). Through the Internet, satellite technology, and cell phones, many of the world's people have access to both mass media and personal accounts of events and experiences as they unfold around the globe. However, in this time of instant messages and global communication, about 775 million or 1 out of 5 young people and adults worldwide do not have the skills to read (Richmond, Robinson, & Sachs-Israel, 2008). Today, advances in transportation technology bring families, friends, migrants, tourists, businesspeople, and strangers closer together more rapidly than ever before in the history of human interaction. Yet some have the privilege to enjoy intercultural experiences through leisure, recreation, and tourism, while other people travel far from home and engage with others who are different from themselves out of economic necessity and basic survival.

People from different cultural backgrounds have been interacting with each other for many millennia. What makes intercultural communication in our current times different from other periods in history? The amount and intensity of intercultural interactions; the degree of intercultural interdependence; the patterns of movement of people, goods, and capital; and the conditions that shape and constrain our intercultural interactions distinguish our current context—the context of globalization—from other periods in history. Consider the following:

- About 214 million people live outside their country of origin (International Organization for Migration, n.d.).
- U.S. cultural products and corporations—films, TV programs, music, and Barbie, as well as McDonalds, Walmart, Starbucks, and Disney—saturate the world's markets, transmitting cultural values, norms, and assumptions as they dominate the global economy (Yúdice, 2003).
- "Minorities, now roughly one-third of the U.S. population, are expected to become the majority in 2042, with the nation projected to be 54 percent minority in 2050. By 2023, minorities will comprise more than half of all children" (U.S. Census Bureau, 2008).
- According to U.S. Treasury data, in June 2011, $4.49 trillion in U.S. Treasury securities were owned by foreign banks with China, the biggest buyer of U.S. Treasury debt, holding $1.15 trillion (Crutsinger, 2011).
- In a *New York Times* op-ed article, columnist David Brooks (2005) wrote " . . . while global economies are converging, cultures are diverging, and the widening cultural differences are leading us into a period of conflict, inequality and segmentation."
- The gap between the wealthy and the poor is increasing within countries and around the world. The wealth of the top 1% in the United States has doubled in the past 20 years. One percent of the population in the United States owns more than the bottom 90% of the population (Lui, Robles, Leondar-Wright, Brewer, & Adamson, 2006).
- After the attacks of September 11, 2001, former president Bush proclaimed that "they" were attacking "our" culture, our way of life. Who is "us" and who is "them"? How are these categories constructed?
- At the beginning of the new millennium, open conflict between ethnic groups and the use of force by governments against nonstate groups has increased (Eller, 1999).

Clearly, cultural interaction is occurring. And intercultural communication matters. The goal in writing this book is to position the study and practice of intercultural communication within the context of globalization. This enables us to understand and grapple with the dynamic, creative, conflictive, and often inequitable nature of intercultural relations in the world today. This book provides theories, conceptual maps, and practical tools to guide us in asking questions about, making sense of, and taking action in regard to the intercultural opportunities, misunderstandings, and conflicts that emerge today in the context of globalization. Throughout the book, intercultural communication is explored within this broader political, economic, and cultural context of globalization, which allows us to foreground the important roles that history, power, and global institutions—political, economic, and media institutions—play in intercultural communication today.

This first chapter is called "Opening the Conversation" because the relationship between you, the readers, and me, the author, is a special kind of interaction. I start the conversation by introducing various definitions of culture that provide different ways to understand intercultural communication today. Then, some of the opportunities and challenges of studying intercultural communication are addressed by introducing positionality, standpoint theory, and ethnocentrism. This chapter ends with a discussion of intercultural praxis. As we "open the conversation," I invite you to engage with me in an ongoing process of learning, reflecting, and critiquing what I have to say about intercultural communication and how it applies to your everyday experiences.

DEFINITIONS OF CULTURE

Culture is a concept that we use often yet we have a great deal of trouble defining. In the 1950s, anthropologists Clyde Kluckhohn and Arthur Kroeber (1952) identified over 150 definitions of culture. Culture is central to the way we view, experience, and engage with all aspects of our lives and the world around us. Thus, even our definitions of culture are shaped by the historical, political, social, and cultural contexts in which we live. Historically, the word *culture* was closely linked in its use and meaning to processes of colonization. In the 19th century, European anthropologists wrote detailed descriptions of the ways of life of "others," generally characterizing non-European societies as less civilized, barbaric, "primitive," and as lacking "culture." These colonial accounts treated European culture as the norm and constructed Europe as superior by using the alleged lack of "culture" of non-European societies as justification for colonization. By the beginning of WWI, nine tenths of the world had been colonized by European powers—a history of imperialism that continues to structure and impact intercultural communication today (Young, 2001).

The categorization system that stratified groups of people based on having "culture" or not, with the assumption of the superiority of European culture, translated within European societies as "high" culture and "low" culture. Those in the elite class, or ruling class, who had power, were educated at prestigious schools, and were patrons of the arts such as literature, opera, and ballet, embodied **high culture.** Those in the working class who enjoyed activities such as popular theater, folk art, and "street" activities—and later movies and television—embodied **low culture.** We see remnants of these definitions of culture operating today. Today, the notion of culture continues to be used in some situations to stratify groups based on the kinds of activities people engage in, reinforcing beliefs about superior and inferior cultures. Over the past 50 years, struggles within academia and society in general have legitimized the practices and activities of common everyday people, leading to the use of **popular culture** to refer to much of what was previously considered low culture. However, in advertising, in media representations, and in everyday actions and speech, we still see the use of high and low cultural symbols not only to signify class differences but also to reinforce a cultural hierarchy. The growing and overwhelming appeal and consumption of U.S. culture around the world, which coincides with the superpower status of the United States, can be understood, at least partially, as a desire to be in proximity to, to have contact with, and to exhibit the signs of being "cultured."

Anthropologic Definition: Culture as a Site of Shared Meaning

The traditional academic field of intercultural communication has been deeply impacted by anthropology. In fact, many of the scholars like Edward T. Hall (1959), who is considered the originator of the field of intercultural communication, were trained as anthropologists. In the 1950s, Edward T. Hall, along with others at the Foreign Service Institute, developed training programs on culture and communication for diplomats going abroad on assignment. Hall's applied approach, focusing on the micro-level of human interaction with particular attention to nonverbal communication and tacit or out-of-awareness levels of information exchange, established the foundation for the field of intercultural communication (Rogers, Hart, & Miike, 2002).

Clifford Geertz, another highly influential anthropologist, emphasized the pivotal role symbols play in understanding culture. According to Geertz, culture is a web of symbols that people use to create meaning and order in their lives. Concerned about the colonial and Western origins of anthropology, he highlighted the challenges of understanding and representing cultures accurately. Anthropologists engage in interpretive practices that, for Geertz, are best accomplished in conversation with people from within the culture. In his widely cited book, *Interpretation of Culture*, Geertz (1973) said culture "denotes an historically transmitted pattern of meaning embodied in symbols, a system of inherited conceptions expressed in symbolic forms by means of which men communicate, perpetuate and develop their knowledge about and attitudes towards life" (p. 89).

Culture, then, from an anthropological perspective, is **a system of shared meanings** that are passed from generation to generation through symbols that allow human beings (not only men!) to communicate, maintain, and develop an approach and understanding of life. In other words, culture allows us to make sense of, express, and give meaning to our lives. Let's look more closely at the various elements of this definition.

At the core of this definition is the notion of symbols and symbol systems. **Symbols** stand for or represent other things. Words, images, people, ideas, and actions can all be symbols that represent other things. For example, the word *cat* is a set of symbols (the alphabet) that combine to represent both the idea of a cat and the actual cat. A handshake—whether firm or soft, simple or complex—a raised eyebrow, a hand, a finger, a veil, a tie, or bling are all symbolic actions that carry meaning. An image or an object like the

U.S. flag, a T-shirt with the image of Che Guevara on it, or the Golden Arches are also symbols that stand for ideas, beliefs, and actions. How do we know what these and other symbols represent or what they mean? Are the meanings of symbols somehow inherent in the things themselves, or are meanings assigned to symbols by the people who use them? While the meaning of symbols may seem natural or inherent for those who use them, the anthropological definition that was previously offered indicates that it is the act of assigning similar meanings to symbols and the sharing of these assigned meanings that, at least partially, constitutes culture.

The definition by Geertz (1973) also suggests that culture is a system. It is a system that is expressed through symbols that allow groups of people to communicate and develop knowledge and understanding about life. When we say culture is a system, we mean that the elements of culture interrelate to form a whole. The shared symbols that convey or express meaning within a culture acquire meaning through their interrelation to each other and together create a system of meanings. Consider this example: As you read the brief scenario that follows, pay attention to what you are thinking and feeling.

Imagine a young man who is in his mid to late 20s who works at a job making about $70,000 a year. OK, what do you think and how do you feel about this man? Now, you find out that he is single. Have your thoughts or feelings changed? For the majority of students like you in the United States, the picture of this man and his life is looking pretty good. Generally, both female and male students from various cultural backgrounds in the classroom think and feel positively about him. Now you find out that he lives at home with his parents and siblings. Have your thoughts or feelings about him changed? Without fail, when this scenario is used in the classroom, an audible sigh of disappointment comes from students when they learn that he lives with his parents. What's going on here? How does this information contradict or challenge the system of meaning in the dominant U.S. culture that was being created up to that point? This young man, who was looking so good, suddenly plummets from desirable to highly suspect and, well, according to some students "weird," "strange," and "not normal." The dominant U.S. culture is a system of shared meanings that places high value and regard on individualism, independence, consumerism, and capitalism, which are symbolically represented through the interrelated elements of income, age, sex/gender, and in this case living arrangements. Students in the classroom who ascribe to the dominant cultural value system ask questions like the following: Why would he want to live at home if he has all that money? Is he a momma's boy? What's his problem? Does he have low self-esteem? Others, operating from similar assumptions, suggest that he might be living at home in order to save money to buy a house of his own. In other words, he may be sacrificing his independence temporarily to achieve his ultimate (and of course, preferable) goal of living independently.

After the disappointment, disbelief, and concern for this poor fellow has settled down, I often hear alternative interpretations from students who come from different cultural backgrounds or who straddle multiple cultural systems of meaning-making. The students suggest that "he lives at home to take care of his parents," or that "he likes living with his family," or "maybe that's just the way it's done in that culture." These students' interpretations represent a different system of meaning-making that values a more collectivistic than individualistic orientation and a more interdependent than independent approach to life.

The students who do speak up with these alternative interpretations may feel a bit ambivalent about stating their interpretation because they realize they are in the minority and yet they have no problem making sense of the scenario. In other words, the scenario is not viewed as contradictory or inconsistent; rather, it makes sense. My purpose in giving this example at this point is to demonstrate the ways in which culture operates as a system of shared meanings. The example also illustrates how we—human beings—generally assume that the way we make sense of things and the way we give meaning to symbols is the "right," "correct," and often "superior" way. One of the goals in this book is to challenge these ethnocentric attitudes and to develop the ability to understand cultures from within their own frames of reference rather than interpreting and negatively evaluating other cultures from one's own cultural position.

In summary, a central aspect of the anthropological definition of culture is that the patterns of meaning embodied in symbols that are inherited and passed along through generations are assumed to be shared. In fact, it is shared meaning that constitutes culture as a unit of examination in this definition of culture. The cultural studies definition of culture from a critical perspective offers another way to understand the complex notion of culture (see Figure 1.1).

Cultural Studies Definition: Culture as a Site of Contested Meaning

While traditional anthropological definitions focus on culture as a system of shared meanings, cultural studies perspectives, informed by Marxist theories of class struggle and exploitation, view **culture as a site of contestation** where meanings are constantly negotiated (Grossberg, Nelson, & Treichler, 1992). Cultural studies is a transdisciplinary field of study that emerged in the post–WWII era in England as a challenge to the positivist approaches to the study of culture, which purported to approach culture "objectively." The goals of Richard Hoggart, who founded the Birmingham Centre for Contemporary Cultural Studies, and others who followed, such as Stuart Hall, are to develop subjective approaches to the study of culture in everyday life, to examine the broader historical and political context within which cultural practices are situated, and to attend to relations of power in understanding culture. Simon During (1999) suggested that as England's working class became more affluent and fragmented in the 1950s, as mass-mediated culture began to dominate over local, community cultures, and as the logic that separated culture from politics was challenged, the old notion of culture as a shared way of life was no longer descriptive or functional.

Through a cultural studies lens, then, the notion of culture shifts from an expression of local communal lives to a view of culture as an apparatus of power within a larger system of domination. A cultural studies perspective reveals how culture operates as a form of **hegemony,** or domination through consent, as defined by Antonio Gramsci, an Italian Marxist theorist. Hegemony is dominance without the need for force or explicit forms of coercion. In other words, hegemony operates when the goals, ideas, and interests of the ruling group or class are so thoroughly normalized, institutionalized, and accepted that people consent to their own domination, subordination, and exploitation. Developments in cultural studies from the 1980s forward focus on the potential individuals and groups have to challenge, resist, and transform meanings in their subjective, everyday lives.

Figure 1.1   Are the meanings associated with these images shared or contested within cultures and across cultures?

Source: Flag © Can Stock Photo Inc./Brandon Seidel; Veiled Woman © Can Stock Photo Inc./Gina Sanders; Che Guevara © Can Stock Photo Inc./Claudiodivizia; Fries and Drink © Can Stock Photo Inc./Tilly design; Thumb's Up © Can Stock Photo Inc./Cristovao.

John Fiske (1992) stated, "The social order constrains and oppresses people, but at the same time offers them resources to fight against those constraints" (p. 157), suggesting that individuals and groups are both consumers and producers of cultural meanings and not passive recipients of meanings manufactured by cultural industries. From a cultural studies perspective, meanings are not necessarily shared, stable, or determined; rather, meanings are constantly produced, challenged, and negotiated.

Consider, for example, the images of nondominant groups in the United States such as African American; Latino/Latina; Asian American; American Indian; Arab American; or lesbian, gay, bisexual, and transgender (LGBT) people. Nondominant groups are often underrepresented and represented stereotypically in the mass media leading to struggles to affirm positive identities and efforts to claim and reclaim a position of respect in society. When any of us—from dominant or nondominant groups—speak or act outside the "norm" established by society or what is seen as "normal" within our cultural group, we likely experience tension, admonition, or in more extreme cases, shunning. As we engage with media representations and confront expected norms, we challenge and negotiate shared and accepted meanings within culture and society. Meanings associated with being an African American, a White man, or Latino/Latina are not shared by all in the society; rather, these meanings are continuously asserted, challenged, negotiated, and rearticulated. From a cultural studies perspective, meanings are continually produced, hybridized, and reproduced in an ongoing struggle of power (S. Hall, 1997). Culture, then, is the "actual, grounded terrain" of everyday practices—watching TV, consuming and wearing clothes, eating fast food or dining out, listening to music or radio talk shows—and representations—movies, songs, videos, advertisements, magazines, and "news"—where meanings are contested.

While older definitions of culture where a set of things or activities signify high or low culture still circulate, the cultural studies notion of culture focuses on the struggles over meanings that are part of our everyday lives. Undoubtedly, the logic of understanding culture as a contested site or zone where meanings are negotiated appeals to and makes sense for people who experience themselves as marginalized from or marginalized within the centers of power, whether this is based on race, class, gender, ethnicity, sexuality, or nationality. Similarly, the logic of understanding culture as a system of shared meanings appeals to and makes sense for people at the centers of power or in a dominant role, whether this position is based on race, class, gender, ethnicity, sexuality, or nationality. This, itself, illustrates the struggle over the meaning of the notion of culture.

Nevertheless, it is important to note that we all participate in and are constrained by oppressive social forces. We all, at some points in our lives and to varying degrees, also challenge and struggle with dominant or preferred meanings. From a cultural studies perspective, culture is a site of analysis—in other words, something we need to attend to and critique. Culture is also a site of intervention, where we can work toward greater equity and justice in our lives and in the world in the ongoing struggle of domination and resistance.

The initial aim of the transdisciplinary field of cultural studies to critique social inequalities and work toward social change remains today; however, the academic field of cultural studies as it has traveled from England to Latin America, Australia, the United States, and other places has taken on different forms and emphases. In the mid-1980s, communication scholar Larry Grossberg (1986) identified the emerging and significant impact cultural studies began to have in the United States, particularly in the communication discipline. Today, as we explore intercultural communication within the context of globalization, a cultural studies approach offers tools to analyze power relations, to understand the historical and political context of our intercultural relations, and to see how we can act or intervene critically and creatively in our everyday lives.

Globalization Definitions: Culture as a Resource

Influenced by cultural studies, contemporary anthropologist Arjun Appadurai (1996) suggested in his book *Modernity at Large: Cultural Dimensions of Globalization* that we need to move away from thinking of culture as a thing, a substance, or an object that is shared. The concept of culture as a coherent, stable entity privileges certain forms of sharing and agreement and neglects the realities of inequality, difference, and those who are marginalized. He argued that the adjective *cultural* is more descriptive and useful than the noun *culture*. Focusing on the cultural dimensions of an object, issue, practice, or ideology, then, is to recognize differences, contrasts, and comparisons. Culture, in the context of globalization, is not something that individuals or groups possess but rather a way of referring to dimensions of situated and embodied difference that express and mobilize group identities (Appadurai, 1996).

George Yúdice (2003) suggested that culture in the age of globalization has come to be understood as a **resource**. Culture plays a greater role today than ever before because of the ways it is linked to community, national, international, and transnational economies and politics. As we enter the 21st century, culture is now seen as a resource for economic and political exploitation, agency, and power to be used or instrumentalized for a wide range of purposes and ends. For example, in the context of globalization, culture, in the form of symbolic goods such as TV shows, movies, music, and tourism, is increasingly a resource for economic growth in global trade. Mass culture industries in the United States are the major contributor to the gross national product (GNP) (Yúdice, 2003). Culture is also targeted for exploitation by capital in the media, consumerism, and tourism. Consider how products are modified and marketed to different cultural groups; how African American urban culture has been appropriated, exploited, commodified and yet it operates as a potentially oppositional site; or how tourism in many parts of the world uses the resource of culture to attract foreign capital for development. While the commodification of culture—the turning of culture, cultural practices, and cultural space into products for sale—is not new, the extent to which culture is "managed" as a resource for its capital generating potential and as a "critical sphere for investment" by global institutions such as the World Bank (WB) is new (Yúdice, 2003, p. 13).

Culture, in the context of globalization, is conceptualized, experienced, exploited, and mobilized as a resource. In addition to being invested in and distributed as a resource for economic development and capital accumulation, culture is used as a resource to address and solve social problems like illiteracy, addiction, crime, and conflict. Culture is also used today discursively, socially, and politically as a resource for collective and individual empowerment, agency, and resistance. Groups of people in proximity to each other or vastly distant due to migration organize collective identities that serve as "homes" of familiarity; spaces of belonging; and as sites for the formation of resistance, agency, and political empowerment. Consider how the Zapatista movement in Chiapas, Mexico, that emerged in resistance to the oppressive and disenfranchising policies and practices of the North American Free Trade Agreement (NAFTA) articulates and claims its right to autonomous indigenous social, political, and economic organization. Or consider the ways that Black youth in the *favelas,* poverty-stricken areas of Rio de Janeiro in Brazil, use their funk music as a means to challenge racial discrimination and as a platform for activism as they access funding from nongovernmental organizations and foundations that support cultural empowerment (Yúdice, 2003). Today, in the context of globalization "the understanding and practice of culture is quite complex, located at the intersection of economic and social justice agendas" (p. 17).

COMMUNICATIVE DIMENSIONS
COMMUNICATION AND CULTURE

What is the relationship between communication and culture? The three different approaches to culture illustrate different assumptions about communication.

According to the *anthropological definition* of culture as a shared system of meaning, communication is a process of transmitting and sharing information among a group of people. In this case, communication enables culture to be co-constructed and mutually shared by members of a group.

In the *cultural studies definition,* culture is a contested site of meaning. According to this view, communication is a process through which individuals and groups negotiate and struggle over the "agreed upon" and "appropriate" meanings assigned to reality. Through verbal and nonverbal communication as well as the use of rhetoric, some views are privileged and normalized while others perspectives are marginalized or silenced. Thus, communication is a process of negotiation, a struggle for power and visibility, rather than a mutual construction and sharing of meaning.

Finally, in the *globalization definition,* culture is viewed as a resource. In this case, communication can be viewed as a productive process that enables change. We usually associate the word *productive* with positive qualities. However, "productive" here simply means that communication is a generative process. People leverage culture to build collective identities and exploit or mobilize for personal, economic, or political gain. Communication is a process of utilizing cultural resources.

As you can see from our previous discussion, there are various and different definitions of culture. The concept of culture, itself, is *contested*. This means that there is no one agreed upon definition, that the different meanings of culture can be understood as being in competition with each other for usage, and that there are material and symbolic consequences or implications attached to the use of one or another of the definitions. The definitions presented here—(1) culture as shared meaning, (2) culture as contested meaning, and (3) culture as resource—all offer important and useful ways of understanding

[handwritten margin note: meaning of culture "meanings" 1. shared 2. contested 3. Resource contested]

culture in the context of globalization. Throughout the book, all three definitions are used to help us make sense of the complex and contradictory intercultural communication issues and experiences we live and struggle with today.

STUDYING INTERCULTURAL COMMUNICATION

In recent years, when I ask students to speak about their culture, many find it a highly challenging exercise. For students who come from the dominant culture, the response is often "I don't really have a culture." For those students from nondominant groups, responses that point to their ethnic, racial, or religious group identification come more readily; however, their replies are often accompanied by some uneasiness. Typically, people whose culture differs from the dominant group have a stronger sense of their culture and develop a clearer awareness of their cultural identity earlier on in life than those in the dominant group. **Cultural identity** is defined as our situated sense of self that is shaped by our cultural experiences and social locations. What definitions of culture do you think are operating in the minds of my students when asked to speak about their culture and what accounts for the different responses among students from dominant and nondominant cultures?

We can see how the anthropological definition of culture as shared meaning and culture as something that groups possess is presumed in the students' responses. Students who identify with U.S. dominant culture are encouraged to see themselves as "individuals," which often underlies their claim that they "have no culture." Those students in nondominant groups see themselves as having culture or a cultural identity based on the ways in which they are different from the dominant group. Those in the dominant group see the difference of those who are in nondominant groups and label it "culture" and identify their own seeming lack of "difference" as not having culture. While the dominant culture is also infused with "difference," it is not as evident because the cultural patterns of the dominant group are the norm. Additionally, we can see how those from the dominant culture understand culture as a resource, which others have but which they, rather nostalgically, are lacking. Interestingly and importantly, the fact that people from the dominant group do not see their culture as a resource is highly problematic. When members of the dominant group do not recognize their culture as a resource, their knowledge and access to cultural privilege and White privilege are erased and invisibilized by and for the dominant group (Frankenberg, 1993; Nakayama & Martin, 1999). We can see the cultural studies definition of culture as contested meaning manifested in the differences between these students' responses.

Culture or cultural dimensions of human interaction are, to a great extent, unconsciously acquired and embodied through interaction and engagement with others from one's own culture. When one's culture differs from the dominant group—for example, people who are Jewish, Muslim, or Buddhist in a predominantly Christian society or people who identify as African American, Asian American, Latino/Latina, Arab American, or Native American within the predominantly White or European American culture—he or she is regularly, perhaps daily, reminded of the differences between his or her own cultural values, norms, history, and possibly language and those of the dominant group. In effect, people from nondominant groups learn to "commute" between cultures, switching verbal and nonverbal cultural codes, as well as values and ways of viewing the world as they move between two cultures. If you are from a nondominant group, the ways in which the dominant culture is different from your own are evident.

This phenomenon is certainly not unique to the United States. People of Algerian or Vietnamese background who are French, people who are Korean or Korean–Japanese in Japan, or people of Indian ancestry who have lived, perhaps for generations, in Africa, the Caribbean, or South Pacific Islands are likely to experience a heightened sense of culture and cultural identification because their differences from the dominant group are seen as significant, are pointed out, and are part of their lived experience.

On the other hand, people from the dominant cultural group in a society are often unaware that the way things are—the norms, values, practices, and institutions of the society—are, in fact, deeply shaped by and infused with a particular cultural orientation and that these patterns of shared meaning have been normalized as "just the way things are" or "the way things should be." So, to return to our earlier question, what accounts for the differences in responses of my students when asked about their culture?

Positionality

The differences in responses can be understood to some extent based on differences in students' **positionality**. Positionality refers to one's social location or position within an intersecting web of socially constructed hierarchical categories such as race, class, gender, sexual orientation, religion, nationality, and physical abilities, to name a few. Different experiences, understanding, and knowledge of oneself and the world are gained, accessed, and produced based on one's positionality. Positionality is a relational concept. In other words, when we consider positionality, we are thinking about how we are positioned in relation to others within these intersecting social categories and how we are positioned in terms of power. The socially constructed categories of race, gender, class, sexuality, nationality, religion, and ableness are hierarchical systems that often define and connote material and symbolic power. At this point, consider how your positionality—your positions of power in relation to the categories of race, gender, class, nationality, and so on—impacts your experiences, understanding, and knowledge about yourself and the world around you. How does your positionality impact your intercultural communication interactions?

Standpoint Theory

The idea of positionality is closely related to **standpoint theory** (Collins, 1986; Harding, 1991; Hartsock, 1983) as proposed by feminist theorists. A standpoint is a place from which to view and make sense of the world around us. Our standpoint influences what we see and what we cannot, do not, or choose not to see. Feminist standpoint theory claims that the social groups to which we belong shape what we know and how we communicate (Wood, 2005). The theory is derived from the Marxist position that economically oppressed classes can access knowledge unavailable to the socially privileged and can generate distinctive accounts, particularly knowledge about social relations. For example, German philosopher G. W. F. Hegel, writing in the early 19th century, suggested that while society in general may acknowledge the existence of slavery, the perception, experience, and knowledge of slavery is quite different for slaves as compared to masters. One's position within social relations of power produces different standpoints from which to view, experience, act, and construct knowledge about the world.

All standpoints are necessarily partial and limited, yet feminist theorists argue that people from oppressed or subordinated groups must understand both their own perspective and the perspective of those in power in order to survive. Therefore, the standpoint of marginalized people or groups, those with less power, is unique and should be privileged as it allows for a fuller and more comprehensive view. Patricia Hill Collins's (1986) notion of "outsiders within" points to the possibility of dual vision of marginalized people and groups—in her case of a Black woman in predominantly White institutions. On the other hand, people in the dominant group—whether due to gender, class, race, religion, nationality, or sexual orientation—do not need to understand the viewpoint of subordinated groups and often have a vested interest in not understanding the positions of subordinated others in order to maintain their own dominance. Standpoint theory as put forth by feminist theorists is centrally concerned with the relationship between power and knowledge and sees the vantage point of those who are subordinated as a position of insight from which to challenge and oppose systems of oppression.

Standpoint theory offers a powerful lens through which to make sense of, address, and act upon issues and challenges in intercultural communication. It enables us to understand the following:

- We may see, experience, and understand the world quite differently based on our different standpoints and positionalities.
- Knowledge about ourselves and others is situated and partial.
- Knowledge is always and inevitably connected to power.
- Oppositional standpoints can form, challenging and contesting the status quo.

Ethnocentrism

The application of standpoint theory and an understanding of the various positionalities we occupy may also assist us in avoiding the negative effects of ethnocentrism. Ethnocentrism is derived from two Greek words—(1) *ethno,* meaning group or nation, and (2) *kentron,* meaning center—referring to a view that places one's group at the center of the world. As first conceptualized by William Sumner (1906), **ethnocentrism** is the idea that one's own group's way of thinking, being, and acting in the world is superior to others. While some scholars argue that ethnocentrism has been a central feature in all cultures throughout history and has served as a mechanism of cultural cohesion and preservation (Gudykunst & Kim, 1997), the globalized context in which we live today makes ethnocentrism and ethnocentric approaches extremely problematic. The assumption that one's own group is superior to others leads to negative evaluations of others and can result in dehumanization, legitimization of prejudices, discrimination, conflict, and violence. Historically and today, ethnocentrism has combined with power—material, institutional, and symbolic power—to justify colonization, imperialism, oppression, war, and ethnic cleaning.

One of the dangers of ethnocentrism is that it can blind individuals, groups, and even nations to the benefits of broader points of view and perceptions. Ethnocentrism is often marked by an intensely inward-looking and often nearsighted view of the world. On an interpersonal level, if you think your group's way of doing things, seeing things, and believing about things is the right way and the better way, you are likely to judge others negatively and respond arrogantly and dismissively to those who are different from you. These attitudes and actions will likely end any effective intercultural communication and deprive you of the benefits of other ways of seeing and acting in the world. If you are in a position of greater power in relation to the other person, you may feel as if it doesn't matter and you don't really need that person's perspective. From this, we can see how ethnocentrism combines with power to increase the likelihood of a more insular, myopic perspective.

On a global scale, ethnocentrism can affect perceptions of one's own group and can lead to ignorance, misunderstandings, resentment, and potentially violence. In late December 2001, the *International Herald Tribune* reported the results of a poll of 275 global opinion leaders from 24 countries. "Asked if many or most people would consider US policies to be 'a major cause' of the September 11 attacks, 58 percent of the non-US respondents said they did, compared to just 18 percent of Americans" (*Agence France Presse*, 2001). According to the report, findings from the poll indicate "that much of the world views the attacks as a symptom of increasingly bitter polarization between haves and have-nots." In response to the question of how there can be such a difference in perception between what Americans think about themselves and what non-Americans think about Americans, authors Ziauddin Sardar and Meryl Wyn Davies (2002) suggested the following:

> Most Americans are simply not aware of the impact of their culture and their government's policies on the rest of the world. But, more important, a vast majority simply do not believe that American has done, or can do, anything wrong. (p. 9)

Being a student of intercultural communication in the United States at this point in history presents unique opportunities and challenges. On the one hand, the increasing diversity of cultures within the United States provides an impetus and resource in educational settings, workplaces, entertainment venues, and communities for gaining knowledge and alternative perspectives about cultures that are different from one's own. The accelerated interconnectedness and interdependence of economics, politics, media, and culture around the globe also can motivate people to learn from and about others. On the other hand, rhetoric proclaiming the United States as the greatest and most powerful nation on Earth can combine with an unwillingness to critically examine the role of the United States in global economic and political instability and injustice. This can result in highly problematic, disturbing, and destructive forms of ethnocentrism that harm and inhibit our intercultural communication and global intercultural relations. Ethnocentrism can lead to one-sided perceptions as well as extremely arrogant and misinformed views, which are quite disparate from the perceptions of other cultural and national positions and dangerously limit knowledge of the bigger global picture in which our intercultural communication and interactions take place.

The study and practice of intercultural communication inevitably challenge our assumptions and views of the world. In fact, one of the main benefits of intercultural communication is the ways in which it broadens and deepens our understanding of the world we live in by challenging our taken-for-granted beliefs and views and by providing alternative ways to live fully and respectfully as human beings. Ethnocentrism may provide temporary protection from views, experiences, and realities that threaten one's own, but it has no long-term benefits for effective or successful intercultural communication in the context of globalization.

CULTURAL IDENTITY
CONSTRUCTING CULTURAL IDENTITIES

Cultural identity refers to our situated sense of self that is shaped by our cultural experiences and social locations. Our cultural identities develop through our relationships with others—our family, our friends, and those we see as outside our group. Cultural identities are constructed by the languages we speak and the nonverbal communication we use. Histories passed along from within our cultural group as well as representations of our group by others also shape our cultural identities. In the context of globalization, cultural identities are not fixed; rather, our identities are complex, multifaceted, and fluid.

Positionality, standpoint, and ethnocentric views are closely tied to our cultural identities. Our identities, which are based on socially constructed categories of difference (i.e., middle class, white male, an American citizen) also position us in relation to others. Our positionality gives us a particular standpoint (i.e., "in American society, anyone can become successful if they work hard"). Ethnocentric views may emerge (i.e., "American culture is more advanced and civilized than other cultures") if we have limited understanding of others' positionalities and standpoints. When cultural identity is understood as a situated sense of the self, we see how our positionality is not neutral, our standpoint is never universal, and our ethnocentric views are always problematic.

INTERCULTURAL PRAXIS IN THE CONTEXT OF GLOBALIZATION

One of my goals in this book is to introduce and develop a process of critical, reflective thinking and acting—what I call **intercultural praxis**—that enables us to navigate the complex and challenging intercultural spaces we inhabit interpersonally, communally, and globally. I hope that by reading this book you not only learn "about" intercultural communication but also practice a way of being, thinking, analyzing, reflecting, and acting in the world. At all moments in your day—when you are interacting with friends, coworkers, teachers, bosses, and strangers; when you are consuming pop culture in the form of music, clothes, your favorite TV shows, movies, and other entertainment; when you hear and read news and information from the media and other outlets; and in your routines of what and where you eat, where you live, how you travel around and where—you have the opportunity to engage in intercultural praxis.

To begin to understand intercultural praxis, I offer six interrelated points of entry into the process: (1) inquiry, (2) framing, (3) positioning, (4) dialogue, (5) reflection, and (6) action. The purpose of engaging in intercultural praxis is to raise our awareness, increase our critical analysis, and develop our socially responsible action in regard to our intercultural interactions in the context of globalization. These six points or ports of entry into the process direct us toward ways of thinking, reflecting, and acting in relation to our intercultural experiences, allowing us to attend to the complex, relational, interconnected, and often ambiguous nature of our experiences. The six points of entry into intercultural praxis are introduced here and developed in greater depth through the following chapters (see Figure 1.2).

Figure 1.2   Intercultural Praxis

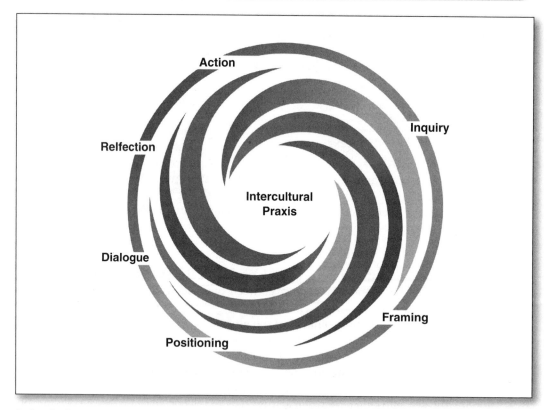

Design: Jessica Arana (www.jessicaarana.com)

Inquiry

Inquiry, as a port of entry for intercultural praxis, refers to a desire and willingness to know, to ask, to find out, and to learn. Curious inquiry about those who are different from ourselves leads us to engagement with others. While it may sound simple, inquiry also requires that we are willing to take risks, allow our own way of viewing and being in the world to be challenged and perhaps changed, and that we are willing to suspend judgments about others in order to see and interpret others and the world from different points of view. A Vietnamese American student, Quynyh Tran, recounted an intercultural experience she had before enrolling in one of my intercultural classes. When being introduced in a business setting to a man she did not know, she extended her hand to shake his. He responded that it was against his culture and religion to shake hands. She remembers feeling rather put off and offended by his response, deciding without saying anything that she was not interested in talking or working with him!

Reflecting on this incident in class, she realized that she missed an incredible opportunity to learn more about someone who was different from herself. She realized that if she could have let go of her judgments about those who were different and had not reacted to the man's statement as "weird, strange, or unfriendly," she may have been able to learn something and expand her knowledge of the world. She regretted not stepping through one of the doors of entry into intercultural praxis. Yet she learned from this experience that simple inquiry, curiosity, a willingness to suspend judgment, and a desire to learn from others can be tremendously rewarding and informing.

Framing

I propose **framing** to suggest a range of different perspective-taking options that we can learn to make available to ourselves and need to be aware of in intercultural praxis. First, the concept and action of "framing" connotes that our perspectives and our views on ourselves, others, and the world around us are always and inevitably limited by frames. We see things through individual, cultural, national, and regional frames or lenses that necessarily include some things and exclude others. As we engage in intercultural praxis, it is critical that we become aware of the frames of reference from which we view and experience the world.

Secondly, "framing" means that we are aware of both the local and global contexts that shape intercultural interactions. Sometimes it is very important to narrow the frame—to zoom in—and focus on the particular and very situated aspects of an interaction, event, or exchange. Take, for example, a conflict between two people from different cultures. It's important to look at the micro-level differences in communication styles, how nonverbal communication may be used differently, the ways in which the two people may perceive their identities differently based on cultural belonging, and the ways in which the two may have learned to enact conflict differently based on their enculturation. However, in order to fully understand the particular intercultural interaction or misunderstanding, it is also necessary to back up to view the incident, event, or interaction from a broader frame. As we zoom out, we may see a history of conflict and misunderstanding between the two groups that the individuals represent; we may observe historical and/or current patterns of inequities between the two groups; and we may also be able to map out broader geopolitical, global relations of power that can shed light on the particular and situated intercultural interaction, misunderstanding, or conflict. As we zoom in and foreground the micro-level of intercultural communication, we need to keep the wider background frame in mind as it provides the context in which meaning about the particular is made. Similarly, as we zoom out and look at larger macro-level dimensions, we need to keep in mind the particular local and situated lived experience of people in their everyday lives. "Framing" as a port of entry into intercultural praxis means we are aware of our frames of reference. It also means we develop our capacity to flexibly and consciously shift our perspective from the particular, situated dimensions of intercultural communication to the broader, global dimensions and from the global dimensions to the particular while maintaining our awareness of both.

Positioning

Where are you positioned as you read this sentence? Your first response may be to say you are lounging in a chair at home, in a café, in the break room at work, or in the library. If you "zoomed out" utilizing the framing strategy in the previous discussion, you may also respond by stating what part of a neighborhood, city, state, nation, or region of the world you are in. **Positioning** as a point of entry into intercultural praxis invites us to consider how our geographic positioning is related to social and political positions. As you read these sentences, where are you positioned socioculturally? The globe we inhabit is stratified by socially constructed hierarchical categories based on culture, race, class, gender, nationality, religion, age, and physical abilities among others. Like the lines of longitude and latitude that divide, map, and position us geographically on the earth, these hierarchical categories position us socially, politically, and materially in relation to each other and in relation to power.

Understanding how and where we are positioned in the world—the locations from which we speak, listen, act, think, and make sense of the world—allows us to acknowledge that we are, as human beings, positioned differently with both material and symbolic consequences. It is also important to note that your positionality may shift and change based on where you are and with whom you are communicating. For example, it could vary over the course of a day, from occupying a relatively powerful position at home as the oldest son in a family to having to occupy a less powerful positionality in your part-time job as a personal assistant. Sometimes the shift may be even more drastic, as in the case of someone who is a doctor and part of a dominant group in her home culture and then shifts class and power positions when she is forced to migrate to the United States for political reasons. She finds herself not only part of a minority group but also positioned very differently when her medical degree is not recognized, forcing her into more manual work and part-time student positionalities.

Positioning, as a way to enter into intercultural praxis, also directs us to interrogate who can speak and who is silenced; whose language is spoken and whose language trivialized or denied; whose actions have the power to shape and impact others and whose actions are dismissed, unreported, and marginalized. It demands that we question whose knowledge is privileged, authorized, and agreed upon as true and whose knowledge is deemed unworthy, "primitive," or unnecessary. Positioning ourselves, others, and our knowledge of both self and others allow us to see the relationship between power and what we think of as "knowledge." Our knowledge of the world—whether knowledge of meridians of longitude and latitude or hierarchical categories of race, class, and gender—is socially and historically constructed and produced in relation to power.

Dialogue

While we have all heard of **dialogue** and likely assume that we engage in it regularly, it's useful to consider the derivation of the word to deepen our understanding of dialogue as an entry port into intercultural praxis. A common mistake is to think "dia" means two and dialogue, then, is conversation between two people. However, the word *dialogue* is derived from the Greek word *dialogos*. *Dia* means "through," "between," or "across," and *logos* refers to "word" or "the meaning of the word" as well as "speech" or "thought." Physicist and philosopher David Bohm (1996) wrote the following:

> The picture or the image that this derivation suggests is of a *stream of meaning* among and through us and between us. This will make possible a flow of meaning in the whole group, out of which may emerge a new understanding. It's something new, which may not have been in the starting point at all. It's something creative. (p. 6)

Anthropologist Vincent Crapanzano (1990) suggested that "dialogue" necessarily entails both an oppositional as well as a transformative dimension. Given the differences in power and positionality in intercultural interactions, engagement in dialogue is necessarily a relationship of tension that "is conceived as a crossing, a reaching across, a sharing if not a common ground of understanding . . . " (p. 277).

According to philosopher Martin Buber, dialogue is essential for building community and goes far beyond an exchange of messages. For Buber, dialogue requires a particular quality of communication that involves a connection among participants who are potentially changed by each other. Buber refers to such relationships as I–Thou, where one relates and experiences another as a person. This relationship is quite different from an I–It relationship where people are regarded as objects and experienced as a means to a goal. Dialogue occurs only when there is regard for both self and other and where either/or thinking is challenged allowing for the possibility of shared ground, new meaning, and mutual understanding.

Dialogue offers a critical point of entry into intercultural praxis. Cognizant of differences and the tensions that emerge from these differences, the process of dialogue invites us to stretch ourselves—to reach across—to imagine, experience, and creatively engage with points of view, ways of thinking and being, and beliefs different from our own while accepting that we may not fully understand or come to a common agreement or position.

Reflection

While cultures around the world differ in the degree to which they value reflection and the ways in which they practice **reflection,** the capacity to learn from introspection, to observe oneself in relation to others, and to alter one's perspectives and actions based on reflection is a capacity shared by all humans. Many cultures, including the dominant culture of the United States, place a high value on doing activities and accomplishing tasks, which often leaves little space and time for reflection. However, reflection is a key feature of intercultural praxis. Consider how reflection is central to the other points of entry into intercultural praxis already addressed. To engage in curious inquiry, one must be able to reflect on oneself as a subject—a thinking, learning, creative, and capable subject. The practices of framing and positioning require that one consciously observe oneself and critically analyze ones relationships and interrelationships with others. Similarly, reflection is necessary to initiate, maintain, and sustain dialogue across the new and often difficult terrain of intercultural praxis.

Brazilian educator and activist Paulo Freire (1998) noted in his book *Pedagogy of Freedom* that critical praxis "involves a dynamic and dialectic movement between 'doing' and 'reflecting on doing'" (p. 43). Reflection is what informs our actions. Reflection that incorporates critical analyses of micro- and macro-levels of intercultural issues, which considers multiple cultural frames of reference and that recognizes our own and others' positioning, enables us to act in the world in meaningful, effective, and responsible ways.

Action

Influenced by the work of Paulo Freire (1973/2000), the concept of intercultural praxis refers to an ongoing process of thinking, reflecting, and acting. Intercultural praxis is not only about deepening our understanding of ourselves, others, and the world in which we live. Rather, intercultural praxis means we join our increased understanding with responsible **action** to make a difference in the world—to create a more socially just, equitable, and peaceful world.

Each one of us takes multiple and varied actions individually and collectively that have intercultural communication dimensions and implications every single day of our lives. We take action when we decide to get an education, to go to class or not, and when we select classes or a field of study. Our actions in an educational context are influenced by cultural, gendered, national, and class-based assumptions, biases, or constraints. We take action when we go to work and when we speak out or don't about inequity, discrimination, and misuses of power. Watching or reading the news is an action that affords opportunities to understand how cultural and national interests shape, limit, and bias the news we receive. Our consumption of products, food, and entertainment are all actions. When we know who has labored to make the goods we consume and under what conditions, we confront ourselves and others with the choices we make through our actions. We take action when we make decisions about who we develop friendships and long-term relationships with and when we choose not to be involved. When we feel strongly enough about an issue, we are moved to organize and take action.

What informs our choices and actions? What are the implications of our actions? In the context of globalization, our choices and actions are always enabled, shaped, and constrained by history; relations of power; and material conditions that are inextricably linked to intercultural dimensions of culture, race, class, religion, sexual orientation, language, and nationality. Intercultural praxis, then, offers us a process of critical, reflective thinking and acting that enables us to navigate the complex and challenging intercultural spaces we inhabit interpersonally, communally, and globally. Intercultural praxis can manifest in a range of forms such as simple or complex communication competency skills, complicit actions, and oppositional tactics, as well as through creative, improvisational, and transformational interventions.

SUMMARY

As we "open the conversation," it is evident that there is a critical need for skillful and informed intercultural communicators in the current context of globalization. To assist us in making sense of intercultural communication in the rapidly changing, increasingly interdependent, and inequitable world we inhabit, I introduced various definitions of culture: (1) culture as shared meaning, (2) culture as contested meaning, and (3) culture as resource. Each definition provides different and necessary ways of understanding culture in our complex age. Studying intercultural communication in the context of globalization offers opportunities and challenges. To guide our approach and to increase our awareness, the basic concepts of positionality, standpoint theory, and ethnocentrism were introduced. Because we want to become more effective as intercultural communicators, thinkers, and actors in the global context, intercultural praxis—a set of skills, processes, and practices for critical, reflective thinking and acting—was outlined to navigate the complex, contradictory, and challenging intercultural spaces we inhabit. In the next chapter, we explore the historical, political, and economic factors and forces that have contributed to globalization and discuss various dimensions of intercultural communication in the context of globalization.

KEY TERMS

high culture
low culture
popular culture
culture as shared meaning
symbols
culture as contested meaning
hegemony
resource culture as resource
cultural identity
positionality

standpoint theory
ethnocentrism
intercultural praxis
inquiry
framing
positioning
dialogue
reflection
action

DISCUSSION QUESTIONS AND ACTIVITIES

Discussion Questions

1. Based on the anthropological definition of culture, how are shared meanings created? Using a concrete example to illustrate your answer, discuss who constructs systems of shared meanings and how shared meanings change over time.

2. Following the cultural studies definition of culture, how are meanings contested in your everyday life practices? Can you think of examples of how meanings are negotiated and contested?

3. Hegemony, defined as domination through consent, is at work in our everyday practices of culture. Can you think of examples in which you consent—consciously or unconsciously—to forms of domination? How do you think we can resist?

4. Do you think there are universal human values? If so, what are they? Is the belief in universal human values inherently ethnocentric?

Activities

1. Exploring the Cultural Dimensions That Shape You

   a. Write a brief paragraph exploring the cultural dimensions that shape you using the definitions of culture discussed in this chapter. How do you understand your culture as a system of shared meanings? As a site of contestation? As a resource?

      (For example, as an American, I value independence and individualism, which are cultural values that I share with many others from the United States. As a woman, I feel like I am constantly negotiating representations of what it means to be a woman. My gender culture is a site of contestation. Women, in this society, are often turned into objects like resources that can be exploited, packaged, and sold. Yet I am proud to be a woman and experience this cultural dimension of myself as an empowering resource. As a White American, I know my experiences are different from other racial groups. I am learning how I am different from others and not just how they are different from me as a member of the dominant group. The privileges I have from being White are resources even or especially when I can't see these invisible advantages.)

   b. Share your paragraph responses with your classmates, and discuss the similarities and differences among your cultural dimensions.

   c. Discuss the usefulness and limitations of each definition of culture.

2. Positioning Yourself and Your Cultural Dimensions

   a. Using your responses to the first activity, develop your ideas on how you are positioned in terms of race, class, gender, ethnicity, sexuality, nationality, religion, and ableness in relation to others.

   b. Discuss how your positionality influences your standpoint on the world around you and how you engage in intercultural communication.

3. Intercultural Praxis—Group Activity

   In a group of four to five students, consider and discuss the following:

   a. Inquiry: What do you already know about each other? What stereotypes, preconceptions, and assumptions might you have about students in your class or those in your group? What would you like to know about the cultural background of those in your group? What skills and experience do you bring to the process of inquiry?

   b. Framing: In what ways does your cultural background frame the way you see and experience others in your group? What frames of reference are useful in understanding the members of your group? What can you see if you "zoom in" and look at the micro-level in terms of the cultural dimensions of your group? What can you see if you "zoom out" and look at the macro-level in terms of the cultural dimensions of your group?

c. Positioning: How are you positioned sociohistorically in relation to others in your group? How does your positionality change in different contexts and frames of reference?

d. Dialogue: With whom do you frequently engage in dialogue? How can you expand the circle of people with whom you engage in dialogue? What qualities are required to engage effectively in dialogue? How do relationships of power shape the process of dialogue?

e. Reflection: As you reflect on your inquiry, framing, positioning, and dialogue, what have you learned about yourself, your group, and intercultural praxis?

f. Action: How and when can you engage in intercultural praxis? How can you use what you have learned in this chapter to effect change for a more equitable and just world? What are the consequences and implications of lack of action?

g. Finally, discuss the challenges of engaging in intercultural praxis. Keep your dialogue and reflections from this group activity in mind as you read the following chapters.

REFERENCES

Agence France Presse. (2001, December 20). Global poll: US policies played "significant role" in terror attacks. Retrieved from http://www.commondreams.org/headlines01/1220-01.htm

Appadurai, A. (1996). *Modernity at large: Cultural dimensions of globalization.* Minneapolis: University of Minnesota Press.

Bohm, D. (1996). *On dialogue.* New York: Routledge.

Brooks, D. (2005, August 10). All cultures are not equal. *Global Policy Forum.* Retrieved from http://www.globalpolicy.org/globliz/cultural/2005/0810allcultures.htm

Collins, P. H. (1986). Learning from the outsider within: The sociological significance of black feminist thought. *Social Problems, 33*(6), S14–S32.

Crapanzano, V. (1990). On dialogue. In T. Maranhão (Ed.), *The interpretation of dialogue* (pp. 269–291). Chicago: University of Chicago Press.

Crutsinger, M. (2011). China increases holdings of US Treasury securities. *Associated Press.* Retrieved from http://www.aolnews.com/story/china-increases-holdings-of-us-treasury/862636/

During, S. (1999). Introduction. *The cultural studies reader.* London: Routledge.

Eller, J. D. (1999). *From culture to ethnicity to conflict: An anthropological perspective on international ethnic conflict.* Ann Arbor: University of Michigan Press.

Fiske, J. (1992). *Introduction to communication studies: Studies in culture and communication.* London: Methuen & Co.

Freire, P. (1998). *Pedagogy of freedom: Ethics, democracy, and civic courage.* Lanham, MD: Rowman & Littlefield.

Freire, P. (2000). *Pedagogy of the oppressed.* New York: Continuum. (Original work published 1973)

Frankenberg, R. (1993). *White women, race matters: The social construction of whiteness.* Minneapolis: University of Minnesota Press.

Geertz, G. (1973). *The interpretation of culture: Selected essays.* New York: Basic Books.

Global Issues. (2010, September 20). *Poverty facts and stats.* Retrieved from http://www.globalissues.org/article/26/poverty-facts-and-stats

Grossberg, L. (1986). History, politics and postmodernism: Stuart Hall and cultural studies. *Journal of Communication Inquiry, 10*(2), 61–77.

Grossberg, L., Nelson, C., & Treichler, P. (1992). *Cultural studies.* New York: Routledge.

Gudykunst, W., & Kim, Y. Y. (1997). *Communicating with strangers: An approach to intercultural communication* (3rd ed.). New York: McGraw-Hill.

Hall, E. T. (1959). *The silent language.* New York: Doubleday.

Hall, S. (Ed.). (1997). *Representation: Cultural representations and signifying practices.* Thousand Oaks, CA: Sage.

Harding, S. (1991). *Whose science, whose knowledge: Thinking from women's lives.* Ithaca, NY: Cornell University Press.

Hartsock, N. (1983). The feminist standpoint: Developing the ground for a specifically feminist historical materialism. In S. Harding & M. B. Hintikka (Eds.), *Discovering reality: Feminist perspectives on epistemology, metaphysics, methodology, and the philosophy of science* (pp. 283–310). London: D. Riedel.

International Organization for Migration. (n.d.). *About migration.* Retrieved from http://www.iom.int/jahia/page3.html

Internet World Stats. (2011). *Internet usage statistics: The big picture.* Retrieved from http://www.internetworldstats.com/stats.htm

Kluckhohn, C., & Kroeber, A. (1952). *Culture: A critical review of concepts and definitions.* Cambridge, MA: Harvard University Peabody Museum of American Archeology and Ethnology Papers 47.

Lui, M., Robles, B., Leondar-Wright, B., Brewer, R., & Adamson, R. (2006). *The color of wealth: The story behind the U.S. racial wealth divide.* New York: The New Press.

Nakayama, T. K., & Martin, J. N. (Eds.). (1999). *Whiteness: The communication of social identity.* Thousand Oaks, CA: Sage.

Richmond, M., Robinson, C., & Sachs-Israel, M. (Eds.). (2008). *The global literacy challenge.* Paris, France: UNESCO.

Rogers, E. M., Hart, W. B., & Miike, Y. (2002). Edward T. Hall and the history of intercultural communication: The United States and Japan. *Keio Communication Review, 24,* 3–26.

Sardar, Z., & Davies, M. W. (2002). *Why do people hate America?* New York: The Disinformation Company.

Sumner, W. (1906). *Folkways.* New York: Ginn.

U.S. Census Bureau. (2008). *An older and more diverse nation by midcentury.* Retrieved from http://www.census.gov/newsroom/releases/archives/population/cb08-123.html

Wood, J. T. (2005). *Gendered lives* (6th ed.). Belmont, CA: Wadsworth.

Young, R. C. (2001). *Postcolonialism: An historical introduction.* Malden, MA: Blackwell.

Yúdice, G. (2003). *The expediency of culture: Uses of culture in the global era.* Durham, NC: Duke University Press.

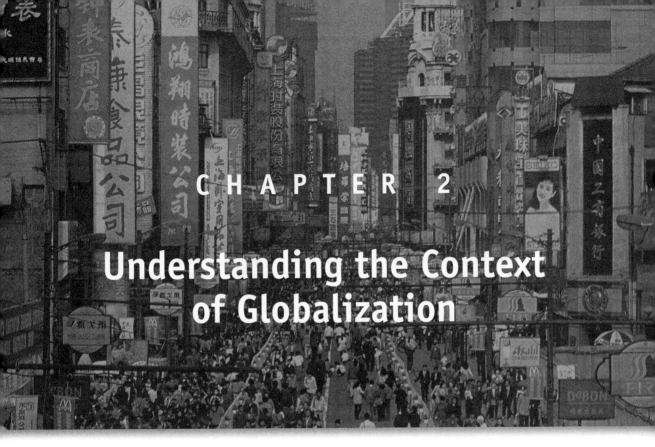

CHAPTER 2

Understanding the Context of Globalization

How do you imagine life in Shanghai, China, as different from or similar to your life?

Scenario One: *In the hallway of a university in Southern California, three students—Hamza, an international student from Morocco; Cathy, who came to the United States 4 years ago from France; and the third, Immaculee from Rwanda, who immigrated 17 years ago—spend the 15-minute break during their intercultural communication class speaking with each other in French, relishing in the comfort that speaking a language of "home" offers and forming an intercultural relationship, however temporary and transitory.*

Scenario Two: *While Brazil, Mexico, Chile and Argentina historically have produced more than 80 per cent of Latin American gross domestic product and 90 per cent of Australia's trade with Latin America, new opportunities are arising in adjoining economies led by economic reforms to reducing trade barriers and encouraging foreign direct investment. . . . This will see new and ongoing opportunities for Australian businesses in the region across a range of sectors including mining, mining technology, education, tourism, agribusiness, animal genetics and education. (Harcourt, 2008)*

(Continued)

Source: Chapter-opening photo © Goodshoot/Goodshoot/Thinkstock.

(Continued)

Scenario Three: Mumbai's (Bombay) film industry is the biggest in the world, producing more than 1,000 films viewed in Russia, China, Africa, the Middle East, Europe, the United States, and Canada. Amitabh Bachchan, internationally revered Indian film star, said of his fans in Africa and Russia, "very surprising . . . the entire northern belt of Africa. So, Morocco, Algeria, Ethiopia, Sudan, down to Egypt. . . . And Russia. Massive. Massive. . . . When I first went to Moscow for the first time, I was received by Russian female fans, who were actually dressed in our Indian dress and wore the bindi and the jewelry and everything, and spoke Hindi . . . and said that they were going to university to study the language so they could follow our films. Remarkable." (Rose, 2005)

Scenario Four: Environmentalists, human rights activists, indigenous groups, students, religious groups, farmers, labor activists, union workers, and teachers were among the 40,000 people from around the globe who converged on Seattle in November 1999 to protest against the third meeting of the World Trade Organization (WTO). The Washington Post *describes the protesters: "What they all seem to agree on is that giant corporations have gone too far in gaining control over their lives and defining the values of their culture and that the WTO has become a handmaiden to those corporate interests." (Editorial Board, 1999)*

Scenario Five: Filipina American Grace Ebron recalls, "I arrive at the Rome Airport, thrilled at the notion of living in Italy. As I step out of the customs hall, I immediately see my boyfriend, waiting to meet me. His parents, whom I've never met, are with him and as I turn to them with my perfectly-rehearsed Italian greeting, they appear very confused. 'No- no' they stammer, a perplexed expression on their faces. They turn to Massimo: 'But where is your girlfriend—the American? Why did she send the maid?'" (Ebron, 2002)

W hat themes are interwoven through the fabric of all of these scenarios? Without erasing the obvious and more subtle differences between the situations, what common factors and forces shape the world that these scenarios describe? Hamza, Cathy, and Immaculee made personal journeys from different parts of the globe to the United States and find themselves relating to each other through a common language and connected to each other through a history of colonization. Through worldwide distribution of Hindi films and through numerous websites online, fans from around the world can stay up to date on Amitabh Bachchan's latest public appearance and movie. Businesspeople in Latin America are linked through rapid communication technology and transportation with businesses in Australia, Europe, Asia, the Middle East, and North America. Australians view Latin America as an "attractive environment" with "great potential" for investment and markets. In November 1999, people from around the globe representing widely varying interests organized together to publicly challenge the increasing control of global financial institutions such as the **World Trade Organization (WTO)** over their lives and cultures. Grace Ebron, excited to reconnect with her Italian boyfriend, benefits from her global mobility and yet is confronted with stereotypes and racialized assumptions due to colonial histories and the migration of Filipina laborers to Italy as part of a development policy based on the export of labor.

All the scenarios illustrate the dynamic movement, confluence, and interconnection of peoples, cultures, markets, and relationships of power that are rooted in history and yet are redefined and rearticulated in our current global age. Through advances in technology—both communication technology and transportation technology—and open markets, people from around the globe with different cultural, racial, national, economic, and linguistic backgrounds are coming into contact with each other; consuming each others' cultural foods, products, and identities; developing relationships and struggling through conflicts; building alliances and activist networks; and laboring with and for each other more frequently, more intensely, and with greater impact today than ever before. In the workplace and the home, through entertainment and the Internet, in politics and the military, and through travel for leisure, work, pleasure, and survival, intercultural communication and interaction have become a common experience.

This chapter begins with an introduction of the central roles history and power play in intercultural communication and explores the broader context of globalization within which intercultural communication occurs today. To grasp the complexity of globalization, we examine the facets of economic globalization, political globalization, and cultural globalization. While these three facets of globalization are inextricably intertwined, each is treated separately to highlight the intercultural communication dimensions.

THE ROLE OF HISTORY IN INTERCULTURAL COMMUNICATION

Certainly, as we know from a study of history, people have traveled and moved great distances exchanging cultural goods, ideas, and practices and experiencing significant intercultural contact for several millennia. While both the Islamic and Mongol empires had broad reaches, Held, McGrew, Goldblatt, & Perraton (1999) noted in their book *Global Transformations: Politics, Economics and Culture* that the European conquest starting in the 16th century transformed global migration patterns in ways that continue to impact us today. During the European colonial era, people moved from Europe—Spain, Portugal, and England primarily but also from France, Holland, Belgium, and Germany—to the Americas, Oceania, Africa, and Asia for the purpose of conquest, economic expansion, and religious conversion. Settlers from these countries then followed, reinforcing the flow from Europe to the outlying colonies. Between the 1600s and the 1850s, 9 to 12 million people were forcibly removed from Africa and transported to the colonies—primarily in the Americas—to serve as enslaved laborers during the transatlantic slave trade. In the 19th century, Indians subjected to colonial British rule were relocated as laborers—often as indentured servants—to British colonies in Africa and Oceania. The process of colonization, which was based on the extraction of wealth through the exploitation of natural and human resources, established Europe as the economic and political center of the world and the colonies as the periphery (Young, 2001).

Later in the 19th century, after the British and Spanish colonies in the Americas had gained independence from colonial rule, a mass migration occurred with the expulsion of working class and poor people from the economically stretched and famine-torn centers of Europe to the United States, Canada, and the Southern Cone including Argentina, Chile, Brazil, Uruguay, and others. Movements of indentured laborers from Asia—primarily China, Japan, and the Philippines—to European colonies and former colonies—mainly the United States and Canada—swelled the number of migrants to over 40 million during the 25 years before WWI.

WWI brought the unprecedented closure of national borders and the implementation of the first systematic immigration legislation and border controls in modern times. The ethnically motivated violence of WWII led to the movement of Jews out of Europe to Israel, the United States, and Latin America. In the wake of unprecedented devastation of human lives, economies, and natural habitats experienced across Europe, Russia, and Japan as a result of WWII, the first institutions of global political and economic governance—the United Nations, the **World Bank (WB)**, and the **International Monetary Fund (IMF)**—were established.

Since the 1960s with the rebuilding of European economic power and the rise of the United States as an economic and political center, we see a shift in migratory patterns. While earlier periods saw the movement of peoples from the center of empires to the peripheries, increasingly people from the former colonies or peripheries are migrating toward the centers of former colonial power. In search of jobs and in response to demands for labor, migrants are moving from Turkey and North Africa to Germany and France, respectively, and from more distant former colonies in Southeast Asia and East and West Africa to England, France, Germany, Italy, and the Scandinavian countries. The transatlantic migration from Europe to the United States at the turn of the 20th century is matched today by the numbers of immigrants from Latin America and Asia to the United States.

We also see flows of people to the oil-rich countries of the Middle East from Africa and Asia and new patterns of regional migration within Latin America, Africa, and East Asia. In the later part of the 20th century, the numbers of people seeking asylum, refugees fleeing internally strife-stricken countries in the developing world, and those who have been displaced for a variety of political reasons in Africa, the Middle East, and Latin America have risen exponentially (Held et al., 1999).

As noted earlier, people have engaged in intercultural contact for many millennia, yet the European conquest starting in the 16th century transformed global migration patterns in ways that continue to impact intercultural relations today. The brief historical overview of world migrations since the colonial period reminds us that movements of people and therefore intercultural interactions are directly related to economic and political forces. It also suggests that the networks of connection and global relationships of power that we experience today are a continuation of worldwide intercultural contact and interaction over the past 500 years. Therefore, in order to understand the dynamics of intercultural communication today, we must place them within a broad historical context. The process of colonization by Europe of much of the world, which included the exploitation of natural resources and human labor, established Europe and later the United States as the economic and political centers of the world. The colonial process initiated the division between "the West and the Rest" that we experience today. Colonization and the global expansion of the West propelled the development of capitalism, which required then and continues to require today the expansion of markets and trade, and the incorporation of labor from the former colonies or what have been referred to as the Third World or developing countries (Dussel, 1995; Wallerstein, 2003; also see Figures 2.1 and 2.2).

Figure 2.1   Colonized World in 1800

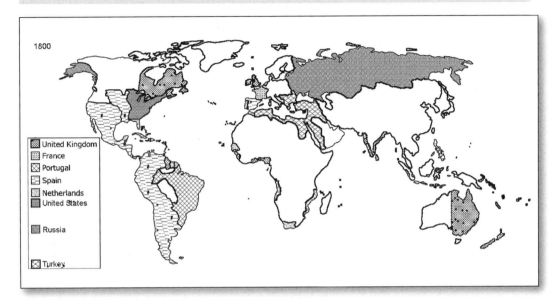

Source: Wikimedia Commons (2008a).

Figure 2.2   Colonial Powers 1914

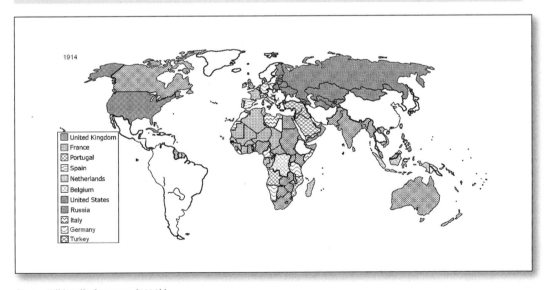

Source: Wikimedia Commons (2008b).

The concept of the First World, Second World, and Third World is a relic of the Cold War period initially used to describe the relationship between the United States and other countries. The **First World** referred to countries friendly to United States and were identified as capitalist and democratic. The **Second World** referred to countries perceived as hostile and ideologically incompatible with the United States—the former Soviet bloc countries, China, and their allies—and were identified as communist. The **Third World** referred to countries that were seen as neutral or nonaligned with either the First World (capitalism) or the Second World (communism). While the relationship between the First World and Third World was ostensibly positive, the history of the last half of the 20th century reveals the so-called "Third World" as sites of anticolonial struggles and battlegrounds between the First and Second Worlds. Since the fall of the Soviet Union and the end of the Cold War, the meaning of First and Third Worlds is less clearly defined and more closely associated with levels of economic development. The terms *developing country* and *developed country*, more commonly used today, are based on a nation's wealth (gross national product [GNP]), political and economic stability, and other factors. The terms *Global South* and *Global North,* also in usage today, highlight the socioeconomic and political division between wealthy, developed nations (former centers of colonial power) in the Northern Hemisphere and poorer, developing nations (formerly colonized countries) in the Southern Hemisphere. As is evident, the labels, products of historical moments, are flawed and limited in their accuracy and represent a particular standpoint. As the book unfolds, significant historical periods that have shaped and continue to shape our world today—such as European colonization and the period immediately following WWII—are discussed in greater depth.

THE ROLE OF POWER IN INTERCULTURAL COMMUNICATION

Let's return to the scenarios again. While intercultural interactions can be engaging, delightful, informing, and even transformative, they are also often challenging, stressful, contentious, and conflicting. What else can we say about these scenarios? What other themes or threads are evident? Are Hamza, Cathy, and Immaculee positioned equally in terms of power? Are their claims of "French-ness" the same? Are they likely to experience similar or different receptions from people in the United States based on race, nation of origin, gender, class, religion, and post–9/11 attitudes? Is Australia positioned equally in terms of economic and geopolitical power with Brazil, Argentina, and Mexico despite the fact that they are all former colonies? Are international business relations influenced by these inequities? Well, sure, most of us would answer. Therefore, it is important to consider the impact on intercultural relations when the people communicating come from different and inequitable positions of power.

Have you heard of Amitabh Bachchan? If you said, "no," you are not alone among people from the United States. Named "Superstar of the Millennium" by an online BBC poll ahead of Marlon Brando and Buster Keaton and other American film idols, Amitabh Bachchan enjoys worldwide renown. So, how, in this global age with highly advanced mass communication technology, is it that so few Americans outside the Indian American community know about this superstar? While Bollywood (the film industry in India is primarily centered in Mumbai and is often referred to as "Bollywood," a melding of the city's colonial name, Bombay, with Hollywood) produces over 1,000 films per year, three times more than Hollywood, and reaches a larger audience worldwide, U.S. films continue to dominate the U.S. market. Why do you think that is?

Power = physical & ideological

INTERCULTURAL PRAXIS
COMMUNICATION AND POWER

Intercultural praxis is a kind of exercise—both mental and embodied—to investigate and transform unequal relations of power embedded in our culture. Power can be conceptualized as a constraining *and* enabling force that regulates our culture and communication. Power may be physical (i.e., violence and coercion) or ideological (i.e., persuasion and representation). The concept of power implies that the world as we know it is not neutral or natural. Rather, the world as we know and understand it is constructed and regulated by people throughout history. Thus, intercultural communication both produces and reflects relations of power.

The six ports of entry into intercultural praxis allow us to investigate the way our culture and communication are regulated and constrained by physical and ideological power. You may inquire who produces knowledge and regulates social relations, examine your position of privilege or disadvantage in relation to other cultural groups, and understand how your frame of reference is shaped by relations of power. At the same time, intercultural praxis is about using our power to enable more equitable and socially just relationships across different cultures by engaging in dialogue, reflecting, and taking informed action.

Protests against the WTO in Seattle in 1999—and later in Prague, Quebec City, and Geneva—highlight the inequities in power that characterize globalization. However, it should be noted that the WTO protest in Seattle with over 1,300 trade organizations and social movements from over 80 countries represented was not, by any means, the first major protest against the inequitable effects of global capitalism. While generally glossed over or erased by the U.S. corporate media, protests against and resistance to the devastating human, social, and environmental effects of multinational corporations and the practices and policies of global financial institutions such as the WTO have taken place in Bolivia, Venezuela, India, Nigeria, and South Korea, to name only a few (Yuen, Katsiaficas, & Rose, 2002). Why is this? In the age of global exchange of information, why was the protest against the WTO in Seattle viewed by many as the first major challenge to multinational corporate control and the power of global financial institutions?

In our study of intercultural communication in the context of globalization, we must consider how global movements of people, products, cultural forms, and cultural representations are shaped and controlled by relationships of power. What and who is controlling these positions and practices of power, and how have these power relationships been established? It is important for us to ask and investigate, for example, who are the media giants who shape the content and the distribution of news, information, and popular culture? Who are the global actors who occupy the seats at the table when the WTO and other global financial institutions meet? How are people in small villages in southern France; in the oil-rich but poverty-stricken Delta of Nigeria; in the indigenous land of Chiapas, Mexico; and in cities around the world building power bases, independently and together, to challenge global capitalism? In later chapters, we delve into how differences in power among individuals, groups, nations, and global regions have come about historically and what trends we see for the future.

INTERCULTURAL COMMUNICATION IN THE CONTEXT OF GLOBALIZATION

As illustrated in the five scenarios, intercultural communication in the context of globalization is characterized by the following:

- An increasingly dynamic, mobile world facilitated by communication and transportation technologies, accompanied by an intensification of interaction and exchange among people, cultures, and cultural forms across geographic, cultural, and national boundaries
- A rapidly growing global interdependence socially, economically, politically, and environmentally, which leads both to shared interests, needs, and resources and to greater tensions, contestations, and conflicts
- A magnification of inequities based on flows of capital, labor, and access to education and technology, as well as the increasing power of multinational corporations and global financial institutions
- A historical legacy of colonization, Western domination, and U.S. hegemony that continues to shape intercultural relations today

These characteristics of globalization outlined point to the centrality of intercultural communication in our current age. In face-to-face interactions, our differences across cultures in values, norms, verbal and nonverbal communication, as well as communication styles often lead to misunderstanding and misperceptions. Our assumptions and attitudes based on differences in physical appearance—socially constructed as racial, gender, class, and religious systems—frequently condition our responses and shape who we communicate with, build friendships and alliances with, as well as who we avoid, exclude, and engage in conflict with. The increased exposure today through interpersonal and mediated communication to people who differ from ourselves deeply impacts how we make sense of, constitute, and negotiate our own identities as well as the identities of others. Additionally, histories of conflict among groups, structural inequities that are rooted in the past and exacerbated today, as well as ideological differences frequently frame and inform our intercultural interactions.

Globalization refers to the complex web of forces and factors that have brought people, cultures, cultural products, and markets, as well as beliefs and practices, into increasingly greater proximity to and interrelationship with one another within inequitable relations of power. The word *globalization* is used here to address both the processes that contribute to and the conditions of living in a world where advances in technology have brought the world's people spatially and temporally closer together; where economic and political forces of advanced capitalism and neoliberalism have increased flows of products, services, and labor across national boundaries; and where cultural, economic, and political ideologies "travel" not only through overt public campaigns but through the mass media, consumer products, and through global institutions such as the WB, the IMF, and the WTO.

I recognize that globalization is an extremely complex concept and perhaps the ideas and vocabulary used here are new to you. For that reason, in the following pages, I start out by "deconstructing" the main forces and factors that contribute to globalization while addressing the consequences of globalization for people's lived experiences and for intercultural communication. As the book progresses, we explore together the multiple and layered meanings of the word and how globalization is understood differently by people and groups with different interests, positionalities, and standpoints.

While the term *globalization* came into common usage in the 1990s, the various factors or forces that constitute globalization have been in play for a much longer time. For the purpose of making sense of this rather unwieldy and highly contested concept, we examine three interrelated facets of globalization: (1) economic globalization, (2) political globalization, and (3) cultural globalization. Throughout all three facets, the intercultural communication dimensions are highlighted.

INTERCULTURAL DIMENSIONS OF ECONOMIC GLOBALIZATION

When a multicultural and multinational team from Chile and Australia engage in business as described in Scenario Two at the beginning of the chapter, what intercultural benefits and challenges can you imagine? Why have U.S. corporations established export production centers, or **maquiladoras,** in Mexico on the United States–Mexico border? When Korean corporations employ Guatemalan women as laborers and Korean women and men as managers, what intercultural communication issues arise? How do cultural differences in values, norms, and assumptions play out when Filipinas leave their homes and country out of economic necessity to work in the homes of middle- and upper-class families in Italy, Greece, or Japan as introduced by Scenario Five?

Global Business and Global Markets

Economic globalization—characterized by a growth in multinational corporations; an intensification of international trade and international flows of capital; and internationally interconnected webs of production, distribution, and consumption—has increased intercultural interaction and exchange exponentially. To get a sense of how you are situated within this web of economic globalization, think about your daily activities, the products and services you consume, and your future dreams. Perhaps, the alarm clock that woke you is a product of Japan with parts from China that was assembled in Indonesia. Your coffee was likely picked by laborers in Brazil, Colombia, or Vietnam. Take a look at the labels on your clothes or shoes. Where does the raw material come from, and where were the products made and under what conditions? How far did the gasoline used to fuel your mode of transportation travel to reach you? How have your job prospects and wages changed since your parents' generation? What country does the person you talk to live in when you dial customer service or answer a telemarketing call? Will you live and work in your country of origin? With whom will you work, and how will cultural differences impact your workplace?

By considering these questions, you begin to see how economic globalization has magnified the need for intercultural awareness, understanding, and training at all levels of business. In the late 1960s, Dutch psychologist Geert Hofstede conducted research at over 50 IBM company sites worldwide to identify and understand differences in national cultures and their impact on workplace culture. Hofstede's (1980/2003) past studies and more recent work (Hofstede & Hofstede, 2004) identify five dimensions of national cultural difference, which include (1) power distance, (2) individualism–collectivism, (3) uncertainty avoidance, (4) masculinity–femininity, and (5) long- and short-term orientation, providing a broad map for understanding intercultural differences and avoiding cultural conflicts in organizations.

These dimensions of cultural difference and the research of other scholars and practitioners are explored and critiqued in depth throughout the book. For now, it is important to recognize that cultural differences in values, norms, and behaviors play a significant role in team building, decision making, job satisfaction, marketing and advertising, as well as many other aspects of doing business in the context of economic globalization. Some intercultural misunderstandings are rather humorous; however, they point to the difficulties of "translating" business practices, products, and markets across cultures. Take, for example, this popular Pepsi slogan: "Pepsi Brings You Back to Life." The slogan, translated into Chinese, reads, "Pepsi Brings Your Ancestors Back From the Grave." Or the Coors beer slogan, "Turn it loose," when translated into Spanish, told the consumer to "Suffer from diarrhea."

Intercultural mistakes may be amusing, but they are also often costly. Researcher and marketing expert at Sejong University in South Korea Choe Yong-shik criticizes the use of "Konglish" in corporate slogans arguing that it damages the image of Korean companies. "The more they invest in marketing overseas, the worse their image may become," referring to the awkward use of Korean cultural values translated into English phrases (Kitae & Staines, 2005). Anticipating the intercultural challenge every multinational communicator must solve, former West German chancellor Willy Brandt stated, "If I'm selling to you, I speak your language. If I'm buying, *dann müssen Sie Deutsch sprechen*" (as cited in Nurden, 1997, p. 39).

The examples direct our attention to the intercultural dimensions of economic globalization. Languages are complex and nuanced repositories of culture. Languages, both verbal and nonverbal, convey meanings about the values, beliefs, and assumptions of a culture. Translation across cultures can lead to confusion, misunderstanding, and communication failures if the culture as a system of meaning, as discussed in Chapter 1, is not understood. The confluence and interplay of languages in the global context also leads to hybrid forms such as *Konglish* and *Spanlish,* which challenge shared systems of meanings within cultures and introduce what may be viewed as "outside" and "undesirable" influences. The former West German chancellor's statement, "If I'm selling to you, I speak your language. If I'm buying, *then you must speak German,*" demonstrates how language and language use are intricately interwoven with relationships of power.

As we have seen, advances in technology—both communication and transportation technology—have enabled the growth of multinational corporations, an increased global interconnection in the production of goods and services, and the distribution of products through global markets. What other forces combine with advances in technology to define economic globalization?

Free Trade and Economic Liberalization

Shifts in international economic policies since WWII and most markedly since the 1990s have dramatically increased the movement of capital (money), commodities (products), services, information, and labor (people) around the globe. A primary factor propelling these economic shifts is **economic liberalization**—also known as trade liberalization, or free trade. Broadly speaking, what this means to us at the beginning of the 21st century is that the movement of goods, labor, services, and capital is increasingly unrestricted by tariffs (taxes) and trade barriers. Historically, taxes and tariffs on foreign products and services were put in place by national governments to protect the jobs, prices, and industries of a nation-state. The countries we consider developed nations, or First World nations, today used protectionist policies (taxation of foreign-made products and services) until they accumulated enough wealth to benefit from free trade. In fact, until the last 30 to 40 years, the United States opposed "free trade" policies in an effort to protect U.S. jobs, products, and services (Stiglitz, 2002). What we see in the 1990s and 2000s, however, is the promotion and support of **free trade agreements** by the United States and other First World nations, which liberalize trade by reducing trade tariffs and barriers transnationally while maintaining protection for some of their own industries.

As a result of economic liberalization or free trade along with advances in transportation and communication technologies, we see an escalating trend toward moving manufacturing sectors and more recently service sectors of the economy offshore or outside the geographic boundaries of the corporate ownership's country of origin. In search of cheaper labor, few if any labor and environmental regulations and tax breaks, U.S.-based multinational corporations, as well as corporations based in other First World nations such as Europe, Australia, Canada, and Japan, are relocating their sites of production to Mexico, Central America, and countries in Asia. In addition, corporations in search of ways to expand their markets turn to populations in other countries. As a result, most all business transactions today have an intercultural component.

With the signing of the **North American Free Trade Agreement (NAFTA)** by Canada, Mexico, and the United States in January 1994, one of the boldest experiments in free trade or economic liberalization, which supports the free movement of goods, services, and capital without trade or tariff barriers, was put into play. Almost two decades after the experiment of NAFTA was initiated, the implications of its policies remain highly controversial and contested. As you can imagine, people with varying standpoints, positionalities, and interests have judged its success and/or failure differently. Communication—on corporate and governmental websites, in the news, in face-to-face interactions, and at protest sites—about the free trade agreement differs greatly based on its impact on people's lives and livelihood:

- The governments of all three nations support it. It has been touted as "the world's largest free trade zone" that has "brought economic growth and rising standards of living for people in all three countries," claims the Canadian government website (Foreign Affairs and International Trade Canada, 2011).

- Multinational corporations are generally strongly in support of NAFTA because it increases profit by significantly reducing labor and facilities costs and offers a deregulation of environmental and labor restrictions (U.S. Chamber of Commerce, n.d.).
- A growing number of organizations, groups, and individuals oppose the liberalization policies including labor unions in the United States and Canada who point to the loss of 3 million manufacturing jobs in the United States alone to cheaper labor in Mexico (Tonelson, 2002).
- More than 2 million farmers in Mexico have been driven out of business due to subsidies provided to U.S. farmers and the appropriation of Mexican farmers' land.
- Environmental and social justice groups in all three countries point to the health and environmental risks and the increasingly inequitable distribution of wealth that has resulted from the agreement (George, 2004).

Clearly, economic globalization and the policies of free trade have dramatically accelerated the amount and intensity of intercultural communication. Individuals, families, for-profit and nonprofit institutions and businesses, as well as nations are increasingly interwoven into a complex web of intercultural relations. From an intercultural communication perspective, it is important to be aware of the broader economic context that propels and shapes intercultural interactions today. Additionally, it is critical to underscore how different actors on the global stage—governments, multinational corporations, labor union representatives, farmers, and environmental and social justice groups—experience and make meaning about economic globalization in vastly different ways.

Global Financial Institutions and Popular Resistance

Scenario Four at the beginning of the chapter described the protest against the WTO in Seattle, Washington, in November 1999, where over 40,000 people from around the globe, representing a wide variety of groups and interests, rallied together to challenge the decision-making power of the WTO. What is the WTO, and why would 40,000 people want to stop discussion of "free trade"? In 1995, the WTO was formed as a successor to the post–WWII General Agreement on Tariffs and Trade (GATT) as "the only international organization dealing with the global rules of trade between nations. Its main function is to ensure that trade flows as smoothly, predictably and freely as possible," according to the WTO website. Free trade agreements are negotiated by governments, but the purpose of these agreements is to assist producers, exporters, and importers in conducting business with the goal to "improve the welfare of the peoples of the member countries" (WTO, 2011). GATT (now the WTO), IMF, and the WB were set up immediately following WWII to maintain global economic stability and to address poverty through development. These three institutions are the primary ones governing economic globalization.

Economic globalization, spearheaded by free trade agreements that are often mandated by the IMF, financed by the WB, and negotiated and monitored by the WTO, certainly has led to increased intercultural business transactions and economic interdependence internationally. From a business perspective, individuals and companies must become effective in communicating interculturally in order to participate and compete in global markets. Multinational corporations are by nature composed of people from different national and cultural backgrounds who are accustomed to "doing business" differently, not to mention the range of languages, managerial styles, work ethics, negotiating styles, and marketing practices that are brought together in multinational and multicultural teams.

The integration of global markets within and across the First and Third Worlds offers some on both sides of the divide an opportunity to increase their wealth. However, economic globalization has resulted in increased economic disparities between the wealthy and the poor not only globally but within the United States and has magnified economic stratification based on race and gender (Lui, Robles, Leondar-Wright, Brewer, & Anderson, 2006; Stiglitz, 2002; also see Figure 2.3).

Figure 2.3   Global Wealth Distribution: World's Richest 1% Own 40% of All Wealth; 50% of World's Poorest Adults Own Just 1% of the Wealth

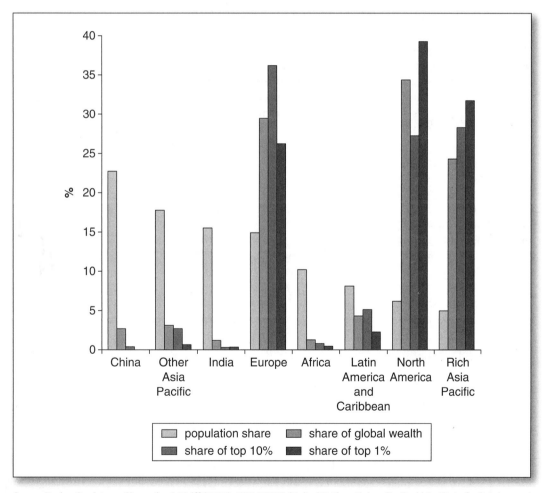

Source: Davies, Sandstrom, Shorrocks, & Wolff (2006); UNU-WIDER (United Nations University-World Institute for Development Economic Research).

After this brief discussion, we clearly see the value of learning about intercultural communication in the context of economic globalization; we have insight into the critical role economic liberalization and free trade agreements play in increasing economic interdependence around the world. We also see the intercultural issues and challenges to social justice of economic globalization including the growing gap between the wealthy and the poor and the economic stratification of both the United States and global society based on race and gender. In the next section, the political dimensions of globalization are explored and the impact on intercultural communication is discussed.

INTERCULTURAL DIMENSIONS OF POLITICAL GLOBALIZATION

As we see an increase in economic interdependence and growing inequities in terms of control of wealth and resources, we also see a trend toward the interconnectedness of nation-state politics, the formation of bodies of global governance, as well as global movements of resistance responding to increasing inequities in political power. Political agendas of democratization are closely linked to free trade agreements and the agendas of the WTO, the WB, and the IMF. Thus, these global financial institutions also serve political purposes.

Democratization and Militarism

Since the fall of the Berlin Wall in 1989, the collapse of the former Soviet Union in 1990, and the end of the Cold War, there has been a widely held belief that democracy and capitalism go hand in hand to bring about both national and global prosperity and peace. Harvard political scientist Samuel Huntington (1993) documented a global trend toward democratization since WWII. While the concept and practice of democracy is contested, **democratization** in this case refers to the transition from an authoritarian to a democratic political system that ensures the universal right to vote. U.S. political economist Francis Fukuyama (1992) wrote what is considered a classic in democratization studies entitled *The End of History and the Last Man,* which argues for the inevitable rise of *Western* liberal democracy in the post–Cold War era.

> What we may be witnessing is not just the end of the Cold War, or the passing of a particular period of post-war history, but the end of history as such: that is, the end point of mankind's ideological evolution and the universalization of Western liberal democracy as the final form of human government. (Fukuyama, 1992, p. 1)

However, in her book *World On Fire: How Exporting Free Market Democracy Breeds Ethnic Hatred and Global Instability*, Yale Law School professor Amy Chua (2003) disputed this assumption, showing that economic globalization and the rapid expansion of free market democracy has led to an increase in interethnic conflict worldwide. Chua identified a phenomenon she calls "market-dominant minorities," groups of people such as the Chinese in Southeast Asia, Whites in Zimbabwe and South Africa, Jews in Russia, and

Indians in East Africa who are ethnically or religiously the minority in terms of population and yet control vastly disproportionate percentages of a country's or region's resources and wealth. In the midst of long-standing poverty experienced by majority groups, the accumulation of wealth by minorities has triggered dramatic interethnic conflicts and genocide such as the massacre of over 1 million Tutsi in less than 100 days by the Hutu majority in 1994 and the slaying of ethnic Chinese in Indonesia. Chua (2003) noted that "the combined pursuit of free markets and democratization has repeatedly catalyzed ethnic conflict in highly predictable ways. This has been the sobering lesson of globalization in the last twenty years" (p. 16).

It is equally important to note the popular resistance movements that emerged in 2011, particularly in the Middle East, where, in Egypt, for example, "people-powered" nonviolent uprisings opposed the repressive authoritarian regime and demanded democratic reform. These movements for social change in the context of globalization are facilitated by advances in communication technologies such as the Internet and social media sites that connect and mobilize protestors both within and across cultures.

Ideological Wars

The attacks on 9/11 illustrate some of the shifting, contradictory, and contested political facets of globalization and the intercultural communication dimensions that have emerged. While it is not my intention to condone any form of violence for political or other purposes, it is useful to examine carefully the historical and political forces that led up to 9/11 and the dynamics that shape our post–9/11 world. In the 1980s, the United States was politically and militarily aligned with the founders of al-Qaeda (Arabic for the "base" or "foundation"), an organization comprised of international independent cells who were credited with the attacks. Called "freedom-fighters" by the United States for their resistance to the Soviet invasion and occupation of Afghanistan, al-Qaeda currently opposes U.S. military occupation of Arab nations (Cooley, 2002). From a geopolitical, international intercultural perspective, we see an increase in the use of military force to address political conflicts and to maintain access to raw materials such as oil, as demonstrated by the extended occupation of Afghanistan and Iraq in the name of the "War on Terror." The challenges of advancing a Western-style democracy in the context of militarization and extended occupation played out in full force as various ethnic, religious, and secular factions in Iraq drafted a constitution in August 2005 and as the country wavered on the verge of civil war in 2007.

Following attacks in London in July 2005, also credited to al-Qaeda, Ayman al-Zawahiri, previously second in command in al-Qaeda, obliquely claimed responsibility in a video to the British and American people, stating, "Our message to you is crystal clear: Your salvation will only come in your withdrawal from our land, in stopping the robbing of our oil and resources, and in stopping your support for the corrupt and corrupting leaders" (Sullivan, 2005). Former president George W. Bush responded by saying the following:

> The Iraqis want to live in a free society. Zawahiri doesn't want them to live in a free society. And that's the clash of ideologies—freedom versus tyranny. . . . People like Zawahiri have an ideology that is dark, dim, backwards. (Sullivan, 2005)

Ideology is defined as a set of ideas and beliefs reflecting the needs and aspirations of individuals, groups, classes, or cultures that form the basis for political, economic, and other systems.

What can we observe about the communication or miscommunication occurring here? Is there any indication that the two communicators are listening to each other? How is the intercultural communication or miscommunication being used intentionally for political purposes? On the one hand, Zawahiri's statement sounded like a militant anticolonial plea. On the other hand, former president George W. Bush's response framed and justified the military invasion and occupation of the Middle East by polarizing Western-style "freedom" with Islamic "tyranny."

In the article "Multiculturalism Fans the Flames of Islamic Extremism," published in the *London Times,* Kenan Malik (2005) claimed that Britain's pursuit of multiculturalism, which stresses identity politics instead of national unity, is the cause of the bombings in three "tubes" (subways) and a bus in July 2005. As an Indian-born British cultural commentator who grew up in Manchester, England, and who now lives in London, Malik recognized the history of racism endured by his parents' generation and directly combated by his generation. At the same time, however, he lamented the lack of a unifying British identity stating the following:

> Of course, there is little to romanticise in old-style Britishness with its often racist vision of belongingness. Back in the fifties policy makers feared that, in the words of a Colonial Office report, "a large coloured community would weaken . . . the concept of England or Britain." That old racist notion of identity has thankfully crumbled. But nothing new has come to replace it. The very notion of creating common values has been abandoned except at a most minimal level. Britishness has come to be defined simply as a toleration of difference. The politics of ideology has given way to the politics of identity, creating a more fragmented Britain, and one where many groups assert their identity through a sense of victimhood and grievance. (Malik, 2005)

On the one hand, globalization is characterized by the opening of borders and the increased flow of people, goods, and ideologies across national boundaries; on the other hand, as evidenced by the call for more restrictive immigration policies in Europe and Australia and the punitive immigration laws proposed by the U.S. Congress in 2006 and Arizona's Senate Bill 1070 in 2010, "free" movement of people across borders is highly conditional and is directly related to political and economic power.

Ideological wars frame issues in the public arena in ways that profoundly impact intercultural communication in people's everyday lives. Ideological battles often employ false dichotomies—requiring adherence to a belief in freedom versus adherence to Islam or support for multiculturalism versus national unity—to galvanize the public while obscuring the complexities and nuances of intercultural issues. Rhetoric that emerges from ideological wars often scapegoats one group—for example, immigrants—for the challenges and ills of a society instilling and perpetuating prejudices and animosity as well as inciting violence among cultural groups.

Global Governance and Social Movements

One of the critical issues of globalization is the question of governance. Questions of governance on global, national, state, and local levels are closely linked to intercultural communication. Who is at the table, literally and figuratively, when decisions that affect people close by and in the far reaches of the world are made? Whose voices are represented, and whose interests are served? What standpoints and positionalities are silenced or dismissed? Whose language, political processes, and economic system dominate? Whose rules, behaviors, communication styles, values, and beliefs are privileged and normalized? Interestingly, in a time of increased "democratization," we see a magnification of the concentration of decision-making power in the hands of a few First World nations. As Stiglitz (2002) noted, most of the activity of IMF and WB is in the developing world, while the control of the global financial institutions is in the hands of developed nations. He argued that the current system run by the IMF, WB, and WTO is "one of taxation without representation" (p. 20). He also said it's a system that could be called:

> global governance without global government, one in which a few institutions—
> the World Bank, the IMF, the WTO—a few players—the finance, commerce, and
> trade ministries, closely linked to certain financial and commerical interests—
> dominate the scene, but in which many of those affected by their decisions are
> left almost voiceless. (p. 22)

Yet individuals, groups, and organizations are coming together across national, ethnic, and cultural lines to form intercultural alliances that challenge the domination of global financial and political institutions and work together to create alternatives to racial, ethnic, and class discrimination and exploitation. Susan George (2004), author of *Another World Is Possible If . . . ,* stated that people opposed to the policies and practices of the WTO, the IMF, and WB:

> refer to themselves collectively as the "social movement," the "citizens'
> movement" or the "global justice movement." In a pinch, if headline space is
> really at a premium, they'll settle for "alter-" or "counter-," as preferable to the
> inaccurate, even insulting, "anti-" globalization. The movement is not "anti" but
> internationalist and deeply engaged with the world as a whole and the fate of
> everyone who shares the planet. (p. ix)

Political globalization is complex and often contradictory. At this point, it is important to note that the forces of globalization have led to the spread of Western-style democracy, an increase in interethnic tension and violence as free market economic policies combine with democratic processes of universal suffrage, an escalation in militarization as a form of conflict resolution and as a means for the imposition of democratic principles, and an increased concentration of power in the hands of international institutions of governance. While some argue that our current times are marked by an increased sense of alienation, powerlessness, and apathy toward political engagement, the wide range of participation in intercultural resistance movements, international labor organizations, and multicultural activism suggests otherwise.

COMMUNICATIVE DIMENSIONS
COMMUNICATION AND GLOBALIZATION

Intercultural communication is central to three aspects of globalization. In the context of economic globalization, attention to cultural differences in communication styles, values, norms, and behaviors is critical to effective business practices. Additionally, economic relationships of power are imposed, negotiated, and changed through communication.

As a result of political globalization, people's lives are increasingly shaped not only by national and local decision making but also by global bodies of governance. Ideological differences, often communicated through opposition rhetoric such as "us vs. them," inform how we think and feel about those who are culturally different. Political globalization also creates conditions for interethnic, interracial or interreligious conflict as well as intercultural alliances for social justice.

The rapid flow of people and cultural forms in the context of globalization generates increasing opportunities for intercultural communication. Communication among people from different cultures—interpersonally and through music, dance, film, clothing, and media—produces new hybrid cultural forms and identities. In this sense, intercultural communication is the process and site of cultural globalization.

INTERCULTURAL DIMENSIONS OF CULTURAL GLOBALIZATION

As people move around the globe—whether for tourism, work, or political asylum; in the military; in search of economic opportunity; or for survival—we carry our culture with us and make efforts, however elaborate or small, to re-create a sense of the familiar or a sense of "home." While the complex notion of culture cannot be reduced to objects that are tucked away in a suitcase or packed in a backpack, the things we take as we move, travel, or flee are significant in representing our culture, just as the languages we speak, the beliefs that we hold, and the practices we enact. In the following section, I introduce a few of the more salient aspects of **cultural globalization** including migration and the formation of cultural connectivities, cultural flows within the context of unequal power relations, and the emergence of hybrid cultural forms and identities.

Migration and Cultural Connectivities

Due to the forces of globalization, people from different cultural backgrounds—ethnic/racial cultures, religious cultures, class cultures, national cultures, and regional cultures—find their lives, their livelihoods, and their lifestyles increasingly intertwined and overlapping. People from different backgrounds have been engaging with each other and experiencing intercultural contact for many millennia; however, the degree and intensity of interaction, the patterns and directions of movement, and the terms of engagement in the context of globalization are different than earlier eras of human interaction. All of this, as anthropologists Jonathan Xavier Inda and Renato Rosaldo (2001) claimed, points to "a world in motion. It is a world where cultural subjects and objects—that is, meaningful forms such as capital, people, commodities, images, and ideas—have become unhinged from particular localities" (p. 11). They argued that culture, in the context of globalization, is **deterritorialized,** which means that cultural subjects (people) and cultural objects (film, food, traditions, and ideas) are uprooted from their "situatedness" in a particular physical, geographic location and **reterritorialized,** or relocated in new, multiple, and varied geographic spaces. Meanings of cultural forms such as Hindi movies that Amitabh Bachchan stars in or TV programs from the United States such as *Friends* or *Survivor* that are broadcast around the world take on different meanings in different locations. Similarly, a person's or group's sense of identity, who migrates from Iran to Israel to the United States, for example, is reinscribed in new and different cultural contexts, altering, fusing, and sometimes transforming that identity.

In previous times, when people moved voluntarily or forcibly to distant locations, they likely stayed there. While they may have had intermittent contact with home, they were unlikely to visit frequently or maintain regular communication as people can today through the Internet, nor were they likely to consider several places in the world as "home." Today, due to advances in communication and transportation technology, we see the emergence of global circuits of cultural connection and community interconnection between multiple geographic locations crossing national and continental boundaries. Someone who migrates from Mexico, Central America, or Latin America to the United States may return regularly to work or visit. We also see the formation of economic and social networks or associations that operate internationally where communities of people from one location, for example, Mexico or South Korea, may unite to support each other in the new location and maintain ties and connections, sending financial support or **remittances** as a community to the city or regional community at home.

The reality of groups of people migrating to new locations and maintaining connections to "home" is not a new phenomenon. Take, for example, the notion of **diasporic communities,** groups of people who leave their homeland and who maintain a longing for—even if only in their imagination—a return to "home," such as the expulsion and dispersion of the Jews during the Babylonian Exile in 700 BCE, the African diaspora that forcibly uprooted and transplanted Africans to the Americas and the Caribbean during the period of British colonization, or the Armenian diaspora in the early part of the 20th century that resulted from the genocide of approximately 1.5 million Armenians. What is different today in the context of globalization is that communities are able to maintain transnational connections that are not only in the imagination but where "home" can literally be in multiple places, where one's neighborhood may cross national boundaries, and where one's community is spread around the globe.

Cultural Flows and Unequal Power Relations

With Starbucks' 16,000 coffeehouses in 50 countries outside North America, McDonald's spread around the world, Coca-Cola ubiquitous in even the most remote areas, and Mickey Mouse the most internationally recognized figure, what are the implications for local and/or national cultures? Responses to global flows of culture and cultural products range from outraged efforts to protect local cultures to a full embrace of the "McDonaldization" of the world, yet what are the effects of the global flow of cultural products on local and national cultures? Is the flow of cultural products such as music, films, food, and media evenly distributed with equitable, multidirectional movement? Most observers, even proponents of economic globalization, recognize an asymmetrical power relationship that magnifies inequities in the flow of culture and cultural forms. What are the implications of dramatically uneven distribution of culture and imbalanced diffusion of cultural products that are ideologically infused?

Some argue that globalization has brought about a homogenization and specifically an **Americanization** of the world's cultures that need to be examined carefully not only from an economic point of view but also from the perspective of U.S. dominance and cultural imperialism. **Cultural imperialism** is the domination of one culture over others through cultural forms such as popular culture, media, and cultural products. Economic globalization has exacerbated an inequitable spread of U.S.-based corporations and cultural products that, while providing additional goods and services, also has led to the bankruptcy of local industries and has had a dramatic impact on local cultural values, traditions, norms, and practices. For example, in France, where finely prepared cuisine is integrally linked to the national cultural identity, there is a resistance to the ways U.S. fast-food chains have invaded the culinary landscape and altered cultural eating rituals and habits. In China, marketing targeted at children by McDonald's and Disney disrupts cultural norms of parental authority, where children are informed through mass advertising that they can make choices about what they want independent of their parents. Grewal (2005) argued that in India, production and consumption of Barbie dressed in a sari (traditional Indian dress) advances notions of universal female subjectivity—what it means to be female in the world today—that is essentially bound to White American norms and values and yet is "veiled" in Indian attire. The former prime minister of Canada Kim Campbell noted the following:

> For Americans, cultural industries are industries like any others. For Canadians, cultural industries are industries that, aside from their economic impact, create products that are fundamental to the survival of Canada as a society. The globalization of the world economy and communications has been a vehicle for the Americanization of the globe. For Canada and other countries, globalization has been a phenomenon within which their distinct, non-American cultures must struggle to survive. (Globalization 101.org, n.d.)

The "struggle to survive" for non-American cultures, and for many nondominant cultures within the United States, is an ongoing, daily contestation among local/national cultural industries, products, and identities and the overwhelming dominance of U.S. cultural products, cultural industries, and culturally produced identities in the world market today. The unequal diffusion of Western, specifically U.S., cultural products, identities, and ideologies and control of mass media can be seen as a form of cultural imperialism, where cultures outside the center of power (those outside the United States or those within who do not identify with the dominant mainstream culture) are saturated through market-driven globalization by American cultural ideals, and become, over time, increasingly "Americanized" and homogenized by and assimilated to American culture.

John Tomlinson (1999) argued that cultural imperialism in the context of globalization is a continuation of earlier forms of imperialism as evidenced in the colonization process of the 16th to 19th centuries and represents "an historical pattern of increasing global cultural hegemony" (p. 144). Cultural imperialism today can be understood as the domination of Western cultural forms—from music to architecture to food to clothing styles—Western norms and practices—from gender norms to dating practices to eating habits—and Western beliefs—from individualism to Western-style democracy to Western notions of "freedom" and human rights—around the globe.

As you can imagine, U.S. cultural imperialism, the Americanization of the world, and the notion that the cultures of the world are becoming homogenized—meaning that cultures, over time, will become the same—are hotly debated topics within the cultural dimensions of globalization. So, what do you think? How does this picture of the world mesh with your experience and understanding? Even those who fervently oppose the notion of homogenization recognize the tremendous impact U.S. popular culture and U.S. cultural industries have on cultures around the globe. However, they also suggest that the cultural imperialism approach is too one-sided, limiting, and simplistic. If the world's cultures are not becoming homogenized and yet are deeply influenced by the distribution and dissemination of U.S./Western cultural products and ideologies, what is going on?

Hybrid Cultural Forms and Identities

Without erasing the asymmetrical power relations and the dominance of U.S. and Western cultural forms, it is important to note the power, voices, and agency of those who are impacted by or are recipients of these dominant U.S. cultural products. Can we assume, for example, that similar meanings are made of television shows like *Friends*, *Sex and the City*, and *Survivor* when they are viewed by people in Turkey, Honduras, and Thailand or in different cultural communities within the United States?

Inda and Rosaldo (2001) identified another important question to ask. Is the flow of culture and cultural products only from the West to rest of the world, or is there movement in multiple directions? The international success of Indian superstar Amitabh Bachchan in Russia, Africa, and the Middle East indicates there are directions of flow and circuits of cultural influence impacting cultures around the world other than those originating from the United States. When we look closely at our lived experience in the context of globalization, we see that the overlap and intersection of cultures create **hybrid cultural forms,** or a mix that produces new and distinct forms, challenging the idea that there is only a unilateral dissemination of culture and cultural forms from the U.S and Western cultures to the rest of the world.

Take, for example, reggaeton, a blend of rap and reggae with Latin influence and origins, which soared into popularity in the mid-2000s. Daddy Yankee, the Puerto Rican reggaeton artist who was nominated for a Latin Grammy in 2005, said in an interview, "In the past year we didn't have a true genre that speaks for the Latino's. Right now we have that with the reggaeton" (Daddy Yankee Interview, n.d.). I am sure that you can think of other music forms that could be considered hybrid or fusion forms such as jazz, rock, Raï—originating from Western Algeria with Arabic, French, and Spanish influence—or Wu-Tang Latino, which is a fusion of hip hop and reggaeton.

Communication scholar Radha Hegde (2002) defined the creation of hybrid cultures and hybrid cultural forms as a type of resistance that nondominant groups employ out of fear of total assimilation and as a means of cultural maintenance in the midst of powerful dominant cultural forces. "Hybrid cultures, therefore, are not always a romantic return to the homeland; they are also cultures that develop and survive as forms of collective resistance" (p. 261). Throughout the book, we will explore in greater detail how individuals, cultural groups, communities, and nations adapt to, resist, and negotiate their collective cultural identities, sense of cultural agency, and cultural productions within the context of U.S./Western cultural imperialism and the global forces of cultural homogenization.

SUMMARY

Do you have a clearer understanding of globalization at this point? As you can tell, it is an extremely complex phenomenon with multiple historical, cultural, political, and economic influences. In this chapter, globalization was defined as the complex web of forces and factors that have brought people, cultures, cultural products, and markets, as well as beliefs and practices into increasingly greater proximity to and interrelationship with one another. Globalization is characterized by an increasingly dynamic and mobile world that has led to an intensification of interaction and exchange among people, cultures, and cultural forms across geographic, cultural, and national boundaries. It has also resulted in a rapidly growing global interdependence, which translates into shared interests, needs, and resources, as well as greater tensions, contestations, and conflicts over resources. A magnification of inequities based on flows of capital, labor, and access to education and technology, as well as the increasing power of multinational corporations and global financial institutions, is a very real part of globalization. These forces and factors did not just develop independently of world history. Rather, globalization must be understood in relation to the **historical legacy of colonization,** Western domination, and U.S. hegemony that shapes intercultural relations today.

While it is somewhat artificial to divide globalization into economic, political, and cultural aspects, we can more easily highlight and understand the intercultural dimensions of globalization by doing this. As workplaces, communities, schools, and people's lives become more intricately interwoven in global webs, intercultural communication is increasingly present in all areas of our lives. To analyze, understand, and effectively act in intercultural situations, we need to be able to take broad macro-level perspectives as well as micro-level views. The purpose of this chapter was to introduce you to global dynamics that shape intercultural communication—the role of global governance systems like the WTO, IMF, and WB as well as the global resistant or "alter-globalization" movements; the processes of democratizing, militarization, and the ideological wars; as well as cultural imperialism and cultural hybridity—that influence who we interact with, frame our attitudes about and experiences of each other, and structure our intercultural interaction in relationships of power. Since intercultural communication is an embodied experience and most often an embodied experience of "difference," our next chapter focuses on understanding how and what our bodies communicate, how our bodies have been marked by difference historically, and how performances of the body communicate in the context of globalization.

KEY TERMS

World Trade Organization (WTO)
World Bank (WB)
International Monetary Fund (IMF)
First World
Second World
Third World
developing country/developed
   country
Global South/Global North
globalization
maquiladoras
economic globalization
economic liberalization
free trade agreements

North American Free Trade Agreement
   (NAFTA)
democratization
ideology
political globalization
cultural globalization
deterritorialized
reterritorialized
remittances
diasporic communities
Americanization
cultural imperialism
hybrid cultural forms
historical legacy of colonization

DISCUSSION QUESTIONS AND ACTIVITIES

Discussion Questions

1. Consider the scenarios at the beginning of the chapter. What themes are interwoven through the fabric of all the scenarios? Without erasing the obvious and more subtle differences between the situations, what common factors and forces shape the world that these scenarios describe? What intercultural communication issues are evident in the scenarios?

2. What is the relationship between colonialism and globalization? What are the similarities, and what are the differences? Using concrete examples, discuss how the legacy of colonialism impacts the process of globalization today.

3. How are economic, political, and cultural globalization interconnected? Using concrete examples from the chapter and/or your own observation/knowledge, discuss the relationships among economic, political, and cultural globalization.

4. Is globalization a process of Americanization and cultural homogenization? Or does globalization produce hybrid culture forms and thus create cultural heterogeneity? What is your position on this debate? What does this debate tell us about the complex nature of globalization?

Activities

1. Historicizing Globalization—Group Activity
   a. The class is divided into three groups. The first group is assigned to research the history of economic globalization, the second group on political globalization, and the last group on cultural globalization.

b. Each group should focus on three to five major historical events, time periods, key individuals, institutions, and so on, that shaped the course of globalization from economic, political, and cultural dimensions.

c. Each group draws a historical timeline.

d. Compare the three timelines, and examine how the three types of globalization are interconnected with each other.

2. Spatializing Globalization—Group Activity

a. In small groups, research the current global movement of people, circulation of information and products, political and economic partnership, international and regional conflicts, and so forth.

b. Draw a map so that people can understand the dynamics of globalization visually.

c. Once the global map is drawn to describe the macro picture of globalization, discuss the following questions:

i. What are the patterns of movements you can see on the map?

ii. What are the relationships of power you can read in the transnational movements of people and commodity shown on the map?

iii. If you were to position yourself in the map of globalization, where would you find yourself geographically, economically, politically, and culturally?

iv. How are the patterns of global movements reflected in the dynamics of intercultural communication at the interpersonal and local levels?

3. Research the IMF, WB, and WTO—Group Activity

a. In small groups, conduct research on the three international organizations that are the powerful players of globalization.

b. Report your findings to the class, and discuss how the roles and functions of international organizations shape the process of globalization today.

REFERENCES

Chua, A. (2003). *World on fire: How exporting free market democracy breeds ethnic hatred and global instability.* New York: First Anchor Books.

Cooley, J. K. (2002). *Unholy wars: Afghanistan, America and international terrorism.* London: Pluto.

Daddy Yankee Interview. (n.d.). *1-Famous-Quotes.com.* Retrieved from http://www.1-famous-quotes.com/quote/1322231

Davies, J. B., Sandstrom, S., Shorrocks, A., & Wolff, E. N. (2006). *The world distribution of household wealth.* Retrieved from http://www.iariw.org/papers/2006/davies.pdf

Dussel, E. (1995). Ethnocentrism and modernity. In J. Beverley, J. Oviedo, & M. Aronna (Eds.), *The postmodernism debate in Latin America* (pp. 65–76). Durham, NC: Duke University Press Books.

Ebron, G. (2002, October). Not just the maid: Negotiating Filipina identity in Italy. *Intersections: Gender, History and Culture in the Asian Context, 8.* Retrieved from http://wwwsshe.murdoch.edu.au/intersections/issue8/ebron.html

Editorial Board. (1999, December 6). The social meaning of the anti-WTO protests in Seattle. *World Socialist Web Site.* Retrieved from http://www.wsws.org/articles/1999/dec1999/wto-d06.shtml

Foreign Affairs and International Trade Canada. (2011). *Canada and the North American Free Trade Agreement.* Retrieved from http://www.international.gc.ca/trade-agreements-accords-commerciaux/agr-acc/nafta-alena/index.aspx?view=d

Fukuyama, F. (1992). *The end of history and the last man.* New York: Avon Books.

George, S. (2004). *Another world is possible if . . .* London: Verso.

Globalization 101.org. (n.d.). *Cultural impact #2: Popular culture.* Retrieved from http://www.globalization101.org/index.php?file=issue&pass1=subs&id=128

Grewal, I. (2005). *Transnational America: Feminisms, diasporas, neoliberalisms.* Durham, NC: Duke University Press Books.

Harcourt, T. (2008). Market opportunities across Latin America remain despite global cooling. *Austrade.* Retrieved from http://www.austrade.gov.au/Market-opportunities-across-Latin-America-remain-despite-global-cooling/default.aspx

Hegde, R. (2002). Translated enactments: The relational configurations of the Asian Indian immigrant experience. In J. N. Martin, T. K. Nakayama, & L. A. Flores (Eds.), *Readings in intercultural communication: Experiences and contexts* (2nd ed., pp. 259–266). New York: McGraw-Hill.

Held, D., McGrew, A. G., Goldblatt, D., & Perraton, J. (1999). *Global transformations: Politics, economics and culture.* Stanford, CA: Stanford University Press.

Hofstede, G. (2003). *Culture's consequences: International differences in work-related values.* Thousand Oaks, CA: Sage. (Original work published 1980)

Hofstede, G., & Hofstede, G. J. (2004). *Cultures and organizations: Software of the mind: Intercultural cooperation and its importance for survival.* New York: McGraw-Hill.

Huntington, S. P. (1993). *The third wave: Democratization in the late 20th century.* Norman: University of Oklahoma Press.

Inda, J. X., & Rosaldo, R. (Eds.). (2001). *The anthropology of globalization: A reader.* Cambridge, UK: Blackwell.

Kitae, K., & Staines, R. (2005). "Konglish" slogans hurt image. *Korea Times.* Retrieved from http://times.hankooki.com/lpage/nation/200506/kt2005062917203311990.htm

Lui, M., Robles, B., Leondar-Wright, B., Brewer, R., & Adamson, R. (2006). *The color of wealth: The story behind the U.S. racial wealth divide.* New York: The New Press.

Malik, K. (2005, August). Multiculturalism fans the flames of Islamic extremism. *London Times.* Retrieved from http://www.kenanmalik.com/essays/times_ bombings. html

Nurden, R. (1997, October 30). Teaching tailored for business people's every demand. *The European,* p. 39.

Rose, C. (2005, April). *Amitabh Bachan on Charlie Rose.* Retrieved from http://twentyonwards.blogs.com/twenty_onwards/2005/04/amitabh_bachan__2.html

Stiglitz, J. (2002). *Globalization and its discontents.* New York: W.W. Norton.

Sullivan, K. (2005, August 5). Al Qaeda's No. 2 blames Blair, issues warning. *Washington Post.* Retrieved from http://www.washingtonpost.com/wp-dyn/content/article/2005/08/04 /AR2005080400514.html

Tomlinson, J. (1999). *Globalization and culture.* Cambridge, UK: Blackwell.

Tonelson, A. (2002). *The race to the bottom: Why a world wide worker surplus and free trade are sinking American living standards.* Cambridge, MA: Westview Press.

U.S. Chamber of Commerce. (n.d.). Retrieved from http://www.uschamber.com/issues/index/international/drcafta.htm

Wallerstein, I. (2003). *The decline of American power: The U.S. in a chaotic world.* New York: The New Press.

Wikimedia Commons. (2008a). *Colonisation 1800.* Retrieved from http://commons.wikimedia.org/wiki/File:Colonisation_1800.png

Wikimedia Commons. (2008b). *Colonisation 1914.* Retrieved from http://commons.wikimedia.org/wiki/File:Colonisation_1914.png

World Trade Organization. (2011). *The WTO.* Retrieved from http://www.wto.org/english/thewto_e/thewto_e.htm

Young, R. C. (2001). *Postcolonialism: An historical introduction.* Malden, MA: Blackwell.

Yuen, E., Katsiaficas, D., & Rose, G. (2002). *Confronting capitalism. Dispatches from a global movement.* New York: Soft Skull Press.

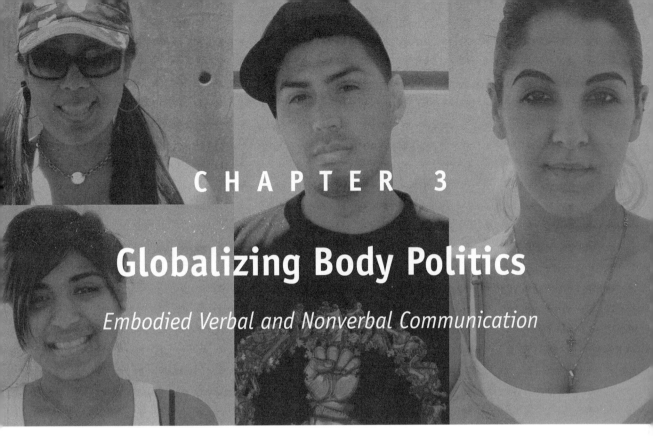

CHAPTER 3

Globalizing Body Politics

Embodied Verbal and Nonverbal Communication

Why are categories based on physical differences so important?
What do differences communicate and why?

Intercultural communication is an embodied experience. Much of our knowledge and under-standing, as well as many of our misconceptions, stereotypes, and prejudices about other cul-tures are exchanged through our physical bodies—in face-to-face interactions or through media images. Similarities and differences in language use, communication styles, and nonverbal communication such as the use of space, gestures, eye contact, and clothes are all conveyed and performed through our bodies. Categories used historically and today to distinguish "us" from "them" and to establish hierarchies of difference are often based on how our bodies appear to be similar to or different from others. Take a look at the photos at the beginning of the chapter. What comes to mind as you look at each picture? Did you consciously or unconsciously place each person into categories based on race, gender, or nationality? Why are these categories so important in our everyday lives and communication? What assumptions, relations of power, and histories of intercultural interaction underlie our processes of categorization?

From a very early age, we are taught implicitly and explicitly how to read, interpret, and assign meanings to our own and others' bodies based on our culturally informed codes. Skin

Source: Chapter-opening photos: © Kathryn Sorrells.

51

color, hairstyles, facial features, and expressions, as well as gestures and clothing, all convey meanings within complex cultural systems of signification, shaping our thoughts, actions, and experiences. Our communication with others is inevitably mediated through our bodies. "Reading" and making sense of the body politics—in other words, how power is written and performed symbolically on and through the body—requires that we understand how socially constructed categories such as race, gender, and culture have been encoded on our bodies historically, how these signification systems are linked to power, and how these categories are recoded in the context of global power structures (Butler, 1993; Foucault, 1978; Winant, 2001).

This chapter starts with our bodies as sites where categories of social difference are constructed. **Body politics,** as used here, refers to the practices and policies through which power is marked, regulated, and negotiated on and through the body. We begin by looking at how "difference" in terms of gender and race is marked and normalized on the body. The concept of social construction and the semiotic approach to understanding difference provide a foundation for examining the history of race, how racial hierarchies were "invented" and imposed on the body in the colonial context, and how these racial codes persist and have changed in the global context. Hip hop culture is introduced as a site where old racial regimes are contested and where alternative spaces for intercultural communication emerge in the context of globalization. Throughout, we point to the ways our everyday communication constructs, reinforces, and sometimes challenges categories of difference.

HIP HOP CULTURE

Yo! Whaz up? What does hip hop culture have to do with intercultural communication? Well, for one thing, hip hop culture is global. You can find hip hop culture around the world—from Japan to Israel, South Africa to Germany; from Chile to Iran, Honduras, Australia, Pakistan, Senegal; and of course, from the urban to suburban and rural settings of the United States. It's a global phenomenon driven not only by corporate interests, commodification, and capitalism but by unique values, norms, behaviors, and beliefs. Hip hop culture also has a complex language, nonverbal codes, and a history born of struggle, creative resistance, and contestation (Chang, 2005; Kitwana, 2003).

For those of you who are suspicious about calling hip hop a "culture," think of hip hop as only a type of music, assume it is a passing "fad" or "phase" of youth culture or perhaps you are so thoroughly disgusted by the violence, misogyny, and homophobia of some of the leading spokespeople and lyricists of hip hop, just hang on. The intercultural space of hip hop culture is, indeed, sometimes messy, sometimes oppressive and exploitative, and sometimes violent—just like the broader global culture, nations, cities, and neighborhoods we all live in. A key entry point into intercultural praxis is the ability to suspend judgment, be curious, and learn from what is different from our own culture, a standpoint or cultural viewpoint that challenges our position, life experience, or point of view. For some of you, this will be relatively easy because you already experience yourself as part of hip hop culture and identify with it. For others, you may be curious and have some exposure to artists or various aspects of the culture. Yet, for others, it will be tremendously difficult to go beyond the stereotypes that you have formed and the assumptions and judgments you hold about hip hop culture. These positions regarding hip hop culture are not so different from attitudes people hold about national, racial, ethnic, and religious cultures. For now, engage in intercultural praxis. Stay open to thinking about the past, present, and future in ways that may challenge your assumed or received knowledge. We're going to "break it down" here—the social constructs of gender and race—and get back to hip hop a little bit later.

MARKING DIFFERENCE THROUGH COMMUNICATION

Gender Difference

Among other things, physical differences in human bodies are used to construct two mutually exclusive gender categories: (1) women and (2) men. A conversation with parents or grandparents, a quick review of films from 50 years ago, or engagement with different cultural groups informs us that what it means to be a woman or a man has changed throughout history and is different across cultural, racial, religious, and class groups. Sociologists Judith Lorber and Susan Farrell (1991) noted that biological differences are not what distinguish the categories of feminine and masculine. Rather, gender differences are constructed through communication and imposed on our bodies. The **social construction of gender** refers to the use of physical differences in human bodies to construct two mutually exclusive gender categories: (1) women/men and (2) femininity/masculinity.

Differences between masculinity and femininity are symbolically embodied, performed, and communicated within our specific cultural contexts through the way we walk; through our gestures, speech, touch, and eye contact patterns; through the way we use physical space and the gendered activities we participate in; through our hairstyles, clothing, the use of makeup or not; and through colors, smells, and adornments (Butler, 1990; Stewart, Cooper, & Stewart, 2003; Wood, 2005).

Within and across cultures, meanings are constructed and assigned through communication to these categories of difference—man/women, masculine/feminine—often as polar opposites or dichotomies of strong/weak, rational/emotional, and significant/insignificant. While the meanings have been "normalized" and "naturalized" historically, they have also been challenged, contested, and changed through communication over time. The notion of what it means to be a woman has changed and is challenged today in societies around the world as a result of women's and feminist social movements. In addition, the "reading" and "marking" of two gender categories based on physical differences is contested by **third gender** people, or people who live across, between, or outside of the socially constructed two-gender system of categorization. **Transgender,** or trans, refers to people whose gender identities differ from the social norms and expectations associated with their biological sex. Misconception and stereotypes about transgender or gender-crossing people abound today, including a common mistaken belief that transgender people have appeared recently on the human stage and only in modern or postmodern societies. Quite to the contrary, gender-crossing people have existed historically and exist today in societies around the world, such as hijras in India and Pakistan, fa'afafine in Samoa, and two-spirits in indigenous North American cultures to mention only a few.

"Normalized" meanings that construct the two-gender system and the differences between men and women reflect and embody relationships of power. Consider how the verbal and nonverbal communication of men and women—language use, who is speaking and who is silent, body positions, gestures, degrees of activity, and so on—in popular cultural forms such as hip hop music videos, video games, and TV soap operas construct gender "difference." These gendered performances, where women generally embody subordinated power positions and men embody dominance, also structure and impact intercultural communication dynamics in the global context. Assumptions about feminine passivity, submissiveness, and subservience allow for and "normalize" the global exploitation of women in the workplace, sex trade, and "marriage" markets. A Chinese woman on a visiting professor program was stopped when walking across a U.S. university campus by a European American man who was a student. After chatting briefly, he said he wanted to marry an Asian woman because Asian women showed more respect toward men than American women. When she asked him what he meant by "respect," he responded, "You know, less assertive and more willing to do what you want."

Communication scholar Julia Wood (2005) noted that while biological differences between men and women exist, there are far more similarities between the two groups than there are differences. Why, then, do cultures around the world persist in marking and performing gender difference and constructing rigid divisions between the categories of men and women? Why are third gender people so demonized and erased? What social, political, and economic purposes are served by constructing and performing differences between men and women and reinforcing a two-gender system? Lorber and Farrell (1991) stated the following:

> The reason for gender categories and the constant construction and reconstruction of differences between them is that gender is an integral part of any social group's structure of domination and subordination and division of labor in the family and the economy. (p. 2)

In societies where gender inequity exists (almost everywhere), women and their social, economic, and political roles are inevitably devalued. Who benefits from the gendered construction and performance of unequal power relations? How does the rigid construction of differences between men and women through communication exclude and erase third gender? The intercultural encounter between the Chinese scholar and the White American student that was just mentioned, leads us to ask this question: How are the social categories of gender, sexuality, and race connected?

Racial Difference

Our bodies and the physical characteristics of our bodies such as skin color, facial features, hair, and body type have been used and are used today to separate people into categories that are customarily referred to as race or racial groups. Yet the majority of scientists and social scientists today agree that race is a social construct (Cohen, 1998; Montagu, 1997). Evolutionary biologist Joseph L. Graves (2005) stated, "The traditional concept of race as a biological concept is a myth" (p. xxv). In other words, the categorization of people into groups based on physical characteristics has no biological basis; the association of physical, mental, emotional, or attitudinal qualities with these socially constructed groups also has no biological basis. Rather, science has been used to normalize, naturalize, and validate a system that was historically and socially constructed and that was and still is linked closely to power in today's global context. If you're thinking this is crazy and you know race exists because you can see it, you're not alone. Most college students in the United States, Graves (2005) reported, think that biological race exists.

There is no question that human differences are visible and physically embodied. Human beings differ in a wide variety of ways including height, weight, eye color, and a preference for using the right or left hand, to mention only a few. Imagine if we grouped people into categories based on these physical differences and attributed innate characteristics to members of these groups. Tall people are smarter than short people. Brown-eyed people are more industrious than green-eyed people. Right-handers are better at sports than left-handers. It sounds absurd, right? Well, the concept of race as it operates today would sound equally absurd to us if it were not for the systematic construction of race and the reinforcement of racial hierarchies through laws, science, medicine, economics, education, literature, and forms of media for the past 500 years. While physical differences of all sorts do, of course, exist, it is the grouping or categorization of people based on these characteristics and the creation of racial hierarchies through the attribution of value-laden qualities (industrious, smart, athletic, lazy, violent, etc.) that is socially constructed through communication. Race is socially constructed within historical, political, and economic contexts, resulting in social inequities that continue to impact us today in the context of globalization.

CONSTRUCTING SOCIAL WORLDS THROUGH COMMUNICATION

A **social construct**, or a **social construction**, is an idea or phenomenon that has been "created," "invented" or "constructed" by people in a particular society or culture through communication. Social constructs exist only because people agree to act like and think like they exist and agree to follow certain conventions and rules associated with the construct (Berger & Luckman, 1966; Searle, 1995). For example, languages are social constructs. Languages are developed by the people who use them and carry meaning because the people who use them agree to the meanings and follow certain rules of the language. Money is another fairly easy example to understand. Think of a note or coin of any national currency—a yen, a peso, a deutschmark (which has been replaced by the euro), a dollar, a pound, or a yuan. The value and meaning of the currency is not in the note itself but rather is constructed by people through their conventional social usage within an economic system that places value on the note as currency. Peter L. Berger and Thomas Luckmann (1966) introduced their sociological theory of knowledge in their book *The Social Construction of Reality.* The core idea of their theory is that human beings participate in the creation of our own realities. Our knowledge about ourselves, the world, and everyday reality is created through communication about our ongoing, dynamic social interactions. In other words, knowledge about the world does not exist "out there" in the external world waiting to be found or discovered. Rather, knowledge about ourselves and the world around us is created or constructed through our social interaction and communication with others.

Semiotic Approach to Difference

In the late 1800s, Swiss linguist Ferdinand de Saussure introduced an approach to understanding how things—objects, words, ideas, and actions—come to mean what they do. Saussure contributed the groundwork for the field of study called **semiotics**, or the study of the use of signs in cultures, which provides a useful way to understand how meaning is socially constructed. **Signs**—a stoplight, clothes, or more complicated social phenomenon such as race—are composed of a signifier and signified. The body, things, actions, images, or words are understood as **signifiers** and what they represent—the idea or concept—as the **signified**. Saussure noted several key features about signs. First, the relationship between the signifier and signified is arbitrary. In a stoplight, for example, the fact that the red light means "stop" and the green light means "go" is arbitrary, right? These meanings have been assigned, fixed, and normalized by convention and use. Signs do not have permanent or essential meanings. Second, signs belong to systems, and their meaning comes from their relationship to other signs within the system. The red and green lights are part of a traffic control system, and their meaning—go or stop—is derived from their relationship to each other. Third, the meaning of signs is created through the marking of difference. What signifies or has meaning is the *difference* between green and red (Saussure, 1960). Cultural studies scholar Stuart Hall (1997) summarized, "Meaning does not inhere *in* things, in the world. It is constructed, produced. It is a result of a signifying practice—a practice that produces meaning, that *makes thing mean*" (p. 24).

Therefore, in order to understand social constructs like race, we have to examine how difference is marked and how meaning is associated with differences through communication within the racial signification system. To do this, we need to examine the historical construction of race as a sign; study how different meanings have been associated with racial categories through communication over time and place; and explore how preferred meanings regarding race have been constructed, negotiated, contested, and changed. It is also imperative to look at how the preferred meanings of social constructs are linked to power; how groups who benefit from a preferred meaning and hegemony work hard to maintain these meanings; and how people and groups who are negatively impacted may work even harder to resist, challenge, and change the social construction of our realities (Barthes, 1972; Foucault, 1975; Hall, 1997). One of the implications of analyzing signs and making apparent the social construction of reality is that if our perceived reality is created through social interaction and communication, we, as human beings, are powerful agents who can alter and change our worlds. Let's take a look at how race has become a sign with tremendous impact on people's lives over the past 500 years.

THE SOCIAL CONSTRUCTION OF RACE: FROM COLONIZATION TO GLOBALIZATION

Race has been fundamental in global politics and culture for half a millennium. It continues to signify and structure social life not only experientially and locally, but national and globally. Race is present everywhere: it is evident in the distribution of resources and power, and in the desires and fears of individuals from Alberta to Zimbabwe. Race has shaped the modern economy and nation-state. It has permeated all available social identities, cultural forms, and systems of signification. Infinitely incarnated in institution and personality, etched on the human body, racial phenomena affect the thought, experience, and accomplishments of human individuals and collectives in many familiar ways, and in a host of unconscious patterns as well. (Winant, 2001, p. xv)

As with all social constructs, what "race" means and what it signifies have changed during different historic periods and across geographic areas of the world. Certainly groups of people throughout human existence have distinguished themselves from others based on a wide range of differences including linguistic, regional, religious, and in some cases, physical differences. Precursors also exist for the idea of a hierarchy of human beings that place one group in a position of superiority in relation to others as articulated by Plato's concept of the natural scale. Yet the systematic categorization of people into a relatively small number of groups or "races" based on physical qualities and the ascription of qualities—intelligence, character, physical, as well as emotional and spiritual capacities—was not developed until the colonial era of the past 500 years (Todorov, 1984; Winant, 2001). How is it that into the 21st century a system of racial/cultural hierarchy still exists that assumes the natural or cultural superiority of people who are light-skinned or "White" and the inferiority or lack of cultural development of people with darker skin? How is it that some nonverbal practices—giving a firm handshake, wearing a shirt and tie, and using direct eye contact, for example—have come to signify "professionalism" and "the right way to do business" in the global workplace? As you read the following sections, consider how systems of meaning regarding race and racial superiority, rooted in colonization, are communicated and persist in the global era.

Inventing Race and Constructing the "Other"

Conquest, colonization, and the rise of capitalism were the terrain upon which race, racial identities, and racial hierarchies were forged. As Europeans expanded their reach around the globe in the 15th to 19th centuries, intercultural contact on a scale previously unknown occurred. In these "encounters," "difference" and most especially differences as they were marked or represented through the body were constructed as significant and were infused with meaning through a hierarchical racial system that justified and promoted domination and exploitation.

Undoubtedly, the physical bodies, as well as the cultural, linguistic, and nonverbal practices of people were different, for example, when the indigenous peoples of the Americas came in contact with the Portuguese, Spanish, and British and when Africans and Asians first came in contact with the Dutch, French, and Germans. However, the meanings that were given over time to these differences—in other words, what, how, and why these physical differences and communication practices came to signify what they did—are what we want to understand as we deconstruct race and racial hierarchies.

Just as the notion of "race" differs from place to place today—for example, a student is considered White in Costa Rica and a person of color in the United States—the process of inscribing the body with racial signification varied in different parts of the colonial world.

The Spanish colonizers of the Americas, assisted by the Catholic Church, developed a highly complex hierarchical racial scale or system—starting with the Spanish at the top and descending to Criollo, mestizo, castizo, mulatto, morisco, coyote, lobo, and so on—that linked "racial purity" with socioeconomic class. To maintain social order and control and to protect the economic and political interests and supremacy of the ruling Spanish "pure-blood" class, the signification system promoted "racial whitening" or blanqueamiento, a process by which racial mixing would produce lighter-skinned children and improve social status (Garcia Saiz, 1989). In North America, European Americans or Whites instituted the "one-drop" rule that legalized the racial signification system such that anyone with even one drop of non-White blood was not White (Lopez, 1996). In South Africa, a four-tiered "racial" system was constructed: Whites, Coloreds, Asians, and Blacks (Davis, 1991). While variation exists, what is the one aspect of the racial hierarchies that was consistent across continents and time?

Yes, the people primarily responsible for narrating the story, developing the discourse, and constructing the text about race—the colonizers, people of European descent—placed themselves at the top of the **racial hierarchy** and relegated the "Other," those designated as non-White to lower and inferior positions in the hierarchy. The marking of difference establishes lines of inclusion within the group through the exclusion of others. Sociologist Howard Winant noted (2001) the following:

> "Othering" came not from national, but from supranational distinctions, nascent regional distinctions between Europe and the rest of the world, between "us" broadly conceived, and the non-Christian, "uncivilized," and soon enough non-white "others," whose subordination and subjugation was justified on numerous grounds—religious and philosophical as much as political and economic. (p. 22)

Constructing the "Other" is a process by which differences marked on or represented through the body are constructed as significant and are infused with meaning through a hierarchical racial system that justify and promote domination and exploitation. With variations across continents, these socially constructed racial systems were based in an advanced a system of White supremacy. **White supremacy** is a historically based, institutionally perpetuated system of exploitation and oppression of continents, nations, and people of color by people and nations of European descent for the purpose of establishing and maintaining wealth, privilege, and power (Martinez, 1998).

Las Casas, a Catholic priest from Spain, witnessing the atrocious treatment of indigenous peoples in the Americas at the hands of the colonizers in the 16th century, initiated a serious debate regarding the native "Indians." The question of the day was as follows: Do Indians have souls? The discussion among the conquistadors, the Spanish Crown, and the Church represented a rigorous debate about whether Indians were humans or not. Could they be saved? Was it acceptable to work them to death and treat them like animals (Las Casas, 1542/1992; Todorov, 1984)? While the nature of this debate sounds archaic, we need to ask ourselves whose humanity—whose inclusion in the human species—is in question today?

Note that the **social construction of race** is not only a question of "difference" but the relationship between signs of difference in a system of power. The hierarchical relationship between the signs—bodies that are constructed as White or red, White or Black, civilized or uncivilized, Western or Other, for example—is where meaning is produced. Marking the body by "race" in the colonial era not only served to demarcate group membership—who was in the dominant group and who was "Other"—but also constructed a stratified labor system that justified and normalized the exploitation of laborers, which was integral to the development of capitalism during the colonial era (Macedo & Gounari, 2006; Winant, 2001). Racial differences came to mark and signify labor relations of owner/slave. Slavery— the selling and purchasing of people as commodities—was the first global business on a grand scale, the prototype of multinational capitalism (Walvin, 1986).

The Power of Texts

By the end of the 1700s, Johann Friedrich Blumenbach, a German anatomist, physician, and anthropologist, extended Linnaeus's system of categorizing all living things by formulating a **hierarchy of difference,** a system of classification of people predicated on the socially constructed idea of superior and inferior races. Based on his analysis of human skulls, Blumenbach (1775/1969) divided the human species into five races as follows: (1) the Caucasians or White race (people of European descent) were placed at the top of the hierarchy; in the middle were (2) the Malay or the brown race (people of Malaysian descent) and (3) the Americans or the red race (people of the Americas); and at the bottom of the hierarchy were (4) the Mongolian or yellow race (people of Asian descent) and (5) the Ethiopian or Black race (people of African descent). The color-coded schema Blumenbach worked out reflected the White supremacist ideologies of his time and was instrumental in legitimizing, codifying, and promoting a system of domination. His "scientific" explanation resonated with popularly constructed beliefs and practices that justified and normalized inequitable social, political, and economic systems.

As European colonial explorers, priests, chroniclers, scientists, and anthropologists scrutinized, studied, labeled, named, and categorized the "Other," they created elaborate texts attesting to the inferiority of non-White groups while implicitly and explicitly inscribing their own White European superiority (Winant, 2001). The process that constructed the "Other" through religious, "scientific," scholarly, and popular texts, as well as through art, law, and philosophy, also created or constructed the colonizers (Said, 1978). As authors in control of the production of written texts in the colonial world, European colonizers and their descendants narrated, consolidated, and legitimized their versions of history, knowledge, and "truth." During the colonial era and well into the 20th century in many parts of the world, access to writing, reading, printing, publishing, and distributing texts or narratives was curtailed or severely limited for the majority of people who were not White. Considering who has control over the production of texts, whose version of history is authorized and preferred, and what perspectives, experiences, and stories are left out draws attention to **the power of texts** in constructing, maintaining, and legitimizing systems of inequity and domination. Control over and access to the production of "official" written texts structured, enforced, and reinforced inequitable relations of power. Yet people from cultures and societies who were colonized did pass along their own histories and create versions of their stories in oral and written forms.

INTERCULTURAL PRAXIS
THE POWER OF TEXTS

In *Exemplar of Liberty: Native America and the Evolution of Democracy*, Donald Grinde and Bruce Johansen (1991) illustrated how Native American societies, particularly the Iroquois, have influenced the development of American democracy, freedom, and political system since the late 18th century. The publication of their book resulted in heated debates among historians and scholars. Some welcomed this revision of history that shed light on the silenced histories of Native American people and their contribution to U.S. society. Others rejected the authors' thesis arguing that their use of "evidence" was inadequate.

The power of texts, evident in this controversy, is foundational to the way we understand history. The lives of people who are considered unimportant or periphery to the history of a nation are excluded from official historical records. Without documented records, critics who are invested in tracing American democracy to its European origin can easily dismiss alternative accounts.

The plight of Native Americans is not solely a tragedy of the past. Today, Native American tribes struggle and fight for economic independence and self-determination as the long history of contestation over federal control of their land, natural resources, and culture continues.

While the Las Casas debate ended with the determination that the indigenous people of the Americas were, indeed, humans with souls, this "fact" was incorporated into the colonial project as a rationale to "civilize" and "save" them. Regardless of how indigenous peoples of the Americas were constructed, over 100 million died from genocide, exposure to disease, and the disruption of their sociocultural systems as a result of conquest (Smith, 2005). In *American Holocaust: Columbus and the Conquest of the New World,* David Stannard (1992) wrote, "The destruction of the Indians of the Americas was, far and away, the most massive act of genocide in the history of the world" (p. x). The devastating genocide of indigenous peoples of the Americas is one of many silenced histories. The phrase **silenced histories** refers to the hidden or absent accounts of history that are suppressed or omitted from official or mainstream versions of history. How can such conspicuous destruction, devastation, and genocide be hidden? Further, what is the impact of silenced histories on intercultural communication and sensitivity to various cultural experiences and perspectives today? Imagine, for example, if Germany celebrated its Holocaust with a "Hitler Day" as the United States does with Columbus Day? While the events of history cannot be reduced to stories, the way we receive and understand history is through stories codified into texts—or better stated, versions of stories that reveal and privilege certain perspectives while concealing others. Understanding how power operates to highlight and hide, reveal and distort certain "truths" about history, as well as current events, is critical to intercultural communication. Lack of knowledge about the historical realities that have created current conditions of inequity perpetuates misunderstanding, stereotypes, and prejudices that fuel and reproduce social, economic, and political injustice.

RESIGNIFYING RACE IN THE CONTEXT OF GLOBALIZATION

Clearly, the social construction of race, racist ideology, and White supremacy has had a devastating and demoralizing impact on non-White people around the globe through genocide, exploitation, and sociocultural destruction. Yet powerful collective identities and social movements for liberation and justice emerged in the late 19th century and continue today to resist the systematic dehumanization, exploitation, and subordination of people of color through economic, political, and social means. The anticolonial and anti-imperialist struggles of the peoples of Latin America since the 19th century, the anticolonial movements in Africa and Asia that culminated in independence from colonial rule in the middle part of the 20th century, the civil rights movement of the 1950s and 1960s in the United States, and the long-awaited dismantling of the apartheid system in South Africa in 1994 challenged the myth of race and the global ideology of White supremacy. Struggle and resistance to oppressive conditions forged collective race-based and nation-based identities for mobilization and empowerment. Anticolonial, national independence and civil rights movements were monumental collective actions where colonized, oppressed, and disenfranchised people demanded the rights of democratic participation, self-governance, and self-determination around the globe (see Figure 3.2). These movements, coalescing in the post–WWII era, forced a major rupture in the world racial order (Winant, 2001). Race has been resignified in the context of globalization in complex, shifting, and contradictory ways (see Figure 3.1).

Figure 3.1   Civil rights march on Washington, D.C., 1963

Source: © Warren K. Leffler/ U.S. News & World Report Magazine Photograph Collection/Library of Congress.

In the early 21st century, the notion of race as a biological concept has been scientifically debunked, yet race as it was constructed in the colonial era and marked on the body continues to have real consequences for people around the globe today. No biological or genetic difference exists between so-called "races" that determines intelligence, sexual appetite, reproduction, or athletic abilities. Yet these common myths about race persist with weighty consequences (Graves, 2005). At the same time, claims circulate that we now live in a raceless society and have reached "the end of racism"; however, stratification, discrimination, profiling, and exclusion based on racial categories persist in our society. Discourses of a color-blind society collide with representations of diversity that depict images of one person from each "racial" group. How can we make sense of these competing claims, discourses, and realities?

From Race to Culture: Constructing a Raceless, Color-Blind Society

David Theo Goldberg (2006) delineated two dominant ideologies that inform our understanding of race today. He argued that **racial naturalism,** or the claim that White people of European descent are "naturally" or biologically superior to non-White people, lingers today. However, in the post–WWII era, this ideology was challenged as a premodern relic from an earlier period and gave way in many parts of the world to racial historicism. **Racial historicism,** as a dominant ideology, shifts the focus from biological deficiencies to cultural ones, claiming the lack of "cultural development" or "progress" in non-White peoples and nations. In the worldwide pursuit of modernization, progress, and development, the rationale of racial historicism goes something like this: *Through education, the less advanced, less modern, and backward cultures are capable of developing civilizing behaviors, democratic values, and self-determination, which will, over time, allow them to be absorbed into society.*

Racial historicism insists upon and constructs a "racelessness" and "color-blind" society. How frequently we hear people say things like the following: I'm not racist. I don't see color. I'm color-blind. Racial historicism, where "race" is recoded as "culture," challenges the old racial signification system and at least on the surface, appears to go beyond race, leading to claims of "the end of racism." But let's take a closer look. Read the italicized sentence (at the end of the previous paragraph) again. What are the underlying assumptions behind this statement? Who is the invisible narrator? Whose cultural (racial) standards are used to determine and judge this hierarchy of development? We know that the construction of "race" structured, justified, and normalized stratified and exploitative economic, social, and political conditions during the colonial era. What does the construction of "racelessness" and a "color-blind" society do today?

The claims of a raceless and color-blind society erase or neutralize the centuries of historical injustice, exploitation, and asymmetrical relations of power during the colonial era that have produced current conditions of race-based inequity. Authors of the book *The Color of Wealth: The Story Behind the U.S. Racial Wealth Divide,* wrote this in 2006:

For every dollar owned by the average white family in the United States, the average family of color has less than one dime." Why do people of color have so little wealth? Because for centuries they were barred by law, by discrimination, and by violence from participating in government wealth-building programs that benefited white Americans. (Lui, Robles, Leondar-Wright, Brewer, & Adamson, 2006, p. 1)

The notion of racelessness also serves to mask the unmarked elevation of Whiteness— White norms and ways of thinking, knowing, being, and doing—as the standard for all (Goldberg, 2006). Whiteness is difficult to define because it is a default category, the category of the invisible narrator. Whiteness is a category that people who are White do not need to name given that it is the dominant norm. Part of the privilege of being White is the position to define, describe, and evaluate others based on a dominant White norm or standard that is invisibilized, a position of power that extends from the colonial era forward. Feminist sociologist Ruth Frankenberg (1993) outlined three interlocking dimensions of Whiteness: **Whiteness** is as a location of structural advantage, a standpoint, and a set of core values, practices, and norms.

A location of structural advantage means that the systems in place within society— political, economic, and social systems that take on concrete forms in education, laws, law enforcement, medicine, employment, and many others—benefit or advantage people who are White. Of course, not all White people have equal advantage or privilege. Whiteness is mediated by class, gender, and sexuality among other things. Yet the point is that the systems that are in place within U.S. society were constructed historically and continue to perpetuate advantage and privilege for the dominant White group today. Erasing or at least masking the existence of these privileges and advantages perpetuates the power conferred through locations of advantage.

Another dimension linked to locations of structural advantage that defines Whiteness is a particular standpoint or point of view from which to see the world and oneself. While great diversity exists within and across the group of people who are categorized as White, White people in the United States often espouse similar perspectives and are often blind to other perceptions. For example, a poll taken just before the court decision showed that 77% of White Americans thought that O. J. Simpson was guilty of murder. Nearly 72% of Black Americans thought he was innocent. The American public watched the same trial, so how can we explain this difference in perspective? A standpoint informed by life experiences where the institutions in place—schools, police, courts, and media—treat you and those around you fairly, equitably, and justly constructs a very different standpoint from life experiences where these same institutions treat you and those around you unfairly, inequitably, and unjustly. The motto of the police "to protect and to serve" is understood and experienced quite differently for Whites than for Blacks (and other minorities) in the United States. Whiteness and the power it gives to the dominant group are maintained by not marking a particular standpoint that is linked to locations of structural advantage.

The third dimension of Whiteness outlined by Frankenberg is a set of core symbols, norms, and labels. Due to the location of structural advantage of Whites and White culture, many of these core values, behaviors, and symbols are hard to identify simply because they are seen and accepted as the norm, just the way things are. A strong adherence to individualism, an emphasis on doing and accomplishing tasks, and an orientation to thinking and to time that is linear are just a few of the core values associated with

White American culture. These values are often seen by those who share and practice them as universal human values, as the "right way" or the "best way," and are used subtly as standards to measure other cultures. In this way, White American cultural norms are invisibly elevated to universal human norms and standards to which all should strive and by which all are judged. A position of structural advantage enables the dominant group, Whites in the United States, to label, generalize, and make claims about others while remaining in a position that is unnamed, individually unique, and outside of generalization and categorization. Delineating the concept of Whiteness is one step toward describing and disrupting a system that creates and sustains inequity. The three dimensions of Whiteness—(1) a location of structural advantage, (2) a standpoint, and (3) a set of core symbols and labels—interlock to invisibilize, mask, and normalize the maintenance and promotion of White American hegemony. The ways in which Whiteness and White hegemony function in the global context are discussed in depth in later chapters. It is critical to note that Whiteness can be practiced by non-White people and is not inevitably attached to White bodies. In a supposedly "raceless" society, Whiteness is an ideological perspective or position to which people who are not White can and do ascribe. Whiteness is also an ideological perspective that people who are White can confront and attempt to change (Carrillo Rowe & Malhotra, 2006).

From Race to Class: Rearticulating Race in the Neoliberal Context

We often hear comments like this: "Race doesn't matter anymore. All that matters is money." In societies like the United States that are ideologically constructed as raceless and color-blind, race is rearticulated in the neoliberal context in terms of class. In other words, it's all about the color of money! Yet Goldberg (2006) argued that there is an invisibilized process of Whitening that is required as people of color rise to the middle and upper classes. Membership in these classes is predicated upon assimilation and allegiance to Whiteness. People of color who accept these conditions benefit from the privileges and advantages of Whiteness, often espouse standpoints that support Whiteness and associate with values, practices, and norms of the dominant White culture. We might understand this as modern or postmodern "cultural whitening" based on accepting, performing, and supporting the dominant White culture. The "absorption" into society is complete as people of color achieve highly visible positions of power in the government, military, on the Supreme Court and in multinational corporations, serving, in rather contradictory ways, as icons for diversity in a raceless society.

Intersectionality

Yet, class does not provide complete protection against racism, sexism, and other forms of exclusion, even in or perhaps especially in, a supposedly raceless society. Socioeconomic class assists, limits, and denies access to everything from basic human needs of food, water, safety, and housing to health care, education, and property ownership to the ability to accumulate luxury items and wealth. But class alone does not determine access. Socioeconomic class intersects with race, as well as with gender, sexuality, and culture to create complex forms and degrees of exclusion and inclusion. **Intersectionality,** introduced by feminist theorists (Collins, 1990; Moraga, Anzaldúa, & Bambara, 1984), is an approach to understanding how socially constructed categories of difference—race, gender, class, and sexuality—operate in relationship to each other. These markers of difference do not function separately or independently in society but rather interrelate and intersect with each other magnifying and complicating positions of disadvantage and privilege.

CULTURAL IDENTITY
INTERSECTION OF RACE AND CLASS

The intersection of race, class, gender, sexuality, and other socially constructed categories of difference shape our cultural identities and impact our access to employment, decent wages, and wealth. Racism and classism, the historical legacy as well as current discriminatory practices and policies, result in continued economic disparities and social inequalities today. Consider the following facts:

- As of December 2009, 16.2% of African Americans and 12.9% of Latinos/Latinas are unemployed, compared to 9% of Whites.
- Blacks earn 62 cents for every dollar of income earned by Whites, and Latinos earn 68 cents for every dollar earned by Whites.
- The average hourly wage of newly hired White workers in jobs that did not require a college education was $13.08. Newly hired Black workers in the same jobs averaged only $10.23, while newly hired Latino/Latina workers averaged $11.46 an hour.
- Blacks and Latinos/Latinas are 2.9 and 2.7 times as likely, respectively, to live in poverty as Whites.

Source: Adapted from Dillahunt, Miller, Prokosch, Huezo, & Muhammad (2010).

These statistics clearly show how race and class intersect to shape people's social location, positionality, and experience in the United States today.

In the context of globalization, resignifying "race" as "culture" allows for the invention of a raceless and color-blind society that masks how race, as it is written on the body, persists as a marker for social, economic, and political stratification. It also invisibilizes Whiteness as the universal standard and norm. Rearticulating "race" as "class" in the global context hides the way that race and gender intersect with class and how the intersectionality of these social categories continues to structure the lives, material conditions and access to opportunities of people around the world today. In an article entitled "Of Race and Risk," Patricia J. Williams (2004) recounted her experience of buying a house.

After talking with a mortgage broker on the phone, she was quoted a mortgage interest rate. When she received the forms, she saw that the racial category of White was marked and that the broker must have assumed, apparently based on her use of Received Standard English, that she was White. When she changed it to Black and returned the form, suddenly the bank wanted more money, more points, and a higher interest rate. In her negotiations to contest this, the justification used by the bank was that she represented a financial "risk." Patricia Williams was made aware through this process that she, as a Black woman, *is* the "risk" not in terms of her financial ability to follow through with the loan (that had not changed when she shifted from White to Black). Rather, she is the risk as her home ownership as a Black woman in the neighborhood diminishes the value of the property owned by White residents. Historically, when a Black person or family moves in, Whites flee and take funding and social resources with them. Race, in an ideologically constructed "raceless" society, is rearticulated as "financial risk," masking through economic language a system that perpetuates racism and hiding a system that sustains Whiteness.

Intercultural interactions in the context of globalization are deeply embedded in the legacy of colonization, intersecting systems of oppression, and inequitable relations of power. Yet struggles against racism and White supremacy also continue. While mass media representations draw attention to and exacerbate the violent, criminal, and destructive aspects of hip hop culture, many people around the world experience hip hop culture as offering possibilities for disrupting the hegemonic racial order and providing spaces for new forms of coalition building across racial lines. We turn now to the contested cultural space of hip hop culture.

HIP HOP CULTURE: ALTERNATIVE PERFORMANCES OF DIFFERENCE

Figure 3.2   Hip hop culture offers an alternative to the existing racial order.

Source: © Kathryn Sorrells.

Meet Darren Dickerson, who identifies as Black (not pictured); Sun Yu Young, who is Korean American (left); Jani (Janithri) Gunaesekera (second from left), whose parents immigrated to the United States from Sri Lanka; Izzy (Israel) Perez (second from right), whose mother is Mexican American and father is Puerto Rican American; and Sheh (Venoosheh) Khaksar (right), who identifies as Iranian American. These folks were presented at the beginning of the chapter (see chapter opening photo). Each one of them acknowledges that the gender and racial codes marked, performed, and constructed on and through their bodies impact their lives every day. Each also identifies as being part of hip hop culture and experiences hip hop culture as an alternative to the existing racial order. Let's see what they had to say when asked this question: What does hip hop culture mean to you?

Darren Dickerson: I was born into hip hop culture. I am hip hop culture. Hip hop culture is speaking out and expressing what's real. The values of hip hop culture? Honesty, truth, respect, courage, and credibility. Hip hop culture comes out of a history of struggle, a history of having been denied and forgotten. It's fundamentally about the struggle—the struggle against powerful forces that have marginalized all sorts of people. But at the end of the day, it's about keeping it real.

Sun Yu Young: Hip hop to me isn't just a genre of music. It truly is an entire culture in every sense of the word, with its own individual language, music, fashion, and most important, history. I don't just "listen" to hip hop—I feel like I really live it. I also don't consider myself just a casual listener. I'm pretty good about knowing about and enjoying an artist's or producer's entire body of work, not just the songs that are released on the radio. Sometimes I think that my life is like one huge soundtrack—hip hop culture has truly influenced every aspect of my life. I don't think I would be the same person I am today without it. It's helped me understand different viewpoints and cultures other than my own, and it's helped me come together with people of different cultures, solely based on the fact that we both are a part of hip hop culture. So answering the question "what hip hop means to me," I guess can be summed up in a word: life.

Jani (Janithri) Gunaesekera: Since I am Sri Lankan, it is very hard for me to identify with a certain group. I want to say I can relate to the American side of me, but sometimes I feel it is limited. Then when I try to relate to my Sri Lankan side, I feel there is a big gap. When I was introduced to hip hop, I felt there was finally something that doesn't see me as a race or ethnicity. I felt like it took me in and gave me an identity that I could deal with . . . being different and not having a certain group to be part of was hard.

Izzy (Israel) Perez: Hip hop culture is so many things—like all cultures it's pretty hard to define. Hip hop brings people together—some who normally wouldn't get along can share a common interest. It connects people from all over the globe. Because it's different every place, you can learn about different experiences from others—it's a collaboration and expression from all over the world. But then there's the whole masculine side of hip hop with the "beefs" and rivalries. The whole point is to emasculate the other person, character assassination, "dis" and embarrass the other person. A lot of this is about setting the record straight about false accusations. It's also pretty homophobic. But what so many people can relate to is that it's about constant struggle, the ability to rise up, and overcome. It creates solidarity between people and groups who can relate—the poor, immigrants, and other struggling people.

Sheh (Venoosheh) Khaksar: As an Iranian, it wasn't easy being different growing up in a small town in Washington—I call it Pleasantville. An Asian American girl and a few Hispanic students and I were the only ones who were not like the rest. When I first heard Tupac, I thought, yeah, he's saying something to me and about me. He's talking about things I feel and putting them into word—expressing them so well. He's talking about the experience of minorities. It may not be exactly what I experienced, but I can relate. Hip hop culture is about struggle and overcoming obstacles. Hip hop is the voice of a people—a voice that speaks in various ways.

As you can see from these statements, hip hop culture clearly offers an alternative to the old racial signification system. The folks here do not seem to buy into the myth of a race-less society. They see and experience race as it is written on their bodies every day. Yet, in the context of a racialized society, they experience hip hop as a cultural space where, as Darren says, people can speak out and "struggle against powerful forces that have marginalized all sorts of people." Darren and Sheh see hip hop as the voice of the people—people who have been forgotten, disenfranchised, and oppressed by interlocking systems of exclusion based on race, class, and gender. Izzy notes that hip hop culture is fundamentally about "the ability to rise up and overcome" the challenges and obstacles that people face. Hip hop culture is a site where meanings about race, class, gender, sexuality, love, hate, violence, history, the government, family, and many other things are challenged, negotiated, and transformed. Hip hop tells the stories of resistance and resilience—stories of how people live their lives and how they challenge and survive powerful forces that work to silence their voices and diminish their lives. In 1989, Public Enemy's Chuck D said, "Rap is the Black CNN," offering an alternative interpretation of current events as well as history. Jay Woodson (2006) from Z-Net noted that "hip hop articulated something so universal and revelatory that White kids wanted (to listen) in. Some even began to question the skin privilege into which they had been born."

Sun finds that hip hop culture is a place where racial hierarchies break down and connection and coalition across socially constructed lines of race are made possible to provide a source of learning and pleasure, as well as political and economic empowerment. Hip hop culture offers hope for coalition-building across historically divided and stratified groups. In rural Washington, Sheh discovered that hip hop spoke to and about her and offered her a place of connection and identification. Jani articulates the ways in which she is caught between various racial and ethnic identifications—American and Sri Lankan—not feeling like she fits in either. For her, hip hop culture is a site where colonial constructions of race and racial hierarchies are contested and new body politics based on inclusion rather than exclusion are created. Jani states, "Hip hop did something to me that made me feel like it was okay to be different and that no matter what race I was I could be part of that world." Darren argues, "That's why so many people around the world connect with it—it's about creating a new system, an alternative system." Bakari Kitwana (2005), former editor of *The Source* and author of several books, agrees that hip hop culture has the potential to challenge and disrupt the old racial politics. As a powerful tool for social, economic, and political change, hip hop is doing just that. He stated the following:

> As young people worldwide gravitate to hip-hop and adapt it to their local needs, responding to the crises of our time, they are becoming equipped with a culture that corporate and political elites can't control. It's a youth-centered culture that is self-motivating and only requires its participants to have a mouth, the ability to listen and frustration with business as usual. This cultural movement is currently making way for hip-hop's emerging political movement. Given the way the culture is being absorbed by young people around the globe, these movements may be the catalysts necessary to jump-start an international human rights movement in this generation, a movement with the potential to parallel if not surpass yesterday's civil rights successes. (pp. 10–11)

The goal here is not to uncritically valorize hip hop culture. As Izzy noted, hip hop culture is troubled by a hypermasculinity that often denigrates, objectifies, and violates women, sexual minorities, and men. Hip hop culture often idealizes and glamorizes violence, drugs, and rampant consumerism. Aspects of the culture play off of and reinforce centuries-old racial stereotypes, promoting deeply ingrained patterns of domination and subordination. In these ways, hip hop culture reflects, normalizes, and advances the racist, patriarchal, homophobic, and capitalist ideologies of our larger society. Tricia Rose (1994) stated that hip hop "brings together a tangle of some of the most complex, social, cultural, and political issues in contemporary American society" (p. 2). So the point here is not to gloss over the difficult, ugly, controversial, or contested nature of hip hop culture. After all, at the core, hip hop culture is about keeping it real. Intercultural communication in the context of globalization situates us in the midst of complex and messy tensions. We need to learn how to hold contradictions and address the muddled, chaotic, and difficult challenges that arise in the nexus of oppositional realities. For example, we need to see how hip hop culture is *both* a site of inclusion across racial and cultural groups *and* a site where exclusion based on gender and sexuality occurs. Hip hop is *both* a space of empowerment *and* a space where oppressive and exploitative conditions are enacted and performed. Taking a **both/and approach** guards against essentializing, stereotyping, and enacting closure and allows us to step into rather than away from the complex, confusing, and untidy terrain of intercultural communication today.

SUMMARY

Our goal in this chapter was to introduce the process and practice of "reading" body politics in the age of globalization. We began with the assumption that intercultural communication is an embodied experience. Since our engagement with others is through our bodies, we looked at how differences are marked on the body—how our bodies are signs that communicate—in the socially constructed systems of race, gender, and class that impact global and local intercultural interactions. We provided an overview of the historical construction of race to show how social constructs are linked to power—social, political, and economic power. Since social constructs are invented, used, and institutionalized by people through communication, they can and have changed over time, yet we note how the preferred meanings of deeply engrained signification systems that benefit those in power are difficult to disrupt and change. The social constructions of race and racial hierarchies through communication, which are linked historically to colonization, capitalism, and national/regional identities, have been resignified in the global context. In a supposedly raceless society, race is rearticulated as culture and class; however, in these barely masked forms, race as it intersects with class, gender, and culture continues to impact the lives of people around the globe today. As we take on the project of analyzing our intercultural encounters and understanding the global context of intercultural relations, the semiotic approach and the concept of intersectionality are useful tools for critical analysis. Voices and visions born out of hip hop culture suggest that alternative spaces exist that resist and transform the old, colonial regime of racial naturalism and the more recently constructed racial regime of a raceless society. Yet hip hop culture also points to the complex and contradictory nature of intercultural communication today where sites that resist and contest hierarchies of difference can also reinscribe and reproduce racism, sexism, classism, and homophobia.

KEY TERMS

body politics
social construction of gender
third gender
transgender
social construct
social construction
semiotics
signs
signifiers
signified
racial hierarchy

constructing the "Other"
White supremacy
social construction of race
hierarchy of difference
the power of texts
silenced histories
racial naturalism
racial historicism
Whiteness
intersectionality
both/and approach

DISCUSSION QUESTIONS AND ACTIVITIES

Discussion Questions

1. How is your body a site where your identity, in terms of race, gender, sexuality, and so on, is constructed and communicated? Provide specific examples.

2. Why is there a rigid binary gender system? Why are gender and sexual identities outside of heterosexuality demonized and erased from mainstream society?

3. What does it mean when we say that race is a social construct? Aren't our skin color, hair texture, and facial features all biological? Why is race not biological?

4. Race, gender, and sexuality are all socially constructed and communicated through the body. How do race, gender, and sexuality interrelate in terms of the body? How do differences marked on the body intersect?

5. Why is the color-blind ideology problematic? Why can't we ignore "color" and create a raceless society?

6. How does Whiteness influence the process of intercultural communication? How does Whiteness operate in different cultures and countries through the process of globalization?

Activities

1. "Reading" the Body Politics
   a. Find visual images of the body (photographs, advertisements, paintings, movie posters, etc.).
   b. Address the following questions using the semiotic approach:
      i. In the particular visual image of the body, what signifiers can you identify? Pay close attention to gesture, eye contact, posture, clothing, physical type, size, colors, and so forth.
      ii. What do the signifiers mean? In other words, what is signified?
      iii. How are racial and gender differences constructed on and through the body?
      iv. How is "hierarchy of difference" constructed through the visual image?

2. Unpacking the Everyday Performance of Race and Gender—Group Activity
   a. Think about specific examples in which you perform your race and gender in everyday practices—consciously or unconsciously.
   b. Enact the performance in front of the class.
   c. Now think about specific examples in which you violate the expected norms of gender/race performances.
   d. Enact the performance in front of the class.
   e. After the performance from each group, discuss the following questions:
      i. How does it feel to enact your everyday performance of race and gender?
      ii. How does it feel to violate the norms of race/gender performance?
      iii. What happens when you violate the norms of gender/race performance?
      iv. How does the body communicate? How does the body set the context for intercultural encounter?

3. Unpacking Whiteness—Group Activity
   a. Whiteness is defined as "a location of structural advantage, a standpoint and a set of core values, practices and norms in which White ways of thinking, knowing, being and doing are normalized as the standard."

b. Write down a scenario in which Whiteness may manifest in intercultural communication.

c. Enact the scenario in front of the class.

d. Address the following questions:

    i. How does Whiteness shape intercultural interactions?

    ii. Can people of color enact Whiteness?

    iii. Can we disengage from and challenge Whiteness?

REFERENCES

Barthes, R. (1972). *Mythologies*. London: Cape.

Berger, P. L., & Luckmann, T. (1966). *The social construction of reality: A treatise in the sociology of knowledge*. New York: Doubleday

Blumenbach, J. F. (1969). *On the natural varieties of mankind*. New York: Bergman. (Original work published 1775)

Butler, J. (1990). *Gender trouble: Feminism and the subversion of identity*. New York: Routledge.

Butler, J. (1993). *Bodies that matter*. New York: Routledge.

Carrillo Rowe, A., & Malhotra, S. (2006). (Un)hinging whiteness. In M. P. Orbe, B. J. Allen, & L. S. Flores (Eds.), *The same and different: Acknowledging the diversity within and between cultural groups* (pp. 166–192). Washington: National Communication Association.

Chang, J. (2005). *Can't stop, won't stop: A history of the hip hop generation*. Boston: St. Martin's.

Cohen, M. N. (1998). *Chauvinism, class, and racism in the United States*. New Haven: Yale University.

Collins, P. H. (1990). *Black feminist thought: Knowledge, consciousness and the politics of empowerment*. Boston: Unwin Hyman.

Davis, F. J. (1991). *Who is black: One nation's definition*. University Park: Pennsylvania State University Press.

Dillahunt, A., Miller, B., Prokosch, M., Huezo, J., & Muhammad, D. (2010). *State of the dream 2010: Drained, jobless and foreclosed in communities of color*. Retrieved from www.faireconomy.org

Foucault, M. (1975). *Discipline and punish: The birth of the prison*. London: Penguin.

Foucault, M. (1978). *The history of sexuality: An introduction*, vol. 1. New York: Random House.

Frankenberg, R. (1993). *White women, race matters: The social construction of whiteness*. Minneapolis: University of Minnesota Press.

Garcia Saiz, M. C. (1989). *Las Castas Mexicanas: Un género pictórico Americano* (The Mexican castas: A genre of American paintings). Milan, Italy: Olivetti.

Goldberg, D. T. (2006). The global reach of raceless states. In D. Macedo & P. Gounari (Eds.), *The globalization of racism* (pp. 45–67). Boulder, CO: Paradigm.

Graves, J. L. (2005). *The myth of race: Why we pretend race exists in America*. New York: Dutton.

Grinde, D. A., & Johansen, B. E. (1991). *Exemplar of liberty: Native America and the evolution of democracy*. Los Angeles: American Indian Studies Center.

Hall, S. (1997). Introduction. In S. Hall (Ed.), *Representation: Cultural representations and signifying practices* (pp. 1–45). Thousand Oaks: Sage.

Kitwana, B. (2003). *The hip hop generation: Young blacks and the crisis in African American culture*. New York: Basic Civitas Books.

Kitwana, B. (2005). *Why white kids love hip hop: Wankstas, wiggers, wannabes, and the new reality of race in America*. New York: Basic Civitas Books.

Las Casas, B. D. (1992). *A short account of the destruction of the Indies*. London: Penguin Books. (Original work published 1542)

Lopez, I. H. F. (1996). *White by law: The legal construction of race*. New York: New York University Press.

Lorber, J., & Farrell, S. A. (Eds.). (1991). *The social construction of gender*. Thousand Oaks, CA: Sage.

Lui, M., Robles, B., Leondar-Wright, B., Brewer, R., & Adamson, R. (2006). *The color of wealth: The story behind the U. S. racial wealth divide*. New York: The New Press.

Macedo, D., & Gounari, P. (Eds.). (2006). *The globalization of racism*. Boulder, CO: Paradigm.

Martinez, E. (1998). *What is white supremacy? Challenge white supremacy workshop presentation*. Retrieved from http://www.prisonactivist.org/archive/cws/betita.html

Montagu, A. (1997). *Man's most dangerous myth: The fallacy of race* (6th ed.). Walnut Creek, CA: AltaMira.

Moraga, C., Anzaldúa, G., & Bambara, T. C. (1984). *This bridge called my back: Writings by radical women of color*. New York: Kitchen Table.

Rose, T. (1994). *Black noise: Rap music and Black culture in contemporary American society*. Hanover, NH: Wesleyan.

Said, E. W. (1978). *Orientalism*. New York: Random House.

Saussure, F. de (1960). *Course in general linguistics*. London: Peter Owen.

Searle, J. R. (1995). *The construction of social reality*. New York: The Free Press.

Smith, A. (2005). *Conquest: Sexual violence and American Indian genocide*. Cambridge, MA: South End.

Stannard, D. E. (1992). *American holocaust: Columbus and the conquest of the New World*. New York: Oxford University Press.

Stewart, L. P., Copper, P. J., & Stewart, A. D. (2003). *Communication and gender* (4th ed.). Boston: Allyn & Bacon.

Todorov, T. (1984). *The conquest of the Americas: The question of the other*. New York: Harper Row.

Walvin, J. (1986). *Questioning slavery*. New York: Routledge.

Williams, P. J. (2004). Of race and risk. In M. L. Andersen & P. H. Collins (Eds.), *Race class and gender: An anthology* (5th ed.) (pp. 108–110). Belmont, CA: Wadsworth/Thomson Learning.

Winant, H. (2001). *The world is a ghetto: Race and democracy since WWII*. New York: Basic Books.

Wood, J. T. (2005). *Gendered lives: Communication, gender, & culture* (6th ed.). Belmont, CA: Wadsworth.

Woodson, J. (2006). Hip hop's black political activism. *Z Net*. Retrieved from http://www.zcommunications.org/znet/viewArticle/3784

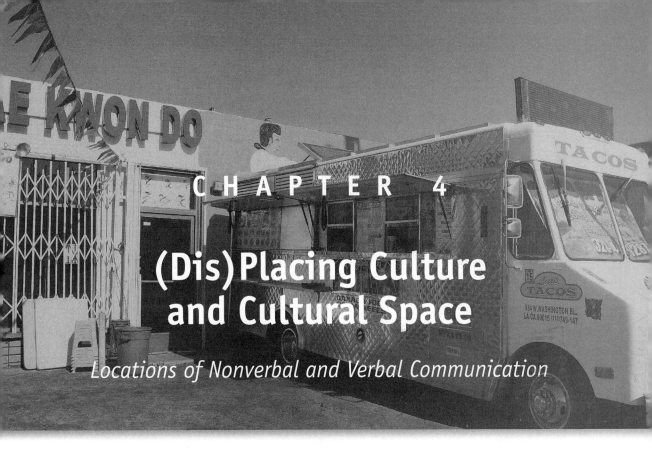

CHAPTER 4

(Dis)Placing Culture and Cultural Space

Locations of Nonverbal and Verbal Communication

Hybrid cultural space in Los Angeles

Take a look around yourself. Notice the place where you are and the space that surrounds you. Perhaps you are in your dorm room, apartment, home, or office. How is this space "cultural" space? How is the use and organization of space, the objects or artifacts that fill the space, and the verbal and nonverbal language used in this space cultural? Is there a sense of gender, ethnic, racial, national, and/or religious identity communicated? Now consider the neighborhood you live in, where you shop, consume food and entertainment, and meet with friends. Can you identify cultural dimensions of these spaces? Don't forget that places and spaces you may see as "normal," "just the way things are," or even "lacking in culture"—a shopping mall or your school campus, for example—are, in fact, products of culture. While spaces of nondominant groups are often marked as "cultural," those unmarked spaces in the United States that are constructed and shaped by the dominant European American or White culture are also cultural. As you imagine moving in a broader circle from where you are to your neighborhood, then to your geographic region to the nation and across national boundaries, do you experience a layering, intersection, or friction between different cultural spaces?

Source: Chapter-opening photo © Marta Lopez-Garza.

Expanding upon the previous chapter, we now move outward from the body to explore and "read" the cultural and intercultural communication dimensions of place, space, and location. In this chapter, we examine how cultures are simultaneously placed and displaced, inevitably located in specific places, and yet dislocated from their sites of origin in the context of globalization. The confluence of forces that shape the terrain of globalization has dramatically accelerated the displacement and replacement of people, cultures, and cultural spaces since the early 1990s. Given this displacement and fragmentation of cultures, we investigate how human beings use communicative practices to construct, maintain, negotiate, reconstruct, and hybridize cultural spaces. Penetration, disruption, and mixing of cultural spaces have occurred on a worldwide scale since the European colonial era. Understanding globalization as a legacy of colonization allows us to recognize how cultural spaces experienced today—segregated, contested, and hybrid cultural spaces—sustain historically forged relations of unequal power. Yet these cultural spaces are also sites where Western hegemony is negotiated, challenged, and changed. Building on the case study introduced in the previous chapter, hip hop culture is used to illustrate the cultural and intercultural dimensions of place, space, and location in the context of globalization.

PLACING CULTURE AND CULTURAL SPACE

Historically, notions of culture have been closely bound to place, geographic location, and the creation of collective and shared cultural spaces. The traditional anthropological definition of culture, as noted in Chapter 1, implies that cultures are bounded entities that are grounded in place, which allows for shared meanings to develop and be passed along. Based on this definition, a reciprocal relationship exists between culture and place. To understand place is to understand culture and vice versa. Introducing an anthology of essays by anthropologists called *Senses of Place*, philosopher Edward S. Casey (1996) argued the following:

> Given that culture manifestly exists, it must exist somewhere, and it exists more concretely and completely in places than in minds or signs. The very word *culture* meant "place tilled" in Middle English, and the same word goes back to Latin *colere*, "to inhabit, care for, till, worship." To be cultural, to have a culture, is to inhabit a place sufficiently intensely to cultivate it—to be responsible for it, to respond to it, to attend to it caringly. Where else but in particular places can culture take root? (pp. 33–34)

Cultural practices, norms, behaviors, and values, then, have historically been understood as emerging from and being defined by ongoing interactions among people who are situated in specific locations and who, through shared interaction, construct cultural spaces. Yet today, culture and cultural spaces have been deterritorialized, removed from their original locations and reterritorialized or resituated in new locations through global flows of people, technology, finance, and ideas (Inda & Rosaldo, 2001). These global flows have created fragmented and disjointed cultural "scapes" and cultural spaces (Appadurai, 1996). What do we mean by cultural space?

COMMUNICATIVE PRACTICES
SPACE AND CULTURAL DIFFERENCES

Na-young, an international student from South Korea, tells a story about space and cultural differences:

A few months after I moved to the U.S., a professor of mine and her husband invited me to their house for dinner. They had just moved into this very nice, big house. When I arrived, they asked me if I wanted to see the house. First, they took me to their living room and kitchen, which was very nicely decorated. In the hallway, they had many pictures framed on the wall with their family and wedding photographs.

I enjoyed the tour very much until they took me to their master bedroom. Then it got really awkward for me. Looking at their king size bed, I was so confused and thought to myself 'why are they showing me their bedroom?' To me, a bedroom is a private space and it was really strange that my professor was showing her student her bedroom.

I have been in the U.S. for a couple of years now and I learned that it is a part of custom here to show your guests around the house—all the house! Some people use their living space to express their identity, lifestyle, and accomplishments.

Cultural Space

Building on Judith Martin and Thomas Nakayama's (2004) definition, **cultural space** is defined as the communicative practices that construct meanings in, through, and about particular places. Let's examine the concept of cultural space more closely. Can you identify some of the verbal and nonverbal communicative practices that define an academic cultural space? Do you use language in the classroom that may not easily translate in conversations with your family or friends outside of campus? The buildings on a campus, the exterior and interior spaces, and the kind and arrangement of furniture certainly all construct academic cultural space. Are there also nonverbal communication norms that are specific to the cultural space of a classroom? When you are in a club—a sports bar, a karaoke club, or a country western bar—or when you go to places of worship such as a synagogue, church, mosque, or temple, there are particular architectural features, artifacts, uses of space, and language, as well as verbal and nonverbal practices that construct the cultural space of these particular places. These are all cultural spaces that are constructed through the communicative practices developed and lived by people in particular places. Communicative practices include the languages, accents, slang, dress, artifacts, architectural design, the behaviors and patterns of interaction, as well as the stories, the discourses, and histories. Places and the cultural spaces that are constructed in particular locations also give rise to collective and individual identities.

Place, Cultural Space, and Identity

In greater metropolitan Los Angeles, residents make broad identity distinctions based on place; for example, people talk about being from "the city" or from "over the hill" in "the Valley." As you can imagine, all sorts of stereotypes, assumptions, and judgments, as well as emotional attachments, feelings of belonging, and identification, underlie being from "the city" or "the Valley." In the Seattle, Washington, area, as in all places around the world, the neighborhood or area where you live—"where you come from"—such as the Central District, Queen Anne Hill, Rainier Valley, Mercer Island, or Kent communicates meaning about your identity, class status, power positions, and history. In small towns in the United States, people use the expression that "they (as opposed to "us") live on the wrong side of the tracks," the "bad" part of town, geographically placing or positioning the "Other" in terms of hierarchies of class and sometimes race or ethnicity. The way people who live in one place talk about and make meaning about their identity and their "home" or cultural space can be very different from how they are labeled, represented, and seen by others. For example, the South Side of Chicago, the South Bronx in New York, or South Los Angeles (formerly South Central Los Angeles) are represented in mainstream media as drug and crime infested, dangerous places. However, residents likely have very different versions of the story about the place called "home." Meanings about places, cultural spaces, and the collective identities that arise from them are constructed, negotiated, and circulated within a context of unequal relations of power. This example illustrates the difference between **avowed identity,** the way we see, label, and make meaning about ourselves, and **ascribed identity,** the way others may view, name, and describe us and our group.

As noted in previous chapters, it is important to consider who has control and power over the texts (in this case, mass media texts) that are constructed. Like the texts that were written and circulated constructing and legitimizing the ideology of race in the colonial era, mass mediated texts disseminating stories about the South Bronx, South Los Angeles, and the South Side of Chicago are narrated by invisible sources who appear to come from neutral positions. Yet just as locations such as the South Bronx, South Los Angeles, or the South Side of Chicago are marked in terms of race, class, and culture, mainstream media texts derive from a position or location literally and figuratively and perpetuate certain interests and points of view. Places or locations marked by the intersection of race, class, gender, and culture as well other categories of difference correlate to **locations of enunciation**—sites or positions from which to speak. An individual's or group's location of enunciation can be a platform from which to voice a perspective and be heard. An individual or group's location of enunciation can also be a site of silencing and erasure—a voiceless place. Differing locations of enunciation that are structured by asymmetrical relations of power impact our intercultural communication in interpersonal, community, national, and global interactions. In the global arena, race and gender combine with nationality and geopolitical regions (the West, the East, the North, or the South) to construct different locations of enunciation that enable and constrain the ability to speak and to be heard for groups and individuals. Territorial maps of difference that connect cultural spaces and identities to particular places are deeply rooted in historical and contemporary intercultural interactions, political contestation, and economic struggle. Consider your city, state, the nation, and the world. How are differences in terms of race and class mapped onto geographic locations? How do these mappings shape locations of enunciation? Now consider how cultural spaces are gendered and how gender impacts locations of enunciation.

CULTURAL IDENTITY
VIEWS ON "HOME" AND IDENTITY

Monica is Japanese American born and raised in Chicago, Illinois. Sayaka is an international student born and raised in Tokyo, Japan. They discuss their views on "home," cultural identity, and location of enunciation:

Monica: "When I came to university in a small town, I had so many people ask me 'where are you from?' When I say 'I'm from Chicago,' they often respond, 'well, where are you really from?' It's frustrating when people do not believe that I belong here. This is the only country I know. My grandparents immigrated to the U.S. from Japan, but I see myself as an American."

Sayaka: "When people ask me where I am from, I'm proud to say, 'I'm from Japan.' It's complicated though when they start asking me all kinds of questions about Japan. I feel like I have to represent all people in Japan. There are so many kinds of people in Japan. It makes me feel like they see me only as Japanese and nothing else."

Monica's avowed identity is American, yet many people ascribe a Japanese or foreign identity to her, which causes tension. An unexamined assumption that "American" means "White" underlies the responses she gets. For Sayaka, congruence exists, in terms of national culture, between her avowed and ascribed identities, yet, in conversations, her cultural "difference" obscures her other identities and she is expected to speak for all Japanese people.

How do each of their identities and positionalities impact what they can say and what others expect to hear?

As mentioned earlier, cultures and cultural spaces have been studied historically as if they were distinct entities bound to particular places and specific geographic locations. While place is central to the construction of cultural spaces and identities, Appadurai (1988) noted that "natives, confined to and by the places to which they belong, groups unsullied by contact with a larger world, have probably never existed" (p. 39). We know that precolonial societies traded with each other creating *regional patterns of intercultural exchange*. Armies of emperors, tribal leaders, and feudal lords fought in regional conflicts resulting in the collision, occupation, and overlap of cultural spaces. Colonization, beginning in the 15th century, linked regional circuits of intercultural exchange creating *worldwide interconnection*, which broadened the scope of displacement of people as well as the mixing and collision of cultural spaces. In other words, the dislocation, intersection, and contestation of cultural spaces we experience today are not entirely new. Yet, while globalization has historical antecedents, the deterritorialization, or uprooting of people and cultural forms, and the reterritorialization, or relocation of people and cultural products, as well as the fragmentation and fusion of cultures on a global scale are exponentially greater than in the past.

DISPLACING CULTURE AND CULTURAL SPACE

Culture has been displaced and unhinged from its geographic moorings in our highly dynamic, mobile, and globalized world. Xavier Inda and Renato Rosaldo (2001) noted, however, that culture is not simply floating out there in some unidentifiable space; rather, culture is constantly and continually replaced in new environments and new places, however temporary, cyclical, or fleeting the replacement may be. I use the phrase **(dis)placing culture and cultural space** in the chapter title to capture the complex, contradictory, and contested nature of cultural space and the relationship between culture and place that has emerged in the context of globalization. As people and cultural products circulate globally, new cultural spaces are created, intersecting and colliding with existing cultural spaces, in locations often quite distant and geographically removed from their places of origin. Imagine walking the narrow Spanish colonial streets in "Old Town" San Juan, Puerto Rico, and stepping through the doorway of Tantra, a restaurant that serves a delicious fusion of Latin and Indian food to tourists and locals while a Puerto Rican woman belly dances. Picture weaving along the bumpy, rutted dirt roads on the outskirts of Bangalore, India, where glass and steel corporate call centers contrast with the bustling street vendors and pedestrians outside. Consider surfing the channels on the TV in Bangkok, Thailand. You can see a collage of "virtual" cultural spaces from the Korean hip hop scene to the U.S. "reality-show" *Survivor* to Thai soap operas. Visualize driving through the capital city of Tegucigalpa in Honduras where Popeye's, T.G.I. Friday's, McDonald's, KFC, and other fast-food chains dot the urban landscape, sometimes adjacent to but often displacing local restaurants and cuisines. What examples of displaced and replaced cultural spaces can you identify in your neighborhood, town, or city? Globalization is characterized by a **time–space compression** bringing seemingly disparate cultures into closer and closer proximity, intersection, and juxtaposition with each other (Harvey, 1990). As cultural spaces are permeated, disrupted, transported, and relocated in new places around the globe, a continuous process of fragmentation, contestation, hybridization, and fusion of cultures and cultural spaces occurs. Yet place and location still matter. Anthropologist Clifford Geertz (1996) stated the following:

> For it is still the case that no one lives in the world in general. Everybody, even the exiled, the drifting, the diasporic, or the perpetually moving, lives in some confined and limited stretch of it—"the world around here." The sense of interconnectedness imposed on us by the mass media, by rapid travel, and by long-distance communication obscures this more than a little. (p. 262)

Our goal, then, is to investigate "the world around here." By "here," I mean the localized and situated embodiments of culture and intercultural interactions in particular places that are inevitably influenced by globalizing forces.

Glocalization: "In Here-ness" and "Out There-ness"

In the context of globalization, "the world around here" is infused with, shaped by, and connected to many different cultures that are both "here" and "there"—both present and distant in space and time. We need to look at both the **"in-hereness"** and **"out-thereness"** of globalization (Giddens, 1994). In other words, we need to investigate how this particular "here" is linked to "there" and how this linkage of places reveals colonial histories and postcolonial realities. **Glocalization** refers to the dual and simultaneous forces of globalization and localization. First introduced in relation to Japanese business practices in the 1980s and later popularized by sociologist Roland Robertson (1992), the concept of glocalization allows us to think about how globalizing forces always operate in relationship to localizing forces. Given that globalization "happens" in specific locals, glocalization points to the intersection of the global and the local in particular places.

For example, on a street in a metropolitan area in the United States, you might find a Korean evangelical church next to an Iranian bakery and across the street a steak house next to a Thai boxing gym. It's likely that migrants from distant or not-so-distant places labor in the back and the people who frequent these sites are from many different cultural backgrounds. How is the juxtaposition of cultural spaces we experience "here," in this particular local intercultural context, related to and interconnected with places around the globe through historic and contemporary webs of connectivity? Contemporary multicultural spaces, "the world around here," are always layered with histories of intercultural interaction and contestation, as well as assimilation and integration of cultural communities and cultural spaces. In order to understand the intercultural dynamics occurring in cultural spaces around us, we need to dig beneath the surface to examine the histories of interaction that literally and figuratively shape and construct meanings about the ground upon which we stand today.

The specific place designated as "here" where a Korean evangelical church, Iranian bakery, steak house, and Thai boxing gym create a multicultural space is in Los Angeles, California. This particular "here" was previously the homeland of indigenous American Indians, which was invaded and conquered by the Spanish at the beginning of the European colonial era in the 16th century. This location was inhabited by citizens of Mexico who were later displaced by the "Westward Movement" of White Americans (experienced as the "Eastern Invasion" by those who were there). In the past 100 years, this place—this particular "here"—has been "home" to Black Americans who moved to the area in the 1920s and 1930s. Fleeing Jim Crow segregation laws of the South, they experienced other types of spatial segregation in their new home. Following WWII, Japanese Americans, attempting to recover their dignity, economic losses, and "place" within U.S. society after their criminalization and detention in "internment camps" (the dominant U.S. phrase for "concentration camps") also made this place home.

This neighborhood in Los Angeles, California, with its layered, negotiated, and contested cultural spaces, reflects and embodies a complex history of intercultural relations. Today it is home to a small Japanese American community, a significant African American population, and a large Latino/Latina population. The growing presence of Latinos/Latinas in this neighborhood and across the United States can be understood as a result of the displacement of people, culture, and cultural space due to the forces of neoliberal globalization. The increasing Latino/Latina population is also interpreted by some in the United States as an "invasion" from the South. Yet if we take a longer historical view, we can also make sense of the changing populations and shifting cultural spaces as a return of people to their home—both a precolonial indigenous ancestral homeland and a Mexican homeland before U.S. annexation. This example illustrates how the patterns and flows of displacement and replacement of peoples and cultural spaces in the context of globalization are not random. An excavation of "the world around here," whether "here" is your neighborhood, the site of your university, or the central cross streets of your city, uncovers histories of overlapping and contested cultural spaces that link particular local places to global historical and contemporary events. A statement popularized by immigrant rights groups in Europe and the United States captures this dynamic: "We are here because you were there." Understanding and "reading" the intercultural dimensions of place, cultural space, and location today requires bifocal vision that attends to the linkages between past and present as well as between "here" and "there."

Let's take a look at hip hop culture to illustrate concepts and issues relating to the intercultural dynamics of place, space, and location discussed thus far in the chapter. As you read the following section, notice how communication is used to construct hip hop cultural spaces, how hip hop cultural spaces that emerge out of particular places define locations of enunciation, and how hip hop youth represent themselves, avowing identities that challenge and contest the ways they have been represented. Also pay attention to how hip hop culture illustrates processes of deterritorialization/reterritorialization and glocalization. Segregated, contested, and hybrid cultural spaces are introduced through the case study and will be addressed in greater depth after the case study.

CASE STUDY: HIP HOP CULTURE

South Bronx

Hip hop culture emerged out of the harsh, burned-out, poverty-stricken, gang dominated urban spaces of the South Bronx. Grandmaster Flash and the Furious Five (1982) described the cultural space as a jungle, where lack of education and escalating inflation made him wonder "how I keep from going under." Black and Puerto Rican youth took what was available to them—their bodies, their cultural forms of expression, and their innovation—to reclaim their "place." The reclaimed place of hip hop culture is a literal geographic space, a cultural space of belonging and identification as well as a location of enunciation—a sociopolitical and economic site from which to speak. Through creative forms of cultural expression with deep ancestral ties such as break dancing, graffiti, and rap music, the South Bronx was transformed into a site of pleasure and protest (Rose, 1994). The youth of the South Bronx used the streets, parks, subways, abandoned buildings, and trains as locations for creating, writing, and voicing their own "texts" about their struggles. Transplanted and resignified in urban contexts around the world today, the communicative practices of hip hop culture are rooted in transatlantic African diasporic colonial history. In "The Roots of Hip Hop" (1986), *RM HIP HOP MAGAZINE* stated the following:

In the beginning there was Africa, and it is from Africa that all today's black American music—be it Jazz, R'n'B, Soul or Electro—is either directly or indirectly descended. The ancient African tribal rhythms and musical traditions survived the shock of the transportation of millions of Africans as slaves to the Americas, and after 300 years of slavery in the so called Land of the Free the sounds of Old Africa became the new sounds of black America. Rapping, the rhythmic use of spoken or semi-sung lyrics grew from its roots in the tribal chants and the plantation work songs to become an integral part of black resistance to an oppressive white society.

The South Bronx in the 1970s was an urban wasteland—"a Necropolis—a city of death" (Chang, 2005, p. 16). Like many urban centers in the United States, New York City was devastated by the loss of jobs as the forces of globalization geared up and manufacturing industries sought cheaper labor conditions outside the United States in a process called **deindustrialization.** New York City's officials mounted a tremendous revitalization program in the 1970, but areas like the South Bronx, home to working-class and poor Blacks and immigrants, were left out of the plan and off the map. Joblessness, slum landlords, economic divestment, and depopulation from the displacement of over 170,000 residents due to the construction of the Cross-Bronx Expressway led to the rapid deterioration of the social and economic fabric of the South Bronx community. Out of these conditions, hip hop culture rose as a vibrant, expressive, and oppositional urban youth culture. Trisha Rose (1994) stated, "Hip hop is a cultural form that attempts to negotiate the experience of marginalization, brutally truncated opportunity, and oppression within the cultural imperatives of African American and Caribbean history, identity and community" (p. 21).

Back in the Day

From the beginning, the communicative practices of hip hop culture—break dancing, graffiti writing, DJing, and rapping—developed in relationship to particular places, an identification with and defense of territory and an awareness of sociopolitical locations. Communication scholar Murray Foreman (2004) quoted Grandmaster Flash, one of the first hip hop DJs, as he identified the division of space and place during the early years of hip hop cultural formation:

> We had territories. It was like, Kool Herc had the west side. Bam had Bronx River. DJ Breakout had way uptown past Gun Hill. Myself, my area was like 138th Street, Cypress Avenue, up to Gun Hill, so that we had our territories and we all had to respect each other. (p. 202)

The original DJs, Kool Herc, Afrika Bambaataa, and Grandmaster Flash of the South Bronx and other Black and Puerto Rican youth who followed, used two turntables; a microphone; sound systems; and the soul, funk, and blues music of earlier times to create new sounds and styles that spoke to, about, and from the inner-city urban Black and Latino/Latina experience. This was their location of enunciation. They borrowed old beats from

Africa and the Caribbean and reterritorialized them in the urban Bronx context in creative and inspiring ways, looping colonial histories of oppression with contemporary, postcolonial struggles for survival. Block parties reminiscent of those in Jamaica brought MCs forward who layered words on top of beats, rapping in ways that recalled African and Jamaican cultural communicative practices of toasting or playing the dozens, where rhyming slang is used to put down enemies or tease friends (George, 1998; Rose, 1994).

Figure 4.1 Towering buildings and graffiti mark cultural spaces in New York

Source: © iStockphoto.com/Terraxplorer.

In the transition from gang affiliations to hip hop culture, gang communicative practices such as "tagging"—the marking of either your own territory to signify authority and dominance or the marking of others' territory to provoke—morphed into graffiti "writing," where individual and group "writers" used the city—walls, buildings, buses and trains—as their canvas. The initial writing of code names (Taki 183, Kase 2, Lady Pink, etc.) that literally inscribed the identities of individuals and graffiti crews on the urban landscape offered previously dispossessed and silenced youth notoriety and credibility. As the numbers and boldness of writers increased and the size and shapes of their work expanded to murals on subway trains, intense resistance from city officials mounted. The South Bronx youth's desire to "talk back," reclaim their space, and represent themselves was criminalized by city offices. The dominant powers spent millions of taxpayer dollars to reassert power, regain control, and take back the "public" space. As Rose (1994) noted, New York City in the mid-1970s was "a city at war to silence its already discarded youths" (p. 45).

Going Commercial

With the recording of "Rapper's Delight" in 1979, hip hop culture catapulted into the complex and contested terrain of commercialization and commodification. As hip hop commercialized and "went national" in the late 1980s, the regional place-based split or "beef" between the East and West Coasts gained prominence. Brian Cross (1993) argued that the rise of hip hop culture on the West Coast and specifically in Compton was "an attempt to figure Los Angeles on the map of hip hop" in a direct communicative "reply to the construction of the South Bronx/Queensbridge nexus in New York" (p. 37). The commercial success of rap has led to artist-owned businesses and independent labels providing employment and economic viability for many African Americans. The industry fosters entrepreneurial endeavors that have advantaged many dispossessed and marginalized people. Yet hip hop is a highly contested cultural space. Mainstream middle- and upper-class Whites and Blacks decry the corrosive moral effects of hip hop culture. Yet the vibrant lyrics of rap and the locations of enunciation pictured and voiced in music videos capture the attention of youth across the United States and the globe.

In rap videos, young mostly male residents speak for themselves and for the community, they speak when and how they wish about subjects of their choosing. These local turf scenes are not isolated voices; they are voices from a variety of social margins that are in dialogue with one another. (Rose, 1994, p. 11)

Fascinated and lured by narratives of rebellion, oppositional identities, and locations on the margin, youth of all ethnic racial backgrounds and particularly White Americans are the primary consumers.

Global Hip Hop Culture

Today, hip hop cultural spaces are materializing around the globe. In urban, suburban, and rural settings in Europe, Africa, Latin America, and Asia, hip hop culture has been deterritorialized from the urban centers of the United States and reterritorialized in new locations creating hybrid cultural spaces that illustrate processes of glocalization. Distinctive communicative practices—particular styles of DJing, rapping, break dancing, and graffiti writing—originally constructed hip hop cultural spaces in the South Bronx, traveled to the urban centers of the U.S. Northeast, the West Coast, across the United States, and now around the globe. While the communicative practices of hip hop cultures around the world are clearly linked to the African diasporic colonial experience, they also rework the qualities of flow, layering, and rupture in their place-based specificity as global forces converge with local forces (Rose, 1994). Hip hop culture and styles developing in France and Italy provide spaces to address local issues of racism and concerns over police brutality. In Sweden, the hip hop scene among ethnic minorities focuses on constructing a collective oppositional identity to resist the White skinhead youth culture (Mitchell, 1996). For Maoris in New Zealand, rap music groups speak out for the rights of indigenous groups around the world. Hip hop in Japan is often used as a means of identity distinction by youth who want to mark themselves as different from the mainstream culture. Sociologist Andy Bennett (2004) noted that:

> the commercial packaging of hip hop as a global commodity has facilitated its easy access by young people in many different parts of the world. Moreover, such appropriations have in each case involved a reworking of hip hop in ways that engage with local circumstances. In every respect then, hip hop is both a global and a local form. (p. 180)

The appropriation of cultural forms and practices originally improvised and created in Black and Puerto Rican inner-city ghettos is central to the global flow of hip hop culture today. The meaning of **appropriation** varies along a continuum from the idea of "borrowing" to "mishandling" to "stealing" and raises questions about authenticity, ownership, and relations of power. Is hip hop essentially a Black thing? Is it disrespectful, inauthentic, or a subtle continuation of colonial practices for White rappers like the Beastie Boys, Eminem, Paul Wall, and rappers in the White working-class town of Newcastle, England, to borrow, mimic, use, and rework Black cultural practices? Sociologist Paul Gilroy (1993) argued that "the transnational structures which brought the black Atlantic world into being have themselves developed and now articulate its myriad forms into a system of global communications constituted by flows" (p. 80). In other words, Gilroy pointed out how the African diaspora is rooted in the development of Western capitalism. Today, hip hop circulates through a global communication system as a result of the networks of connectivity established during the colonial era. "Black" culture becomes global culture as hip hop is deterritorialized and reterritorialized around the globe, and the music and styles mesh with and call forth local responses (Bennett, 2004).

Hip hop cultural spaces, forms, and practices illustrate the complex and paradoxical nature of intercultural communication in the context of globalization. While enabling economic mobility and providing a platform for speaking—a visible and audible location of enunciation—mainstream rap narratives often promote stereotypes about communities of color and valorize danger, violence, misogyny, and homophobia. The commodification of hip hop culture—turning the culture into a product for sale and appropriating a message of rebellion and protest to sell everything from jeans to Jeeps—defuses and neutralizes the potentially resistive and counter-hegemonic message of hip hop. Yet it is through circuits of commodification that hip hop gains global visibility and accessibility. In the corporate-dominated information age, rap music and videos are "public and highly accessible place(s)," providing communication vehicles for the marginalized, yet the ultimate control and largest shares of the profits of both the music and video industries are in the hands of White Americans (Rose, 1994, p. 17).

Today, hip hop cultural spaces are places of belonging and identification, spaces of opposition and resistance, as well as spaces where ideologies of domination and exclusion are disseminated around the globe. Hip hop cultural spaces are locations of enunciation where the stories of the dispossessed and marginalized "Others" spin and spit alternative texts that can and do challenge, resist, and rewrite dominant narratives. Yet the commodification of hip hop culture has manufactured "mainstream" or "commercial" hip hop, which produces texts that comply with and shore up dominant ideologies. The case study on hip hop culture points to the central role of power—economic, social, political, and discursive power—in the formation, maintenance, and disruption of cultural spaces. In the following section, segregated, contested, and hybrid cultural spaces are examined highlighting the way power circulates in each.

CULTURAL SPACE, POWER, AND COMMUNICATION

Throughout history and today, space has been used to establish, exert, and maintain power and control. Power is signified, constructed, and regulated through size, shape, access, containment, and segregation of space. In other words, the use of space communicates. Consider the largest metropolises in the world today—Tokyo, Japan; Mexico City, Mexico; Mumbai, India; San Paulo, Brazil; New York City, United States; Shanghai, China; and Lagos, Nigeria. How do you think power is symbolized through the use of space in these cities today? In the Middle Ages in Europe, churches were the tallest buildings and occupied central locations in cities signifying the importance of religious authority. In the Ottoman Empire, no building was built higher than the minarets of mosques. European colonizers erected churches on top of local religious sites from the Americas to India and Africa to materially and symbolically impose colonial rule. Massive, elaborate, and substantial buildings were constructed in Europe and the colonies during the period of nation-state building, signifying governmental power.

Today, the signs of power in metropolises around the world are the financial buildings—the towering, glitzy, eye-catching economic centers of transnational capitalism. Financial centers around the globe like the Twin Towers in New York City are symbols of wealth, prosperity, and participation in global, transnational flows of capital. In other words, they signify access to resources and communicate power. Like all signs, buildings that are erected with multinational and transnational capital acquire meaning within a signification system that includes its opposite, or the lack of access to wealth and power. Towering skyscrapers also signify unequal relations of economic and political power. As Edward T. Hall (1966) elaborated in his book *The Hidden Dimension*, the way cultures use space communicates. Let's take a look now at how power is exerted and negotiated through communication in the construction of segregated, contested, and hybrid cultural spaces.

Segregated Cultural Space

Spatial segregation exists today and has existed historically in cities and rural areas around the world based on socioeconomic, racial, ethnic, political, and religious differences. Ethnic, racial, religious, as well as sexual minority cultural groups may choose to live in communities in close proximity as a way to reinforce and maintain cultural spaces and to buffer themselves from real or perceived hostile forces around them. These cultural spaces—more appropriately understood as voluntary separation rather than segregation—often provide and reinforce a sense of belonging, identification, and empowerment. Yet there are many historical and contemporary examples of **segregated cultural spaces**: the imposition and use of spatial segregation to maintain the hegemony of the dominant group and to restrict and control access of nondominant groups to power and resources. The word *ghetto,* used primarily today to refer to ethnic or racial neighborhoods of urban poverty, originally referred to an area in Venice, Italy, where Jews were segregated and required to live in the 1500s. The reservation system imposed on Native Americans, the Jim Crow laws that segregated Blacks, and the isolation of Japanese Americans during WWII are examples of forced segregation that maintained the hegemony of European Americans and limited access for nondominant groups in the United States.

On the long road from slavery to freedom that many still walk in the United States, African Americans have encountered tremendous obstacles including various insidious forms of segregation. From the abolition of slavery in 1865 until the civil rights laws of the 1960s, more than 400 state laws, constitutional amendments, and city ordinances were passed by White lawmakers to legalize racial segregation and discrimination against Blacks (and other minorities in the western United States) in the majority of states in the United States. Jim Crow laws segregated Blacks and Whites, first and foremost, restricting interracial marriage and secondly restricting contact between the two groups by imposing legal punishment for those who crossed the color line (Litwack, 1998). Visible signs marked the public spaces where Blacks were allowed. If Blacks entered spaces on trains or buses, in public buildings, hospitals, restaurants, theaters, or schools that were not designed for "coloreds" or crossed the line into the "Whites only" area, they were subjected to beating, arrest, and on occasion, death. Today, the use of the word *colored* to refer to people of color or non-White people is problematic and often experienced as derogatory because of the dehumanizing use of the term historically. Jim Crow laws maintained and managed a system of White supremacy constructed through colonization and slavery (Litwack, 1998).

Real estate covenants restricted where Blacks and people of color could live and "Whites-only" towns officially and unofficially segregated Blacks, forcing them into areas where economic resources from businesses to jobs and public services such as schools and health care were and continue to be substandard and scarce. Sociologist James Loewen (2006) argued that "Whites-only" towns, what are called "sundown towns," exist today. "Sundown towns," so named for their threats of violence aimed at Blacks after the sun sets, are places that have deliberately excluded Blacks for decades and that, today, increasingly exclude Latinos/Latinas. You might think that racial, ethnic, and cultural segregation is a phenomenon of the past in the United States. I often hear students say, "That's history. It's over now. Let's move on." Well, unfortunately, it isn't over. First, systemic inequities and injustices of the past continue to impact the present and the future. Second, while laws that blatantly led to segregation such as the Jim Crow laws have been abolished, other formal and informal practices support de facto (by practice) segregation today. As discussed in Chapter 3, in the context of neoliberal globalization, race is recoded as class. Given the legacy of colonization and the history of systemic discrimination, the contours of class segregation are closely linked to race. Rearticulating race as class obscures the racial, as well as gender, dimensions of class (see Figure 4.2).

Figure 4.2 Racial Wealth Gap

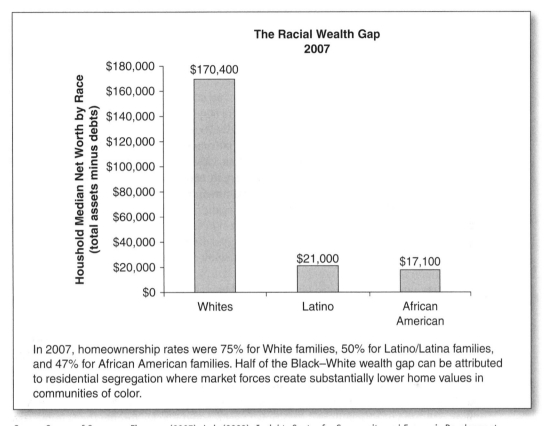

In 2007, homeownership rates were 75% for White families, 50% for Latino/Latina families, and 47% for African American families. Half of the Black–White wealth gap can be attributed to residential segregation where market forces create substantially lower home values in communities of color.

Source: Survey of Consumer Finances (2007); Lui, (2009); Insight: Center for Community and Economic Development.

More than five decades after the Supreme Court issued the decision to desegregate education in the United States, schools today are resegregated to the same level as in 1970s. According to the Civil Rights Project (Orfield & Yun, 1999), across the United States, White students attend schools that are approximately 80% White. The most racially segregated schools are in New York, Illinois, Michigan, and California, where suburban schools tend to be predominantly White and inner-city schools Black and Latino/Latina. Authors of the Harvard Civil Rights Project Gary Orfield and John Yun (1999) reported the following:

Though we usually think of segregation in racial and ethnic terms, it's important to also realize that the spreading segregation has a strong class component. When African-American and Latino students are segregated into schools where the majority of students are non-white, they are very likely to find themselves in schools where poverty is concentrated. This is of course not the case with segregated white students, whose majority-white schools almost always enroll high proportions of students from the middle class. This is a crucial difference, because concentrated poverty is linked to lower educational achievement. . . . When school districts return to neighborhood schools, white students tend to sit next to middle class students but black and Latino students are likely to be next to impoverished students. (p. 3)

Another vivid and compelling illustration is the devastation experienced by victims of Hurricane Katrina. While all people living in New Orleans and the Gulf area were impacted by the natural disaster, low-income, working-class neighborhoods were hit the hardest. Working-class and poor neighborhoods were the least protected from the storm and most vulnerable to the substandard relief efforts that followed. Historically, racial segregation imposed geographic color lines in New Orleans as it did in cities across the United States, and current class segregation maintains these divisions. The New Orleans parish with 67% Black residents was the hardest hit by the storm and floods. Representative Cynthia McKinney (2006) from Georgia reported the following:

Poverty cuts across ethnic divisions, but there is another side to this story . . . whites were evacuated before blacks while blacks were detained or turned back, as happened on the bridge to Gretna. The media stereotyped blacks as "looters" and whites as "takers" and fueled fears of blacks that led to the "invasion" of New Orleans, shockingly by hired mercenaries.

The plight of victims was exacerbated by long-standing and present-day systematic racism and neglect.

These examples illustrate how segregation of cultural spaces structure and reinforce different power positions within socioeconomic, political, and cultural hierarchies. Segregation, whether it is class, race, gender-based, or an intersection of all three, is a powerful means to control, limit, and contain nondominant groups. Spatial segregation is imposed and enforced by systems put in place by a dominant group—in the United States, European Americans or Whites, who maintain White supremacy. Formal and informal institutional systems that restricted access to places and spaces continue to limit the material, social, political, and economic potential of nondominant groups in the United States today. What other examples can you think of that suggest segregated cultural spaces are not relics of the past? As in the case of the forgotten and disenfranchised Black and Latino/Latina youth in the South Bronx, segregated cultural spaces that produce the exclusion of groups from resources—material, symbolic, political, and social resources—have been challenged in the past and are disputed today resulting in contested cultural spaces.

Contested Cultural Space

Chinese immigrants who came to the United States to work from the 1850s onward were forced to live in isolated ethnic enclaves known as Chinatowns in large cities such as

San Francisco and New York. In an article entitled "The First Asian Americans" in the *Asian-Nation: The Landscape of Asian America*, C. N. Le (2006) stated the following:

> Because they were forbidden from owning land, intermarrying with Whites, owning homes, working in many occupations, getting an education, and living in certain parts of the city or entire cities, the Chinese basically had no other choice but to retreat into their own isolated communities as a matter of survival. These first Chinatowns at least allowed them to make a living among themselves.
>
>   This is where the stereotypical image of Chinese restaurants and laundry shops, Japanese gardeners and produce stands, and Korean grocery stores began. The point is that these [occupations] did not begin out of any natural or instinctual desire on the part of Asian workers, but as a response to prejudice, exclusion, and institutional discrimination— a situation that still continues in many respects today.

After the devastating 1906 earthquake and fires in San Francisco, White city leaders and landlords wanted to relocate Chinatown, which was situated on prime real estate in the city center, to the outskirts of town claiming that it was an "eyesore and health hazard." A political battle ensued with the Chinese community leaders strongly protesting the forced displacement. Finally, they were able to convince the White civic leaders that Chinatown could be rebuilt in a "traditional Oriental" style to attract tourists and contribute to the city's revenue and appeal. We can see how Chinatown is a polysemic cultural space as well as a contested cultural space. A **polysemic cultural space** means that multiple meanings have been constructed about Chinatown over time. Chinatown was originally seen as a place to exclude and isolate Chinese immigrants by White city power brokers. It was seen and experienced as a refuge, a safe haven, and "home" by and for Chinese immigrants. Powerful White leaders denigrated Chinatown and its residents calling it an "eyesore and health hazard" with a masked goal of repossessing it as a desirable and valuable piece of property. Chinatown was redefined as a "cultural resource" by Chinese immigrant organizers for community empowerment and a product or commodity for sale. Chinese leaders of the dispute had to agree to represent themselves and their community in ways that would appeal to and be marketable to tourists from the dominant European American culture. In a way, Chinatown was appropriated by city power brokers, whether we understand that as borrowed or stolen, for the purpose of commodifying and selling it. The competition or dispute over various meanings and interests—economic, community, symbolic, political, and social meanings and interests—make Chinatown a contested cultural space. Anthropologists Setha Low & Denise Lawrence-Zúñiga (2003) define **contested cultural spaces** as geographic locations where conflicts engage actors defined by unequal control and access to resources in oppositional and confrontational strategies of resistance.

In the early 2000s, in Hudson, New York, a small town of 7,000 just 100 miles north of New York City, residents joined together in what has been described as a lopsided power battle between David and Goliath. The largest cement company in the world, Swiss-owned Holderbank, planned to build a massive, coal-fired cement manufacturing factory nearby Hudson on the banks of the river. Hudson is a diverse community with European American and African American families dating back to the Civil War, Bangladeshi immigrants who arrived in the 1950s to work in button factories, transplants from failed urban renewal projects in the Bronx, and a wave of newcomers that includes artists and professionals and a strong gay and lesbian community. The film *Two Square Miles* by filmmaker Barbara Ettinger (2005), documented the contested cultural space of the city of Hudson as residents wrestle, like so many towns and cities around the world, with competing economic, social, and political issues in the global context. Competing concerns and interests—the lure of job opportunities, detrimental environmental effects, and political affiliations—divided residents across lines of race, gender, and sexual orientation. In this contested cultural space, key figures work to bridge these divides and build alliances to contest the power politics of city officials and the multinational corporate giant. Setha Low and Denise Lawrence-Zúñiga (2003) noted, "Spaces are contested precisely because they concretize the fundamental and recurring, but otherwise unexamined, ideological and social frameworks that structure practice" (p. 18). Contested cultural spaces like hip hop culture expose how socially constructed ideological frameworks such as race, class, and gender function to divide, segregate, and exclude. Let's take a look at how hybrid cultural spaces are sites of negotiation, resistance, and change.

Hybrid Cultural Space

On the surface, the notion of hybrid cultural spaces appears fairly simple. Most people agree that there is a mixing or blending of cultures in the world today, and through intercultural overlap and intersection, hybrid cultural spaces are constructed. Yet what is the nature of the blending and mixing? Is it simply an equal mix of two or more cultural ingredients—like food preparation—that creates hybridity and hybrid cultural spaces? The following three examples of hybrid cultural spaces help us understand the power dynamics that structure the terms and conditions of mixing in hybrid cultural spaces.

Imagine you are sitting in a McDonald's in Moscow, Russia. You might expect to find a situation similar to what you experience here in the United States—a fast, inexpensive, (fat) filling meal in a familiar and standardized space (each one is pretty much like the next one) where you sit down, eat your meal, and leave *or* take the drive-through option. You might assume you will have an experience of "American" culture in Russia. Yet when Shannon Peters Talbot (as cited in Nederveen Pieterse, 2004, p. 50) conducted an ethnographic study of McDonald's in Moscow, Russia, she found something quite different. Moscowites came to McDonald's to enjoy the atmosphere, often hanging out for more than an hour. They pay more than one third of the average Russian daily wage for a meal and are drawn to this cultural space for its uniqueness and difference. Instead of "one size fits all" management practices that are generally applied in the United States, McDonald's in Moscow offers a variety of incentive options for employees (Nederveen Pieterse, 2004).

The proliferation of multinational entities around the globe suggests a corporatization and homogenization of cultural spaces. This McDonaldization of the world (think 16,000 Starbucks in 50 countries; 8,500 Walmart stores in 15 countries outside the United States; 31,000 McDonald's in 119 countries; etc.) is the result of unequal power relations, which manifests in an asymmetrical global flow of cultural products. Do we see the proliferation of Russian restaurants, coffee shops, and department stores in the United States or around the world? Undoubtedly, this is an example of cultural imperialism or the domination of one culture over others through cultural forms such as pop culture, media, and cultural products. Without erasing the asymmetrical power relations and the dominance of U.S and Western cultural forms, it is important to note the hybrid nature of the cultural space—the mixing of cultural influences, the altered way the space is used, and the new meanings that are produced about the space—in this reterritorialized McDonald's. Sociologist Jan Nederveen Pieterse (2004) used Talbot's ethnography in Moscow as an example of intercultural hybridization. McDonald's in Moscow is a hybrid cultural space. **Hybrid cultural space** is defined as the intersection of intercultural communication practices that construct meanings in, through, and about particular places within a context of relations of power. Digging under the surface appearance of blending and mixing reveals **hybrid cultural spaces as sites of intercultural negotiation.** Hybrid cultural spaces are innovative and creative spaces where people constantly adapt to, negotiate with, and improvise between multiple cultural frameworks.

Communication scholar Radha Hegde (2002) described the hybrid cultural space in an Asian Indian immigrant home:

> The aroma of Indian cooking replete with cinnamon, cardamom, saffron, and ginger rises in the air as friends arrive. The colors of Indian saris stand out, making a statement of embodied difference. The afternoon warms up with an array of appetizers—a tantalizing multicultural spectacle ranging from salsa and chutney to tahini! The conversation also spans a vast geographical and cultural terrain. (p. 259)

Hegde continued by describing the multiple and varied conversations that move from the delicious taste of samosas, reminders of home, to concerns over cholesterol and heart disease. Conversations about mothering in a bicultural world merge into a heated discussion over the stoning of a local Indian temple. Here is how she ended the scenario:

> Just then a new batch of samosas arrives from the kitchen, ready to be savored. There is a roar from the adjoining room. The football game gets intense. "American football is where the action is. What did you say, cricket? Can't take it anymore—just too drawn out." (p. 260)

Hegde argued that the hybrid cultural space described here is constructed by Asian Indian immigrants as a response to what Salome Rushdie (1991) called the triple dislocation: a disruption of historical roots, language, and social conventions. This triple dislocation penetrates to the very core of migrants' experiences of identity, social connections, and culture. The construction of hybrid cultural spaces, then, is an active and creative effort to maintain and sustain one's culture in the context of global displacement and replacement. Constructed in the context of differential power relations, hybrid cultural spaces are forms of resistance to full assimilation into the dominant culture. As noted in the case study about hip hop, hybrid cultural spaces are *both* highly innovative, improvisational, and creative *and* "also cultures that develop and survive as a form of collective resistance" (Hegde, 2002, p. 261). Hybridity—hybrid cultures, spaces, and identities—challenge stable, territorial, and static definitions of culture, cultural spaces, and cultural identities. Therefore, we can understand **hybrid cultural spaces as sites of resistance.**

In a third example, Chicana feminist scholar Gloria Anzaldúa (1987) described the fluid, contradictory, and creative experience of living in the hybrid cultural space she calls the "Borderlands/borderlands":

> . . . the Borderlands are physically present wherever two or more cultures edge each other, where people of different races occupy the same territory, where under, lower, middle and upper classes touch, where the space between two individuals shrinks with intimacy. I am a border woman. I grew up between two cultures, the Mexican (with a heavy Indian influence) and the Anglo (as a member of a colonized people in our own territory). I have been straddling that *tejas*-Mexican border, and others, all my life. It's not a comfortable territory to live in, this place of contradictions. Hatred, anger and exploitation are the prominent features of this landscape. However, there have been compensations for this *mestiza*, and certain joys. Living on borders and in margins, keeping intact one's shifting and multiple identity and integrity, is like trying to swim in a new element, an "alien" element. There is an exhilaration in being a participant in the further evolution of humankind, in being "worked" on. (first page of unnumbered preface)

Amidst the pain, hardship, and alienation, Anzaldúa expressed "exhilaration" at living in, speaking from, and continually constructing hybrid cultural spaces—the Borderlands. In the ongoing confrontation with and negotiation of "hegemonic structures that constantly 'marginalize' the mixtures they create" (Tomlinson, 1999, p. 146), Anzaldúa experienced and constructed a location of enunciation, a position, and a cultural space (both a literal and figurative space) from which to speak and claim an oppositional identity. Nederveen Pieterse (2004) stated, " . . . it's important to note the ways in which hegemony is not merely reproduced but *reconfigured* in the process of hybridization" (p. 74). Therefore, we can understand **hybrid cultural spaces as sites of transformation.** We have explored segregated, contested, and hybrid cultural space through historical and contemporary examples. The discussion of cultural spaces and the excavation of underlying power dynamics here provide a foundation for investigating the intercultural dynamics of border crossing, identity construction, and relationship building in later chapters.

SUMMARY

In this chapter, the cultural and intercultural communication dimensions of place, space, and location were investigated. I discussed the ways that human beings construct, negotiate, contest, and hybridize cultural spaces though communicative practices highlighting the role of power historically and today. The concept of glocalization was introduced to focus attention on how specific places are impacted by globalizing and localizing forces. I also proposed the notion of bifocal vision or the ability to attend to the linkages between "here" and "there" as well as the connections between the present and past to understand the complex, layered, and contested dimensions of places, cultural spaces, and locations today.

The case study on hip hop culture illustrated the pivotal function of place in constructing individual and group identities, locations of enunciation, and relationships of power. Hip hop emerged from the segregated space of the South Bronx—a forgotten and forsaken place. Fusing traditional communicative practices with contemporary technologies and postcolonial realities, the youth of the Bronx created a powerful cultural space. Hip hop cultural spaces give rise to both pleasure and protest that challenge the conditions of marginalized people within societies around the world. Yet hip hop culture's counter-hegemonic messages of resistance and struggle are often defused through processes of commodification. As cultures and cultural spaces are deterritorialized and reterritorialized around the world in the global context, contested and hybrid cultural spaces develop. Segregated, contested, and hybrid cultural spaces expose the context of unequal power relations that structure intercultural communication in the global age. We discovered that hybrid cultural spaces are much more than the blending of multiple cultural traditions and practices. Rather, hybrid cultural spaces are sites of intercultural negotiation, sites of resistance where people reconstitute identities, and sites where creative alternatives challenge and transform oppressive hegemonic forces.

KEY TERMS

cultural space
avowed identity
ascribed identity
locations of enunciation
(dis)placing culture and cultural spaces
time–space compression
"in-hereness"
"out-thereness"
glocalization
deindustrialization

appropriation
segregated cultural space
polysemic cultural space
contested cultural space
hybrid cultural space
hybrid cultural spaces as sites of intercultural
    negotiation
hybrid cultural spaces as sites of resistance
hybrid cultural spaces as sites of
    transformation

DISCUSSION QUESTIONS AND ACTIVITIES

Discussion Questions

1. Think about the neighborhood you grew up in, the street you live on, and the place you work. How do these cultural spaces contribute to your avowed and ascribed identities?

2. Is the city or town you live in segregated? How are the relations of power across class, race, gender, and ethnicity reflected in the segregated map of your city?

3. In the previous chapter, we discussed bodies as sites where difference is constructed. How does cultural space (i.e., neighborhoods, restaurants, shopping malls) shape the meaning of the body and vice versa?

4. How is meaning communicated through cultural space, and how does it influence the process of face-to-face intercultural communication?

Activities

1. Creating a Cultural Map—Group Activity

   a. On a geographical map of the area around your university campus, identify types of cultural space using words, symbols, colors, and pictures. Identify what kind of schools, neighborhoods, museums, businesses, cultural/ethnic/religious sites, and so on, are located in the area.

   b. Address the following questions:

      i. What groups (race, gender, sexuality, ethnicity, age, class, nationality, etc.) are associated with the cultural space? What meanings are attached to the space and people?

      ii. How is the area segregated and/or integrated? How does the segregation translate into or reflect unequal access to resources such as housing, education, and health care?

      iii. Where can you position yourself in the map? How does the way you navigate in the area reflect your identity, belonging, and privilege or lack thereof?

      iv. Can you see the signs of globalization on the map? If so, what concepts from the chapter can you apply to the phenomena?

2. The Body and the Space—Group Activity

   a. Choose a specific cultural space (i.e., restaurant, neighborhood, nightclub, workplace) you are familiar with.

   b. Describe in detail how you communicate verbally and nonverbally in the space, such as your language, greetings, gesture, eye contact, voice, clothing, and use of space.

   c. Address the following questions:

      i. How is your verbal and nonverbal communication shaped by the particular cultural space?

      ii. What are the "codes of conduct" in the cultural space, and what happens if you violate them? Are there different codes based on gender?

      iii. How is your body signified in the particular cultural space? How are your differences marked on the body?

      iv. What is the relationship between the body and the space?

REFERENCES

Anzaldúa, G. (1987). *Borderlands/La Frontera: The new mestiza*. San Francisco: Aunt Lute Books.

Appadurai, A. (1988). Putting hierarchy in its place. *Cultural Anthropology, 3*, 36–49.

Appadurai, A. (1996). *Modernity at large: Cultural dimensions of globalization*. Minneapolis: University of Minnesota Press.

Bennett, A. (2004). Hip hop am Main, Rappin' on the Tyne: Hip hop culture as a local construct in two European cities. In M. Forman & M. A. Neal (Eds.), *That's the joint! The hip hop studies reader* (pp. 177–200). New York: Routledge.

Casey, E. S. (1996). How to get from space to place in a fairly short stretch of time: Phenomenology and prolegomena. In S. Feld & K. H. Basso (Eds.), *Senses of place* (pp. 13–52). Santa Fe, NM: School of American Research.

Chang, J. (2005). *Can't stop, won't stop: A history of the hip hop generation*. Boston: St. Martin's.

Cross, B. (1993). *It's not about a salary: Rap, race and resistance in Los Angeles*. London: Verso Books.

Ettinger, B. (Director). (2005). *Two square miles* [Motion picture]. United States: Niijii Films.

Foreman, M. (2004). "Represent": Race, space and place in rap music. In M. Forman & M. A. Neal (Eds.), *That's the joint! The hip hop studies reader* (pp. 201–222). New York: Routledge.

Geertz, C. (1996). Afterward. In S. Feld & K. H. Basso (Eds.), *Senses of place* (pp. 259–262). Santa Fe, NM: School of American Research.

George, N. (1998). *Hip hop America*. New York: Penguin.

Giddens, A. (1994). Living in a post-traditional society. In U. Beck, A. Giddens, & S. Lash, *Reflexive modernization* (pp. 56–109). Cambridge, UK: Polity.

Gilroy, P. (1993). *The Black Atlantic: Modernity and double consciousness*. Cambridge, MA: Harvard University.

Grandmaster Flash and the Furious Five. (1982). The message. *The message* [CD]. Englewood, NJ: Sugarhill Records.

Hall, E. T. (1966). *The hidden dimension*. New York: Doubleday.

Harvey, D. (1990). *The condition of postmodernity: An enquiry into the origins of cultural change*. Cambridge, MA: Blackwell.

Hegde, R. (2002). Translated enactments: The relational configurations of the Asian Indian immigrant experience. In J. N. Martin, T. K. Nakayama, & L. A. Flores (Eds.), *Readings in cultural contexts* (pp. 259–266). Boston: McGraw-Hill.

Inda, J. X., & Rosaldo, R. (Eds.). (2001). *The anthropology of globalization: A reader*. Cambridge, UK: Blackwell.

Le, C. N. (2006). The first Asian Americans. *Asian-nation: The landscape of Asian America*. Retrieved from http://www.asian-nation.org/first.shtml

Litwack, L. F. (1998). *Trouble in mind: Black southerners in the age of Jim Crow*. New York: Alfred A. Knopf.

Loewen, J. W. (2006). *Sundown towns: A hidden dimension of American racism*. New York: Touchstone.

Low, S. M., & Lawrence-Zúñiga, D. (2003). Locating culture. In S. M. Low & D. Lawrence-Zúñiga (Eds.), *The anthropology of space and place: Locating culture* (pp. 1–47). Malden, MA: Blackwell.

Lui, M. (2009). Laying the foundation for national prosperity: The imperative of closing the racial wealth gap. *Insight: Center for community and economic development*. Retrieved from http://www.insightcced.org/uploads/CRWG/LayingTheFoundationForNationalProsperity-MeizhuLui0309.pdf

Martin, J. N., & Nakayama, T. K. (2004). *Intercultural communication in contexts*. Boston: McGraw-Hill.

McKinney, C. (2006). McKinney warns of new underclass of "Katrina homeless." *The Final Call*. Retrieved from http://www.finalcall.com/artman/publish/article_2440

Mitchell, T. (1996). *Popular music and local identity: Rock, pop and rap in Europe and Oceania*. London: Leicester University.

Nederveen Pieterse, J. (2004). *Globalization and culture: Global mélange*. Lanham, MD: Rowman & Littlefield.

Orfield, G., & Yun, J. T. (1999). Resegregation in American schools. *The Civil Rights Project UCLA*. Retrieved from www.civilrightsproject.ucla.edu

Robertson, R. (1992). *Globalization: Social theory and global culture*. London: Sage.

The roots of hip hop. (1986). *RM HIP HOP MAGAZINE*. Retrieved from http://globaldarkness.com/articles/roots_of_hiphop.htm

Rushdie, S. (1991). *Imaginary homelands*. New York: Penguin.

Rose, T. (1994). *Black noise: Rap music and Black culture in contemporary American society*. Hanover, NH: Wesleyan.

Tomlinson, J. (1999). *Globalization and culture*. Cambridge, UK: Blackwell.

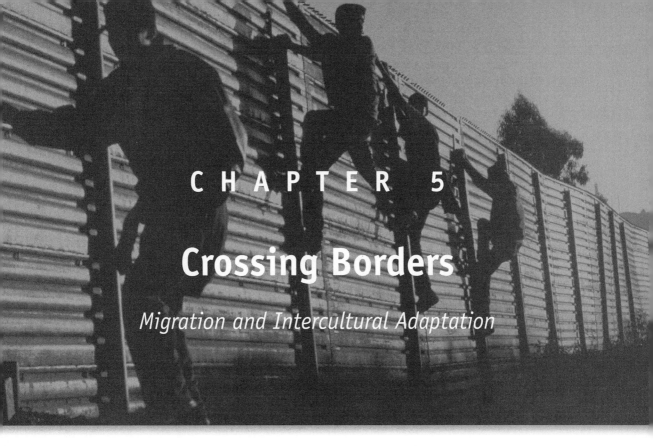

CHAPTER 5

Crossing Borders

Migration and Intercultural Adaptation

Who can move freely across borders, and who is restricted?

Our world, at the beginning of the new millennium, is a world in motion. More people are on the move today crossing cultural boundaries and national borders than ever before in the history of humankind. The International Organization for Migration reported in 2009 that 214 million people live outside their country of origin. With an annual increase of about 3%, migration and relocation are key global issues facing individuals, communities, and nation-states today. In addition, over 940 million people crossed international borders as tourists (for leisure, business, visiting relatives, etc.) in 2010 despite rising oil prices, fluctuating exchange rates, global political uncertainty, and threats of terrorism (United Nations World Tourism Organization, 2011). Globalization has dramatically altered the context for understanding the movement of people around the world. We have moved, as Manuel Castells (1996) told us, from a space of "places" to a space of "flows." Why are so many people on the move today? What is unique about migration in the global context?

First, advances in transportation and communication technologies facilitate frequent, multidirectional flows and the creation of transnational networks of people. Second, the integration of global capital and markets has accelerated the concentration of wealth and

Source: Chapter-opening photo © Todd Bigelow/Aurora/Getty Images.

exacerbated economic inequity both within and across nations, resulting in new patterns of rural to urban and south to north global migration. Third, the implementation of neoliberal policies has displaced millions of people who are compelled to move for jobs and livelihood. Fourth, escalation in intranational and international conflict has propelled unparalleled numbers of people across borders in search of safety, opportunity, and the spoils of war. Additionally, as the cross-border flows of people challenge the power and sovereignty of the nation-state, nation-states struggle to reassert control over national boundaries through increasingly restrictive and punitive immigration policies by erecting walls, utilizing sophisticated surveillance, and mobilizing large numbers of people to police borders. We live in a world in motion driven and disrupted by powerful forces.

In November 2006, Nobel Prize–winning novelist Toni Morrison chose the theme of "A Foreigner's Home" as the guest curator for a multidisciplinary, international conversation among artists and audiences at the Louvre Museum in Paris, France. Films, readings, concerts, and dance performances addressed the pains and rewards of migration, displacement, and exile experienced by millions who search for "home," "like nomads between despair and hope, breath and death," Morrison says (Riding, 2006). Part of the program featured rappers from France, some of them immigrants of sub-Saharan African and Muslim North African descent. Morrison's use of hip hop links the African diaspora with current postcolonial migratory experiences of dispossessed and marginalized North African–French immigrant youth who took to the streets in the suburbs of Paris in fall 2005, protesting racial discrimination and exclusion from French society. Her work connects the multidirectional, complex, and contradictory dynamics of intercultural encounters in the context of globalization with the colonial past. In an article in the *New York Times,* Toni Morrison commented that her theme, "A Foreigner's Home," requires "us to come to terms with being, fearing, and accepting strangers" (Riding, 2006). She focuses our attention not only on population mobility but on the reception, adjustment, and impact of a world in motion for all of us.

What role does intercultural communication play in the adaptation of migrants and in the social, political, and cultural transformations that result from the unprecedented flows of people crossing borders? This chapter begins with a brief discussion of different types of migrants and an overview of the three major waves of world migration, which provide a context for understanding contemporary patterns of migrant mobility, settlement, and the emergence of transnational migrant networks. Various theories of migration and cross-cultural adaptation are introduced and then applied to three case studies pertaining to the experiences of migrants in the global context. Throughout the chapter, the central role of communication in intercultural transitions is highlighted as people navigate the challenges and benefits of crossing borders.

MIGRANTS

Migrants are people who move from their primary cultural context, changing their place of residence for an extended period of time. It is useful to distinguish two dimensions when categorizing migrants. One important dimension is the degree of agency of a migrant in choosing to move or travel and a second is the length of stay or permanence of the relocation of migrants. Migrants who choose to leave home to travel or relocate are called **voluntary migrants. Sojourners** are voluntary migrants who leave home for limited periods of time and for specific purposes such as international students, business travelers, tourists, missionaries, and military personnel. Voluntary migrants who leave one country and settle permanently in another country are called **immigrants.** Europeans who moved along colonial routes during the first wave of world migration and to industrial centers in Europe and the Americas in the second wave are considered voluntary migrants. Migrants who are forced to leave due to famine, war, and political or religious persecution are called **involuntary migrants.** Africans who were traded as slaves during the colonial era, refugees who flee their countries of origin due to war and famine, or those seeking asylum for political reasons today are considered involuntary migrants. **Human trafficking** for sex work and other types of labor is another form of forced or involuntary migration, as people, particularly women, are transported against their will in increasing numbers in the global context. Involuntary migrants—refugees, asylum-seekers, and those forced into labor—may also, over time, seek or obtain permanent residence in the country of destination, making them immigrants.

The categories of voluntary and involuntary migrants underscore how the conditions of migration differ. Making a decision to leave one's place of origin and voluntarily settling in a new location suggests that the migrant has acted upon their own agency with some desire to relocate, which establishes different conditions for relating to the country of destination compared to those who are forced to migrate. Yet the distinction between voluntary and involuntary has always been somewhat ambiguous, and the difference blurs even more today for many people who leave their home countries and resettle either temporarily or permanently. For example, Mexican migrants may "choose" to leave their homes and migrate to the United States, but they often do so only under extreme duress when local economies collapse and jobs are lost. Migration is often the only viable alternative to provide food, clothing, and shelter for families. Let's take a look at how globalizing forces since the 16th century have resulted in three major waves of world migration. As you read, note the similarities and differences among the three migration waves.

HISTORICAL OVERVIEW OF WORLD MIGRATION

The **first wave of world migration** can be traced to the European colonial era from the 16th century through the 19th century. Thousands of migrants—sailors, soldiers, traders, missionaries, administrators, and later farmer–settlers—sailed out of ports of Europe for colonies in Africa, Asia, and the Americas, establishing sea trade routes that continue to structure migration flows today. While the experiences varied in different locations, a general pattern followed as colonizers appropriated the so-called "empty" lands and used indigenous peoples to extract the material wealth of the land. After indigenous labor was almost exhausted or annihilated through genocide and disease, the forced migration of over 15 million slaves from the west coast of Africa provided the labor for the production of commodities in mines and plantations (such as gold, silver, coffee, sugar, and cotton) in the colonies. The African diaspora dispersed people around the world to the Americas, Europe, and Asia. Also part of the first wave of colonial migration, some 12 to 37 million people were transported internationally as indentured servants, representing a significant migratory flow to over 40 countries after the abolition of slavery in the mid-19th century (Potts, 1990). Working under very poor conditions, indentured laborers were recruited—sometimes by force and sometimes voluntarily—and then transported great distances to fill the labor needs of European colonies. The wealth extracted from the colonies not only supported the lavish lifestyles of the ruling

Figure 5.1 Young doffer and spinner boys in Mill

Young textile mill workers at the Seaconnet Mill, Massachusetts, in 1912. Children as young as 6 years old worked long hours in factories during the Industrial Revolution. These immigrant boys couldn't read or write and barely spoke English.

Source: Library of Congress/National Child Labor Committee.

elite in Europe but the exploitation of labor and land was crucial to the rise in economic and political power of European nations that spurred the second large wave of migration (Castles & Miller, 2003; Toro-Morn & Alicea, 2004).

The **second wave of migration** took place from the mid-1800s to the early 1900s during the Industrial Revolution, when peasants from the rural parts of Europe, fleeing poverty and famine, migrated to urban areas in Europe and North and South America. Conditions in factories were severe—long hours, low pay, and unsafe environments—similar to conditions for workers in sweatshops today. Between 1900 and 1930, 40 million people left Europe for North and South America and Australia, first from Britain and Germany, and later from Spain, Italy, Ireland, and Eastern Europe (Castles & Miller, 2003). **Chain migration,** or linkages that connect migrants from points of origin to destinations, led to the segmentation of ethnic groups in the United States. For example, the Irish, Italians, and Jews tended to settle in the ports of the East Coast, while Central and Eastern Europeans were drawn to work in heavy industries in the Midwest. Until the 1880s, immigration to the United States was open; however, as racist campaigns increased and **nativist movements** emerged—movements that called for the exclusion of foreign-born people—Chinese and other Asian immigrants were targeted through the Chinese Exclusion Act of 1887 (Saenz, Morales, & Ayala, 2004). Italian and Irish immigrants, viewed as a threat to American values and as not capable of being assimilated, were also excluded. While the Irish and Italians are categorized racially as White today, their differences from the dominant Anglo-Americans in terms of language and culture were used to classify them racially as non-White in the late 1800s (Ignatiev, 1995). Throughout the history of the United States, immigration policy has served economic interests. The National Network for Immigrant and Refugee Rights (Cho, Puete, Louie, & Khokha, 2004) claims the following:

> Immigration policy in the U.S. has also served as a way to regulate the "character of the nation," limiting entry, citizenship, and economic access while enforcing racial divides. Because immigration can influence the demographic makeup of the nation, policy makers throughout U.S. history have admitted or excluded migrants based on qualifications such as national origin, race, class, gender, political ideology, and sexual orientation. (p. 40)

War, economic depression, and **xenophobia**—defined as the fear of outsiders—dramatically curtailed immigration to the United States until after WWII.

COMMUNICATIVE PRACTICES
RHETORIC OF NATIVISM

In April 2010, Arizona lawmakers passed anti-immigration legislation that spurred a nationwide protest and controversy. The law requires the state and local law enforcement to stop and interrogate people suspected as undocumented migrants. Massive protests and boycotts against the state ensued. The law, from the perspective of those who oppose it, is racist normalizing, racial profiling, and criminalizing undocumented migrants.

Supporters of this law deploy rhetoric of nativism and exclusion to justify their position. They argue that economic recession, increasing prison populations, an overburdened health care system, and unemployment result from the failure of the federal government to protect its border. In other words, undocumented migrants are a burden on U.S. society. Rhetoric of nativism not only leads to stricter laws but also increases the militarization of the border and violence against migrants.

Nativist movements, whether today or in the past, show how people use language and discourse to create hierarchies of belonging and access in terms of citizenship and nation. The immigration debates also demonstrate the shifting and contested ideas about what is considered "criminal" and who is entitled to equal protection under the law. Such rhetoric often appeals to xenophobia and ethnocentrism, shaping historical and cultural contexts of intercultural communication.

The third wave, often labeled the postindustrial wave, is more diverse and multidirectional than previous migrations and encompasses patterns of movement since WWII. Following WWII, large numbers of Jews left Europe for Israel, as well as South and North America. **Guest workers programs** brought workers from the periphery of Europe—Spain, Italy, Turkey, Ireland, and Finland—to fill the labor shortages in industrialized Western Europe due to the war and declining population (Hammer, 1985). Another large wave of voluntary migration occurred as anticolonial movements across Africa and Asia led to independence for former colonies. Labor demands in the former European colonizing countries as well as political and economic instability in struggling recently independent nations resulted in **postcolonial migrants,** migrants who leave former colonies and relocate in colonizing countries. Postcolonial migrants include the movement of Indian, Pakistani, and Caribbean migrants to England; of North African, Tunisian, Moroccan, and West African migrants to France; and of migrants from Indonesia, a former Dutch colony, to the Netherlands.

Postcolonial migration patterns counter the directional flows of the first wave of colonial migration resulting in the unanticipated growth of significant non-White, ethnic minority populations within Europe. While guest workers and postcolonial migrants fueled the economies of host countries and played a major role in the rebuilding of Europe after WWII, their status and acceptance as immigrants within the host countries of Europe varies. Institutional and informal racism and discrimination often limit employment and educational options and create residential separation (Castles & Miller, 2003). From the 1920s to 1965, immigration to the United States was severely restricted. Migrant workers from Mexico were recruited through a guest worker program called the **Bracero Program** in the 1940s to fill labor shortages during WWII. Migrants who participated in this program made tremendous contributions to the agricultural industry in the United States. They provided skilled, low-wage work until the mid-1960s when the program was ended due to protests over harsh working conditions and severe human rights violations. Migration to the United States declined until amendments to the Immigration and Nationality Act in 1965 challenged the discriminatory national origins quota system. The change was not intended or expected to instigate large scale migration from non-European countries. Yet, with the shift to kinship and family reunification with U.S. citizens as the main criteria, the number of Latin American and Asian immigrations increased dramatically (Borjas, 1990).

MIGRATION TRENDS IN THE CONTEXT OF GLOBALIZATION

In the later part of the 20th century and into the new millennium, migration is increasingly rapid, complex, multidirectional, and diverse. Countries in Europe that were, in the first and second waves of migration, primarily sending countries are now receiving migrants from Eastern European countries and from former colonies. While European countries depend on immigrants to fill labor needs and to support the negative population growth, ethnic, racial, and religious demographic changes have heightened cultural and political conflicts and increased anti-immigrant sentiment. Latin America was previously seen as a receiving continent during the colonial and industrial migration waves. However, as a result of macro-level changes such as economic liberalization, Latin America is experiencing massive rural to urban migration within nations, international migration within Latin America (e.g., temporary migrants from Nicaragua to Costa Rica and from El Salvador to Mexico), and international migration to North America. These shifts create major challenges as divided and displaced families and communities struggle to maintain connections and construct regional and transnational networks.

As global economic integration concentrates wealth in more developed countries, Africans from less developed and poverty-ridden countries are driven to more affluent neighboring countries such as the Ivory Coast and South Africa. Africa has a very large refugee population due to unstable political and economic conditions in the struggling former colonies. **Refugees** are people who are forced to flee for safety from their country of origin due to war, fear of persecution, or famine. According to the United Nations High Commissioner for Refugees (UNHCR) (n.d.), the number of official refugees has declined in the past decade from an all-time high of 18 million in the mid-1990s to approximately 10.5 million in 2009. War, human rights violations, and ethnic cleansing in the Balkans, Rwanda, and the Soviet Federation in the 1990s and in Sudan, the Congo, Afghanistan, and Iraq since 2000 have displaced hundreds of thousands of people who move from the poorest and most politically unstable countries in the world. While the number of official refugees has declined in the past decade, the number of **internally displaced persons,** refugees within one's own country of origin, has increased to approximately 25 million.

Migration patterns within and to the Arab region are propelled primarily by the magnet of oil rich countries that draws laborers from India, Pakistan, Sri Lanka, Bangladesh, the Philippines, Thailand, and Indonesia to the Middle East. Most Asians come as **contract workers** through labor agreements established between the governments of the sending and receiving countries. Conditions for employment are often severe and exploitative and do not allow for permanent settlement or family reunification. Known as the "tiger economies," the Asia Pacific region holds half the world's population and two thirds of the world's workforce (Castles & Miller, 2003). While often the case in the global era, migrants within and from Asia can be divided into **high- and low-skilled laborers.** Economic liberalization, the entry of multinational corporations into formerly closed areas, and the creation of free trade zones has promoted rural to urban movement in China, India, Thailand, and Vietnam as low-skilled laborers and particularly women, driven by poverty, seek factory work in export processing zones. Regional economic disparities draw low-skilled workers from poorer countries—the Philippines, India, and Sri Lanka—to wealth-concentrated Asian countries—Japan, Hong Kong, Singapore, and Malaysia—who often perform what is known as the three Ds in Japan: work that is (1) difficult, (2) dangerous, and (3) dirty, such as factory, agricultural, food processing, sex industry, and domestic labor. On the other end of the spectrum, educated, high-skilled workers migrate from Asia, primarily from India and China, to developed countries such as the United States, Canada, England, and Australia to work in high-tech and medical professions. Toro-Morn and Alicea (2004) noted that these migratory flows are two sides of the same coin:

> Global restructuring has led to a global division of labor, where periphery economies have become the source of production and assembly lines while core economies such as the United States, Canada, and Europe have become centers of high finance and technology. (p. xxix)

In summary, multidirectional migration is a central feature of globalization resulting in an increase in and intensification of intercultural interactions, alliances, and conflicts. As areas of the world join and are forced into the interconnected global economy, people are thrust into unparalleled migration flows. The lives of those who are uprooted, the lives of those who remain, and the lives of those in places where people resettle are dramatically transformed. Second, advances in communication and transportation technologies create the conditions for migration networks to form that enable transmigrants to maintain, hybridize, and change the "host" cultures and "home" cultures through global migration flows. Third, approximately 65% of all international migration is to highly developed countries of the north. As south-to-north migrant flows concentrate in urban centers of Europe, the United States, Canada, Australia, and Japan, significant changes and tensions emerge, fueling anti-immigrant campaigns, mobilizing immigrant rights groups, and igniting intercultural tensions and conflicts. Fourth, women across the economic spectrum are entering the paid labor force in unprecedented numbers leading to the **feminization of the workforce.** Women joining the workforce in developed countries creates demand for women from developing countries to migrate great distances to serve as caretakers and surrogate mothers, often leaving their own children with relatives. In export processing zones, women are often preferred for low-skilled work because they can be paid less and are more easily exploited. Today, one half of the 192 million international migrants are women, exacerbating the familial, social, and economic impact of migration and displacement.

The three waves of migration have produced the multicultural societies in which we live today, affording opportunities to engage with and benefit from diverse cultural groups and individuals. Yet many of the challenges faced by societies around the world—racial and ethnic discrimination and tension, intensified economic inequity, and increasing poverty, as well as disputes over immigrant rights and immigration policies—are also embedded in and structured by racist, classist, and ethnocentric ideologies forged and institutionalized through the past 500 years of global migration. We turn now to a range of theories that assist us in making sense of the complex, multidirectional patterns of migration and cultural adaptation in the context of globalization.

THEORIES OF MIGRATION AND INTERCULTURAL ADAPTATION

To understand the experiences of migrants as they move around the globe today, we need to consider migration patterns and intercultural adaptation from three interrelated levels or frames: (1) the macro or large scale economic–political level of nation-states and global, transnational structures; (2) the micro or individual level of migrant adaptation; and (3) the meso or intermediate level of migrant networks and sociocultural group ties that link the macro, structural level and the micro, individual level. While much of the research on cultural adaptation in the field of communication focuses on the individual level of migrants' adaptation to new environments, the micro-level experience is inevitably impacted by social networks on the meso-level and by macro-level political and economic global structures. A multilevel analysis accounts for the structural inequities and sociocultural networks that circumscribe migrants' process of cultural adaptation as they cross borders in the context of globalization.

Macro-Level Theories

Many of the traditional macro-level explanations of migration are variations of the **push-pull theory,** first articulated by a British geographer in the late 1800s, which proposes that circumstances in the country of origin "push" people toward migratory paths—economic hardship, famine, war, or persecution, for example—and conditions in the country of destination "pull" people toward particular locations. The conditions that pull people may be a higher degree of economic opportunities relative to what is available in the country of origin, the opportunity for family reunification, or political stability. While the push-pull theory is useful today, the complexities of migration and migratory patterns in the global context defy simple explanation. **World-systems theory** argues that international migration today is a result of the structure of global capitalism (Sassen, 1994; Wallerstein, 2000). Migration flows from less developed, or Third World, countries to more highly developed, or First World, countries are a result of global structural inequity grounded in colonization. Nation-states and global institutions that act on behalf of capitalists drive migration as they take advantage of land, labor, resources, and markets in peripheral or Third World countries (Massey et al., 1993). Decisions, policies, and treaties made at the global institutional level—the World Trade Organization (WTO), the International Monetary Fund (IMF), and the World Bank (WB)—create conditions where people cannot survive in their countries of origin, propelling migration.

Where migrants go, where they are "pulled" to, is also affected by nation-state immigration policies and transnational economic and political agreements on the macro-level. The orientation of the "host" or "destination" country toward migrants and migrant groups in official and informal terms impact migrants' processes of adaptation in the new country (Castles & Miller, 2003). Are the nation-state's immigration policies and practices directed toward assimilation, exclusion, or integration in a multicultural society? Historically, the primary orientation toward migrant adaptation in United States has been assimilation to the dominant culture with the **melting pot** serving as the metaphor. The melting pot ideology, popularized by Jewish immigrant Israel Zangwill in his play in the early 1900s, assumes that the migrants' adaptation to a new culture requires and allows newcomers to "melt" or "blend" into the mainstream to form a cohesive whole (Postiglioni, 1983). While the notion of the melting pot was, to some extent, descriptive of the experiences of some Europeans who immigrated to the United States, it has never adequately captured the diverse experiences of exclusion and adjustment of non-White migrants, migrants with strong ethnic ties, or many immigrant groups who have lived in the United States for generations. The myth of the melting pot prevails today masking the ways that some migrants are not allowed to "melt" and casting suspicion on those who do not want to shed their cultural norms, values, and practices. More recently, an ideology of **pluralism,** which emphasizes the maintenance of ethnic and cultural values, norms, and practices within a multicultural society, has emerged as a result of the civil rights movement, anticolonial movements, and immigrant rights movements, challenging the inaccurate myth of the melting pot.

Micro-Level Theories

While macro-level theories provide a map for understanding the large scale dimensions of migration and cultural adaptation in the global context, micro-level theories focus our attention on the smaller scale individual and interpersonal dynamics (see Figure 5.2, p. 111). The **U-curve model** of adaptation, based on research conducted with Norwegian international students who traveled to the United States on study abroad programs in the 1950s, was one of first models developed that focused on short-term adaptation. The research measured the level of contentment or happiness experienced by sojourners over time. Norwegian researcher Sverre Lysgaard (1955) noted three significant stages in the cultural adaptation process. The first stage was one of **anticipation,** where excitement about the new culture characterizes the sojourner's experience. The second stage is marked by **culture shock,** or the disorientation and discomfort sojourners experience from being in an unfamiliar environment. Originally theorized as a disease because it is often accompanied by physical symptoms (Oberg, 1960), culture shock has been reinterpreted as a type of transition shock that leads to growth, learning, and personal change (Adler, 1987). The third stage is one of **adjustment** to the new environment as the sojourner learns to negotiate the verbal and nonverbal codes, values, norms, behaviors, and assumptions of the new culture. Adjustment varies considerably based on a range of factors including the sojourner's desire to adapt, the host culture's receptivity, the degree of similarity or difference between home and host cultures, as well as age, gender, race, and socioeconomic background.

Noting the experiences of sojourners and other types of migrants as they return to their countries of origin, the U-curve model has been extended to the **W-curve model,** which addresses the challenges of reentry into one's "home" culture (Gullahorn & Gullahorn, 1963). Reentry, or return, may follow a similar pattern of anticipation, culture shock, and adjustment, yet the changes that an individual has gone through in the cultural adjustment process away from home as well as the fact that the culture the sojourner is returning to has also changed may exacerbate culture shock and adjustment upon return (Martin, 1984).

To understand the cultural adaptation of longer-term migrants, social psychologist John Berry (1992) considered the attitudes of migrants toward their host and own cultures, outlining four **migrant–host modes of relationship,** which include assimilation, separation, marginalization, and integration. **Assimilation** occurs when a migrant values the host's culture more than his or her own culture. Historically and today, Europeans who migrate to the United States generally have developed a migrant–host relationship of assimilation, facilitated by the similarities between their own cultures and the dominant host culture and the receptivity of the host culture to them, along with the migrants' desire to assimilate. **Separation** describes the migrant–host mode of relationship when the migrant values their own or home culture more than the host culture. The desire to maintain one's cultural values, norms, and practices leads some migrants to voluntarily choose separation as a mode of relationship with the dominant host culture, yet, in other cases, migrants have been forced by law or informal discriminatory practices into a migrant–host relationship of separation such as the historical segregation of Chinatowns in major U.S. cities and real estate covenants that excluded minorities. **Marginalization,** according to Berry (1992), occurs when the migrant places little value on either her or his own culture or the host culture. Migrants, who experience a sense of distance from and lack of acceptance by both their culture of origin and the dominant culture, live on the borders of both cultures. Marginalization is often characterized as psychologically isolating and stressful, yet it is also potentially a creative and empowering migrant–host mode of relationship (Bennett, 1993). Someone who is on the margins of both the home and host cultures occupies a unique position that allows for the emergence of fluid and multifaceted standpoints, as well as creative hybridization of the two cultures. **Integration** describes the migrant–host mode of relationship when the migrant values both his or her own culture and the host culture. Migrants who sustain their cultural identity by maintaining their language and cultural practices through social networks and participate in the dominant host culture develop a migrant–host mode of integration. While integration may appear to be the ideal migrant–host mode of relationship, many factors influence the relationship a migrant adopts at any given time.

The attitudes of the migrant to adaptation are not the only factors that influence the migrant–host mode of relationship. The host nation's immigration policies, the institutional practices, and the attitudes of the dominant culture toward the migrant and her or his group also impact migrants' experiences. Additionally, it is important to consider what role racism and ethnocentrism play in the host or majority culture's receptivity to the migrant and his or her culture. Consider how economic stratification in the host country can lead to separation in terms of housing, education, and employment. The relative ease of returning to one's country of origin for work or extended visits also impacts the relationship migrants develop with the host or majority culture as well as the relationship migrants can maintain with their "home" country.

In the context of globalization, as migrants move more frequently and rapidly between "host" and "home" cultures, the modes of relationship that migrants maintain with their own culture *within their country of origin* is increasingly significant in the intercultural adaptation process. "Host" and "home" are put in quotes here to note the complicated nature of labeling the various locations where migrants live, work, develop affinities, and build community in the global context. Traditionally, the host country designated the country of destination where migrants settle either temporarily or permanently. Host carries a connotation of visitors who are treated with hospitality, which does not adequately represent the experiences of many migrants historically or today. The notion of home culture or country is also problematic as migrants today increasingly maintain strong connections to their country of origins and yet may consider their country of resettlement (host country) more their home than their country of origin.

CULTURAL IDENTITY
HOME, FAMILY, AND CULTURE

Leo is a Chinese American man in his late 20s. He explains his changing relationship to his home, family, and culture:

Growing up in San Francisco, all I wanted to be was anything but Chinese. All my life I tried my best not to be associated with Chinese culture.

Things changed drastically when I took a trip to Shanghai to attend my grandmother's funeral when I was 25. I was welcomed by my cousins, relatives, and friends of my parents. To my greatest surprise, I felt like I belonged for the first time in my life. It was so strange that I felt at "home" in a place I had never been or really cared about. The experience in Shanghai made me think about my cultural identity in a completely new way.

I ended up moving to Shanghai for a year. Things were great, but over time, it became clear that I didn't really belong there—I didn't speak the language and I didn't have a job. Although I looked liked them, I began to realize I am still an American. Now I visit Shanghai every year to see my relatives and friends. I hope someday my children will appreciate the history of transnational migration that has shaped my Chinese American identity.

integrative-theory 3

Communication scholar Young Yun Kim (2001, p. 15) noted "that the individual and the environment co-define the adaptation process." She argued for an **integrative theory of cultural adaptation** that addresses the attitudes and receptivity of the host environment, the ethnic communities within the majority culture, and the psychological characteristics of the individual. Taking a general systems perspective, Kim (2001) identified three assumptions about the nature of human adaptation: (1) humans have an innate self-organizing drive and a capacity to adapt to environmental challenges, (2) adaptation of an individual to a given cultural environment occurs in and through communication, and (3) adaptation is a complex and dynamic process that brings about a qualitative transformation of the individual. Kim's process model of cultural adaptation, emphasizing the role of communication as individuals adapt across cultural boundaries, states that individuals experience a process of stress, adaptation, and growth as they interact with and adjust in new and different cultural environments. Encounters with new cultures often challenge our assumed and taken-for-granted ways of thinking, behaving, and understanding ourselves, our communities, and the world around us. As migrants gain new information and insight about the norms and values and adapt their behaviors to the host culture in a process of **acculturation,** migrants also go through a process of **deculturation,** or the unlearning of some aspects of their culture of origin. This dynamic and ongoing movement between stress and adaptation, disequilibrium and readjustment produces growth. Kim (2001) postulated that **intercultural transformation** occurs as a result of this stress-adaptation-growth process and identifies three outcomes: (1) increased functional fitness of the migrant's ability to engage effectively with the host culture; (2) improved psychological health of the migrant in coping with the environment; and (3) a shift toward an intercultural identity, which allows the migrant to connect and identify with multiple cultural groups. All three micro-level theories—the U- and W-curve model, the migrant–host relationship model, and the integrative theory—provide insights that allow us to explain and navigate the challenges and rewards of intercultural adaptation.

Meso-Level Theories

Meso-level theories of migration and cultural adaptation seek to bridge macro-level theories that emphasize structural issues and micro-level theories that focus on individual attributes in the cultural adaptation process. A critical feature of intermediate level theories examines the role migrant networks play in global migration patterns and adaptation processes (see Figure 5.3). **Migrant networks** are defined as "sets of interpersonal ties that connect migrants, former migrants and non-migrants in origin and destination areas through ties of kinship, friendship and shared community origin" (Massey et al., 1993, p. 448). Attention to migrant networks highlights how social groups and collective cultural relationships motivate, sustain, and give meaning to migration and cultural adaptation processes. Meso-level analyses reveal how migrant social networks provide information and support for travel, housing, employment, education, and health care, which are instrumental in mediating both the macro-level structural conditions of global migration and the micro-level individual challenges that migrants face in their cultural adaptation process.

Migrant network approaches draw attention to the ways that migration and cultural adaptation in the context of globalization are embedded in webs of interlocking political, cultural, community, and familial relationships, environments, and locations, where social

Figure 5.2   Multilevel Approach to Intercultural Adaptation

Level/Frame	Theories/Concepts
Macro: Economic–political level of nation-states, global, transnational structures	Push-pull theory World-systems theory
Meso: Intermediate level of migrant networks and sociocultural group ties	Migrant networks Social capital Transmigrants
Micro: Individual level of migrant adaptation	U-curve W-curve Migrant–host relationships Integrative theory

capital develops and is exchanged. **Social capital** refers to the sense of commitment and obligation people within a group or network share to look after the well-being and interests of one another (Gold, 2005). Today, migrants maintain connections to more than one nation, community, and location, reinforcing, breaking, and reconstituting collective identities and migrant networks across national boundaries. A new category of migrants has emerged in the global context often referred to as **transmigrants,** or migrants who move across national boundaries to new locations for work and family reunification and yet also maintain cultural, social, economic, and political ties with their country, region, or city of origin (Basch, Blanc, & Schiller, 1994; Portes, Guarnizo & Landolt, 1999). Transmigrants are able to maintain transnational bonds in the global context through frequent communication and travel and through migrant networks that enable the construction of transnational homes, or transnational spaces, where collective identities, economic support, and empowerment are nurtured and where political resistance across national borders is possible. For example, when a transmigrant from India who lives in the United States is invited to join Facebook by a friend from home, she is instantly added to the Facebook pages of old classmates and relatives, linking her to an expansive transnational network where past, present, and future friends around the world are connected.

Utilizing a multilevel approach that integrates macro-, micro-, and meso-level theories of migration and cultural adaptation allows us to understand the challenges, choices, losses, opportunities, and rewards migrants face as they cross borders and negotiate "homes" in the global context. In the following pages, three case studies are presented. After each, theories of migration and cultural adaptation are used to critically analyze each case. The goal is to develop a process of analysis to make sense of the complex web of individual, social, and geopolitical factors that impact migrants and the globalized environments as we all adapt to a world in motion. I encourage you to empathize with the tremendous challenges migrants face and recognize the relationships among macro-, micro-, and meso-level issues facing migrants today.

CASE STUDIES: MIGRATION AND INTERCULTURAL ADAPTATION

The case studies that follow tell the stories of migrants with a focus on the conditions of migration and the complexities of intercultural adaptation in the global context. As you read these stories, notice the ways in which the experiences of migrants today are both similar to and different from the experiences of migrants in the first and second waves of world migration. Also consider what factors influence migrants' experiences of intercultural adaptation.

Villachuato, Mexico, to Marshalltown, Iowa: Transnational Connections[1]

In 1989, laborers—primarily men—began traveling from the small town of Villachuato in the state of Michoacán, Mexico, to work in a meatpacking plant in

---

[1]Case based on Grey & Woodrick (2002).

Marshalltown, Iowa. As economic conditions in Mexico worsened, larger numbers made the 3,000 mile trek to *el norte*. By the late 1990s, more than half of the employees at the third largest pork processing plant in the world were Latinos/Latinas and about half of those workers were from Villachuato. The meatpacking plant would shut down if not for the migrant laborers. Through remittances and fund drives organized by migrant networks that link several locations in the United States, wages made by workers in the United States are used to improve the Mexican community such as installing water and electricity, paving roads, and renovating the town plaza and church. Workers return to Villachuato frequently for annual religious events, weddings, and funerals often quitting their jobs and returning for rehire. While these practices benefit the plant economically, White American managers view them as disruptive and criticize Latinos/Latinas for being "irresponsible," for not learning English, and for not wanting to settle permanently in the United States. Tensions between Anglos and Latinos flared when the plant was raided by the Immigration and Naturalization Service (INS) with the knowledge of plant supervisors, and undocumented workers were deported. Efforts to build sustainable relations between the two communities improved when Marshalltown community leaders, the chief of police, and others visited Villachuato. Increasingly, as children of migrant families are born in the United States, families make decisions to seek permanent residence.

How can we make sense of the complex dynamics occurring in this scenario? The macro-level push-pull theory explains that high unemployment and poverty in Mexico relative to the United States "push" migrants from Mexico and "pull" them to the United States. But why is there such great economic disparity between Mexico and the United States? A world systems approach argues that historically, colonization and military force were used to establish conditions for the accumulation of capital by European and U.S. powers. Today, the conditions are established and maintained by "free trade agreements" (i.e., North American Free Trade Agreement [NAFTA] and Central America Free Trade Agreement [CAFTA]), negotiated through global governance bodies such as the IMF, WB and WTO. NAFTA has displaced hundreds of thousands of people in Mexico, resulting in at least 8 million undocumented workers seeking employment in the United States (Caulfield, 2010). While working conditions are harsh—difficult, dangerous, and dirty—and legal status for some workers perilous, basic self-survival and the survival of family members remaining in Mexico propel them to their northern neighbor. The globalization of capital, goods, and labor has linked Villachuato and Marshalltown to a global economy dominated by the United States. These communities are no longer marginal to the world economy; rather, they are part of an uneven global capitalist expansion (Grey & Woodrick, 2002; Griffith & Kissam, 1995). Like towns across the United States and Mexico, the lives and livelihoods of people from Villachuato and Marshalltown are intertwined and interdependent in the global context.

How is migration between Villachuato and Marshalltown and cultural adaptation sustained? Meso-level approaches to adaptation suggest that migrant networks pass along knowledge and experience about safe migration routes, work, housing, and other services through interpersonal communication with friends, family relations, and community connections. The establishment of migrant networks clearly support and promote migration and the creation of a transnational community. **Transnational communities** are constructed by transmigrants whose density of movement and social ties over time and across geographic space form circuits of exchange, support, and belonging (Goldring, 1996). Sociologist Luin Goldring noted that transnational communities are characterized by intertwining familial relationships across locations, identification with "home" or sending locations, and the ability to mobilize collective resources. The Villachuato–Marshalltown transnational community exemplifies all three characteristics.

Interestingly, the characteristics that define transnational migration are often the source of intercultural misunderstanding and conflict. First, the transmigrants' social, cultural, economic, and political allegiance to and sustained contact with their community in Mexico challenges the migrant–host mode of relationship of assimilation, where migrants from Europe in previous waves assimilated to the dominant culture (even if it took several generations of struggle). These new patterns of transmigration disrupt and resist hegemonic assumptions of U.S. superiority and the desirability of living in the United States, which further escalates tensions between the dominant group and migrant workers. The individual and collective agency of Villachuato migrants expressed through frequent travel between the two communities, remittances and fund drives to support the community in Mexico, and the ability to quit work are all strategies that challenge and subvert the assumed unidirectional power of U.S. national and corporate interests.

Second, the migrant–host mode of relationship in this case is initially one of separation as migrant laborers and their families from Villachuato are separated from the Marshalltown community. A level of voluntary separation based on migrant networks that affords social, economic, and political support combines with subtle and more blatant forms of segregation in housing and employment as well as social exclusion through stereotypes, prejudice, and racism by the "host" or receiving community. The transmigrants' mode of relationship with the host culture that is sustained through migrant networks is often viewed negatively by the dominant or host culture, commonly giving rise to statements like "they don't want to assimilate." Yet as children of transmigrants are born in the United States, a sense of allegiance to and connection with their Marshalltown home shifts the migrant–host relationship for some to one of integration. Additionally, as community members from Marshalltown take an interest in the community in Villachuato, Mexico, a process of intercultural adaptation occurs not only for migrants but also for Marshalltown residents. Kim's (2001) integrative theory of cultural adaptation explains that through an ongoing process of stress, disequilibrium, and adaptation growth takes place. It is not only the transmigrants from Mexico who are involved in a process of adaptation. As a transnational community is forged, Marshalltown residents and the community as a whole are also changed over time by the interactions and experience a process of intercultural adaptation characterized by stress, adaptation, and growth.

Fujian, China, to New York, New York: Human Smuggling of Low-Skilled Workers[2]

In the early 1990s, Ms. Zhang and her husband arrived in New York and immediately started working long hours for little pay at different Chinese

---

[2]Case based on Zhou (2004).

restaurants in Chinatown, organized by the smuggling network that had arranged their transportation. While excited to finally be in New York after agreeing to pay a considerable amount of money ($30,000 each) for the illegal 17,000 mile 3-month journey, for several months, Ms. Zhang experienced anxiety and fear. She was able to communicate with other Chinese migrants but found the different languages, regional accents, and ways of life in this new urban setting disorienting. For months, she took the same route to and from work, stopping only briefly to purchase food at the same shop each day. Over time, she became more familiar with her surroundings, developed contacts with people in her new environment, and learned some English. Ms. Zhang and her husband came to the United States from a rural area in the Fujian province in southeastern China where they worked in a factory that afforded them enough money to live but no extra money. Three years after coming to New York, she gave birth to their son. Since she could not afford to stop working and one income would not support the family, Ms. Zhang decided to go back to China with her son. She and her husband hoped she could return to the United States with their child when he was old enough to enter public school. In China, she was welcomed home but found it difficult to adjust.

What theories of cultural adaptation shed light on this situation? What conditions of globalization allow for and lead to such risk-taking actions on the part of Fujian Chinese migrants? Clearly, Ms. Zhang experienced the stages of the U-curve model as she progressed through excitement and anticipation, the disorientation and anxiety of culture shock, and an extended period of cultural adjustment as she familiarized herself with her new environment, made connections with people, and gained a degree of intercultural competence. Her story illustrates the processes of entry into new cultural contexts and reentry into familiar and yet changed cultures of origin reflecting the W-curve model. Her experience also points to the potential for ongoing cycles of departure and arrival to and from various "homes" that characterize migration in the global context.

On a macro-level, "push" and "pull" theories of migration provide insight and yet do not explain the whole story. Workers in China, on average, can make about twice as much in cities than in rural areas and as much as eight times more in coastal cities. In the United States, the average income is 20 times that of earnings in coastal cities of China. Yet, on a wage of $3 per hour as undocumented workers, migrants work 80 to 90 hours per week to cover basic needs and pay off debts to their smugglers (Kwong, 2000). Chinese migrants often dream of becoming wealthy in the United States, known as "the Golden Mountain," based upon the relative difference in wages between the United States and China.

In the context of globalization, media images of wealth, lavish lifestyles, and material success circulate around the world creating dissatisfaction with what one has and instilling desires for greater wealth and status. Author of *Smuggled Chinese: Clandestine Immigration to the United States*, Ko-lin Chin (2000) commented, "When people get together they always talk about how their sons or daughters or relatives or husbands or brothers are doing in the United States." Having a family member living in the United States is seen as a status symbol among relatives and neighbors. People are often pressured into making the risky journey and are ridiculed if reluctant. Once in the United States, Chinese migrants are often too embarrassed to talk about their devastating conditions, preferring to appear "successful" even as they toil night and day in miserable conditions. Social networks that link people on the interpersonal, familial, and community level compel migration even as they facilitate it. While the Zhangs in the vignette are by no means wealthy, they are also not poor compared to other regions of China. However, China's transition to a market-oriented economy has dramatically increased overall income inequality (Khan & Riskin, 1998). The increased disparity between income levels combines with heightened exposure to actual and media images of material wealth such that poorer people, people in the lower economic ranks, feel a sense of **relative deprivation.** In other words, in absolute terms, they are not poor. Rather, in a world with increasing inequity, the difference between oneself and those who have more motivates a desire to find ways to make money and become rich. Going to the United States, even with the level of risk and suffering involved, is an alternative way of getting rich (Kyle & Liang, 2001).

On the other end of the economic spectrum, Chinese immigrants to the United States in the past 20 years who have had access to educational and monetary resources have become highly successful professionals in the sciences, technology, medicine, and other fields in the United States. Chinese entrepreneurial families see the United States as an important destination for one or more sons to cultivate links in a growing global web of capital connection and accumulation. Anthropologist Aihwa Ong (1999) noted, "For over a century, overseas Chinese have been the forerunners of today's multiply displaced subjects, who are always on the move mentally and physically" (p. 2). High-skilled migration to the United States from India, China, the Philippines, or Canada has increased since the late 1980s as the elevated demand for knowledge workers, particularly in the areas of information technology, medicine, and science, combines with insufficient supply in the United States.

A controversial aspect of high-skilled migration has been the **brain drain** that results when high-skilled workers migrate temporarily or permanently from one country to another. The movement of high-skilled workers away from their countries of origin represents a huge loss in terms of knowledge, skills, investment, and capital for sending countries (Iqbal, 2000). The large numbers of Indian scientists, doctors, and computer programmers who migrated to the United States and other First World countries in the 1980s and 1990s are an example of brain drain. Yet, today, with the phenomenal growth of high-tech industries in India, many Indian migrants are returning to India. Additionally, there is a new pattern of U.S. migrants going to India to set up branch offices and to serve as English instructors in call centers on 1- to 2-year contracts. High-skilled workers are often accepted more easily than low-skilled workers into the dominant society in host countries due to their educational and economic levels, affording them the option to integrate into the host culture. The formation of ethnic, religious, and national cultural communities within host, or receiving, countries as well as transnational networks supported by communication and transportation technologies allow migrants to maintain connections with their cultural communities while they also develop association and acceptance with the dominant host culture. The migrant–host mode of relationship of integration best describes these migrant experiences.

North Africa–France: Postcolonial Immigrant Experience[3]

Nazim is 25 years old, a French citizen of Algerian descent, whose parents came to France in the 1960s, displaced by the Algerian War of Independence. Nazim, who has a university degree, has diligently searched for jobs sending out hundreds of resumes and following every lead possible. Yet he is unemployed, like 50% of the youth living in La Courneuve, a suburb 5 miles from the center of Paris. The dangerous streets and dilapidated buildings of the immigrant neighborhood contrast sharply with the clean, glitzy avenues of Paris's city center. Growing up, Nazim wanted to be seen as "French," reluctantly participating in his parents' desire to maintain allegiance to their Algerian homeland and culture. He preferred to hang out with friends who were not stigmatized as "immigrants." When the family returned to Algeria for a visit 10 years ago, Nazim was viewed as a foreigner, called derogatory names, and looked down upon because his family had emigrated from Algeria. Nazim did not participate in the uprising that set La Courneuve and other neighborhoods ablaze in the fall of 2005, as North African youth across France protested the racism and exclusion they experience. He didn't participate, but he certainly understands the anger, hopelessness, and disappointment that so many French North Africans feel. As an atheist, he's refused to join Muslim groups mobilized for North African immigrant youth in light of the French government's failure to provide education, employment, and social services.

What role do colonial and diasporic histories play in this scenario? How is culture—in this case, what it means to be "French," what it means to be "Algerian," and who benefits from citizenship—a contested site where meaning is negotiated? As a second generation immigrant to France, what is Nazim's relationship to the "host" country of France and to his "home" or parents' home country of Algeria?

Viewing the scenario from a macro-level, Nazim, like many who have been deterritorialized/reterritorialized in the past 50 to 60 years, is a postcolonial migrant or, more accurately, a second generation postcolonial immigrant. Born into an Algerian family in France, he constantly negotiates national, racial, cultural, religious, and class borders. The colonial relationship between his family's homeland of Algeria and his current "home" of France continues to structure his life, opportunities, and future. Prior to Algeria's independence from France in 1962, Algerians who migrated to France were French *subjects* but not *citizens*. While filling major labor gaps in post–WWII France, Algerians were often represented in the media as criminals, uncivilized, and poor. Algerians fought a long, bloody war of independence from France between 1954 and 1962 in which a half million Algerians died. Bitter memories and untended wounds scar the fabric of both nations fueling prejudices and hindering the integration of Algerians into French society.

On a meso-level, Algerian migrants' segregation from and stigmatization within mainstream French culture was intensified by discriminatory housing and employment

---

[3]Case based on Melvin (2006).

practices, as well as repressive and prejudicial treatment by law enforcement, legal, and educational systems. Spatial segregation into ethnic communities provided Algerian immigrants in France the motive and space to create migrant networks and mobilize resistance to the dominant society's oppressive forces. Immigrant Algerian communities in France played a significant role in the Algerian independence movement leading to brutal conflicts between French authorities and protesters (House, 2006). Since the 1970s, second generation immigrants, the sons and daughters of Algerian migrants, have been targeted in media and governmental discourses as "problems." Young men are depicted as "criminal" and "not capable of being assimilated," and young women are represented as "passive" and "submissive." Protesting the rise in racist killings and their second-class citizenship status even as they hold French nationality, young people from Algerian communities in France organized antiracist social movements in the 1980s. Stereotypes, institutionalized forms of discrimination, and anti-immigrant rhetoric have intensified in recent years as high levels of unemployment and socioeconomic crisis exclude French citizens of Algerian descent (House, 2006). In the global context, French Algerians, like other postcolonial immigrants around the world, develop migrant networks that offer political, economic, and cultural support; identification; and allegiance.

On a micro-level, marginalization best describes the migrant–host–home relationship that Nazim experiences both in France and Algeria. Even as he works toward acceptance and integration into French society, he experiences exclusion due to ethnic discrimination within the host culture. Children of Algerian immigrants like Nazim "experience a displacement of identity . . . suspended between the parents' background and the everyday life of French society" (Marranci, 2000). When he returns to Algeria, he is perceived as "too French," as a "traitor" in the complex postcolonial and neocolonial relationship between Algeria and France. Additionally, in the Algerian community in Paris, he sets himself apart from local groups who have organized based on religious affiliation to meet the needs of the community. As the experiences of Nazim illustrate, marginalization occurs in the complex intersection of the host culture's attitudes and practices toward migrant groups, the migrant or immigrant's desires and choices in relation to both the host and home cultures, and the homeland's attitudes and actions toward those who have emigrated. While marginalization often has a negative connotation and does indeed carry significant challenges, living in or being on the margins of social, cultural, and national groups can be an empowering and creative position.

As illustrated by the case studies, understanding migration and cultural adaptation in the global context requires that we address the intricate web of individual, social, and geopolitical factors that compel and constrain as well as empower and transform migrants and their surroundings. A multilevel analysis that attends to the macro-level historical, political, and economic issues; micro-level individual attributes; and meso-level migrant networks account for the intersection of complex and contradictory conditions that shape a world in motion.

Based on these case studies, a number of factors influence the experiences of migrants crossing borders today. Clearly the history of relations between nations that extends back to the first wave of colonial migration influences the direction of migration and the reception of migrants in host countries. The globalization of capitalism, integration of markets, and the implementation of neoliberal polices have exacerbated economic inequity within countries and across nations catapulting people from the Global South into migratory paths. Legal and economic status affects migrants' experiences and adaptation as well as educational level, language abilities, gender, age, and familiarity with the "host" culture. The reception of the "host" culture to the migrant group also has a tremendous impact. The migrant–host modes of relationship of assimilation, separation, marginality, and integration are directly impacted and shaped by the attitudes and policies as well as the histories of interaction between the host and home countries. In addition, migrant networks impact the cultural adaptation of people who cross cultural borders, offering social and economic support, re-creating collective regional and cultural identities, and providing political alliances.

SUMMARY

In this chapter, we defined various types of migrants from voluntary and involuntary migrants to postcolonial migrants and transmigrants. The purpose of identifying different types of migrants is to highlight the particular conditions that shape the experiences of migrants and draw attention to commonalities and differences across the three waves of migration. World migration from the first wave to the current wave has been integral to the growth of capitalism. Migrants—on a continuum from voluntary to involuntary—have fueled and resuscitated First World economies from the colonial to the industrial and into the postindustrial wave of migration. Viewing migration through a capitalist–labor lens highlights the varying degrees of exclusion and inclusion migrants experience in "host" countries, which significantly affects their ability to participate in "host" countries.

As the forces of globalization converge, unprecedented numbers of people have been displaced, dramatically impacting those who are uprooted, those who remain, and those in places where people resettle. Advances in communication and transportation technologies have created the conditions for migration networks to form that enable transmigrants to maintain, hybridize, and change the "host" cultures and "home" cultures. As south to north migrant flows concentrate in urban centers of Europe, the United States, Canada, Australia, and Japan, significant social and cultural changes as well as economic and political tensions emerge. Anti-immigrant campaigns rally and immigrant rights groups mobilize, fueling racial, interethnic, and intercultural tensions and conflicts. Questions of human rights, civil rights, and immigrant rights coalesce in the global context with complex and unparalleled implications.

Theories of migration and cultural adaptation from macro-, meso-, and micro-levels were introduced that enable us to understand the dynamic and multifaceted nature of migration and cultural adaptation today. Macro-level theories provide insight into the large scale historical, political, and economic structures that shape patterns of migration and adaptation. Micro-level theories enable us to describe and explain individual migrants' experiences of cultural adjustment and intercultural transformation. Bridging these two, the meso-level approach focuses on the role of migrant networks in supporting migration and facilitating the creation of transmigrant communities. As Toni Morrison pointed out, our world in motion requires "us to come to terms with being, fearing, and accepting strangers" (Riding, 2006).

KEY TERMS

migrants
voluntary migrants
sojourners
immigrants
involuntary migrants
human trafficking
first wave of world migration
second wave of migration
chain migration
nativist movements
xenophobia
the third wave of migration
guest workers programs
postcolonial migrants
Bracero Program
refugees
internally displaced persons
contract workers
high- and low-skilled laborers
feminization of the workforce
push-pull theory
world-systems theory

melting pot
pluralism
U-curve model
anticipation
culture shock
adjustment
W-curve model
migrant–host modes of relationship
assimilation
separation
marginalization
integration
integrative theory of cultural adaptation
acculturation
deculturation
intercultural transformation
migrant networks
social capital
transmigrants
transnational communities
relative deprivation
brain drain

DISCUSSION QUESTIONS AND ACTIVITIES

Discussion Questions

1. What are your views on immigration? How does your positionality inform your views and opinions about people who cross borders?

2. How do voluntary and involuntary migrants (sojourners, immigrants, refugees, guest workers, transmigrants, postcolonial migrants, etc.) experience cultural adaptation differently? What are the factors that influence their experience, attitudes, and outcome?

3. Why is the metaphor "melting pot" problematic and/or inaccurate to describe U.S. society? Can you think of other metaphors that describe the United States as a country of people with diverse backgrounds?

4. What role does communication play in understanding global migration and negotiating cultural adaptation?

5. In the previous chapter, we discussed the notion of cultural space. How does global migration impact the construction and transformation of cultural space?

Activities

1. Crossing Borders: Case Study Analysis

   a. Provide a description of someone you know (including yourself, if appropriate) who is a migrant. Address the following questions:

      i. What kind of migrant is she or he?

      ii. What was the social, political, historical, and economic context in which she/he migrated to another country? How did the context shape his or her experience?

      iii. What theories of migration are useful to understand her or his experience as a migrant?

      iv. What role does communication play in his or her process of cultural adaptation?

2. Negotiating Immigration Policies—Group Activity

   a. The class is divided into two independent nation-states located next to each other.

   b. First, name your country and assign each group member to be one of the following categories: political leaders, wealthy elites, educated middle-class, working/lower class, and immigrants.

   c. As a group, decide immigration policies toward the other nation-state to maximize the national interest. Address the following questions, and make sure to include opinions of all citizens:

      i. Who and how many should be allowed to enter the country?

      ii. What are the terms and conditions for migration?

      iii. How can migrants become permanent residents and/or citizens?

      iv. Do you enforce any requirements or restrictions on language skills, educational background, religious beliefs, sexual orientation, nation of origin, and so on?

   d. Share your immigration policies with the other nation-state.

   e. Address the following questions to discuss and debrief the process:

      i. Whose opinions were more powerful and influential in determining the policies, and why?

      ii. What factors were the most important in making the policies?

      iii. How will the immigration policies shape the international relations between the two countries?

      iv. How will the immigration policies shape intercultural interactions between migrants and natives of the country?

      v. What kind of "multicultural society" do you think your country will be?

REFERENCES

Adler, P. (1987). Culture shock and the cross-cultural learning experience. In L. F. Luce & E. C. Smith (Eds.), *Toward internationalism: Readings in cross-cultural communication* (pp. 24–35). Cambridge, MA: Newbury.

Basch, L. G., Blanc, C. S. & Schiller, N. G. (1994). *Nations unbound.* New York: Routledge.

Bennett, J. M. (1993). Cultural marginality: Identity issues in intercultural training. In R. M. Paige (Ed.), *Education for the intercultural experience* (pp. 109–135). Yarmouth, ME: Intercultural Press.

Berry, J. (1992). Psychology of acculturation: Understanding individuals moving between two cultures. In R. W. Brislin (Ed.), *Applied cross-cultural psychology* (pp. 232–253). Newbury Park, CA: Sage.

Borjas, G. J. (1990). *Friends or strangers: The impact of immigration on the U.S. economy*. New York: Basic.

Castells, M. (1996). *The rise of the network society*. Oxford, UK: Blackwell.

Castles, S., & Miller, M. J. (2003). *The age of migration: International population movements in the modern world* (3rd ed.). New York: Guilford Press.

Caulfield, R. (2010). *NAFTA and labor in North America*. Champaign: University of Illinois Press.

Chin, K. (2000). *Smuggled Chinese: Clandestine immigration to the U.S.* Philadelphia: Temple University Press.

Cho, E. H., Puete, F. A., Louie, M. C. Y., & Khokha, S. (2004). Globalization, migration and worker's rights. *BRIDGE: A popular education resource for immigrant & regugee community organizers*. Oakland, CA: National Network for Immigrant and Refugee Rights.

Gold, S. J. (2005). A summary and critique of relational approaches to international migration. In M. Romero & E. Margolis (Eds.), *The Blackwell companion to social inequity* (pp. 257–285). Malden, MA: Blackwell.

Goldring, L. (1996). Blurring borders: Constructing transnational community in the process of Mexican-U.S. migration. *Research in community sociology* (Vol. 6, pp. 69–104). New York: Jai Press.

Grey, M. A., & Woodrick, A. C. (2002). Unofficial sister cities: Meatpacking labor migration between Villachuato, Mexico, and Marshalltown, Iowa. *Human Organization, 61,* 364–376.

Griffith, D., & Kissam, E. (1995). *Working poor: Farmworkers in the United States*. Philadelphia: Temple University Press.

Gullahorn J., & Gullahorn, J. (1963). An extension of the U-curve hypothesis. *Journal of Social Issues, 19*(3), 33–47.

Hammer, T. (1985). *European immigration policy: A comparative study*. Cambridge, UK: Cambridge University Press.

House, J. (2006). The colonial and post-colonial dimensions of Algerian migration to France. *History in Focus*. Retrieved from http://www.history.ac.uk/ihr/Focus/Migration/articles/house.html

Ignatiev, N. (1995). *How the Irish became White*. New York: Routledge.

International Organization for Migration. (2009). *About migration*. Retrieved from http://www.iom.int/jahia/page3.html

Iqbal, M. (2000). The migration of high skilled workers from Canada to the United States: Empirical evidence and economic reasons. *Center for Comparitive Immigration Studies*. Retrieved from http://repositories.cdlib.org/ccis/papers/wrkg20/

Khan, A. R., & Riskin, C. (1998). Income inequity in China: Composition, distribution and growth of household income, 1998-1995. *China Quarterly, 154,* 221–253.

Kim, Y. Y. (2001). *Becoming intercultural: An integrative theory of communication and cross-cultural adaptation*. Thousand Oaks, CA: Sage.

Kwong, P. (2000). *Forbidden workers: Illegal Chinese immigrants and American labor*. New York: New Press.

Kyle, D., & Liang, Z. (2001). Migration merchants: Human smuggling from Ecuador and China. *Center for Comparative Immigration Studies*. Retrieved from http://repositories.cdlib.org/ccis/papers/wrkg43

Lysgaard, S. (1955). Adjustment in a foreign society: Norwegian Fulbright grantees visiting the United States. *International Social Science Bulletin, 7,* 45–51.

Marranci, G. (2000). *A complex identity and its musical representation: Beurs and Raï music*. Retrieved from http://www.umbc.edu/eol/MA/index/number5/marranci/marr_0.htm

Martin, J. (1984). The intercultural re-entry: Conceptualization and directions for future research. *International Journal of Intercultural Relations, 8,* 115–134.

Massey, D., Arango, J., Hugo, G., Kouaouci, A., Pellegrino, A., & Taylor, J. E. (1993). Theories of international migration: A review and appraisal. *Population Development Review, 19* (3), 431–466.

Melvin, D. (2006). Anger still seethes among immigrants in France. *Cox News Service*. Retrieved from http://www.coxwashington.com/reporters/content/reporters/stories/2006/04/28/BC_FRANCE_MUSLIMS27_COX.html

Oberg, K. (1960). Culture shock: Adjustment to new cultural environments. *Practice Anthropology, 7,* 170–179.

Ong, A. (1999). *Flexible citizenship: The cultural logics of transnationality*. Durham, NC: Duke University Press.

Portes, A., Guarnizo, L., & Landolt, P. (Eds.). (1999). The study of transnationalism: Pitfalls and promises of an emerging research field. *Ethnic and racial studies, 2*(22), 217–237.

Postiglioni, G. (1983). *Ethnicity and American social theory: Toward critical pluralism*. Lanham, MD: University Press of America.

Potts, L. (1990). *The world labour market: A history of migration*. London: Zed.

Riding, A. (2006). Rap and film at the Louve: What's up with that? *New York Times*. Retrieved from http://www.nytimes.com/2006/11/21/books/21morr.html

Saenz, R., Morales, M. C., & Ayala, M. I. (2004). The United States: Immigration to the melting pot of the Americas. In M. I. Toro-Morn & M. Alicea (Eds.), *Migration and immigration: A global view* (pp. 211–232). Westwood, CT: Greenwood.

Sassen, S. (1994). *Cities in a world economy*. London: Pine Forge.

Toro-Morn, M. I., & Alicea, M. (Eds.). (2004). *Migration and immigration: A global view*. Westwood, CT: Greenwood.

United Nations High Commissioner for Refugees. (n.d.). *Figures at a glance*. Retrieved from http://www.unhcr.org/pages/49c3646c11.html

United Nations World Tourism Organization. (2011). *UNWTO tourism highlights*. Retrieved from http://mkt.unwto.org/sites/all/files/docpdf/unwtohighlights11enhr_1.pdf

Wallerstein, I. (2000). *The essential Wallerstein*. New York: New Press.

Zhou, Y. (2004). Chinese immigrants in the global economy. In M. I. Toro-Morn & M. Alicea (Eds.), *Migration and immigration: A global view* (pp. 35–52). Westwood, CT: Greenwood Press.

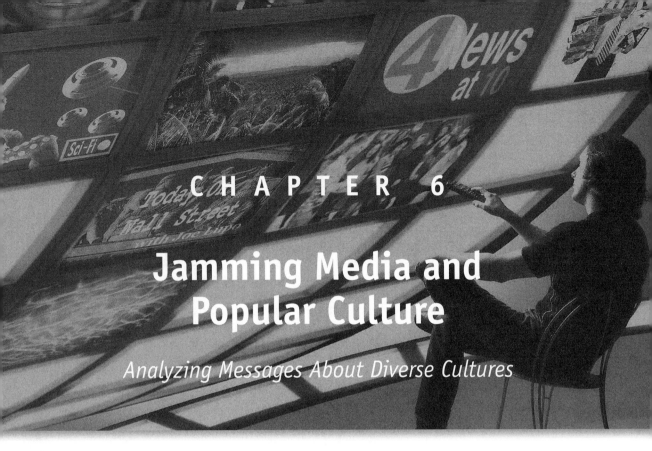

CHAPTER 6

Jamming Media and Popular Culture

Analyzing Messages About Diverse Cultures

How do you know what you know about cultures that are different from your own?

Along with the fast-paced and multidirectional movement of people in the global context discussed in the previous chapter, mediated messages and popular culture also circulate more rapidly, more widely, and with greater degrees of saturation today than ever before. The forces and factors that have given rise to globalization—advances in communication and transportation technology, the integration of global markets, as well as the privatization and deregulation of media outlets in much of the world—combine to intensify the role of media and popular culture in shaping our communication with and understanding of cultures different from our own. Media and popular culture also play pivotal roles in how we make sense of and construct our own cultures and identities.

Often the assumptions, stereotypes, and attitudes we hold about people from different cultures or distant countries come solely or primarily through media and popular culture forms such as movies, TV programs, and celebrities. Take a minute and write down everything you know about the cultures of India, Greece, Brazil, or China. Consider how you know what you do about the cultures of these countries. You may have traveled to one or more of these places

Source: Chapter-opening photo © John Elder/Stone/Getty Images.

or perhaps know someone from there, yet it's likely that much of the information you use to construct your "knowledge" about people and places different from your own comes through mediated forms of communication and popular culture sources. Now imagine people in India, Greece, Brazil, and China watching popular U.S. TV programs such as *Survivor, Friends, Modern Family,* or *American Idol.* What stereotypes and assumptions might people hold about the United States if their primary exposure to the culture is through these mediated texts?

Media and popular culture play central roles in intercultural communication. First, media and popular culture facilitate communication across cultural and national boundaries escalating the flow of information and images interculturally. Second, media frame global issues and normalize particular cultural ideologies. By 2011, five to seven major media monopolies dominated the distribution of mediated images and messages around the globe. The broad reach and global control by a small number of media giants places a few transnational corporations in a position to exert tremendous power over the perspectives, standpoints, and ideologies that are available. Third, the global spread of mass media and popular culture fragments and disrupts national and cultural identities, leading to resistance, opposition, and conflict. Finally, media and popular culture forge hybrid transnational cultural identities in the global context by re-collecting diasporic identities, constructing a global semiculture, and creating intercultural political and social alliances. These four roles of media and popular culture in intercultural communication are addressed throughout the chapter.

The title of this chapter ("Jamming Media and Popular Culture") is used to connote the improvisational and emergent nature of intercultural communication in the technologically advanced, global age—the rapid absorption, adaptation, appropriation, and fusion of verbal and nonverbal languages, and visual and musical codes—that characterizes the mediated popular culture scene as well as new social movements in the context of globalization. We begin by defining media and popular culture and discussing their impact on intercultural communication in the context of globalization. From there, processes of encoding and decoding media messages, questions of power and hegemony, and the representation of nondominant groups are explored. The chapter concludes with steps to heighten our awareness and skills for consuming media and popular culture messages, strategies to resist mainstream corporate messages, and ways to actively produce media messages such as alternative and citizen media that are emerging in the global context.

MEDIA, POPULAR CULTURE, AND GLOBALIZATION

Defining Media

In the broadest sense, the word ***media*** (note that "media" is the plural form of the singular "medium") refers to the modes, means, or channels through which messages are communicated. For example, a telephone or cell phone is a medium of interpersonal communication connecting one point to another; newspapers, magazines, TV, movies, and music recordings are types of mass media, where a source disseminates messages to large audiences. The term ***network media*** refers to media such as the World Wide Web, which connects multiple points to multiple points in addition to serving interpersonal and mass media functions. Technology is a critical feature of media, and advances in technology have dramatically magnified the impact of media on global communication today. Yet media, as channels of communication, are not only technologies. Media—TV, films, the World Wide Web, and e-mail—do not exist "independently of the concepts people have of them, the uses people make of the them, and the social relations that produce them and that are organized around them everyday" (Grossberg, Wartella, Whitney, & Wise, 2006, p. 8). The authors of *MediaMaking* (Grossberg et al., 2006) posited that the media are comprised of three elements: (1) technology; (2) social relationships or institutions such as broadcasting organizations, and music and film companies; and (3) cultural forms. **Cultural forms** refer to the products' format (newscasts, sitcoms, action dramas, or thrillers), structures, languages, and narrative styles that are produced when media technologies and institutions come together.

media= 3 elements

Media bring together technologies, institutions, and cultural forms to create and convey meaning-making products that reflect, construct, and reinforce cultural ideologies. Political scientist Lane Crothers (2007) argued that the popularity of *Titanic*, the second highest grossing film of all times, rested on its embodiment of cultural ideologies of American civil society such as the presumed irrelevance of class distinctions, a tolerance for difference, the centrality of individualism, and the attraction to and fascination with capitalism. Given this, we can see how the global sale, distribution, and consumption of media are not merely economic transactions. When one nation's cultural products—namely, the United States— dominate the world market, the appeal and fascination as well as the concern and resistance focus on the effects on national cultural values, behavior, and identities.

Defining Popular Culture

The term *media* is often confused and conflated with the term *popular culture.* While the media are the source of much of popular culture today and serve to advertise and distribute a broad range of popular cultural forms, the two are not interchangeable. Popular culture as a term has come into common usage in recent years to replace the term *low culture,* which carried a negative connotation as compared to "high culture" as discussed in Chapter 1. Scholars have argued since the 1960s that the mass production of products—TV programs, Barbie dolls, minivans, or hip hop music, for example—does not take away their meaning; rather, groups of people, cultures, and subcultures use mass produced products as a way to make meaning in their lives. People use mass produced forms of popular culture to reflect and construct identities as well as display and enact values. **Popular culture** refers to systems and artifacts that the general populous or broad masses within a society share or about which most people have some understanding (Brummett, 1994). Hamburgers and fries, baggy jeans and bling, tattoos, celebrities, music videos, sports, reality shows, Disneyland, TV evangelists, tourism, video games, and pornography are all forms of popular culture. Three characteristics help define popular culture: (1) popular culture is central and pervasive in advanced capitalist systems, (2) popular culture is produced by culture industries, and (3) popular culture serves social functions. In a world where most everything is commodified, very little is outside of popular culture. From entertainment, fashion, and health to religious rituals, the environment, social causes, and cultural identities, almost everything has been turned into commodities that are packaged, bought, and sold.

popular culture= 3 characteristic

Isolated pockets of what in the past were referred to as **folk culture**—localized cultural practices that are enacted for the sole purpose of people within a particular place—still exist. However, as these practices are sought out by tourists for their "authenticity" as folk culture, such as ritual feast days and dances at the Pueblos in New Mexico or hula dances in Hawaii, they too become commodities in the nostalgic search for the "pure," the "real," and tourist destinations of "authentic" culture (Root, 1996; Sorrells, 2002). As U.S. cultural celebrations such as Halloween, Valentine's Day, and Mother's Day, and culturally rooted coming of age rituals such as quinceañeras and bar mitzvahs, are commodified, they become part of popular culture.

The term *culture industry* refers to industries that mass produce standardized cultural goods such as the Disney Corporation, Time Warner Inc., and Viacom. It is easier to understand these megacorporations as culture industries when we consider the range of products that Disney, for example, produces—amusement parks, adventure tours, cartoons, cable networks, clubs, movies, music, games, toys, clothing, concerts, phones, product tie-ins, and virtual communities. Critical theorists Theodor Adorno and Max Horkheimer (1972), who initially coined the term in the middle of the 20th century, were concerned that culture industries could easily manipulate the masses into docile and passive consumers. Certainly, in a media-saturated culture produced by culture industries, popular culture is a central and pervasive element of advanced capitalist societies. On the streets, airports, buses, subways; in school, in the workplace, and in restaurants; on the Internet; in the dentist and doctor's waiting room; and most especially in our homes and on our bodies, popular culture permeates and penetrates every corner of our lives. The Nielsen Company reports that the average U.S. household took in 8 hours and 18 minutes of TV per day in 2008 (Nielsen Wire, 2009). In 1971, the average American was exposed to 360 advertisement messages per day, and by the late 1990s, the number had catapulted to over 3,000 per day (Shenk, 1997). By the late 2000s, the number was up to 5,000 per day (Story, 2007). Given the centrality and pervasiveness of popular culture, what functions does it serve?

Functions of popular culture

Sociologist Dustin Kidd (2007) noted that the primary function of popular culture within advanced capitalist societies is to generate profit. Yet he argued it also serves to establish social norms, constitute social identities and maintain social boundaries, and create meaning through shared rituals of consumption. Finally, popular culture functions as a site of innovation and social change. Popular culture—whether through TV dramas, radio talk shows, magazine articles and advertisements, sports events, or celebrity stories—is the most central and effective means of defining and disseminating social norms. Portrayals and enactments of interpersonal, intergenerational, gender, and intercultural relationships in popular culture normalize culturally informed ways of interacting, social practices, and hierarchies of power. U.S. dominant cultural values of consumerism, individualism, and competition as well as White American middle-class ideologies of what is proper, acceptable, and desirable are reinforced through popular culture. Note how hip hop culture or heavy metal are demonized as abhorrent and distasteful within the broader cultural discussion while other forms of popular culture are considered acceptable.

Popular culture is a key component in the production of social identities such as class, race, culture, and age where the consumption of popular culture creates and marks social boundaries of inclusion and exclusion (Hall, 1997; Kidd, 2007). Consider how the clothes you buy, the hairstyle you pay for, the music you consume, and the TV programs you enjoy constitute your identity. Additionally, when people collectively participate in the shared consumption of popular culture through rituals—by attending the Coachella Music and Arts Festival; going to watch the Atlanta Hawks, Detroit Pistons, or San Antonio Spurs; or participating in the midnight release of the latest Harry Potter book at Barnes & Noble—the shared sense of meaning of the ritual provides the basis of group solidarity and identity. In other words, in advanced capitalist cultures, the consumption of popular culture serves as shorthand for sets of values, practices, and goals; for individual and group identities; and for inclusion and exclusion in social groups.

CULTURAL IDENTITY
CULTURAL/SELF-EXPRESSION THROUGH FASHION AND POPULAR CULTURE

Rachel, a White American student from Minneapolis, Minnesota, spent a semester teaching English to Somali women who came to the United States as refugees. Minnesota has the largest Somali population in North America. Rachel discusses her observations of how Somali women use popular culture—especially fashion—to express themselves and maintain their culture:

Before I started working with Somali women, I had this stereotype that they are not very fashion-conscious. Because they have to cover their head and dress modestly for religious reasons, I thought they didn't really care about how they dressed. After getting to know some Somali women, I began to realize they actually take great pride in what they wear. They have amazing collections of skirts and dresses. The designs are more subtle than American fashion, but certainly detailed, well-made, and fun in their own way.

A young Somali woman told me that she would never leave Minnesota because the latest Somali fashions come to Minneapolis first. There are three Somali shopping centers where she buys the latest trends from Somalia. To my surprise, she has never lived in Somalia. She was born in a refugee camp in Kenya and then moved to the U.S. She is still deeply connected to her homeland, and fashion is one way for her to maintain her connection as a second generation, diasporic Somali American.

Finally, popular culture can function as a platform for discussion or as an initiating force for social change. When Ellen DeGeneres, star of the popular sitcom *Ellen*, came out as a lesbian (both as the actress and the character she played) in 1997, an international discussion of lesbians and gay men on prime-time TV and the social acceptability of lifestyles that differ from the heterosexual norm ensued. The fact that the enormously popular show—one of the highest rated TV shows ever and winner of an Emmy Award—was cancelled by ABC also generated tremendous discussion about the power of networks to control and censor popular culture. When Don Imus made his now infamous racist and sexist remarks about the Rutgers women's basketball team in 2007, a nationwide discussion and debate about race, gender, and hip hop culture in the United States followed. Additionally, popular culture celebrities have been instrumental in raising awareness and mobilizing economic and political support for natural and social crises through events such as Live Aid, a rock concert known as the "global jukebox" that provided support for famine victims in Ethiopia in 1985; the Rock the Vote campaign that began in the 1990s and has continued in the 2000s and today; and the internationally broadcast benefit concert for Hurricane Katrina victims in 2005. During this event, hip hop artist Kanye West improvised off script saying, "George Bush doesn't care about Black people," generating discussion in public and private spaces about the historically and institutionally embedded racial discrimination in the United States, which was exposed when the levies in New Orleans broke (Dyson, 2006). In 2011, Japanese popular culture celebrities and animators used their influence to gain support for earthquake and tsunami victims. These examples illustrate how popular culture, in addition to generating profit, defining social norms, and constituting social identities, provides a stage for discussion of social issues and can be instrumental in initiating social change. Given its centrality socially and economically, let's take a look at how popular culture impacts intercultural communication in the context of globalization.

POPULAR CULTURE, INTERCULTURAL COMMUNICATION, AND GLOBALIZATION

From the first pages of his book *Globalization & American Popular Culture,* political scientist Lane Crothers (2007) noted the seemingly odd juxtaposition of popular culture, which is often characterized as light, fun, and "just entertainment" with the weighty and important set of issues associated with globalization. Yet he argued that what may appear at first glance as inconsequential forms of entertainment—films, TV programs, and popular music—are, in fact, key elements in contemporary globalization that alternately promote deeply felt desires for global integration and also mobilize adamant resistance to integration.

Consider the fact that popular culture is the largest U.S. export and that more than 50% of the revenue for U.S. films is generated from international sales (Thussu, 2006). Consider also that the United States dominates the production and dissemination of popular culture globally. Given its position as a global leader in the production of popular culture, the United States has led the international battle to reduce or remove restrictions on the flow of popular culture around the world claiming popular culture is a commodity like any other. Yet popular culture forms are not simply commodities like corn, cars, or computers. Many, including representatives of nation-states as well as local culture industries, argue that popular culture products are embedded with cultural values, norms, and ideologies. What may seem like harmless and frivolous entertainment actually disseminates core U.S. cultural values such as individualism, personal freedom, and consumerism around the globe; through the distribution and consumption of U.S. popular culture globally, particular cultural views on gender norms and gender relationships, sex, sexuality, and violence, as well as racial stereotypes and intercultural relations are normalized (Dines & Humez, 2003; Durham & Kellner, 2006; Gitlin, 2002). Thus, in addition to purely economic objections to U.S. global dominance of popular culture that drives national and local producers of cultural products out of business, various countries, notably France, Canada, and Australia initially, and Italy, Spain, Malaysia, Hungary, and South Korea subsequently, have resisted the unregulated flow of cultural products arguing that popular culture can lead to cultural corruption, cultural homogenization, and cultural imperialism (Crothers, 2007).

Cultural corruption refers to the perceived and experienced alteration of a culture in negative or detrimental ways through the influence of other cultures. **Cultural homogenization** is the convergence toward common cultural values and practices as a result of global integration, and **cultural imperialism** is the domination of one culture over others through cultural forms such as popular culture, media, and cultural products. All three objections— cultural corruption, cultural homogenization, and cultural imperialism—focus on the dominance today of U.S. popular culture globally and the potentially significant ways this dominance may contribute to the loss, change, and/or undermining of national and local cultural practices, values, and identities. In 1993, French president François Mitterand captured the rising fear, stating the following:

> Creations of the spirit are not just commodities; the elements of culture are not pure business. What is at stake is the cultural identities of all of our nations—it is the freedom to create and choose our own images. A society which abandons the means of depicting itself would soon be an enslaved society. (Shapiro, 2000)

Globalization has often enabled and sometimes forced the integration of markets, politics, and cultures globally. Integration on a global scale has led to the fragmentation and disruption of economic, political, and cultural cohesiveness within nation-states and communities. Just as the massive and multidirectional migration of people around the globe discussed in the previous chapter has disrupted and fragmented economic, political, and social norms, so too the increased movement of cultural products and popular cultural forms has fragmented local and national cultural identities, values, norms, and practices. Political scientist James Rosenau (2003) has coined the word *fragmegration* to describe the dual and simultaneous dynamic of integration and fragmentation that has emerged in the context of globalization. The term *fragmegration* helps explain the dual, simultaneous, and often contradictory tensions of integration and fragmentation that accompany the spread of and resistance to U.S. popular culture in the context of globalization. Having defined basic terms and highlighted the contested intercultural issues of popular culture and globalization, we turn now to a discussion of global and regional media circuits.

COMMUNICATIVE DIMENSIONS
POPULAR CULTURE AND GLOBALIZATION

The following examples of fragmegration, the simultaneous dynamic of integration and fragmentation, illustrate how popular culture is experienced in the context of globalization. Many in France are outraged by what they experience as the corrosive influence of U.S. popular culture. English is increasingly part of casual conversations and daily business practices in France as evidenced by terms such as *le deal* and *le cash flow*. Outcries that U.S. popular culture is an assault on French language and national identity exemplify the concern about *cultural corruption*.

In Iran today, where more than two thirds of the population is under the age of 30, U.S. popular culture and messages are very alluring. Adaption by youth of cultural practices and values expressed through music, movies, and fashion from the United States and the West illustrates the tendency toward *cultural homogenization* as a result of global integration.

In a move to resist what was seen as *cultural imperialism*, the Venezuelan government passed a law in 2005 requiring 50% of all music played on the radio to be Venezuelan. Sales of Venezuelan music soared while previously popular stars like Britney Spears and the Backstreet Boys plummeted. Some see this move as narrowing choices for Venezuelans; others argue that it increases their choices by drawing attention to Venezuelan products that were previously overshadowed by the immense marketing power of the U.S. culture industries.

GLOBAL AND REGIONAL MEDIA CIRCUITS

Jeremy Tunstall (2008), author of *The Media Were American,* argued that we need to understand global flows of media today in terms of Euro-American dominance rather than focusing solely on the United States as the primary force. He used the term *Euro-American* to refer to the continents of Europe and South and North America, which are the main importers and exporters of media around the globe. While the United States remains central to the production of media and popular culture, many of the films made in Hollywood are collaborations with British and Canadian partners. In the past decade, a number of TV programs immensely popular with U.S. audiences did not originate in the United States. Programs such as *Who Wants to Be a Millionaire?* and *The Weakest Link* were British, and the reality show *Big Brother* was created in the Netherlands. Additionally, over the past decades, South American **telenovelas** produced in countries with large viewing audiences such as Brazil, Mexico, Venezuela, and Chile are now imported to over 130 countries around the world; they are especially popular in Russia, Romania, and Bosnia. Martinez (2005) stated, "In all, about two billion people around the world watch *telenovelas*. For better or for worse, these programmes have attained a place in the global marketplace of culture, and their success illuminates one of the back channels of globalization." While U.S. soaps are still shown regularly around the world, Tunstall (2008) noted that Latin American telenovelas, despite or perhaps because of their rags-to-riches plots, are finding greater appeal than depictions of glitzy affluence in U.S. soap operas.

As telenovelas are exported around the globe, they not only expose people in distant places and different cultures to the narratives, social realities, and cultural practices of Latin America but they also serve a central function for diasporic Latin American communities. Forms of popular culture such as TV programs and movies from migrants' countries of origin allow migrant communities to stay in touch with, remember, and re-create their cultural identities. While telenovelas produced in Latin America have long been popular among U.S. Latinos/Latinas, in 2006, TV executives from the top two Spanish-language networks—Univision and Telemundo—began writing and producing shows in Miami. *Washington Post* writer Peter Whoriskey (2006) reported that executives hope to hook more Hispanics " by depicting the realities of U.S. life, where dating and class distinctions—the staples of many a melodrama—adhere to different rules than in other countries." Whoriskey quoted Telemundo President Don Browne:

> A lot of our audience came from Mexico, they're Mexican, but their life experiences are much different than people who haven't emigrated. The humor is different. The pacing is different. It was critical for us to be more relevant. Everyone reduces their appeal down to language—and it's not just language. It's cultural relevance.

Increasingly, the 41 million Latinos/Latinas in the United States, including bilingual viewers who could be watching the major U.S. networks, are drawn to telenovelas such as Univision's blockbuster *Amor Real*.

While Euro-American media and popular culture remain dominant in the global flow of media today, the world's most densely populated countries—India and China—represent significant audiences of regional importance, especially when combined with the large diasporic communities from each country living around the world. Tunstall (2008) noted that large population countries like India and China as well as the United States, Mexico, and Brazil are much less likely to import media because they have the capacity to produce media for their internal audiences. Large population countries, however, do generally export their media regionally and increasingly, in the current context, globally. International communication scholar Daya Kishan Thussu (2006) noted that India is one of the only non-Western countries that has impacted the global cultural market. In terms of production and viewership, India's film industry, based in Mumbai (formerly Bombay giving rise to the name "Bollywood"), is the largest in the world. Annually, 1 billion more tickets are sold to Indian films than Hollywood films (Thussu, 2006). In 2007, the United States produced about 435 feature films while India produced roughly 1,160 films, yet Indian "Superstar of the Millennium" Amitabh Bachchan remains relatively unknown outside India and the diasporic Indian communities around the world. Nevertheless, the popularity of films like *Monsoon Wedding*, *Bend It Like Beckham*, and *The Namesake* suggests that as Indian films address the challenges of diasporic communities in England, Canada, and the United States, they increasingly appeal to a broader crossover audience.

Like telenovelas for the Latino/Latina audiences living outside Latin America, Indian films play a critical role in the lives of many diasporic Indians. A participant in communication scholar Anjali Ram's (2004) research commented that Hindi films allow "our children to be educated in their own culture, to know about our own childhood, how we grew up—children get to understand about our culture and that in reality, we are foreigners here" (p. 128). Ram noted the following:

> It is clear that Hindi cinema functions as much more than entertainment. Rather, it facilitates and shapes recollections, it allows the past to be reconstructed within the present context, and it provides an emotionally charged technocolor medium through which the past can be shared and communicated with others, both in everyday contexts and shared commemorative events. (p. 129)

China, like India, represents a large viewer and consumer audience for media and popular culture, with much of its media produced either within China for national and regional consumption or imported from geographically and culturally close countries such as Taiwan and Hong Kong in the 1990s and increasingly from Singapore, Japan, and South Korea. With a population of over 1 billion—600,000 of whom speak one language, Mandarin—China remains self-sufficient as a media producer and relatively impenetrable to Western imports (Tunstall, 2008). In contrast, small population countries in Central America, the Caribbean, Africa, and Asia are solely dependent upon media imports. More than one third of the countries of the world produce no films at all and are dependent upon regional and global sources for much of their TV programming. Interestingly, in both small and large population countries, people around the world prefer to watch the news, soap operas, and dramas in their own languages, with culturally relevant content and culturally familiar formats when possible.

The predominance of the Euro-American media circuit combines with regional and diasporic media circuits to create dynamic and contradictory challenges for intercultural communication in the global context. Tunstall (2008) stated the following:

> Most people in almost all other countries spend a tenth or more of their media time with media imported, typically, from the United States and/or from one or two other countries. Consequently, most of the world's people have some sustained exposure to the history, culture, and mythology of one or two other countries. (p. xiv)

Clearly, the circulation of media regionally and globally escalates the flow of information and images interculturally, which exposes people to different cultures, yet this exposure can fragment and disrupt local and national cultural identities. Also, as noted in the examples of Latinos/Latinas in the United States and the diasporic Indian communities, the circulation of media and popular culture creates hybrid transnational cultural identities in the global context by re-collecting and reconstituting diasporic identities. Additionally, the predominance of U.S. media and popular culture internationally has been instrumental in constructing a global semiculture where people from far-reaching countries and cultures—in France, India, Guatemala, Thailand, Korea, and the United States, for example—share some aspects of U.S. popular culture, yet the pervasiveness of U.S. popular culture and

English (more particularly American English) has led to the decline and hybridization of local cultures and languages, threatening cultural and linguistic diversity around the world. Tunstall (2008) succinctly articulated another concern:

> The United States remains unique in that most Americans are exposed almost entirely to their own nation's history, culture, and mythology. What do they know (of a supposedly global reality) who only American media know? (p. xiv)

While the dominance of the United States in terms of media and popular culture may appear beneficial to the United States and to Americans, a lack of understanding of other cultures' perspectives, histories, lifestyles, values, and ideologies is a distinct disadvantage and disturbing danger of this asymmetrical flow. The one-sided view that many people in the United States have as a result of consuming only or primarily U.S. media and popular culture can and often does lead to misperceptions, misunderstanding, ignorance, stereotypes, and prejudice about other ethnicities/races as well as national cultural groups. One of the contradictions of globalization for people living in the United States is that while the world is increasingly interconnected and integrated, Americans can and do live relatively uninformed about the perspectives, and insulated from the conditions, of others around the world due to the inequitable and uneven flows of media and popular culture. Now that we have a broad picture of how media and popular culture circulate globally and regionally, we examine in greater depth the processes of meaning-making involved in the production and consumption of popular culture.

PRODUCING AND CONSUMING POPULAR CULTURE

When studying popular culture, media, and communication, scholars often look at three areas: (1) the production or encoding of popular culture, where the institutions, the people, and the relationships of power involved in making popular culture products or texts are studied; (2) textual analysis, where the actual product or text—the TV program or film such as *Desperate Housewives* or *Avatar,* for example—is analyzed for symbolic meaning and narrative content; and (3) audience analysis, where the meanings and interpretations that viewers/readers/listeners decode from popular culture text are investigated. It may seem a bit odd to ask what meanings are constructed by particular forms of popular culture, yet the production and consumption of popular culture involves ongoing meaning-making processes that establish social norms, constitute identities, disseminate dominant ideologies, and allow for oppositional meanings to emerge. Given the asymmetrical distribution of popular culture around the globe that has led to claims of cultural corruption, cultural homogenization, and cultural imperialism, it is important to understand the meaning-making processes and their consequences in the production and consumption of popular culture.

Cultural studies scholar Stuart Hall (1980), in his article titled "Encoding/Decoding," offered a model that helps us understand the processes of meaning-making that occur as popular culture is produced and consumed. His original research in the 1970s focused on understanding the meanings people made of TV programs in Britain. He examined the ways in which people in England decoded mass mediated messages that were encoded by program producers. Hall noted that **decoding,** or the active interpretative and sense-making processes of audiences, is as important as **encoding,** or the construction of mass mediated meaning by culture industries. Further, Hall (1980) argued that "decoding does not necessarily follow from encoding" (p. 136), emphasizing the interpretative agency audiences have in producing meaning. Let's take a look at his model (see Figure 6.1).

Figure 6.1   Are Encoded and Decoded Meanings the Same? Are Meanings Negotiated?

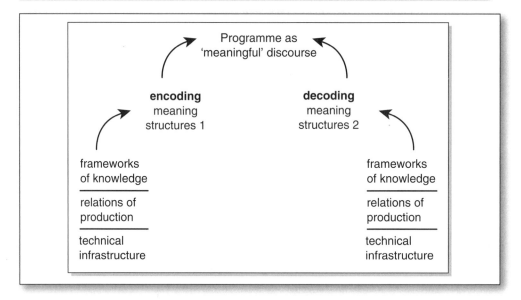

Source: Hall (1980), p. 120.

According to Hall, "meaning structures 1" and "meaning structures 2" may not be the same. Agreement between the meanings that are encoded and those that are decoded depends upon the degree of symmetry between the social and institutional positions of the encoder–producer and the decoder–receiver. The structural differences of relation and position between the media/popular culture producer (meaning structures 1) and the audience (meaning structures 2) may lead to the creation of different meanings. While Hall argued that all stages of the meaning-making are imprinted within complex structures of dominance, he stressed the important role that social, economic, cultural, and political positionality plays in both the encoding and decoding of popular culture texts. Hall outlined three broad ways of "reading" popular culture texts: (1) a dominant or hegemonic reading, (2) a negotiated reading, and (3) an oppositional reading. A **dominant reading** is one where the viewer or reader shares the meanings that are encoded in the text and accepts the preferred reading, which generally naturalizes and reinforces dominant ideologies. A **negotiated reading** is one where the reader or viewer generally shares the codes and preferred meanings of the texts but may also resist and modify the encoded meaning based on her or his positionality, interests, and experiences resulting in a contradictory reading of the text. An **oppositional reading** is one where the social position (in terms of class, race, gender, religion, nationality, ideology, etc.) of the viewer or reader of the text places them in opposition to the dominant code and preferred reading of the popular culture text. The reader understands the dominant code yet brings an alternative frame of reference, which leads him or her to resist the encoded meaning.

Let's take the Spider-Man film series (*Spider-Man* was released in 2002, *Spider-Man 2* in 2004, and *Spider-Man 3* in 2007) to illustrate the concept of dominant, negotiated, and oppositional readings of popular culture texts. The Spider-Man film series is based on the Marvel Comics character created in the 1960s—a groundbreaking comic in that the main character was a teenage superhero with all the insecurities of rejection and loneliness to which a growing adolescent comic book market could relate (Wright, 2001). In the three films to date, the "geeky" Peter Parker from Queens struggles to balance choices and responsibilities presented by his human desires and his superhuman abilities. As he transforms into Spider-Man to fight an array of evil villains that threaten New York City including Green Goblin, Dr. Octopus, Sandman, New Goblin, and Venom, he also negotiates a romantic relationship with his childhood crush, Mary Jane Watson. The monstrous villains are human-made mistakes. They are accidents produced when exaggerated ambitions and inflated egos of men combine with futuristic science and technology. Parker's best friend, Harry Osborn, is torn between friendship and avenging the death of his father, a scientist and CEO of Oscorp who morphed into the Green Goblin and died in a duel with Spider-Man. Mary Jane is "the girl next door," a victim of domestic abuse and an aspiring actress who plays the role of girlfriend to four different men in the three films as her love for Peter Parker waxes and wanes. As the true love of Spider-Man, she is the target of numerous captures by various villains and heroic rescues by Spider-Man and Harry (who has become the New Goblin).

A dominant reading of the Spider-Man film series is as follows: The world we live in is a dangerous and treacherous place divided between forces of good and evil. People need protection from evil or villainous forces, which can take many different forms—even science, which is usually considered a force of progress and good, can be turned to disastrous ends. Fortunately, however, average or even nerdy, working-class boys can grow up to be superheros and can serve as role models if they believe in themselves and take responsibility for the power they have. Making the right choices is difficult in the complex, competitive, capitalist-driven world, but individuals, by making the right decisions, can succeed, saving and protecting others less capable or fortunate.

A negotiated reading of the Spider-Man film series is as follows: Yes, the world is a dangerous place divided between good and evil, but why is the superhero always a boy/man, and why are all the main characters in the film White? Are the only people who can save or destroy the world White men? The female characters in the film—from Mary Jane to the secretaries in the newspaper office—are presented as passive "damsels-in-distress" in stereotypically domestic roles or revered and prized for their beauty and bodies. Fortunately, Mary Jane *is* represented as making some choices in her dedication to her career, as well as which boyfriend she wants. Women, apparently, do have choices—just more limited ones than men.

An oppositional reading of the Spider-Man film series is as follows: All the evil or "bad" things that are presented in the films—from the demonic villains, to the misrepresentation of Spider-Man in the media, to the foreclosure of Aunt May's house—were caused by the greed for money, power, and fame in a capitalist, corporatized, militarized society. The situations people were in had less to do with their individual decisions and more to do with the oppressive and exploitative corporate, media, criminal, and military systems that are depicted as "normal" in the films. The emphasis on individual choice masks the systemic oppression that creates the "evil" from which Spider-Man—the young, White, superhero male—must rescue and protect the vulnerable masses.

The example illustrates how dominant, negotiated, and oppositional readings of the text differ. The varied readings of the Spider-Man film series also demonstrate how ideologies central to U.S. culture—such as individualism; freedom of choice; equality; the irrelevance of class, gender, and race; and the valorization of capitalism—are encoded and normalized in the text. Consumers of media and popular culture texts can make decisions to resist or challenge dominant readings; however, the ability to develop a negotiated or oppositional reading depends upon being conscious of how one's individual or group-based interests are undermined by the passive acceptance of dominant ideologies. People or groups for whom the dominant reading is less than beneficial—people who are disadvantaged or oppressed in the capitalist system, non-White people and women, for example—may be more likely to negotiate and oppose the dominant reading. Now that we have a general overview of the process of producing and consuming popular culture, let's look more closely at how cultural and racial groups are represented in popular culture and the ways individuals and groups negotiate these representations.

POPULAR CULTURE, REPRESENTATION, AND RESISTANCE

Media and popular culture serve as primary channels through which we learn about groups who are different from ourselves as well as make sense of who we are. Through the consumption of media and popular culture, children, teenagers, and adults are fed a steady diet of images that often promote and reinforce stereotypes and misinformation about cultural groups. A study of the 2001 to 2002 TV season by Children Now showed that while programming in the United States had become more diverse, casting was still 90% White and Black with only 5% of lead roles played by other diverse groups. Interestingly, the 8:00 p.m. prime-time viewing hour in the United States, when children are most likely to watch, was the least racially diverse. Additionally, programs with all-Black casts were all situational comedies whereas those with White casts dominated other genres such as dramas, real-life, and comedic dramas (Wilson, Gutiérrez, & Chao, 2003). Psychologist Sherryl Browne Graves (1999) noted that "the limited inclusion of visible racial/ethnic groups in TV programming and advertising conveys to children and youth the relative lack of power and importance of these groups in the larger society" (p. 709).

Limited representations of non-White groups in U.S. media have damaging effects as nondominant groups are more frequently represented as criminals, crime victims, and in limited roles in terms of work (Browne Graves, 1999). Therefore, while the number of representations of Blacks has increased on TV and in films over the past 30 years, the preponderance of images of African American males in stereotypically negatives roles such as criminals, pimps, drug dealers, and gang members continues a 200-year tradition of denigrating, dehumanizing, and devaluing Blacks in the U.S. media. A panel of experts at a forum on Black women in the media at Harvard University in 2002 reported that African American women are more visible in the media today than in the past, yet the images are still very narrow, frequently depicting Black women as overly protective mammies, excessively sexualized Jezebels, and as "naturally" dependent welfare queens.

Latinos/Latinas, Asian Americans, Native Americans, Arab Americans, and other non-dominant groups have been relatively invisible in U.S.-produced TV programs and films. According to communication researcher Martha Lauzen (1999), "Viewers are more likely to see a female alien (from outer space) or angel in prime-time TV than they were a female Asian or Latina character." When appearing, non-White groups are frequently cast as socially deviant elements; as less moral, less intelligent, or "primitive"; as comic figures; or as threats to dominant U.S. or White cultural norms, values, and superiority. Latinos appeared early on in TV history in programs such as *I Love Lucy* and *Cisco Kid*, in a few situational comedies appearing in the 1970s (*Chico and the Man* and *Viva Valdez*), in star roles in the 1980s and 1990s (notably Edward James Olmos in *Miami Vice* and Jimmy Smits in *L.A. Law*); however, the first network series featuring an all-Latino/Latina cast, *Kingpin*, appearing in 2002, depicted "a Mexican drug lord and his family of stereotypical characters" (Wilson et al., 2003, p. 104). Representations in popular culture depict Asians and Asian Americans alternately as dangerous, crafty, devious, and sadistically violent (especially in the use of martial arts), as the "yellow peril"—serving political ends during WWII, the Korean War, the Cold War, and the Vietnam War—and as subservient and comic or as model minorities. Interestingly, while Asian men are depicted as feminized with their sexuality all but erased, images of Asian women as exotic, sexual, and submissive continue to serve the erotic fantasies of White men.

In 2002, a series of six T-shirts were sold at Abercrombie & Fitch, featuring caricatures of Asian men with slanted eyes wearing rice paddy straw hats and Asian women in stereotypically subservient postures that shocked and offended Asian Americans and Buddhists across the country. One, depicting two Asian males, read, Wong Brothers Laundry Service—Two Wongs Can Make It White. Another read, Abercrombie & Fitch Buddha Bash—Get Your Buddha on the Floor. After citizen protests, e-mail petitions, and calls for boycotts, the line was pulled off the shelves of all Abercrombie & Fitch stores, despite the fact that representatives of the company said they were attempting to interject humor and levity assuming Asian American customers would like the line. University of California, Santa Barbara, reporter Christine Bai (2002) noted the following:

> A & F spokesperson Hampton Carney claims that they make fun of everyone, but I'm sure Abercrombie would never even dare to put out an image of blacks picking cotton or Hispanics selling oranges on the street. This only shows how Asian-Americans are viewed to be apathetic and passive about such racial issues. It upsets me that they think they can get away with making a public mockery of Asians when in fact they know very little about the negative effects it can have on them. . . . They're bashing on a religious icon strongly valued throughout many Asian families. If A & F were to make a joke out of an image of Jesus Christ on the cross, I bet many people would be incredibly offended by it. I think religion is a touchy subject that they shouldn't even mess around with in the first place.

The nondominant group with the longest history of being targeted for stereotypical and dehumanizing treatment in the media in the United States is American Indians. Centuries ago, images appeared in print media, paintings, and literature that vilified Native Americans; then, films and TV programs depicted American Indians as brute and primitive savages who were barely considered human (epitomized by films such as *The Searchers*, released in 1956, featuring protagonist John Wayne). More sympathetic depictions of Native Americans have appeared in the past 20 years. Yet such portrayals as those found in Disney's animated film *Pocahontas,* which claimed to challenge racism and intolerance and promote respect for other cultures, were criticized for masking the brutal realities of the intercultural encounter between Europeans and Native Americans and for reinforcing racial and gender stereotypes (Buescher & Ono, 1996). To evaluate Disney's claim of positive representations of Native Americans and women and to explore possible readings of the movie from the standpoint of different cultural groups, communication scholar Amy Aidman (1999) compared the responses to the movie of Native American girls ages 9 to 13 from both urban and rural settings and European American girls from an urban setting. She concluded the following:

> While the Euro-American girls produced a reading that could be labeled as "negotiated" in some respects, they appeared to accept the colonist lesson about U.S. history and to view the movie as somewhat comical. For the urban Native American girls, "Pocahontas" was an important movie to which they related strongly. The Native American girls from the reservation were not as enthusiastic about the movie, perhaps because the culture of their everyday lives strengthened their personal and cultural identities in such a way as to make media representations of Native Americans less significant to them. (pp. 154–155)

Aidman's research highlights the ways our positionality in terms of culture, race, class, and geographic location impact our reading of a movie text. It also demonstrates the significant role media representations play in making sense not only of groups that are different from our own but also in how we make sense of our own identities. The Native American girls who had few real-life role models that reflected and embodied their cultural identities in their urban setting showed a high level of identification with *Pocahontas*. With limited, stereotypical, and often negative representations of nondominant groups in the media, communication scholar Robin R. Means Coleman (2003) noted that "the positive, at times, must be carved out of imagery of exaggeration and ridicule" (p. 88).

In the wake of U.S. military invasions in the Middle East in the 1990s and 2000s and the catastrophe of 9/11, a series of films featuring Arabs, Arab Americans, and Muslims have reflected and fueled negative racial, cultural, and religious stereotypes against these groups. Tremendous controversy, protest, and debate accompanied the debut of *The Siege* in 1998 as the Arab Americans Anti-Discrimination League argued that the film was "insidious, incendiary and dangerous," and proponents of the film claimed it provided a platform for discussing stereotyping, terrorism, and the balance between personal freedoms and collective security (as quoted in Hasian, 2002, p. 227). Communication scholar Marouf Hasian (2002) noted that by the 1980s depictions of Islamic fundamentalists and Muslim fanatics had become stock characters in media and popular culture. By the mid-1990s,

Arabs, Islamic fundamentalists, and Muslims had replaced communism as the perceived threat to Western democracy to the extent that Arabs were immediately assumed to be responsible for the bombing of the Federal Building in Oklahoma City in 1995. The bombings were, in fact, perpetrated by two European American members of an antigovernment militia movement, yet White Americans have not been represented collectively as "terrorists," subjected to racial profiling, and been targets of hate crimes for their racial or national identities.

Anthropologist Suad Joseph's (2006) study of the *New York Times* and the *Wall Street Journal* from 2001 to 2003 points to the critical role media outlets play in racializing and essentializing Arabs and Muslims in general and Arab and Muslim Americans by association. Joseph's research found that media representations of Arab and Muslim Americans in the two most prominent, agenda-setting print media sources in the United States erase the diversity and humanity within Arab and Muslim groups while emphasizing their distinctiveness and "otherness" from Americans. For example, Arab Americans are depicted in the U.S. media as Muslims. Yet the majority of Arab Americans are Christian. Muslims are represented in the U.S. media as Arabs. Yet only about 12% of Muslims worldwide are Arabs. There are more Muslims in Indonesia than in all the Arab countries combined (DiscoverTheNetworks.org, 2005). Further, Muslim Americans are depicted as Arabs when in fact the largest group of Muslims in the United States is African American Muslims. Additionally, Joseph's (2006) research reveals that Arab Americans and Muslims are portrayed in the media as having greater ties to their countries of origin than other immigrants and having greater ties to their countries of origin than to the United States. Muslim Americans and Arab Americans are also represented as devoutly religious as compared to other Americans and as likely to be associated with international Muslim movements. Continuous and repeated misrepresentation and misinformation in the media fuels ignorance and stereotypes about vastly diverse populations of Muslims and Arab Americans, resulting in discrimination, violation of civil rights, and hate crimes.

As previously illustrated, media and popular culture representations of nondominant groups are often negative and stereotypical. While negative representations of dominant group members also exist, these representations appear as attributes of the individual within the group among a broad range of other options. For example, White men are, in some instances, represented as criminals, yet they are also represented as doctors, lawyers, political leaders, teachers, and in other positive roles. Therefore, the element of criminality is attributed to the individual character of the person rather than to the racial or ethnic group as a whole. The final section offers examples and concrete strategies for analyzing, challenging, and re-creating media and popular culture.

RESISTING AND RE-CREATING MEDIA AND POPULAR CULTURE

Given the issues presented in this chapter, concern that culture industries can manipulate the masses into docile and passive consumers is understandable. What are the consequences of the consolidated control of the media by a few powerful multinational corporations and the asymmetrical distribution of popular culture around the globe? To what extent are you an active interpreter of popular culture and media texts as Hall (1980) suggested? What actions can individuals and organized groups take to make a difference? The following three-step process is designed to develop our competence as "readers" or decoders and as "producers" or encoders of media and popular culture texts.

Step One: Increased Awareness

An initial and significant step in improving our competence is to become conscious of the role of the media and popular culture in shaping our views of the world, in normalizing dominant ideologies, and in perpetuating denigrating stereotypes and misrepresentations. Lessons from media literacy offer a framework that can help us navigate and make sense of the media-saturated culture in which we live in the context of globalization. Figure 6.2, modified from the Center for Media Literacy (n.d.), identifies five keywords and core concepts with corresponding key questions that assist us in critically analyzing the production and consumption of media and popular culture messages or texts.

Figure 6.2 Core Concepts and Key Questions for Media Literacy

	Key Words	Core Concepts	Key Questions
1	Authorship	Media/popular culture messages or texts are constructed.	Who created the message?
2	Format	The form or format of media/popular culture messages/texts is cultural.	What cultural messages are conveyed by the media/popular culture format?
3	Audience	People read the same media/popular culture text differently.	What is a dominant, negotiated, and oppositional reading of this text?
4	Content	Media/popular culture are embedded with values, points of view, and ideologies.	What values, points of view, and beliefs are represented or omitted from this text?
5	Function/ Purpose	Media/popular culture messages are created for profit and establish social norms, constitute identities, and create shared meanings and sites of innovation.	What purpose does the media/popular culture text serve?

Source: Adapted from Center for Media Literacy (n.d.).

Step Two: Informed Action

As we develop a critical process of analysis, we have choices about how we consume and act in relation to media and popular culture. Engaging in intercultural praxis, we may continue to consume the same media and popular culture texts that we have before, yet, with our increased awareness, we bring a critical reading of these texts to our consciousness. When we share our critical analysis with others and present our alternative readings to friends, family, coworkers, and others, we take informed action. We may also choose to seek out alternative points of view or media and popular culture texts that offer perspectives that differ from the dominant view. **Alternative media or independent media** refers to media practices that fall outside of or are independent from the mainstream corporate-owned and controlled mass media (Waltz, 2005). In recent years, due to the consolidation of media ownership and the publishing industry and the alignment of mass produced forms of media with multinational corporate interests in the global context, obtaining perspectives independent from corporate interests is increasingly difficult. Accessing news from radio and Internet sources that are independent from corporate interests, searching for news stories and commentary from countries outside the United States, and seeking information from nondominant groups can provide insight into negotiated and oppositional readings that question and challenge dominant perspectives on current and historical events and issues.

Making a decision *not* to consume media or popular culture that reinforces stereotypical and dehumanizing portrayals or that presents racist, sexist, classist, and ethnocentric messages is another type of informed action. It may not seem like individual acts such as refusing to consume media and popular culture can make a difference. However, when organized collectively—such as the boycott campaign launched by Asian Americans who opposed Abercrombie & Fitch—the act of not consuming products, brands, or popular culture forms can and does make a difference in a capitalist-driven world. Historic examples such as the boycott of British goods by Philadelphia merchants in 1769 who opposed "taxation without representation"; the bus boycott in Montgomery, Alabama, in 1955 that initiated the civil rights movement; and the boycott of grapes and lettuce organized by the United Farm Workers Union to protest inhumane working conditions for Mexican migrants in the 1970s attest to the power of collective action to promote change. More recent illustrations of collective consumer resistance include the Just Do It! Boycott Nike Now campaign to bring attention to and change Nike's sweatshop working conditions in Vietnam and other Asian countries, campaigns at universities across the United States to investigate the working conditions for laborers within and outside the United States who make campus and athletic apparel, and the No Sweat campaign in Canadian public institutions. Educating yourself and others, organizing with people who agree that opposition is necessary, and implementing a plan to challenge media and popular culture can lead to social change. By writing letters; signing online petitions; addressing local, state, national, and international officials; and targeting corporate/multinational interests, people's actions—particularly by organized groups of people—can result in movement toward social justice.

Step Three: Creative Production

The first two steps outline our progress from passive consumers to informed actors as we develop increased awareness and skills to critically analyze and consume media and popular culture. A third step in the process of developing strategies for intercultural praxis in relation to media and popular culture is to redefine ourselves as creators who can and do produce texts. With advanced technologies in the global context, average citizens in many parts of the world increasingly have access to producing media and popular culture texts. **Citizen media or participatory media** are media texts created by average citizens who are not affiliated with mainstream, corporate media outlets (Rodríguez, 2001), including videos that appear on YouTube, zines (web-based and print fan magazines), and blogs (weblogs).

Citizen or participatory media texts document and provide commentary on current events and issues that produce alternative viewpoints to mainstream media (Atton, 2002). Blogs from Iraqi citizens to U.S. military personnel, video footage from antiwar activists to pro-war supporters around the world, and zines like *Bust* that produce and publish feminist messages and *GR2* that creates and disseminates popular culture images from Asians and Asian Americans represent perspectives and experiences of issues, events, and groups that are often distorted, filtered out, and excluded from mainstream corporate media.

Culture jamming, or the act of altering or transforming mass media and popular culture forms into messages or commentary about itself, is another way to resist dominant mainstream media and produce alternative popular culture texts. Publisher of *Adbusters,* a magazine aimed at challenging and disrupting the "media trance" of our consumer addicted world and author of *Culture Jam,* Kalle Lasn (2000) argued that culture jamming is a form of public activism that challenges, subverts, and redefines dominant, hegemonic meanings produced by multinational culture industries. Consider the examples of culture jamming in Figure 6.3.

The transgressive practices of "culture jamming" are creative efforts to block or jam and subvert mainstream messages. Culture jamming challenges dominant readings or interpretations of mainstream popular culture and media texts by producing and negotiating oppositional readings that "talk back to" centers of economic, political, and symbolic power such as multinational corporations. Through increased awareness, informed action, and creative production, we transform ourselves into active interpreters and producers of media and popular culture texts as opposed to passive consumers.

Figure 6.3   Culture Jamming Spoof Ads

Source: Adbusters (2011).

SUMMARY

This chapter title ("Jamming Media and Popular Culture") suggests the spontaneous, creative, and evolving nature of intercultural communication in the technologically advanced global age. In the context of globalization, media and popular culture are venues for entertainment, information, and social change that are characterized by rapid adaptation, appropriation, and fusion of verbal and nonverbal languages, as well as visual and musical codes. Amidst this vibrant, constantly changing context, the chapter highlighted the central role of media and popular culture in intercultural communication. Undoubtedly, media and popular culture *facilitate* communication across cultural and national boundaries escalating the flow of information and images interculturally. Media also *frame* global issues and normalize particular cultural ideologies. Popular culture forms such as *Spider-Man* may seem like innocent entertainment, yet they are encoded with dominant ideologies that normalize and naturalize particular ways of being, thinking, and understanding the world. The global distribution of Euro-American and particularly U.S. media and popular culture—embedded with cultural values, beliefs, and norms—has disrupted and *fragmented* national and cultural identities, leading to resistance, opposition, and conflict. Yet the global distribution of media and popular culture has also *forged* hybrid transnational cultural identities in the global context.

The process of encoding and decoding media messages was outlined to assist us in understanding how media and popular culture messages are produced and consumed. Dominant, negotiated, and oppositional readings were illustrated to reveal the ways prevailing ideologies are represented and reinforced through popular culture and to bring to awareness the possibility of alternative interpretations based on the positionality of readers of media and popular culture texts. The links between power and hegemony in mediated intercultural communication and the representation of nondominant groups were explored. Stereotypical and negative representations of nondominant groups serve to maintain the supremacy of dominant groups in terms of race, culture, class, gender, sexuality, and other forms of socially constructed difference. Borrowing from media literacy, the chapter concluded with steps to heighten our awareness and skills for consuming media and popular culture messages, strategies to resist and redefine mainstream corporate messages and ways to become active producers of media in the global context.

KEY TERMS

media
network media
cultural forms
popular culture
folk culture
culture industry
cultural corruption

cultural homogenization
cultural imperialism
fragmegration
telenovelas
decoding
encoding
dominant reading

negotiated reading
oppositional reading
alternative media or independent media

citizen media or participatory media
culture jamming

DISCUSSION QUESTIONS AND ACTIVITIES

Discussion Questions

1. Why is popular culture an important aspect of intercultural communication in the context of globalization?

2. American people are exposed to the media images produced almost entirely by the U.S. media industry. How does this asymmetrical flow of popular culture forms influence the processes of intercultural communication?

3. In the previous chapter, we addressed issues of migration and border crossing. How do you think globalization of popular culture and cultural imperialism shape migrants' cultural adaptation in the "host" culture?

4. Adorno and Horkheimer (1972) argued that culture industries can manipulate the masses into docile and passive consumers. Do you agree with this? Why, or why not?

5. How is popular culture a site of resistance and power negotiation? How can the definition of culture as resource (Chapter 1) be applied to the process of culture jamming?

Activities

1. Critical Analysis of Media Representation
   a. Choose a movie, and analyze it for its authorship, format, audience, and content using the table of media literacy in the chapter.
   b. Address the following questions:
      i. Who created the message?
      ii. What cultural messages are conveyed by the media/popular culture format?
      iii. What is a dominant, negotiated, and oppositional reading of this text?
      iv. What values, points of view, and beliefs are represented or omitted from this text?
      v. What purpose does the media/popular culture text serve?

2. Producing Alternative Media—Group Activity
   a. Create a list of specific problems you see in how different groups are represented in media and popular culture today.
   b. Assuming a position as a producer and writer, create a proposal for a new TV program, movie, song, novel, magazine, website, and so forth, that provides alternative views and representations.

c. Propose the plan to your class, and vote on the best proposal that challenges, resists, and transforms existing views, stereotypes, and misrepresentations.

REFERENCES

Adbusters. (2011). *Adbusters spoof ads*. Retrieved from www.adbusters.org

Adorno, T. W., & Horkheimer, M. (1972). *Dialectic of enlightenment*. New York: Herder and Herder.

Aidman, A. (1999). Disney's Pocahontas: Conversations with Native American and Euro-American girls. In S. R. Mazzareall & N. O. Pecora (Eds.), *Growing up girls: Popular culture and the construction of identity* (pp. 132–158). New York: Peter Lang.

Atton, C. (2002). *Alternative media*. Thousand Oaks, CA: Sage.

Bai, C. (2002). No one is laughing at racist Abercrombie & Fitch shirts. *University of California Santa Barbara Daily Nexus, 117,* 82. Retrieved from http://www.dailynexus.com/article.php?a=2994

Browne Graves, S. (1999). Television and prejudice reduction: When does television as a vicarious experience make a difference? *Journal of Social Issues, 55*(4), 707–727.

Brummett, B. (1994). *Rhetoric in popular culture*. New York: St. Martin's.

Buescher, D. T., & Ono, K. (1996). Civilized colonialism: Pocahontas as neocolonial rhetoric. *Women's Studies in Communication, 19,* 127–153.

Center for Media Literacy. (n.d.). *CML MediaLit Kit*. Retrieved from http://www.medialit.org/bp_mlk.html

Coleman, R. R. M. (2003). Black sitcom portrayals. In G. Dines & J. M. Humez (Eds.), *Gender, race and class in media* (pp. 79–88). Thousand Oaks, CA: Sage.

Crothers, L. (2007). *Globalization & American popular culture*. Lanham, MD: Rowman & Littlefield.

Dines, G., & Humez, J. M. (Eds.). (2003). *Gender, race, and class in media: A text-reader*. Thousand Oaks, CA: Sage.

DiscoverTheNetworks.org. (2005, February 14). *American-Arab Anti-Discrimination Committee*. Retrieved from http://www.discoverthenetworks.org/groupProfile.asp?grpid=6173

Durham, M. G. & Kellner, D. (2006). *Media and cultural studies*. Malden, MA: Blackwell.

Dyson, M. E. (2006). *Come hell or high water: Hurricane Katrina and the color of disaster*. New York: Basic Civitas.

Gitlin, T. (2002). *Media unlimited: How the torrent of images and sounds overwhelms our lives*. New York: Henry Holt.

Grossberg, L., Wartella, E., Whitney, C. D., & Wise, J. M. (2006). *MediaMaking: Mass media in a popular culture* (2nd ed.). Thousand Oaks, CA: Sage.

Hall, S. (1980). Encoding/decoding. In S. Hall, D. Hobson, A. Lowe, & P. Willis (Eds.), *Culture, media and language* (pp. 128–138). London: Hutchinson.

Hall, S. (1997). Introduction. In S. Hall (Ed.), *Representation: Cultural representations and signifying practices* (pp. 1–45). Thousand Oaks, CA: Sage.

Hasian, M. (2002). The siege and American media portrayals of Arabs and Moslems. In J. N. Martin, T. K. Nakayama, & L. A. Flores (Eds.), *Readings in intercultural communication* (pp. 227–243). New York: McGraw-Hill.

Joseph, S. (2006). *In black and white: Representations of Arab and Muslim Americans and Islam in US print news media*. Retrieved from http://www.iue.it/RSCAS/Research/Mediterranean/mspr2006/pdf/joseph-bio-abstract.pdf

Kidd, D. (2007). Harry Potter and the functions of popular culture. *The Journal of Popular Culture, 40*(1), 69–89.

Lasn, K. (2000). *Culture jam: How to reverse America's suicidal consumer binge—and why we must*. New York: HarperCollins.

Lauzen, M. (1999). *Reel News, Nov./Dec. 1999*. Retrieved from http://www.mediawatch.com/wordpress/?p=11

Martinez, I. (2005). Romancing the global. *Foreign Policy*. Retrieved from http://www.foreignpolicy.com/users.login.php?story_id=3269&URL

Nielsen Wire. (2009, November 10). *Average TV viewing for 2008-09 TV season at all-time high.* Retrieved from http://blog.nielsen.com/nielsenwire/media_entertainment/average-tv-viewing-for-2008-09-tv-season-at-all-time-high/

Ram, A. (2004). Memory, cinema, and the reconstitution of cultural identities in the Asian Indian diaspora. In M. Fong & R. Chuang (Eds.), *Communicating ethnic & cultural identity.* Lanham, MD: Rowman & Littlefield.

Rodríguez, C. (2001). *Fissures in the mediascape: An international study of citizens' media.* Cresskill, NJ: Hampton Press.

Root, D. (1996). Cannibal culture: Art, appropriation, and the commodification of difference. Boulder, CO: Westview Press.

Rosenau, J. N. (2003). *Distant proximities: Dynamics beyond globalization.* Princeton, NJ: Princeton University Press.

Shapiro, S. F. (2000). The culture thief. *New Rules Project: Exploring community, mobility, scale and trade.* Retrieved from http://www.newrules.org/journal/nrfall00culture.html

Shenk, D. (1997). *Data smog: Surviving the information glut.* New York: HarperEdge.

Sorrells, K. (2002). Embodied negotiation: Commodification and cultural representation in the U.S. southwest. In M. J. Collier (Ed.), *Intercultural alliances: International and intercultural communication annual* (Vol. 25, pp. 17–47). Thousand Oaks, CA: Sage.

Story, L. (2007, January 15). Anywhere the eye can see, it's likely to see an ad. *New York Times.* Retrieved from http://www.nytimes.com/2007/01/15/business/media/15everywhere.html?_r=1&ei=5094&en=612610efd7f8f6ef&hp=&ex=1168923600&partner=homepage&pagewanted=all

Thussu, D. K. (2006). *International communication* (3rd ed.). London: Hodder Arnold.

Tunstall, J. (2008). *The media were American: U.S. mass media in decline.* New York: Oxford University.

Waltz, M. (2005). *Alternative and activist media.* Edinburgh: University of Edinburgh.

Whoriskey, P. (2006, August 4). Latin American melodramas that are made in the U.S. *Washington Post.* Retrieved from http://hispanic7.com/latin_american_ melodramas_that_are_made_in_the_u_s_a_.htm

Wilson, C. C., Gutiérrez, F., & Chao, L. M. (2003). *Racism, sexism and the media: The rise of class communication in multicultural America.* Thousand Oaks, CA: Sage.

Wright, B. W. (2001). *Comic book nation.* Baltimore: Johns Hopkins University Press.

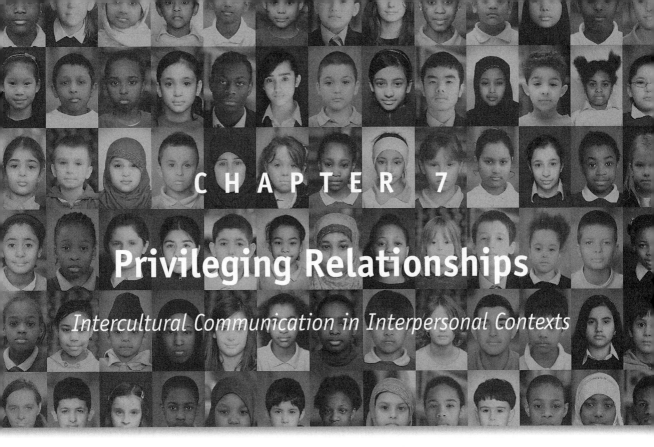

CHAPTER 7

Privileging Relationships

Intercultural Communication in Interpersonal Contexts

In the global context, the proximity of people from different cultures increases the likelihood of intercultural relationships.

R elationships within families, among friends, with romantic partners and coworkers, as well as acquaintances made in schools, service sectors, entertainment, and religious groups have become increasingly diverse and multicultural in the age of globalization. Enhanced mobility, economic interdependence, and advances in technology bring people from very diverse cultural, socioeconomic, linguistic, and social positions together in unprecedented ways, creating both opportunities and challenges for intercultural relationships (Burawoy et al., 2000). Norms regarding friendships, family relationships, gender roles, romance, and sexuality are often questioned, disrupted, and reconfigured as a result of escalating flows of people, capital, and cultural products occurring in the context of globalization (Bell & Coleman, 1999; Sassen, 1999; Shohat, 1998).

One out of every 35 people in the world lives outside her or his country of origin accelerating the potential for and necessity of developing intercultural relationships (International Organization for Migration, n.d.). Intercultural family, friendship, and longer-term romantic

Source: Chapter-opening photo © Gideon Mendel/Corbis.

relationships also result from improved access to travel and tourism that epitomize the mobility of the global context. In her book *Romance on a Global Stage,* anthropologist Nicole Constable (2003) investigated intercultural heterosexual romantic relationships noting that:

> meeting marriage partners from abroad is not new, the Internet has fueled a global imagination and created a time-space compression that has greatly increased the scope and efficiency of introductions and communication between men and women from different parts of the world. (p. 4)

The proliferation of advanced communication and media technology from cell phones to the Internet to global media has also revolutionized and transformed the lives and lifestyles of lesbian, gay, bisexual, transgender, and queer (LGBTQ) communities in Asia and around the globe. For example, toy cartoons like Hello Kitty hang on mobile phones in Japan to signify queer identity and Cyberjaya, an online outlet in Malaysia, subverts harsh antigay laws as a virtual queer community forms (Berry, Martin, & Yue, 2003).

Clearly, globalizing forces—the integration of capital and markets, the implementation of neoliberal policies, and advances in technology—have magnified the frequency and intensity of intercultural relationships. Yet the complexities and contestations surrounding and impacting intercultural relationships in the context of globalization are also deeply embedded in the history of colonization as well as the anticolonial and civil rights movements of the second half of the 20th century. The rise of intercultural friendships and intimate relationships in the United States is attributable, to a great extent, to the historic and monumental changes brought about by the civil rights movement in the 1950s and 1960s that challenged long-standing, colonial era laws inhibiting interracial interactions and prohibiting interracial marriages.

As early as 1660, legislation was enacted in the United States banning interracial marriage between Whites and Blacks. **Miscegenation** comes from Latin roots meaning "mixed" and "kind" and was used historically to refer to "mixed-race" relationships, specifically intermarriage, cohabitation, and sexual relationships between people of different socially constructed races. **Antimiscegenation** laws, which prohibited marriage between people of different so-called "racial" groups, existed in over 40 states until 1967 when the laws were overturned in the landmark *Loving v. Virginia Supreme Court* case (Roberts, 1994). Antimiscegenation laws normalized and maintained the socially constructed categories of "race" based on physical characteristics and promoted a belief that intermarriage across racial groups was deviant and would taint the "racial purity" of the dominant White, European American "race" (Childs, 2005; Lopez, 1997). As recently as 1970, only 1 out of 1,000 marriages in the United States were interethnic or interracial (Kalmijn, 1993). In 2005, approximately 7% of the 59 million couples in the United States were interracial (Rosenfeld, 2007). Research suggests that attitudes toward intercultural marriage are changing (Peterson, 1997; Troy, Lewis-Smith, & Laurenceau, 2006). Interracial and interethnic relationships and marriages are increasing in the United States with each generation. Yet they continue to be shaped by deeply embedded myths, stereotypes, assumptions, and prejudices forged in historical and current relationships of inequitable power that impact the initiation, development, and maintenance of these relationships (Childs, 2005; Orbe & Harris, 2001).

In this chapter, relationships are "privileged" in the sense that we foreground interpersonal relationships in our study of intercultural communication. The chapter title, "Privileging Relationships," also draws attention to how intercultural relationships in the global context are sites where cultural differences, power, privilege, and positionality are negotiated, translated, and transformed. The term *intercultural relationships* encompasses a broad and complicated terrain, so we begin our discussion by exploring the topography of intercultural relationships. An overview of theories and models that help us understand how intercultural friendships and intimate, romantic relationships are formed and sustained follows. The impact of computer mediated communication (CMC), specifically the Internet, on intercultural relationships is then addressed. A central goal of this chapter is to understand the critical role intercultural relationships can play in improving intercultural communication, challenging prejudices and stereotypes held by individuals and communities, and building alliances that advance social justice.

TOPOGRAPHY OF INTERCULTURAL RELATIONSHIPS

Interpersonal relationships are a vital and dynamic aspect of human interaction. People in all cultures initiate, develop, and at times dissolve relationships with others. To a great extent, our blueprints for interpersonal relationships come from our families of origin, which are profoundly shaped by cultural dimensions. Along with personal and contextual differences, we bring different culturally informed expectations, norms, and assumptions about relationships as well as historical and political influences into our interpersonal relationships. For our purposes, intercultural interpersonal relationships include relationships between people from different racial, ethnic, national, and religious as well as class and sexual orientation groups. A brief description and discussion of these types of intercultural relationships follows.

Interracial Intercultural Relationships

Intercultural relationships, as defined here, encompass **interracial relationships,** or relationships that cross socially constructed racial groups—for example, a friendship or romantic relationship between a person who is grouped racially as Black and a person who is categorized racially as White or between a person who is considered racially as Asian and someone who is Native American. Historically, interactions between different racial groups in the United States and particularly between Blacks and Whites were vigorously discouraged, curtailed, and in many cases prohibited by law. While laws have changed and interracial contact has increased in the United States, attitudes, stereotypes, and prejudices passed along, sanctioned, and policed by families and friends as well as through media representations continue to present barriers and challenges for interracial friendships and intimate relationships today (Foeman & Nance, 1999; Orbe & Harris, 2001; Thompson & Collier, 2006).

As outlined in Chapter 3, "race" is a social construct. Notions and perceptions of "race," as well as the meanings and significance attached to race differ across countries and regions in the world. Therefore, the impact of race on the formation and maintenance of intercultural relationships varies in different locations around the globe. For example, the experiences of an interracial couple composed of a Black or African American man and a Japanese woman who is racially constructed as Asian are likely to be different if the couple lives in the United States than if they live in Japan. Different social meanings are associated with race and with interracial unions in the two places resulting in different social, political, and economic impact.

Interethnic Intercultural Relationships

Interethnic relationships are relationships between people who identify differently in terms of ethnicity or ethnic background. A relationship between an Italian American and Irish American, between a Filipino American and Chinese American, or between a Serbian and Croatian in the former Yugoslavia would be considered interethnic. These examples illustrate interethnic relationships between people who are generally categorized as being of the same racial group. Interethnic relationships can also refer to relationships that cross both ethnic and racial group categories such as between a White or European American and a Chinese American or between a Latino/Latina and a Black or African American. In other words, these relationships cross lines that distinguish and separate groups based on socially constructed lines of race as well as **ethnicity,** which refers to shared heritage, place of origin, identity, and patterns of communication among a group.

Lines that divide ethnic groups within the racial category of White in the United States—Anglo/English American, Irish American, or Italian American, for example—have blurred through generations of assimilation and admission to the dominant racial group making the distinctions between ethnic groups within the racial category of White less significant today than in the past. Yet it is important to note that people who avow or are ascribed an identity as White do have an ethnicity. While the distinct and specific languages, heritages, and histories may be lost or only faintly remembered, a shared ethnic/racial culture does exist for European Americans, which manifests in communication patterns, values, norms, and practices. Ethnicity is salient among many groups in the United States in terms of a shared group identity, heritage, and connection to place of origin. Ethnicity, as it is both distinct from and combines with race, plays a role in choices that are made regarding who develops and sustains friendships and romantic relationships (Halualani, Chitgopekar, Morrison, & Dodge, 2004).

International Intercultural Relationships

International relationships refer to relationships that develop across national cultural and citizenship lines such as a relationship between someone who is from Turkey and someone who is from Germany or between someone who is Brazilian and a U.S. American. Many international relationships are also interracial and/or interethnic and therefore must address a complex intersection of socially constructed differences, positionalities, and influences from society in their relationships. In an article on international intercultural friendship development, researchers (Sias et al., 2008) found that cultural similarity, understood as similarities in ethnicity and race, for example, between Chinese and Korean participants, was an important factor in the relationship development process.

In many cases, international intercultural relationships enrich the lives of both partners through exposure and experience of multiple countries, languages, and cultures, yet international intercultural romantic long-term relationships are often challenged by questions of where to live, legal rights of citizenship, and power imbalances if one partner is perpetually perceived as a "foreigner." In addition, international intercultural relationships partners may confront differences in access to social and institutional power and assumptions of superiority (or inferiority) based on perceptions about countries of origin and race from the social networks surrounding the friends or partners.

Interreligious Intercultural Relationships

Interreligious or interfaith relationships refer to relationships where people from two different religious orientations or faiths such as Judaism, Buddhism, Christianity, and Hinduism or Catholic Christians and Protestant Christians form interpersonal relations. Changes in immigration laws within the United States since the 1965 Immigration and Naturalization Act along with the forces of globalization have brought large numbers of practicing Buddhists, Muslims, Sikhs, and Hindus to the United States dramatically increasing the religious diversity in the United States (Fredericks, 2007). Graces-Foley (2007) noted that much attention is placed on the influx of immigrants from religious groups that differ from the dominant Christian religion in the United States, yet Christian immigrants from developing countries outnumber immigrants of other religious traditions with two thirds of all new immigrants being Christian. Research based on a survey of 35,000 Americans found that 37 % of adults in the United States are involved in interreligious or interdenominational marriages (The Pew Forum on Religion & Public Life, 2008). Research also suggests that interfaith marriages are correlated with less religious participation and higher divorce rates than same-faith marriages (Kosin, Mayer, & Keysar, 2001). Yet religious studies scholar Kate McCarthy (2008) argued the following:

> Out of the tension between commitments to each other and to differing religious identities, interfaith couples and their children are crafting religious lives with extraordinary creativity and have a great deal to tell theorists of religious pluralism about strategies for conceptualizing and managing religious difference. (p. 189)

Class Differences in Intercultural Relationships

Differences in class culture and how class culture intersects with and manifests differently based on ethnic, racial, and national differences also impact intercultural relationships. Class culture is a significant dimension of intercultural relationships from seemingly mundane issues such as where one chooses to eat, hang out, and socialize to manners learned as appropriate in given settings and from versions of the language spoken at home to what is expected in the university classroom. Class also affects meanings and attitudes attributed to public displays of wealth as well as norms of raising children. Class culture translates into the social capital to which one has access and manifests in our everyday lives in terms of our *habitus*—our patterns of perceptions, actions, sensibilities, and tastes (Bourdieu, 1984). Communication scholars Dreama Moon and Gary Rolison (1998) analyzed forms of nonverbal communication such as proxemics—the use of space—and fashion to illustrate how "styles of consumption come to define and communicate class and further posit that the roots of classism are partially to be found in the communication, contestation and evaluation of 'class-culture commodities'" (p. 123). While **class prejudice** refers to personal attitudes individuals of any class culture may hold about members of other classes, **classism** is defined as the systemic subordination of class groups by the dominant, privileged class.

| **Figure 7.1** | Lesbian, gay, bisexual, and transgender (LGBT) couples experience varying degrees of acceptance and exclusion in different locations in the United States and throughout the world. |

Source: © BananaStock/BananaStock/Thinkstock.

Sexuality in Intercultural Relationships

Intercultural relationships are often sites where notions of sexuality and sexual identities intersect, collide, and coalesce with ethnic, racial, religious, and national cultural differences. Attitudes, norms, stereotypes, and assumptions regarding sexuality vary along a vast continuum and are deeply shaped by culture; histories of colonization; imperialism; economic, political, and social interests; as well as by the emergence of religious fundamentalism in the global context (Lovaas & Jenkins, 2007; Weeks, Holland, & Waites, 2003). Socially constructed sexual identities such as heterosexual, homosexual, gay, lesbian, bisexual, transsexual, transgender, and queer—whether ascribed, avowed, or both—position us differently in our relationships to each other and to institutions. Our differing positionalities enable and constrain access to power, privileges, and resources with particularly salient consequences for intercultural communication.

Issues of sexual orientation in society and in interpersonal relationships are often experienced as either completely invisible or hypervisible. When dominant norms of heterosexuality—including socially constructed gender roles, opposite-sex romantic attraction, and displays of physical affection—are followed and practiced, sexuality is generally unquestioned and heterosexuality is assumed. Yet when an individual or couple challenge the dominant norms of heterosexuality—in terms of gender norms, same-sex affection, or attraction—then their sexuality is marked, underscored, and made highly visible (Nakayama, 1998). **Heteronormativity** refers to the institutionalization of heterosexuality in society and the assumption that heterosexuality is the only normal, natural, and universal form of sexuality. Communication scholar Thomas Nakayama (1998) argued, "We are bombarded by messages that tell us how to regulate our communicative behavior and to support the supremacy of heterosexuality if not in action, then in communication" (p. 115). Social, economic, educational, media, legal, and religious institutions—as well as family and cultural attitudes—establish, reinforce, and regulate heteronormativity. **Heterosexism** is an ideological system that denies and denigrates any nonheterosexual behavior, identity, or community. Like sexism and racism, heterosexism not only entails individual biased attitudes but refers to the coupling of prejudicial beliefs with institutional power to enact systemic discrimination. For example, international lesbian or gay couples, who may experience homophobia on a daily basis, are also systematically excluded from marriage in most states in the United States and therefore do not have access to spousal petitions for citizenship.

Multidimensional Cultural Differences in Intercultural Relationships

As you no doubt can see, intercultural relationships can and often do involve multiple and intersecting ethnic, racial, national, religious, class, and sexual orientation differences. An intimate, long-term romantic relationship between a White American Jewish woman, for example, and an Indian Hindu man is likely to entail ongoing negotiations over cultural differences in verbal and nonverbal communication styles, norms, and expectations of families, intimacy, sexuality, and gender roles, as well as social pressures, alienation, and sanctions from friends, family, and society regarding their interracial relationship. Depending upon the various geographic, cultural, and national landscapes through which the couple moves, institutional and individual racism, exclusion, and differences in their access to power and privilege may test their relationship. The couple's relationship may require them to address questions of citizenship, where they will live as well as where they can create a shared home in this globally mobile world. Additionally, their interfaith relationship may be a contested site particularly during life transitions such as marriage, birth of children, and death, which are often marked by cultural and religious practices and rituals. Jeremy Caplan (2004), author of the article "Om-Shalomers Come of Age: Children of Jewish and Hindu Parents Are Emerging as a New Cultural Subset," noted that children of intercultural, interracial, interethnic, and interreligious marriages are faced with both challenges and rewards as they cross, blend, and blur cultural, linguistic, national, and religious boundaries.

CULTURAL IDENTITY
INTERCULTURAL RELATIONSHIPS

Soraya and Marcus are in an intercultural relationship. Soraya is from Kuala Lumpur, Malaysia, and Marcus is an African American from Atlanta, Georgia. They discuss the rewards and challenges of their intercultural relationship:

Soraya: "I think the best part of intercultural relationships is that you get to make your own version of culture. As a woman, there are gender norms and expectations I learned from my parents and teachers back home. When I am with Marcus, I do not have to worry too much about whether I'm being 'proper' enough to meet these standards. I sometimes wonder, however, how we are going to raise our children and what kind of values they are going to have."

Marcus: "The best part of intercultural relationship for me is that I get to learn about a new culture and language. It helps me broaden my perspective and see things beyond my culture. Intercultural relationships can also be challenging because some people view interracial dating as a taboo, and there is always a possibility that getting married is the only way for us to stay in the same country. But at least we have that option . . . gay and lesbian couples don't even have that!"

As illustrated here, intercultural relationships do not occur in a vacuum. Interpersonal relationships between people of different racial, ethnic, religious, national, class, and sexuality groups take place within historical, cultural, and political contexts, which are instrumental in how we interpret and make sense of them. The meanings attached to intercultural relationships—whether they are considered taboo, tolerated, or celebrated—are socially constructed by individuals, families, and communities with real consequences. Intercultural interpersonal relationships, therefore, become sites where we develop and communicate shared and contested meanings of our identities, our sense of belonging to and exclusion from groups and where we learn through our communication how we are positioned in relation to others. In the next section, we investigate in more depth processes of relationship formation and maintenance in the context of globalization.

FORMING AND SUSTAINING INTERCULTURAL RELATIONSHIPS

Intercultural Friendships

Friendship is a unique type of interpersonal relationship. Today, in the context of globalization where we frequently come in contact with people from diverse cultures, we are more likely to have friends who are culturally different from ourselves. Intercultural friendships often require us to navigate unknown terrain where our comfort and familiarity with interpersonal norms, communication styles, values, and expectations, as well as our language and meaning-making systems, are thrown into question. These differences can increase anxiety, uncertainty, misunderstanding, and conflict (Gudykunst, 1995; Sias et al., 2008). Maintaining intercultural friendships often means we have to negotiate deeply embedded stereotypes and assumptions held not only by ourselves but also by our network of friends, families, communities, and society. Intercultural relationships may also expose us very personally and with great impact to the ways privilege, positionality, and power operate within society to advantage and include some while disadvantaging and excluding others. These challenges can translate into both personal and societal benefits by increasing our understanding of other ethnic, racial, and cultural groups as well as deepening our understanding of our own; assisting us in challenging and breaking down misconceptions, stereotypes, and prejudices; and developing skills and strategies for intercultural alliances that create a more just and equitable world.

Cultural Notions of Friendship

Unlike relationships with family and relatives, friendships are typically characterized as voluntary—in other words, they involve some element of choice by relational partners. While this is frequently the case, the concept of friendships as "chosen relationships" assumes a typically Western, individualistic orientation to friendship. In more group-oriented or collectivist cultures, friendships are often recognized as growing out of group associations, longer-term connections to place, community, and a sense of mutual obligation.

Communication scholar Mary Jane Collier's (1991) research on African American, Latino/Latina, and European American students found that for all groups the notion of friendship revolved around qualities of trust and acceptance. In a more recent study, Collier (1996) found that while similar in many respects, conversational rules in close friendships among ethnic groups differ. Specifically, while European Americans reported that close friendships developed in a few months, Asian Americans, African Americans, and Latinos/ Latinas report taking approximately a year for close friendships to develop. Collier (1996) further noted morality and cultural respect are important for Latinos/Latinas, family is critical for Asian Americans, while African Americans focus on pride in ethnic heritage. In Krumrey-Fulks' (2001) research comparing Chinese and American expectations of friendship, Chinese participants viewed friends as those who provided help or assistance while Americans tended to look toward friends as good listeners. Notions of what constitutes a friend, what behaviors are appropriate, and what we expect to share in friendship relationships are shaped by the various age, gender, ethnic, racial, cultural, class, and national groups in which we participate and with which we identify (Adams, Blieszner, & DeVries, 2000; Collier, 1996).

Intercultural Relationship Development Processes

It is useful to think about intercultural relationships developing in three phases comprised of an initial encounter phase, an exploratory interactional phase, and ongoing involvement phase. In the initial encounter phase, people who initiate intercultural relationships are drawn to each other based on (1) proximity to each other; (2) similarities in interests, values, and goals as well as cultural, racial, and socioeconomic backgrounds;

encounter phase

(3) the ways in which the two complement and are different from each other; and (4) physical attraction to one another.

Given the increased proximity of people from different cultures in the context of globalization, we would expect an increase in intercultural encounters and interactions. In a study titled "Who's Interacting? And What Are They Talking About?—Intercultural Contact and Interaction Among Multicultural University Students," communication scholar Rona Halualani and her colleagues (2004) found that, rather ironically, in a context that promotes diversity, students have relatively limited intercultural interaction. In this study, students interact interculturally one to two times per week, yet their intercultural interactions revealed distinct patterns based on the following: (1) the racial/ethnic group involved in contact, (2) the location of contact, (3) the topic of interaction, and (4) socioeconomic class.

The researchers (Halualani et al., 2004) noted that people from diverse ethnic/racial backgrounds enter into intercultural interactions from different starting points shaped by socioeconomic class, previous contact with ethnic/racial groups, and historical memory of intercultural encounters between groups, which position individuals and groups differently in relation to each other. Different positionalities—rooted in hierarchies of social, economic, and political difference—impact the amount and frequency of interaction as well as the nature of intercultural contact. The study further suggests that people from different ethnic/racial groups may use "different sense-making logics" when engaging interculturally. For example, African Americans/Blacks may view intercultural interactions as a site of differentiation where cultural distinction and uniqueness is emphasized whereas Asian Americans, Latinos/Latinas, and Whites/European Americans may interact interculturally using a logic of similarities stressing sameness in the encounter (Halualani et al., 2004, p. 369).

The tendency to seek similarity in friendship formation presents an undeniable challenge in the initial encounter phase of intercultural relationship development. Language barriers, cultural differences in our orientation to strangers, and culturally coded conversational rules about what is appropriate to discuss and how much to disclose make initial encounters difficult and anxiety-producing. Discomfort regarding the unfamiliar, ambiguity about what is expected, and fear of difference may lead to confusion, mistrust, and retreat from intercultural encounters and friendships. Additionally, our socially constructed and learned distinctions of race may also inhibit intercultural interactions in the initial phase. How others in our social network perceive our relationship with someone from outside our racial, ethnic, or cultural group is also important. "Because racial alliances are socially constructed as negative and taboo, children are more likely to avoid these relationships because of the consequences of such behavior" (Orbe & Harris, 2001, p. 156).

In the **initial encounter phase** of intercultural relationship development, it is important to challenge preconceived assumptions, stereotypes, and prejudices regarding racial, cultural, and ethnic differences. At the same time, we need to acknowledge, seek to understand, and learn from the differences in communication styles; interactional patterns; and cultural, racial, and ethnic histories that do exist. If we do not take the risk to move outside our comfort zones, we miss the opportunity to develop a more in-depth knowledge, understanding, and experience of the world from the position of those who are different from us.

INTERCULTURAL PRAXIS
LEARNING FROM INTERCULTURAL RELATIONSHIPS

In intercultural relationship development, engaging in intercultural praxis through curious inquiry about people who are different from oneself means that we suspend our judgments, challenge our preconceived notions of others, and take risks to initiate interactions outside our comfort zone. Misunderstandings that result from cultural differences, different histories, and different worldviews can motivate us to use the points of entry of framing and positioning in intercultural praxis to broaden our knowledge, deepen our empathy, and increase our understanding of the world.

While different experiences and resultant standpoints provide opportunities for learning in intercultural friendships, members of the dominant group often find it easier to excuse and rationalize incidents of racism, sexism, or homophobia experienced by nondominant groups rather than grapple with the reality of the differences and the underlying systemic inequity revealed. Lack of recognition of White privilege, male privilege, heterosexual privilege, and U.S. privilege by dominant group members can be a source of tension and conflict in intercultural friendships. A willingness to understand how forms of privilege operate to disadvantage nondominant groups and to normalize the standpoint of the dominant group is critical.

In the **exploratory interaction phase,** intercultural relationships move toward greater sharing of information, increased levels of support, and connection and growing intimacy. A significant challenge for intercultural friendship relationships at this stage is the different culturally coded ways in which individuals from different groups have been socialized to achieve support, connection, and intimacy. In a well-known cross-cultural study, psychologist Kurt Lewin (1948) identified three spheres of information that people share with each other regarding the personal/private self. Imagine three concentric circles that model levels of information about the self. The larger, outer circle contains superficial information about one's self such as interests and regular activities. The middle circle contains more personal information about family and background. The inner circle holds even more personal and private information that we are likely to share with fewer people. What information is held in each of these spheres—what is considered superficial and shared more freely as compared to what is more protected—may vary across cultures. Additionally, the degree to which we self-disclose information from each sphere and the amount of time it takes in the relationship development process to reach the inner core may also vary across cultures. International students in the United States frequently comment on the ease with which U.S. Americans share and self-disclose personal information about themselves. Confusion often arises as international students in the United States are unsure how to make sense of high levels of self-disclosure, which are sometimes mistaken for increased intimacy and closeness, signaling a movement toward a deeper friendship. Additionally, those who are accustomed to a more rapid pace and higher degrees of self-disclosure, often common in the United States, may find the lack of reciprocal disclosure from their relational partner off-putting and unrewarding. In early cross-cultural studies, communication scholar Dean Barnlund (1975) noted that Japanese tended to hold a relatively small layer of information as part of their public self, whereas much more information constituted the private self. In contrast, U.S. Americans tended to have a larger layer of self that would be shared more broadly and less that was considered part of the private self.

As connection and affinity grow in intercultural friendships, relational partners typically spend more time together sharing experiences that expose them to each others' cultures and offers opportunities for intercultural learning. In this phase, friendships are also more susceptible to external pressures and societal perceptions regarding race, gender, culture, and nationality, as well as differences in access to power and privilege that each friendship partner may experience. A friendship between a White American and an African American may reveal through firsthand experience the different positionalities afforded each friend within society and the consequent differences in standpoint each holds. Common experiences of people of color in the United States, such as being singled out for surveillance in a store, pulled over by police for no apparent reason, ignored in conversations, or passed over in hiring processes because "you just don't fit in" may not be shared by a person who is White. The friendship partners are likely to make sense of these experiences in different ways based on different personal and cultural histories, which contribute to their divergent standpoints. The success of continuing intercultural friendship relationships often depends upon a willingness to "value difference and affirm the other person as a member of a culturally different group" (Collier, 2002a, p. 308).

The transition to the **ongoing involvement phase** in intercultural relationship development as noted by Lee (2008) and others is often marked by a turning point that promotes greater connection, intimacy, and involvement between the relational partners. Turning points could include sharing a significant event such as meeting family members, taking a trip together, or having conversations that engage greater levels of self-disclosure, vulnerability, and sharing. Being willing to stay in difficult conversations where one's limited knowledge of others' experiences and vulnerability is exposed and where one's privilege is challenged is critical. As friendship partners move into the ongoing involvement phase, shared rules of engagement that guide their interaction with each other emerge. Julia Wood (1982) used the term *relational identity/culture* to refer to the system of understanding that is developed between relational partners as they coordinate attitudes, actions, and identities within the relationship and with the world outside the relationship. Collier (2002a) noted that intercultural relationships involve the constant and ongoing negotiation of both the friendship relational identity "while simultaneously maintaining divergent cultural identities" (p. 307).

Intercultural Romantic Relationships

The number of people in the United States in intercultural romantic relationships as defined in this chapter—interracial, interethnic, international, and interreligious as well as interclass intimate relationships—is unknown given that existing research tends to study these groups separately. We do know that attitudes toward interracial marriage and intercultural dating are changing. In 2007, a Gallup poll revealed the highest approval rating ever with 77% of Americans approving marriage among Blacks and Whites (Carroll, 2007). Yet there may be a difference between attitude changes toward intercultural marriage and actual intercultural dating and practices. Research indicates that only approximately 40% of White participants in a study at a Southwestern and a Midwestern university had dated interculturally, which suggests little or no increase in intercultural dating in these regions over the past 20 years (Martin, Bradford, Drzewiecka, & Chitgopekar, 2003). Participants who had dated interculturally were more likely to have grown up in racially and ethnically diverse neighborhoods and had family members who had dated interculturally (Martin et al., 2003).

Even with the increased ethnic, racial, and cultural diversity within the United States and greater acceptance of intercultural relationships, most people still live, work, worship, and socialize in largely segregated groups (Childs, 2005). Even though legal barriers to integration and laws prohibiting intermarriage are relics of the past, borders between ethnic, racial, cultural, religious, and class groups still remain. Psychologist Maria Root (2001) noted that opposition to intercultural marriage may not only reflect bigotry but also fears about the loss of long-held cultural traditions, histories, and norms as well as concerns about the challenges children and grandchildren may face.

Individuals who enter into intimate, romantic relationships interculturally cross multiple boundaries and social worlds. Orbe and Harris (2001) noted the continued pervasiveness of racism in contemporary life: "When the two were friends, everyone saw their relationship as positive and nonthreatening, but when it looked as if the relationship was becoming romantic, it became a threat" (p. 169). Historically embedded prejudices held by those surrounding the couple—family, friends, and society—may force people to choose between family and partner. As Childs (2005) made clear, it is not only the couple who navigate borders in intercultural relationships; rather, friends, families, and racial/ethnic communities are central in monitoring and creating the experiences of and meanings about intercultural couples. Typically, research has focused attention on the intercultural or interracial couple—the characteristics of individuals who choose intercultural unions and their psychological problems—promoting the assumption that intercultural relationships are deviant and reinforcing beliefs that romantic relationships within the same culture should be the standard and norm. Childs (2005) proposed that interracial couples are significant not so much for what they tell us about the particular individuals but rather for the meanings produced about them in society and the roles these meanings play in the constructing, maintaining, and dismantling racial borders.

Intercultural Romantic Relationships Development

Much of the early research on interracial romantic or intimate relationships from the 1960s and 1970s reflected the stereotypes of the time and reinforce myths about race and sexuality. In a review of literature on Black–White couples, communication scholars Foeman and Nance (1999) identified five myths that have informed research, societal perceptions, and media representations regarding interracial couples. Many of these myths originated during the colonial period functioning then to rationalize and justify the inequitable and exploitative relationships of slavery and operating now to shape perceptions of intercultural relationships as deviant. The first myth is that Black people have an extraordinarily potent sex drive. Viewed as highly sexual, Black men are feared by White men and portrayed as wanting revenge for White wrongdoing by sexually exploiting White women. Black women are also depicted as highly sexual, which served to alleviate the guilt of White slave owners for their abuses and rape of Black women (Smith, 1966) and absolves White men of their sexual aggressiveness and stereotypes of women of color today (Collins, 1990). A second myth is that Blacks marry Whites for status, a type of socioeconomic trade-off. While this may happen in some cases, research suggests that Black and White couples come from similar educational and socioeconomic backgrounds (Schoen & Wooldredge, 1989). A third myth, often perpetuated in popular culture but unsubstantiated through research, is that Whites choose Black partners out of rebellion, spite for their parents, or as an effort to act out (Childs, 2005; Foeman & Nance, 1999). The assumptions that underlie these myths are that individuals who choose interracial romantic relationships are deviant and disturbed seeking only social or economic advancement or sex.

Other myths include the genetic inferiority of children from interracial marriages and the psychological problems, particularly in terms of identity, of biracial or multiracial children (Stonequist, 1937). Recent research advances a more positive interpretation of biracial individuals highlighting their receptivity and adaptability to multiple cultures (Stephan & Stephan, 1991). While biracial and bicultural people are often challenged by society's obsessive need to categorize them and may experience marginalization in both ethnic/racial/cultural groups, bicultural and multicultural people use their ambiguous positionalities in constructive and creative ways (Anzaldúa, 1991; Bennett, 1993). After interviewing hundreds of biracial/bicultural people, clinical psychologist Maria P. P. Root (1996) wrote the "Bill of Rights for People of Mixed Heritage" to resist racial and cultural myths, stereotypes, and hierarchies that have served to divide and oppress people and groups in the United States (see Figure 7.2).

Foeman and Nance (1999) proposed a four-stage model for understanding interracial romantic relationships and the role communication plays in the relational development process. While their research focuses specifically on interracial relationships, the model is extended here to address intercultural relationships as defined in this chapter. The first stage is **racial/cultural awareness,** where relational partners become aware of their similarities and differences and develop awareness of four coexisting perspectives: (1) their own, (2) their partner's, (3) their collective racial/cultural group's perspective, and (4) their partner's racial/cultural group's perspective. While these perspectives may not be discussed openly, the various individual and group-based viewpoints likely impact decisions such as where to eat out and with whom to socialize. Communication plays a critical role at this stage as partners negotiate new awareness of themselves and outsiders' perceptions of them as a couple as well as the roles race, ethnicity, culture, or class play in their initial attraction. Race and/or culture may be highlighted or minimized in the way the couple talks about their relationship; they are nevertheless negotiating their racial/cultural/ethnic

Myths of interracial couples [handwritten margin note]

Figure 7.2   Bill of Rights for People of Mixed Heritage

Bill of Rights

for

People of Mixed Heritage

I HAVE THE RIGHT . . .

Not to justify my existence in this world.

Not to keep the races separate within me.

Not to justify my ethnic legitimacy.

Not to be responsible for people's discomfort with my physical or ethnic ambiguity.

I HAVE THE RIGHT . . .

To identify myself differently than strangers expect me to identify.

To identify myself differently than how my parents identify me.

To identify myself differently than my brothers and sisters.

To identify myself differently in different situations.

I HAVE THE RIGHT . . .

To create a vocabulary to communicate about being multiracial or multiethnic.

To change my identity over my lifetime–and more than once.

To have loyalties and identification with more than one group of people.

To freely choose whom I befriend and love.

Source: © Maria P. P. Root, PhD, 1993, 1994

differences in this initial phase. Differences in the couple's assumptions, standpoints, and privilege may be revealed, requiring explanations, a willingness to see oneself and the world differently, and "sensitivity to a sometimes uncomfortable alternative perspective" (Foeman & Nance, 1999, p. 550).

The second stage is the **coping stage**, where the couple develops proactive and reactive strategies to manage the challenges of their intercultural relationship and to protect themselves as a couple and individuals from harmful external forces such as negative attitudes, stereotypes, and actions of friends, family, and society. Intercultural couples use communication to develop a shared understanding of situations, develop various responses to hostile environments, and seek out support. While dealing with these challenges can be stressful and can lead to the dissolution of the relationship, working through the difficulties also strengthens the relationship to ensure its survival (Foeman & Nance, 1999).

The third stage, **identity emergence,** occurs as interracial or intercultural couples take charge of the images of themselves, challenge negative societal forces, and reframe their relationship. "Instead of looking at their differences as obstacles to be overcome, interracial couples view the unique racial configuration of the families as a positive source of strength (e.g. 'Being biracial is a gift')" (Foeman & Nance, 1999, p. 553). Interracial and intercultural couples may choose, in fact, to see themselves as unusual or different but frame their uniqueness in positive and supportive ways instead of as "deviant" or "deficient." "Communication functions to provide the voice and words to recast their world: We are the inevitable family of a truly multicultural society" (Foeman & Nance, 1999, p. 553).

The final stage in the interracial/intercultural relationship development is **relational maintenance.** The communication skills, strategies, and perspectives that couples have developed through earlier stages are used to negotiate differences between themselves and with the society at large. Foeman and Nance (1999) noted that each individual within the couple may start the relationship at a different stage or revisit earlier stages as issues internal or external to the relationship emerge. As the couple moves through different life stages—having children, for example—new challenges and opportunities for increased awareness and deepened perspectives, additional coping strategies, and a sense of family identity also emerge.

As people from different ethnic, racial, class, and national cultures maintain friendships and intimate relationships, complex and often contradictory issues and tensions arise based on differing intersectional identities, positionalities, and relationships to power and privilege. Negotiating variations in cultural notions of friendships and intimacy, different norms of relationship development and cultural meaning-making are key to sustaining intercultural friendships and intimate relationships. Attention to how power and privilege operate both within the relationship and in society; an awareness of the roles cultural group histories play and the varied importance placed on history; and affirmation of the relational partner's culture and cultural identities all advance intercultural friendships and romantic relationships (Collier, 2002a).

CYBERSPACE AND INTERCULTURAL RELATIONSHIPS

In the context of globalization, advances in technology—particularly expanded access to the Internet—have dramatically accelerated the likelihood of engaging in intercultural interpersonal relationships through CMC. Cyberspace interactions and relationships have become increasingly popular as the Internet provides new contexts and alternative ways to meet strangers, engage in dyadic conversations, develop relationships, and participate in virtual communities.

In many parts of the world—notably in Japan, South Korea, Europe, Canada, and Australia—the percentage of the population online and the frequency of online interactions are as high if not higher than in the United States (Internet World Stats, 2011). Yet a digital divide persists globally and within nation-states. Less than 25% of the 7 billion people inhabiting the planet are connected through virtual superhighways (Internet World Stats, 2010). Also, within countries, huge discrepancies in access exist. India has an estimated 100 million active Internet users, yet this represents only 8.4% of the population (Internet World Stats, 2011). In a report titled "Are We Really a Nation Online? Ethnic and Racial Disparities in Access to Technology and Their Consequences," Robert Fairlie (2005) found that more than two thirds of White Americans have access to the Internet at home while only 40% of Blacks, Latinos/Latinas, and Native Americans have Internet access at home.

While some researchers argue that the Internet allows communicators to shed traditional constraints in relationship building and transcend barriers of time and place, CMC also presents communicative challenges such as higher levels of uncertainty given the lack of nonverbal cues, an absence of shared relational history, and common interactional norms (Lea & Spears, 1995). While the lack of nonverbal cues is considered a detriment in relationship building in online communication, it may have benefits interculturally. In online environments, communicators express themselves and respond primarily in written text, which may serve, at least initially, to open up channels of communication. The degree of anonymity afforded in online communication can promote greater levels of self-disclosure and more honest, forthright communication. Yet abrasive, impulsive, or abusive behavior called **flaming** is also common in CMC and can threaten online relationship development (Witmer, 1997). *Washington Post* columnist Victoria Shannon (1997) observed that African Americans have experienced comments and postings from European Americans in online conversations "that reflect cultural ignorance and racist ideology" (Orbe & Harris, 2001, p. 251). Researchers have found that online interactions in cyberspace often reflect and reinforce social problems and issues of inequity and can serve to further mask dynamics of power and privilege that exist in face-to-face communication (Gajjala, 2004).

Based on an extensive review, Childs (2005) found that interracial websites on the Internet can be categorized into three groups: (1) sites related to multiracial organizations/support, (2) interracial dating sites and pornography sites, (3) and sites of hate groups. The three categories provide a useful way to understand the complex role the Internet plays in intercultural relationships in the global context. The first grouping of sites includes multiracial organizations that celebrate interracial relationships, provide information about issues for biracial and multiracial individuals and couples, and serve as virtual communities that connect interracial couples and multiracial families. Childs (2005) noted that the prominent multiracial websites mirror the fluctuating discourse between race consciousness and color blindness used by interracial couples and in society at large. For example, the existence of these websites is based on an acknowledgment that interracial couples are treated differently in society, yet the websites and communication in their virtual communities tend to downplay the impact of race and privilege in a racialized society particularly for historically disenfranchised groups.

Interracial dating sites, the second category of websites, offering opportunities to meet partners or find love across color lines, are on the rise. While the sites explicitly market to those who are interested in interracial dating, at the same time, the websites claim that love is color-blind and that dating interracially is a personal preference not a racial one (Childs, 2005). Anthropologist Nicole Constable (2003) noted the Internet greatly facilitates opportunities to meet and develop marriage partners from abroad. Constable conducted Internet ethnography and face-to-face fieldwork with several hundred men and women involved in Internet correspondence courtship relationships. A complex web of over 350 Internet marriage-oriented introduction agencies as well as chat rooms and news groups provide introductions, virtual linkages, and support between U.S. men and Chinese and Filipina women. Internet correspondence courtships conjure images of "mail-order brides" and stereotypes of Asian women as either sweet, innocent "oriental dolls," who are desperate victims or shrewd "dragon ladies" motivated to snatch a husband only for economic reasons. Assumptions and stereotypes also abound about White American men who seek Asian brides—they must be losers unable to find a partner, they only want women they can dominate, and they are "consumers of women as commodities" (Constable, 2003, p. 9). Constable found that neither the women nor the men fit these media-produced stereotypes. Rather, through her in-depth research, she found the individuals involved in Internet correspondence courtships were "a diverse group, with different opinions, experiences, and motivations" and that their relationships must be seen "within a particular historical and global context as people who both exert power and are subject to it" (p. 9). Constable argued that it is critical to take into account how desire, attraction, history, and broader structures of inequitable power are intertwined in the choices made by intercultural couples while also acknowledging the depth and dignity of their decisions.

Internet dating sites and pornography sites are different, yet Childs (2005) argued both are motivated by people who are seeking interracial encounters. In the hugely profitable Internet pornography industry, interracial sex is often turned into a **fetish**, a spectacle that is represented as a commodity that is sought after, purchased, and consumed. Images on these sites tend to play on and reinforce historical myths about race and sexuality such as the hypersexuality of Black men and women; that Black men are out to steal White men's wives; that White women are either sluts or innocent, pure girls seduced by men of color; and that Black women are erotic, sexual objects for White men (Childs, 2005). These websites not only reflect long-standing stereotypes and assumptions of interracial relationships as deviant but they also construct meanings about race, interracial relations, and sexuality.

The third category of websites related to interracial relationships is hate groups. The Internet has played a significant role in expanding the accessibility and networking of White supremacist groups in the United States (Brown, 2009). Individuals or small groups who were previously isolated can now connect with each other, reinforce their racist ideologies, and acquire a sense of identity as a national movement (Southern Poverty Law Center, 2005). Interracial sexuality is presented as a threat to Whiteness, White identity, and White power, and biracial children are seen as destroying Whites and White culture (Ferber, 1998). Undoubtedly, the White supremacist websites promoting ideas that interracial relationships are deviant, unnatural, and destructive are extreme, yet Childs (2005) argued these ideas are similar to and extensions of comments, beliefs, and ideologies she found in her research of White communities.

Clearly, advances in communication technology in the global context facilitate intercultural communication allowing friends and intimate partners to meet, develop relationships, and maintain contact particularly at great geographic distance. Mediated communication through e-mail, chat rooms, and virtual communities enables individuals and groups to find support, expand social networks, and build political alliances. Nonetheless, communication in "virtual" space is not immune to the social, political, and economic barriers that detrimentally impact intercultural communication in face-to-face encounters.

INTERCULTURAL ALLIANCES FOR SOCIAL JUSTICE IN THE GLOBAL CONTEXT

In the global context, intercultural relationships are sites where cultural differences, positionalities, and issues of power and privilege are negotiated, translated, and potentially transformed. Intercultural friendships and intimate relationships can play a critical role in improving intercultural communication, challenging prejudices and stereotypes, developing allies, and building alliances that advance social justice. An ally is a supporter or partner who can be counted on to work in collaboration with another person, group, or community toward a common goal. An **intercultural ally,** then, is a person, group, or community who works across lines or borders of nationality, culture, ethnicity, race, gender, class, religion, or sexual orientation in support of and partnership with others. Given that socially constructed categories of difference inevitably position individuals and groups unevenly within systems of power and privilege, intercultural allies work to challenge inequity and marginalization of nondominant groups. Communication scholar Mary Jane Collier (2002b) defined **intercultural alliance** as a "relationship in which parties are interdependent and responsible to and for each other. Intercultural allies recognize their cultural difference and their interdependence, and often seek similar goals, but they are not necessarily friends" (p. 2). Communication scholar Brenda Allen (2004), an African American heterosexual woman, described her alliance with her colleague and friend, Anna, a White lesbian woman:

> We swap stories and perspectives on the socially constructed aspects of our identity for which society would condemn us, and we find beauty and awe in our differences. We collaborate with one another. We report to one another. We share challenges, victories, and failures together . . . As I review my friendship with Anna, an interracial relationship that is much more than that, I notice that it contains many elements of the classic model of interpersonal attraction. Despite our similarities in personal style and background, Anna and I would probably not have been such good fiends if she were straight. Because of her sexual orientation she can be empathetic with me in ways that my other white, straight friends cannot. Thus, I believe that our marginalized positions in society and academia have been a major factor in forming the center of our friendship. (pp. 200–201)

In a cyberdialogue, scholar–practitioners examine and share their personal experiences of building and facilitating intercultural alliances on interpersonal, community, and international levels (Allen, Broome, Jones, Chen, & Collier, 2002). The authors emphasized the importance of developing trust, a sense of interdependence, and dialogue, where the space to speak openly and the ability to sit with the pain and difficulties of others is critical in intercultural alliance building. Tremendous potential for personal growth as well as movement toward social justice can occur in intercultural alliances. Having the interest and skills to identify and work through misunderstandings, tensions, and conflicts are crucial to developing and sustaining intercultural alliances. All points of entry in intercultural praxis— inquiry, framing, positioning, as well as dialogue and reflection—can lead to collaborative action that serves the interests and needs of both or multiple individuals or groups.

Intercultural alliances often call on individuals to bridge and translate different cultural standpoints, positionalities, struggles, and histories. In the book *This Bridge Called My Back: Writings by Radical Women of Color*, a collective of women of color—scholars, poets, and activists—use the metaphor of serving as a "bridge" between and across socially constructed groups (Moraga & Anzaldúa, 1981). Serving as a "bridge" often means translating languages, values, norms, ways of thinking and being, as well as standpoints and positionalities between disparate groups.

Engaging in **intercultural bridgework** means developing sensitivity, understanding, and empathy and extending vulnerability to traverse multiple positions, creating points of contact, negotiation, and pathways of connection. Our "backs"—as the title of the book implies—our lives, our identities, our experiences, and our access to material, emotional, and spiritual resources are bridges that can carry us across worlds divided by culture, race, ethnicity, nationality, gender, class, religion, and sexual orientation. Yet, historically, the hard work, weight, and cost of intercultural bridgework have fallen disproportionately on the backs of nondominant groups. In a volume dedicated to intercultural alliances, Collier (2002b) drew three conclusions. First, there are more institutions, norms, practices, and ideological forces operating in society to maintain hierarchies of difference than there are ones that encourage and support intercultural alliances; therefore, analysis, reflection, and dialogue on power, privilege, and dominance are necessary first steps toward change. Second, intercultural alliances are complex and dynamic. Attention to the intersecting, overlapping, and multifaceted nature of individual and group identities and histories is needed. Third, intercultural alliances across lines of culture, race, class, gender, nation, and sexual orientation are hard work demanding vulnerability and risk-taking. Yet, as sites of intercultural praxis, alliances have the potential to open up a range of new possibilities, dismantle inequitable relations of power, and move toward social justice on interpersonal, community, and global levels.

SUMMARY

This chapter examined the complicated, contradictory, and contested ways in which intercultural relationships in the global context are sites where cultural differences, power, privilege, and positionality are negotiated, translated, and transformed. A typology of intercultural relationships was offered. The cultural dimensions of interpersonal relationship formation as well as the roles of power, privilege, and history in intercultural relationships were presented to enhance our understanding, develop more effective strategies for relating across cultures, and increase our awareness of the benefits and challenges of intercultural relationships in the global context. The impact of the

Internet in initiating and sustaining intercultural friendship and intimate relationships and the emerging role Internet websites play in constructing collective identities and creating virtual communities was addressed. The chapter concluded with a discussion of intercultural relationships as potential sites of alliances for social justice in the global context.

KEY TERMS

miscegenation
antimiscegenation
intercultural relationships
interracial relationships
interethnic relationships
ethnicity
international relationships
interreligious or interfaith relationships
class prejudice
classism
heteronormativity
heterosexism
initial encounter phase

exploratory interaction phase
ongoing involvement phase
relational identity/culture
racial/cultural awareness
coping stage
identity emergence
relational maintenance
flaming
fetish
intercultural ally
intercultural alliance
intercultural bridgework

DISCUSSION QUESTIONS AND ACTIVITIES

Discussion Questions

1. What kind of intercultural relationships/friendships do you have?

2. What are the benefits and/or challenges of having intercultural relationships?

3. What are the historical contexts and/or relations of power that shape your intercultural relationships?

4. We addressed issues of the media and popular culture in the previous chapter. How does media influence the way people engage in intercultural relationships?

5. How do you think intercultural praxis may help us have more effective and fulfilling intercultural relationships?

Activities

1. Unpacking the Relationship Development Process

   a. Using the stages of intercultural friendship/romantic relationship development models, consider how your intercultural relationships have developed over time.

b. Describe specific incidents, feelings, and stages you and your friend/partner have gone through to develop the relationship.

c. Now consider if you can make connections between your experience and any of the key concepts/issues discussed in the chapter.

2. Performing Intercultural Relationships—Group Activity

a. In a group of five people, come up with a scenario in which cultural differences function as either a challenge or an advantage in intercultural relationships.

b. Act out the scenario in front of the class.

c. Now discuss the following questions:

i. What worked and/or what went wrong and why?

ii. What historical issues and power relations shape the relational interactions in your scenario?

iii. How does globalization influence the way people form intercultural relationships?

REFERENCES

Adams, R., Blieszner, R., & DeVries, B. (2000). Definitions of friendship in the third age: Age, gender and study location effects. *Journal of Aging Studies, 14*(1), 117–133.

Allen, B. (2004). Sapphire and Sappho: Allies in authenticity. In A. González, M. Houston, & C. Chen (Eds.), *Our voices: Essays in culture, ethnicity, and communication* (4th ed., pp. 198–202). Los Angeles, CA: Roxbury.

Allen, B., Broome, B. J., Jones, T. S., Chen, V., & Collier, M. J. (2002). Intercultural alliances: A cyberdialogue among scholar-practitioners. In M. J. Collier (Ed.), *Intercultural alliances: Critical transformations* (pp. 279–319). Thousand Oaks, CA: Sage.

Anzaldúa, G. (Ed.). (1991). *Making face, making soul: Haciendo caras.* San Francisco: Aunt Lute.

Barnlund, D. (1975). *Public and private self in Japan and the United States: Communicative styles of two cultures.* Tokyo, JP: Simul Press.

Bell, S., & Coleman, S. (1999). *The anthropology of friendship.* Oxford, UK: Berg.

Bennett, J. M. (1993). Cultural marginality: Identity issues in intercultural training. In R. M. Paige (Ed.), *Education for the intercultural experience* (pp. 109–135). Yarmouth, ME: Intercultural Press.

Berry, C., Martin, F., & Yue, A. (Eds.). (2003). *Mobile cultures: New media in queer Asia.* Durham, NC: Duke University Press.

Bourdieu, P. (1984). *Distinction: A social critique of the judgment of taste.* Cambridge, MA: Harvard University Press.

Brown, C. (2009). WWW.HATE.COM: White supremacist discourse on the Internet and the construction of whiteness ideology. *Howard Journal of Communication, 20*(2), 189–208.

Burawoy, M., Blum, J. A., George, S., Gille, Z., Gowan, T., Haney, L., et al. (2000). *Global ethnography: Forces, connections, and imaginations in a postmodern world.* Berkeley: University of California Press.

Caplan, J. (2004). *Om-Shalomers come of age: Children of Jewish and Hindu parents are emerging as a new cultural subset.* Retrieved from http://www.forward.com/articles/6137/

Carroll, J. (2007). Most Americans approve of interracial marriage. *Gallop News Service.* Retrieved from http://www.gallup.com/poll/28417/most-americans-approve-interracial-marriages.aspx

Carrillo Rowe, A. M. (2002). Bridge inscriptions: Transracial feminist alliances, possibilities and foreclosures. In M. J. Collier (Ed.), *Intercultural alliances: Critical transformations* (pp. 49–80). Thousand Oaks, CA: Sage.

Childs, E. C. (2005). *Navigating interracial borders: Black-White couples and their social worlds.* New Brunswick, NJ: Rutgers University Press.

Collier, M. J. (1991). Conflict within African, Mexican and Anglo American friendship. In S. Ting-Toomey & F. Korzeny (Eds.), *Cross-cultural interpersonal communication* (pp. 132–154). Newbury Park, CA: Sage.

Collier, M. J. (1996). Communication competence problematics in ethnic friendships. *Communication Monographs, 63*(4), 314–336.

Collier, M. J. (2002a). Intercultural friendships as interpersonal alliances. In J. N. Martin, T. K. Nakayama, & L. A. Flores (Eds.), *Readings in intercultural communication* (2nd ed., pp. 301–310). New York: McGraw-Hill.

Collier, M. J. (2002b). Negotiating intercultural alliance relationships: Towards transformation. In M. J. Collier (Ed.), *Intercultural alliances: Critical transformations* (pp. 1–15). Thousand Oaks, CA: Sage.

Collins, P. H. (1990). *Black feminist thought: Knowledge, consciousness and the politics of empowerment.* New York: Routledge.

Constable, N. (2003). *Romance on a global stage: Pen pals, virtual ethnography, and "mail order" marriage.* Berkeley: University of California Press.

Fairlie, R. W. (2005, September 20). Are we really a nation online? Ethnic and racial disparities in access to technology and their consequences. *Report for the Leadership Conference on Civil Rights Education Fund.* Retrieved from http://www.civilrights.org/publications/nation-online/

Ferber, A. (1998). *White man falling: Race, gender and white supremacy.* Lanham, MD: Rowman & Littlefield.

Foeman, A. K., & Nance, T. (1999). From miscegenation to multiculturalism: Perceptions and stages of interracial relationship development. *Journal of Black Studies, 29*(4), 540–557.

Fredericks, J. (2007). Dialogue and solidarity in a time of globalization. *Buddhist-Christian Studies, 27,* 51–66.

Gajjala, R. (2004). Negotiating cyberspace/negotiating RL. In A. González, M. Houston, & C. Chen (Eds.), *Our voices: Essays in culture, ethnicity, and communication* (4th ed., pp. 82–91). Los Angeles, CA: Roxbury.

Graces-Foley, K. (2007). New opportunities and new values: The emergence of the multicultural church [Electronic version]. *The Annals of the American Academy of Political Science, 612*(1), 209–224.

Gudykunst, W. B. (1995). Anxiety/Uncertainty management (AUM) theory. In R. L. Wiseman (Ed.), *Intercultural communication* (pp. 8–58). Thousand Oaks, CA: Sage.

Halualani, R. T., Chitgopekar, A., Morrison, J. H. T. A., & Dodge, P. S. (2004). Who's interacting? And what are they talking about?—intercultural contact and interaction among multicultural university students. *International Journal of Intercultural Relations, 28*(5), 353–372.

International Organization for Migration. (n.d.). *About migration.* Retrieved from http://www.iom.int/jahia/page3.html

Internet World Stats. (2010). *Internet top 20 countries: Percent of world users 2010.* Retrieved from http://www.Internetworldstats.com/top20.htm

Internet World Stats. (2011, June 30). *Top 20 countries with the highest number of Internet users.* Retrieved from http://www.Internetworldstats.com/top20.htm

Kalmijn, M. (1993). Trends in Black/White in intermarriage. *Social Forces, 72,* 119–146.

Kosin, B. A., Mayer, A., & Keysar, A. (2001). American religious identification survey. *The Graduate Center of the City of New York.* Retrieved from http://www.gc.cuny.edu/faculty/research_briefs/aris.pdf

Krumrey-Fulks, K. S. (2001). *At the margins of culture: Intercultural friendship between Americans and Chinese in the academic setting.* Unpublished doctoral dissertation, University of Kentucky, Lexington.

Lea, M., & Spears, R. (1995). Love at first byte? Building personal relationships over computer networks. In J. T. Wood & S. Duck (Eds.), *Understudies relationships: Off the beaten track* (pp. 197–233). Newbury Park, CA: Sage.

Lee, P.-W. (2008). Stages and transitions of relational identity development in intercultural friendship: Implications for identity management theory [Electronic version]. *Journal of International and Intercultural Communication, 1,* 1, 51–69.

Lewin, K. (1948). Social psychological differences between the United States and Germany. In G. Lewin (Ed.), *Resolving social conflicts.* New York: Harper.

Lopez, I. F. H. (1997). *White by law: The legal construction of race.* New York: New York University.

Lovaas , K. E., & Jenkins, M. M. (Eds.). (2007). *Sexualities & communication in everyday life.* Thousand Oaks, CA: Sage.

Martin, J. N., Bradford, L. J., Drzewiecka, J. A., & Chitgopekar, A. S. (2003). Intercultural dating patterns among young white U.S. Americans: Have they changed in the past 20 years? *Howard Journal of Communications, 14*(2), 53–73.

McCarthy, K. (2008). Pluralist family values: Domestic strategies for living with religious difference [Electronic version]. *The ANNALS of the American Academy of Political and Social Science, 612*(1), 186–203.

Moon, M., & Rolison, G. (1998). Communication of classism. In M. L. Hecht (Ed.), *Communicating prejudice* (pp. 122–135). Thousand Oaks, CA: Sage.

Moraga, C., & Anzaldúa, G. (Eds.). (1981). *This bridge called my back: Writings by radical women of color.* New York: Kitchen Table.

Nakayama, T. K. (1998). Communication of heterosexism. In M. L. Hecht (Ed.), *Communication prejudice* (pp. 112–121). Thousand Oaks, CA: Sage.

Orbe, M. P., & Harris, T. M. (2001). *Interracial communication: Theory into practice.* Belmont, CA: Wadsworth.

Peterson, K. S. (1997, November 3). *USA Today,* p. 1A.

The Pew Forum on Religion & Public Life. (2008). *U.S. religious landscape survey.* Retrieved from http://religions.pewforum.org

Roberts, R. E. (1994). Black-White inter-marriage in the United States. In W. R. Johnson & D. M. Warren (Eds.), *Inside the mixed marriage* (pp. 25–79). Lanham, MD: University Press of America.

Root, M. P. P. (1996). A bill of rights for racially mixed people. In M. P. P. Root (Ed.), *Racially mixed people in the new millennium.* Newbury Park, CA: Sage.

Root, M. P. P. (2001). *Love's revolution: Interracial marriage.* Philadelphia: Temple University Press.

Rosenfeld, M. (2007). *The age of independence: Interracial unions, same-sex, and the changing American family.* Cambridge, MA: Harvard University Press.

Ruskin, D. K. (1981). The bridge poem. In C. Moraga & G. Anzaldúa (Eds.), *This bridge called my back: Writings by radical women of color* (pp. xxi–xxii). New York: Kitchen Table.

Sassen, S. (1999). *Guests and aliens.* New York: New Press.

Schoen, R., & Wooldredge, K. (1989). Marriage choices in North Carolina and Virginia, 1969–1971 and 1979–1981. *Journal of Marriage and the Family, 51*(2), 465–481.

Shannon, V. (1997). Networking: When race meets life on-line, there's a disconnection. In S. Biagi & M. Kem-Foxworth (Eds.), *Facing difference: Race, gender and mass media* (pp. 258–260). Thousand Oaks, CA: Sage.

Shohat, E. (Ed.). (1998). *Talking visions: Multicultural feminism in a transnational age.* Cambridge, MA: MIT Press.

Sias, P. M., Drzewiecka, J. A., Mears, M., Bent, R., Konomi, Y., Ortega, M., et al. (2008). Intercultural friendship development. *Communication Reports, 21*(1), 1–13.

Smith, C. E. (1966). Negro-White intermarriage: Forbidden sexual union. *Journal of Sex Research, 2*(2), 169–177.

Southern Poverty Law Center. (2005). *Intelligence report: Electronic storm.* Retrieved from http://www.splcenter.org/intel/intelreport/article.jsp?pid = 919

Stephan, W. G., & Stephan, C. W. (1991). Intermarriage: Effects on personality, adjustment and intergroup relations in two samples of students. *Journal of Marriage and the Family, 53*(1), 241–250.

Stonequist, E. V. (1937). *The marginal man: A study in personality and culture conflict*. New York: Russell & Russell.

Thompson, J., & Collier, M. J. (2006). Toward contingent understandings of intersecting identifications among selected U.S. interracial couples: Integrating interpretive and critical perspectives. *Communication Quarterly, 54*(4), 487–506.

Troy, A. B., Lewis-Smith, J., & Laurenceau, J. (2006). Interracial and intraracial romantic relationships: The search for differences in satisfaction, conflict and attachment style. *Journal of Social and Personal Relationship, 23*(1), 65–80.

Weeks, J., Holland, J., & Waites, M. (Eds.). (2003). *Sexuality and society: A reader.* Cambridge, UK: Polity.

Witmer, D. F. (1997). Risky business: Why people feel safe in sexually explicit on-line communication. *Journal of Computer-Mediated Communication, 2*(4). Retrieved from http://jcmc.indiana.edu/vol2/issue4/witner2 .html

Wood, J. T. (1982). *Human communication: A symbolic interactionist perspective*. McAllen, TX: Holt, Rinehart, and Winston.

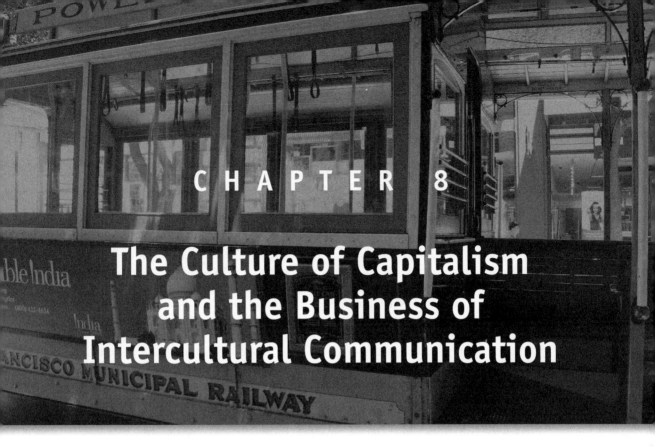

CHAPTER 8

The Culture of Capitalism and the Business of Intercultural Communication

Culture for sale! A streetcar in San Francisco, a nostalgic commodification of culture itself, serves to sell a romantic view of "Incredible India."

The financial crisis that erupted in the United States in the fall of 2008 sent shock waves throughout the entire global financial system with devastating consequences for billions around the world. The economic crisis illustrates well the intricate web of financial interdependence, the frailty of the global economic system, and the ubiquitous yet uneven impact of economic globalization. Around the globe and in the United States, the economic crisis dramatically increased the ranks of the unemployed and the number of people living in poverty. In 2011, the overall unemployment rate in the United States was nearly 9% down from 10% in 2009, which was the highest in the past 30 years (U.S. Department of Labor, 2011). Globally, the economic crisis pushed some 200 million people into extreme poverty. Approximately 40% of the world's employed population, or 1.2 billion people, receive wages of less than $2 per day (International Labour Office, 2011). Nearly 25,000 children under the age of 5 die each day from poverty, disease, and hunger (UNICEF, 2009). At the epicenter of the collapse were U.S. financial giants like Bear Stearns, Morgan Stanley, and Lehman Brothers, which led to devastating

Source: Chapter-opening photo © Sheena Malhotra.

declines and ongoing volatility in stock markets around the world. This precipitated the withdrawal of international capital from global circulation, which put tremendous pressure on developing nations and necessitated the emergency intervention of the International Monetary Fund (IMF) in Iceland, Hungary, the Ukraine, Pakistan, and other countries.

Foreclosed homes, lost jobs, reduced credit to meet payroll, diminished investments, shrinking consumption, corporate closures, furloughs and layoffs, bank collapses, reduced remittances that increase hardship for people dependent on money from migrants, a dramatic slowdown in world trade . . . what does all this have to do with intercultural communication? An immediate and obvious connection is the differential impact of the economic crisis on racial, class, and national cultural groups around the globe. For every dollar an average White family owns in the United States, the average family of color has less than a dime (Lui, Robles, Leondar-Wright, Brewer, & Adamson, 2006). While many in the United States, particularly Whites, think that racial discrimination ended during the 1960s civil rights movement, the racial wealth divide continues (Lui et al., 2006). Globally, the economic crisis squeezed advanced and emerging economies from Europe and Japan to Brazil, India and China. Yet the global trade shock led to a slower-paced devastation of the economies and lives of people from low-income countries, over 90 countries in sub-Saharan Africa, Asia, and Latin America (IMF, 2009).

In a longer-term and more deeply rooted sense, economic realities, material conditions, and the culture of capitalism provide an ever-present backdrop for intercultural communication (Tomlinson, 1999). From the basics of food, clothing, and shelter to the construction of identities, pleasure, and desire to the ways we show love, celebrate holidays, engage in conflict and fight wars, commodities are central to all cultures and intercultural interactions in the context of global capitalism. James Ridgeway (2004), author of *It's All for Sale: The Control of Global Resources* noted the following:

> Commodities seldom draw much attention in the interpretation of today's world events. And yet they played an important role in the evolution of colonialism and empire, and in the waging of small and large wars. They have influenced the flow of migration and emigration. People were enslaved to exploit commodities. They have always been at the heart of things. (p. ix)

The trade of commodities has brought people and things from different cultures into contact and collision since antiquity. From the ancient Silk Road to Columbus's expeditions in the New World and from the 19th-century British opium trade to the U.S. support of coups and military interventions, commodities have been integrally linked to intercultural exchange, nation-state building, and international conflicts.

This chapter addresses the linkages between intercultural communication and capitalism historically and today in the global context. We begin with a history of capitalism and discuss the emergence of the culture of capitalism in the United States and globally. A discussion of cultural dimensions in the workplace as well as trends in managing "diversity," multicultural teams, and virtual teams follows. The global intercultural marketplace is our next stop where we explore the commodification of culture, tourism, and the consumption of cultural "Others." The chapter concludes with a discussion of economic responsibility and intercultural communication in the context of globalization.

HISTORICAL CONTEXT: CAPITALISM AND GLOBALIZATION

French economist Michel Beaud (2001) argued that **capitalism** is a complex social logic that cannot be reduced to economic dimensions alone; rather, in order to understand capitalism, we must take social, cultural, political, ideological, and ethical issues into account. While some argue that capitalism has evolved naturally, the assumption in this chapter is that capitalism is a product of historical processes. Capitalism is best understood as sets of relationships between capitalists, laborers, and consumers. Robbins (2002) noted the following:

> The culture of capitalism is devoted to encouraging the production and sale of commodities. For capitalists, the culture encourages the accumulation of profit; for laborers, it encourages the accumulation of wages; for consumers, it encourages the accumulation of goods. In other words, capitalism defines sets of people who, behaving according to a set of learned rules, act as they must act. (p. 10)

There is nothing "natural" or "inevitable" about these roles, behaviors, and goals. Human beings are not driven by "nature" to accumulate wealth or to continuously acquire things. The culture of capitalism, like all cultures, has developed over time through historical processes where behaviors, beliefs, and values as well as relationships of power are learned and normalized. At times, the culture of capitalism has been equated with "civilization" and with "modernization" implying that nations or groups who do not participate are "uncivilized" or "primitive" (Robbins, 2002). Capitalism has provided relative comfort for large numbers of people; spurred advancements in medicine, food production, communication, and transportation technologies; and engineered or forced global economic integration. Yet ethnocentric assumptions that the culture of capitalism is superior to all others mask the exploitative and dehumanizing consequences of the culture of capitalism. These assumptions ignore how capitalism is central to many of the world's problems today such as unparalleled inequality, unprecedented hunger, poverty, racial and ethnic conflict, as well as irreversible environmental degradation (Beaud, 2001; Harvey, 2005; Robbins, 2002).

Capitalism 101: The Historical Emergence of the Culture of Capitalism

In precapitalist or noncapitalist societies, people make or obtain commodities for use. If you need food, clothing, or shelter, you grow, gather, or make it out of the materials available to you. According to economists, these commodities have **use value.** If you need something you cannot make or grow, you trade for it. Yet the main purpose of the trade is for the *use* of the commodity. Precapitalist forms of commerce, where goods are bought in one place at a certain price and then sold at another site for a profit, extend far back into human history in many societies around the world. In this case, the commodity has what economists call **exchange value.** The purpose of the exchange is not for use but to get money or capital. While this type of exchange involves a critical element of capitalism—the goal of obtaining capital rather than the commodity itself—it is still commonly considered precapitalist. A unique element—the way of combining labor and the means of production—in capitalism is still missing.

Capitalism and Colonialism: Capital Accumulation and the Nation-State

At the beginning of the 1400s, China was the most technologically advanced society in the world with sophisticated trade practices and military as well as political and social organization (Robbins, 2002). While Europe was still under a feudal economic and political system, China and India were likely the wealthiest countries in the world. By the 16th century, economic dominance shifted to Europe. As outlined in Chapter 3, the extraction of immense wealth in the form of raw materials from the New World and later from colonies such as India financed Europe's emerging economic and political power. Slavery provided the exploitable mass labor to extract raw materials to produce commodities, which were sold for profit developing the modern capitalist economy (Winant, 2001). This profit, then, was recycled to extract more raw materials, finance the movement of more slave labor, and exponentially expand the coffers in the centers of colonial power. The world racial hierarchy was foundational to the accumulation of capital and the concentration of wealth in Europe and the United States.

By the 17th century, the nobility and merchant class in European nation-states enacted policies and practices, which economists refer to as **mercantilism,** to enhance and control economic prosperity for the state and to keep the wealth acquired through trade in the nation-state. Mercantilism involved the implementation of protectionist polices that excluded foreign goods and subsidized cheap labor in certain industries. At this time, trading companies like the East India Trading Company and the Hudson's Bay Company, precursors to today's corporations, joined forces with nation-state militaries to ensure the continued extraction of wealth around the world. Intercultural encounters with trading companies dramatically altered the way of life, economic livelihood, and social organization of indigenous communities in the New World and Africa. Material things made locally such as pottery, clothing, tools, and weapons were, over time, replaced by imported goods, which increased dependence on world trade and contributed to the loss of cultural knowledge. Integration into the world economy, then as now, has significant and irreversible impact on cultures.

Mahatma Gandhi, the preeminent political and spiritual leader of the Indian independence movement, understood well the link among world trade, exploitation, and colonial power. He used the spinning wheel, a locally available tool, as the symbol for the independence movement. Gandhi recognized that in order to resist the economic hold of the British Empire, Indians needed to spin their own cloth instead of depend upon British imports. His famous Salt March in 1930, which opposed British taxation of salt, is another illustration of how Gandhi's strategy of nonviolent resistance to the British Empire was based on Indians reclaiming the means of production for goods produced and consumed by Indians (Ackerman & Duvall, 2000).

Capitalism and the Industrial Revolution: Creating the Working Class

The Industrial Revolution in England between the 1800s and 1900s initiated a new means of capital accumulation. Wolf (1982) argued that for capitalism to exist money must be able to purchase labor power by severing the link between producers and the means of production. Control of the means of production—land, materials, tools, and equipment—must be taken from peasants, craftspeople, and workers. Consequently, workers have no alternative but to negotiate agreements to use the land and the tools they need, receiving wages for their labor. Since capitalists control the means of production and the goods that are produced, laborers who produce the goods must buy what they need from capitalists. Therefore, people not only become laborers but also consumers. Thus, through the Industrial Revolution of the 19th century, the working class was forged.

Robbins (2002) identified four characteristics of the working class. First, members of the working class must be mobile, allowing them to move, unfettered by property ownership, to places where work is needed. In 19th-century Europe, the sale of common domain land to large landowners forced the movement of peasants to urban centers—a story similar to what is occurring today in Mexico, Latin America, and parts of Asia. The second character- istic of members of the working class is that they are segmented by race, ethnicity, gender, religion, and age. For example, Irish were pitted against English workers in British factories and Black workers against Irish in the U.S. workforce. A third characteristic is that the work- ing class must be disciplined. Modeled after prisons, the factory was a central site of con- trol. Through constant supervision, rewards, and punishments, laborers were disciplined in new concepts of work and time with far-reaching implications for the whole society. The culture of capitalism established a distinct orientation to time as ruled by the clock, equated with money, and exploited like commodities and laborers for maximum profit. The fourth characteristic is that members of the working class often resisted the conditions imposed upon them by the capitalist class (Robbins, 2002).

Capitalism and Consumption: Creating the Consumer

By the late 1800s, capitalism had reached a defining moment with panic gripping busi- nesspeople and governments. The construction of the capitalist and labor classes led to the overproduction of goods and economic depression loomed. Thus, in the early 20th century, the consumer was born. The consumer culture that envelops the United States today—a culture where more and bigger is better, where identities and lifestyles are constructed through consumption, and where human value is measured by the acquisition of things— has not always characterized U.S. culture.

> In fact, the culture of nineteenth century America emphasized not unlimited consumption but moderation and self-denial. People, workers in particular, were expected to be frugal and save their money; spending, particularly on luxuries, was seen as "wasteful." People purchased only necessities—basic foodstuffs, clothing, household utensils, and appliances—or shared basic items when they could. (Robbins, 2002, p. 12)

In essence, to accommodate the excess production of goods accomplished through the Industrial Revolution, luxuries had to be transformed into necessities. Novel marketing strategies such as department stores designed for consumer enjoyment were introduced transforming spending from an act of necessity to one of pleasure (Leach, 1993). Advertising in the form of company catalogs, newspaper ads, celebrity promotions, and fashion were all unleashed in the early part of the 20th century constituting the consumer.

INTERCULTURAL PRAXIS
CULTURE AND CONSUMERISM

Using intercultural praxis, we can understand how the construction of the consumer in Western industrial countries, which took about a century, is replicated within decades in much of the rest of the world.

Adiya Mehta (2009) reporting in *Nazar,* a South Asian online magazine, classified Indian consumers into four broad categories. The first group, born before Indian independence in 1947, are reluctant consumers who may even feel guilty enjoying things on a regular basis that were previously considered luxuries. The second group, born between 1947 and 1965, is very frugal saving and recycling consumer products whenever possible. A third group, born from 1965 to 1988, was old enough in 1991 when India opened its economy to see and experience the tremendous social changes that resulted. "They generally believe in working hard and spending hard, and are responsible for the current boom in consumerism. They have no qualms about borrowing and spending money, showing it off, or being materialistic." The fourth group, born since 1988, is described as being:

culturally closer to the developed world and unfortunately will spend like them too once they start earning money in the next three to five years. For instance, most urban kids play less cricket and more video games than the third group. They have tremendous choice in what they want to eat, wear, play with and study. They have add-on credit cards that their parents give them.

Americans had to be socialized through rewards and enticements to consume and the desire for things developed through the culture of capitalism. Dan Neil (2009) of the *Los Angeles Times* noted the following:

Longtime Chairman Alfred Sloan's program of "planned obsolescence"—making annual, often minor changes in the products in such a way as to make last year's mode hopelessly unfashionable—put Americans on the acquisitive treadmill they are panting on yet today. (p. A1)

Institutions such as universities, museums, governmental agencies, and financial organizations also facilitated the advance of consumer capitalism by incorporating education and training on how to market and consume and by extending credit to increase the buying power of consumers (Robbins, 2002).

Capitalism, Corporations, and Global Bodies of Governance

Corporations have their origins in the trading companies of the 17th century, which allowed groups of investors to avoid the risk of individual debt and loss though backing by the nation-state. "Corporations used this power, of course, to create conditions in which they could make money. But in a larger sense, they used this power to define the ideology or ethos of the emerging culture of capitalism" (Robbins, 2002, p. 89). Today, corporations exercise power through campaign contributions, lobbying for legislation such as "free" trade agreements, environmental, health care, and labor policies, as well as military contracts that serve corporate interests and by using the media to influence public opinion (Beaud, 2001).

At the end of WWII, President Roosevelt invited government financial leaders from 44 countries to Bretton Woods, New Hampshire, to lay out plans to rebuild war-torn economies and to insure economic stability. Out of these meetings, three very significant bodies of global governance, with far-reaching implications, were formed: (1) the IMF, established to ease currency exchange across nations, provides short-term loans to member countries that face debt crises; (2) the World Bank (WB) provides loans to developing countries to support economic growth; and (3) the General Agreement on Tariffs and Trade (GATT), later the World Trade Organization (WTO), negotiates free trade agreements and disputes among nations.

While providing needed financial assistances, these financial bodies have forced the integration of recipient countries in Latin America, Asia, Africa, and eastern Europe into the global economy (Stiglitz, 2002). Loans are accompanied by stipulations that require indebted countries to increase exports of designated products and reduce or eliminate support for social services, education, and health care. The IMF and WB admit they have only had limited success. After trillions of dollars in loans, indebtedness in developing nations has increased and the social, economic, and environmental impact of the imposed policies has been devastating (Stiglitz, 2002).

Capitalism, Neoliberalism, and Globalization

At the end of the 20th century, neoliberalism, an economic and political ideology endorsed by Prime Minister Thatcher of England and President Reagan of the United States in the 1980s, dramatically increased the movement of capital, commodities, services, information, and labor around the globe. **Neoliberalism,** or the reassertion of liberal ideologies, advocates reducing state intervention, deregulating all aspects of the market, privatizing public resources, decreasing social protection, and dismantling labor unions (Harvey, 2005). Historically, colonization and military force were used to establish conditions for the accumulation of capital by European and U.S. powers; today, in the context of globalization, political leaders, capital controllers, and global financial institutions such as the IMF, WB, and WTO create conditions for multinational corporations to accumulate capital, exploit mobile labor, and create consumers around the world (Wallerstein, 2000). Corporations benefit from the **surplus value** or the profit that is made by reducing labor costs as they move their manufacturing and assembly sites offshore to countries like Mexico, China, and Indonesia where cheaper labor is available and where few if any labor laws or environmental restrictions exist. Dispossessed of their land and means of production, similar to the Industrial Revolution in Europe, farmers and craftspeople in developing nations have no choice but to seek work in factories at less than living wages. The labor force is segmented or stratified based on various forms of social discrimination—most notable is the increased flow of women into the workforce who are paid lower wages than men (Naples & Desai, 2002). In the logic of capitalism, sexism, racism, bias against immigrants, and exploitation of the working class are profitable.

The historical emergence of capitalism from its embryonic phase in the colonial era to its full-blown manifestation in a globalized world has transformed human culture. As a result, today we live in a vastly unequal world with immensely productive and destructive powers where asymmetrical intercultural interactions and international relationships are the norm. Capitalism, as a continually transforming social logic, integrally shapes and informs U.S. culture and cultures that are touched or engulfed by its catalytic and consuming powers.

THE CULTURE OF CAPITALISM

The culture of capitalism as it has evolved historically in the United States promotes individualism, competitiveness, and the pursuit of personal goals and interests. It encourages an orientation to life where the fundamental purpose and meaning is focused on consumption. In the current culture of capitalism, social relations are structured by consumer relations. Interpersonal relationships are theorized, assessed, and experienced in terms of costs and benefits. Often human relationships are mediated and expressed through commodities, where relationships with people are secondary to relationships with things—the house, car, wedding ring, vacation, credit card, or HDTV. Students see themselves as consumers or customers, term papers and curricula are called "deliverables," universities market themselves as desirable playgrounds, and graduates are encouraged to "brand" themselves to commence into the global job market. The power and control of commodities is not only in the accumulation of things; "the commodity's reign is evident, rather, in the submission to market forces of all aspects of mankind's [sic] life and all aspects of society's functioning" (Beaud, 2001, p. 292).

In capitalist culture, segmentation and stratification of labor as well as consumers is normalized. While the culture of capitalism reinforces and profits from sexism, racism, classism, and other forms of social discrimination, today these deeply embedded systems of inequity are masked and rationalized through the rhetoric of "colorblindness," "cultural difference," and the market logic of capitalism. Due to geographic distance and production fragmentation, no relationship exists between consumers of commodities and those who labor to produce them, which further mystifies the practices that sustain capitalism.

COMMUNICATIVE DIMENSIONS
COMMUNICATION AND IDEOLOGY

"Greed is good," Gordon Gekko proclaimed in the movie *Wall Street* (Stone, 1987). The infamous or now famous phrase exemplifies the values and norms that have shaped U.S. financial markets and culture since the 1980s. The sequel of Wall Street was released in 2010 after the biggest financial crisis since the Great Depression. Mr. Gekko commented on his remark: "Someone reminded me I once said greed is good. Now it seems it's legal."

Our everyday cultural communication is embedded with capitalist ideologies. With a hint of sarcasm, phrases on bumper stickers such as "He who dies with the most toys wins," "When the going gets tough, the tough go shopping," or "Life is short, buy the shoes!" point to the underlying belief in material possessions, wealth, and consumerism.

The following proverbs from different parts of the world also communicate beliefs about the power of money to shape social and cultural realities: "When money speaks, the truth keeps silent" (Russian). "When gold speaks every tongue is silent" (Italian). "The saving man becomes the free man" (Chinese). "One hand full of money is stronger than two full of truth" (Danish).

In the postindustrial capitalist society of the United States, identities are defined through the things we consume. Inundated with marketing strategies aimed at grabbing our attention and coding our sense of self through consumer items and consumable experiences—T-shirts, shoes, cars, computers, package tours, cell phones, accessories, and music—our identities and worldviews are constructed and branded by corporations. For example, are you a PC or a Mac person? We are simultaneously laborers, consumers, products, and advertisements thoroughly articulated in capitalism. The concept of "citizen" in democratic societies is appropriated and conflated with consumer identities with deep-seated implications for democratic participation. Clearly, the values we often identify as U.S. cultural values are deeply intertwined with and influenced by the culture of capitalism as it has emerged historically in this country. We turn now to a look at intercultural dimensions of the contemporary workplace.

INTERCULTURAL COMMUNICATION AT WORK

In the context of globalization, the workplace—in both physical and virtual spaces—has become increasingly diverse and multicultural. In the United States and globally, escalating migration, increased access for nondominant groups, advanced communication, and transportation technologies, as well as policies removing barriers to global business, have accelerated the number and magnitude of intercultural challenges and opportunities in the world of business. Meeting with international clients, managing diverse workplaces, developing global strategies, negotiating multinational contracts, and tapping global markets all entail intercultural communication with vast uncertainty and likelihood of misunderstanding as well as possibilities for learning and growth. For example, communication scholar Prue Cruickshank (2007) noted that today New Zealand is increasingly recruiting skilled workers from China, India, and other parts of Asia, as well as from the Middle East to address the country's skill shortage, to strengthen international connections, and to encourage innovation. Communication barriers including lack of fluency in English, cultural differences, interpersonal skills, and lack of social networks are identified by both immigrants and companies as significant workplace challenges. Today, global strategies developed by international managers must account for differences in cultural environments, make arguments for comparative advantage, and infuse cultural sensitivity in the values and decision making of multinational corporations (Grachev & Bobina, 2007a). The following section offers conceptual frameworks to understand the cultural dimensions of the workplace.

Cultural Dimensions of the Workplace

In the late 1960s, Dutch psychologist Geert Hofstede (1980) was contracted by IBM to conduct research with over 100,000 employees in 40 countries worldwide to identify and understand differences in national cultures and their impact on workplace culture. Based on problems faced by all cultures, four dimensions were identified. In the 1980s, prompted by criticism from researchers that the dimensions failed to address the influences of Confucianism on Eastern cultures, a fifth dimension was added. **Hofstede's** (2001) **cultural dimensions** provide broad maps for comparing national cultures, understanding the impact of national culture on organizations, and developing strategies to address differences. The five dimensions are as follows:

1. **Individualism–collectivism:** Individualistic cultures are ones where the interests of the individual are placed before the interest of the group. Individual identity, personal autonomy, individual rights, and responsibility tend to be valued. Collectivistic cultures tend to focus on the needs, interests, and goals of the group. Individuals are socialized from an early age into cohesive, lifelong in-groups where relational interdependence and harmony within the group are stressed. According to Hofstede's (2001) research, countries in Asia, Latin America, Africa, and the Middle East tend to be collectivist while northern European and North American countries tend to be individualistic.

2. **Power distance:** Power distance is the tendency of individuals with less power in an organization to accept the unequal distribution of power. Small or low power distance cultures tend to emphasize equality, self-initiative, and consultation with subordinates in decision making. Rewards and punishment are expected to be distributed equitably based on individual merit and performance. On the other hand, high power distance cultures tend to accept unequal status among members, respect those in higher status positions, and expect managers or authority figures to make decisions. High power distance cultures reward age, rank, and status.

3. **Uncertainty avoidance:** Uncertainty avoidance refers to the tendency to feel threatened by the unknown and the inclination to steer clear of such situations. High uncertainty avoidance cultures tend to be more formal and rule oriented while low uncertainty avoidance cultures tend to be more informal and less structured. In high uncertainty avoidance cultures, innovation is less acceptable, and conflict is seen as a threat to both group harmony and effectiveness. Low uncertainty avoidance cultures tend to encourage new and creative approaches.

4. **Masculinity–femininity:** According to Hofstede's (2001) dimensions, masculinity refers to societies that emphasize distinct differences in gender roles between men and

women. On the other hand, femininity refers to cultures where gender roles overlap and the gender characteristics are shared. Sensitivity to distinct and complementary gender role norms and rules as well as a focus on work-related achievements and results is important in masculine organizational culture. Flexible and interchangeable gender norms and balancing work/life, community, and environmental issues is important in feminine organizational cultures.

5. **Confucian dynamism:** This dimension addresses cultural characteristics of East Asian countries such as persistence and long-term orientation to time, the importance of status, thriftiness, and collective face-negotiation strategies. The tremendous economic growth of Singapore, Taiwan, Japan, Hong Kong, and Korea in the 1990s and of China at the beginning of the 21st century is often attributed to Confucian values of perseverance, hard work, frugality, respect for elders, and hierarchical structures.

Hofstede's (2001) cultural dimensions have found wide application in international and intercultural organizational settings including the areas of decision making, employee compensation and benefits, negotiation, and work teams. For example, the cultural dimension of low to high uncertainty avoidance points to types of compensation preferred by employees, which assists employers in managerial decisions (Rogovsky & Schuler, 1997). Low uncertainty avoidance cultures tend to prefer higher level pay-for-performance compensation with limited benefits while high uncertainty cultures prefer seniority-based compensation with generous benefit packages. In addition, autonomy in work roles and tasks is more highly valued in individualistic, low power distance, low uncertainty avoidance, and low masculine cultures and therefore, serves more effectively in these cultures to motivate employees.

More recent research conducted by GLOBE (Global Leadership and Organizational Behavior Effectiveness) has been used by over 170 researchers in 62 countries to investigate the interrelationship among societal culture, organizational culture, and leadership (House, Hanges, Javidan, Dorfman, & Gupta, 2004). About 17,000 middle managers in telecommunication, financial services, and food processing industries responded to questionnaires aimed at assessing cultural values and cultural practices based on nine cultural dimensions. Six of the nine **GLOBE dimensions** are similar to those offered by Hofstede (2001) addressing institutional and group collectivism, gender egalitarianism, power distance, uncertainty avoidance, and future orientation. The remaining three include **assertiveness,** or the degree to which individuals in organizations or societies are assertive and confrontational; **performance orientation,** which indicates the extent to which an organization/society rewards and encourages members for their quality of performance and level of involvement; and **humane orientation,** which refers to the degree to which an organization/society rewards people for being fair, generous, and kind to others (House et al., 2004). Rankings using these dimensions allow researchers to cluster countries according to high levels of similarity and distance as show in Figure 8.1. Cultural similarity is higher among societies within a cluster. Cultural difference is higher the farther the clusters are from each other on the chart.

Grachev and Bobina (2007b) argued that conceptual frameworks outlined by Hofstede and GLOBE provide managers in multinational corporations with knowledge about both

Figure 8.1   Country Clusters According to GLOBE

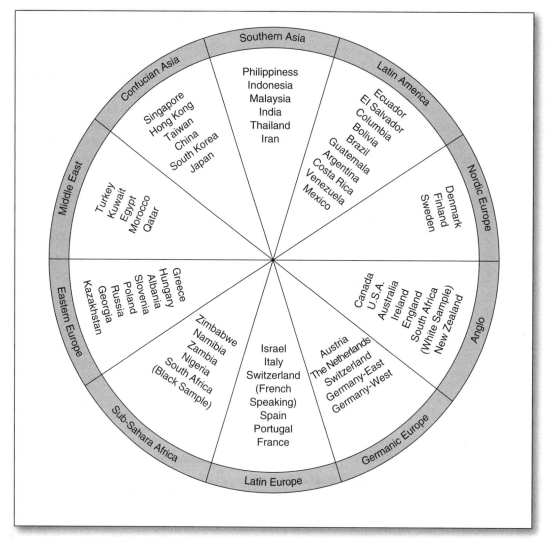

Source: House et al. (2004).

host and home cultures, offer tools to compare and cluster cultural groups, and provide rationale for strategic decision making that enable them to avoid cultural challenges while maximizing cultural advantages.

While Hofstede's (2001) cultural dimensions have been regarded positively within management research and have been used widely in international management, critics point out that data gathered in the late 1960s and early 1970s as well as foundational assumptions may be outdated. Given the complexities of intercultural interactions in the 21st century, the diversity of cultural tendencies within nations and the dramatic geopolitical shifts that have occurred particularly in the last 30 years, frameworks of cultural variation based on national culture such as Hofstede's dimensions, and the GLOBE program can lead to overgeneralization and stereotyping. International management scholar David Thomas (2008) argued that "the ability to profile national cultures along a limited number of dimensions also opens up the possibility for a dramatic oversimplification of the effect of culture" (p. 68). As noted throughout the book, there are many subcultures and cultural variations within national cultures. Often sophisticated stereotypes of national cultures substitute for multifaceted cultural realities limiting rather than explaining the effects of culture on human interaction. While typologies of cultural variation may provide a first yet limited step toward understanding difference in the intercultural business environments, attention to situational contexts and cultural histories is needed (Osland & Bird, 2000).

Managing Diversity, Multicultural Teams, and Virtual Teams

Managing "diversity" in the workplace, ubiquitous today in multicultural organization and corporate boardrooms, was a new idea in the 1990s. With roots in the Affirmative Action and Equal Opportunity Employment policies of the 1970s, the notion of managing diversity attempts to move beyond numbers and quotas for the inclusion of nondominant groups toward recognizing diversity as a resource (R. Thomas, 1990).

Early research categorized organizations based on their approaches and strategies for addressing diversity. Powell (1993) noted that some organizations approach diversity in the workplace through benign neglect, where issues of diversity are ignored. Some organizations are reactive, responding when necessary to conflicts or lawsuits, while other organizations take a proactive approach to diversity by developing strategies to address challenges and maximize the benefit of a diverse workforce. Jackson (2006) argued that multicultural organizational development (MCOD) requires systemic intervention to eradicate social injustice in all forms. The goal of MCOD is to create an inclusive organizational culture that maximizes access and input from members across all socially defined categories of difference (see Figure 8.2, next page).

In the global context, working effectively in multicultural and multinational teams has become a priority as multinational organizations penetrate deeper into distant markets and as workplaces become increasingly diverse. **Multicultural teams** are defined as task-oriented groups composed of members from different national and ethnic groups. Today, the complexity of jobs is increasing exponentially requiring more coordination and cooperation of people working in groups. Compression of space and time accelerated by advances in technologies and the removal of trade barriers in the global context translate into work groups that are increasingly culturally diverse.

D. Thomas (2008) noted that the cultural composition of work groups impacts group effectiveness in three interrelated ways: (1) cultural norms about how work groups function and how they are structured; (2) cultural diversity, or the number of different cultures in the group; and (3) relative cultural distance, or the degree to which members of the group are culturally different from one another. Individuals bring mental maps, metaphors, and scripts to group work and use these to make sense of behaviors, events, tasks,

Figure 8.2 The Multicultural Organizational Development Model

Monocultural		Transitional		Multicultural	
Exclusionary	Passive Club	Compliance	Positive Action	Redefining	Multicultural
Committed to the dominance, values and norms of one group. Actively excludes in its mission and practices those who are not members of the dominant group.	Actively or passively excludes those who are not members of the dominant group. Includes other members only if they "fit" the dominant norm.	Passively committed to include others without making major changes. Includes only a few members of other groups.	Committed to making a special effort to include others, especially those in designed protected "classes." Tolerates the differences that others bring.	Actively works to expand its definition of inclusion, diversity and equity. Tries to examine and change practices that may act as barriers to members of non-dominant groups.	Actively includes a diversity of people representing different groups' styles and perspectives. Continuously learns and acts to make the systemic changes required to value, include and be fair to all kinds of people.
Values and promotes the dominant perspective of one group, culture or style.		Seeks to integrate others into systems created under dominant norms.		Values and integrates the perspectives of diverse identities, cultures, styles and groups into the organization's work and system.	

Source: Holvino © 2008 Chaos Management, Ltd.

expectations, and other group members. For example, in one study, people from more collectivistic cultures tended to use metaphors of the family with clearly defined roles to describe the work group, whereas those from individualistic cultures tended to use metaphors such as sports teams, where membership is voluntary and team goals were clear (Gibson & Zellmer-Brunh, 2001).

Cultural diversity, which often manifests as differences in perceptions, communication styles, and patterns, tends to increase the time required for multicultural groups to complete tasks and initially lower performance rates as compared to homogeneous groups. However, over time, greater cultural diversity can also increase creativity and broaden the group's perspectives and resources resulting in higher quality decision making. In brainstorming, ethnically diverse groups have been shown to generate more creative, high-quality ideas, and diverse teams are more effective than homogeneous teams in identifying problems and producing solutions (Matveen & Nelson, 2004). Yet relative cultural distance between group members has proven to affect members' assessment of group cohesion, their satisfaction, their interpretation of conflicts, and members' willingness to express ideas (D. Thomas, 2008).

In the context of globalization, work groups with members who are geographically dispersed and who rely on technology-mediated communication are referred to as **virtual teams** (Gibson & Cohen, 2003). Across time zones, national borders, and cultural frames, virtual teams use a wide variety of technologies to bridge potentially vast differences and discontinuities. For example, in an Internet technology firm with half of its 1,200 employees in the United States and half in Israel, the company's California-based director of human resources says, "People in Tel Aviv asked me why their U.S. counterparts would sometimes seem upset by email exchanges" (Snyder, 2003). Israelis who tend to be very direct in their communication sent e-mails that seemed "rude" and "blunt" to their U.S. counterparts. On the other hand, e-mails sent by U.S. employees were interpreted as "wishy washy" by the Israelis. Realizing that a relatively minor communication difference could escalate into conflict that would impact the effectiveness of the virtual team, an Israeli-born consultant worked with U.S. employees to understand Israeli communication styles. The U.S.-based employees learned to be more direct and less offended by the short, assertive communication style of Israeli employees.

Based on in-depth qualitative and quantitative research on virtual teams across national and organizational cultures, Gibson and Manuel (2003) emphasized that trust is critical. Many factors that contribute to building and repairing trust such as proximity, similarities in background and experience, as well as interpersonal affective cues are lacking in virtual interactions. While cultural differences are identified as a significant impediment to building trust, using communication to create a supportive climate, engaging in active listening, being aware of differences in communication styles such as implicit and explicit communication, empathizing or taking the other person's frame of reference, and offering constructive feedback can improve the effectiveness of virtual teams. Notions of "trust"—what behaviors and attitudes are needed to develop, maintain, and repair it—also vary across cultures.

It is fairly likely that you work in a diverse workplace, have participated at one time or another in multicultural teams, and have faced challenges communicating with others in the workplace. In order to facilitate more effective working relationships, we can increase our awareness of cultural differences; establish group norms for communicating; and build trust among work group members by learning about each others' cultural histories, experiences of discrimination or exclusion, values, assumptions, and practices. Additionally, a focus on balancing the task at hand with relational needs can enhance productivity, creativity, and intercultural understanding. Next we examine issues related to the intercultural marketplace.

THE INTERCULTURAL MARKETPLACE AND ECONOMIC RESPONSIBILITY

Today, cultural experiences—from music, cuisine, art, and sports to religious holidays, weddings, bar mitzvahs, and funerals, as well as cities and communities—are commodified. The **commodification of culture** refers to the ways cultural experiences—local practices, festivals, arts, rituals, and even groups—are produced and consumed for the market. As cultural practices and cultural groups circulate within the logic of capitalism, they become sites of contestation. Both constrained and propelled by market forces, cultural commodification gives rise to questions of authenticity, appropriation, identity, and resistance. Journalist Jeremy Rifkin (2001) wrote this in the *Los Angeles Times:*

> A great transformation is occurring in the nature of capitalism. After hundreds of years of converting physical resources into goods, the primary means of generating wealth now involves transforming cultural resources into paid-for personal experiences and entertainments. (para 1)

Commodification of Culture

Today, culture is a product that is invented, packaged, and consumed. The marketability of cultural practices, objects, and groups frequently depends upon the ways in which they embody difference—difference from the dominant consumer culture. "It has been argued that under conditions of globalization, difference rather than homogenization infuses the prevailing logic of accumulation" (Yúdice, 2003, p. 28). This "difference" between the culture that is commodified and those who consume it must be constructed as "real," offering the consumer a taste of the authentic and exotic. When the dynamics of cultural commodification are in motion, representations of cultures are often "fixed" or "frozen" in the past, perpetuating stereotypical and limiting images of the cultural Other. Let's take a look at a case study that examines the commodification of cultural forms made by Pueblo and Navajo women in New Mexico (Sorrells, 2002).

For generations, Pueblo and Navajo women have represented themselves and their cultures through their pottery and weaving, respectively. Pueblo women gather the earth around them molding vessels that hold their culture as well as represent the complex intercultural interactions that characterize the colonial history of New Mexico. Navajo women collect material from their environment transforming it into weavings that tell cultural stories of the Navajo people as well as visually depict the dynamics of power in the Southwest region of the United States. Today, in upscale galleries in Santa Fe and well-publicized street markets, in gas stations and curio shops, and on websites accessible around the world, Pueblo pottery and Navajo weavings are packaged, bought, and sold as iconic representations of these cultural groups and of New Mexico.

In face-to-face "sales" interactions, the most common questions Pueblo potters and Navajo weavers receive from consumers or tourists are, "Did you make these?" "Are they made by hand?" and "Are they traditional?" Emma Yepa (personal communication, April 23, 1999) from Jemez Pueblo said that sometimes when she makes her more contemporary designs, customers ask her to make them more traditional: "We want more tradition. And I say, 'This is traditional.' You know?. . .You're telling me what is tradition and what is not." The commodification of indigenous cultural forms in New Mexico is not new. Anthropologist Evelyn Hatcher (1967) observed that by the early 1900s Navajo weavings showed "the Indian's idea of the trader's idea of what the white man thought was Indian design" (p. 174).

In the early part of the 20th century, the successful commodification of New Mexico's cultures depended upon creating an image of an exotic and unusual yet safe place to consume the Other. Ambivalence and anxiety toward cultural difference—the combination of fear and fascination—was neutralized and palatably packaged for tourists from the eastern United States to purchase a glimpse of the exotic (Howard & Pardue, 1996). Through advertisements, museum exhibits, and scholarship, an idealized view of the "picturesque," the "authentic," and the "spiritual" aspects of indigenous cultures was constructed and touted as offering aesthetic, moral, and spiritual salvation from the depravities of contemporary life.

Thus, New Mexico was reimagined and re-created to present a "romantic" image with a distinctive regional and cultural identity. Through their articulation into the marketplace, Pueblo pottery and Navajo weavings are viewed as symbols or signs of their respective cultures. Yet the creative forms are as much a representation of the dominant culture's notion of the Other as they are representations of the cultures for which they are marketed. Difference, or Otherness, from the dominant group is what signifies and sells (Hall, 1997). The stereotypes of Indian people as "quaint," "primitive," and "traditional" produced through processes of commodification reduce the complexity of individuals and groups to easily identifiable and often denigrating characteristics.

The "cultural" art created by Pueblo and Navajo women is a contested site where issues of representation, identity, and notions of tradition are negotiated and transformed. Even as difference is marketed as exotic and enticing for the consumption of the dominant culture (hooks, 1992), women artists in New Mexico exert personal, cultural, and economic agency as they challenge the restrictive stereotypes and characterizations as the Other.

The commodification of cultures often creates barriers for intercultural communication. As anthropologist Dean McCannell (1976) argued, commodification of cultural symbols "represents an end to the dialogue, a final freezing of ethnic imagery which is both artificial and deterministic" (p. 375). When consumers from nonnative cultures demand that cultural forms of representation fit their notions of what Indian art is, a superficial level of engagement is established that can preclude intercultural exchange. The relationship is defined by and often limited to the consumption of one group by another within a system of inequitable power. What could be a space for intercultural connection—the shared appreciation of beauty between consumer and artist, the recognition of struggle and survival in a changing world, and the layering of cultural influences manifest in artistic forms—is frequently reduced to a monetary exchange. Travel to new places, whether international or domestic, offers incredible opportunities for intercultural communication. Yet the ways cultures, communities, and cultural spaces have been commodified through the logic of capitalism often works against intercultural exchange and genuine intercultural dialogue. As Yúdice (2003) noted, in the context of globalization, culture plays a greater role today than in the past because of the ways it is linked to local and transnational economies and politics. Culture, as it is commodified in the marketplace, is a resource that is exploited for economic and political power and agency.

Tourism and Intercultural Communication

In 2010, the global travel industry generated over $877 billion. Despite economic slowdowns, the industry projects an increase of 4% annually until 2019 (United Nations World Tourism Organization [UNWTO], 2010). Approximately 20% of annual travel is by young people, predominantly students, from the ages of 15 to 25, which represents a huge market to which governments and tourist industries target their appeals (UNWTO, 2008). Comparing attitudes and behaviors of student tourists across cultures, researchers found that undergraduate students from the United Kingdom and China had similar interests in beach holidays, sampling local foods, and discovering new places and both preferred to travel in groups (Xu, Morgan, & Song, 2008). Chinese students, however, thought it was more important to visit famous sights, learn about the history and culture, and experience the natural scenery. British students, on the other hand, were more interested in having fun, socializing, shopping, finding entertainment, and enjoying outside adventures. How can we explain these differences? The researchers suggest that differences in the tourism markets, economic conditions, and access to financial resources in the two countries combine with more deeply rooted cultural differences to explain the variation in behaviors and attitudes between Chinese and British students. Drawing on Hofstede's dimensions of individualism/collectivism, power distance, and long-term orientation provides some explanation for the differences in behaviors and attitudes. Yet current conditions such as access to travel and to natural environments as well as sources of funding (British students tended to fund their own trips through part-time work while Chinese students were supported by their families) may explain the differences in attitudes and behaviors regarding travel for the two groups (Xu et al., 2008).

Travel can provide opportunities for intercultural engagement, learning about the unknown and appreciation of the different ways human beings around the world live and make sense of their lives. Yet today, tourists increasingly choose options that limit their exposure and access to the very places they pay to visit. Pat Thomas (2009), British editor of the *Ecologist,* observed the following:

> Most of us are not travelers at all—as vulnerable to processes of commodification as the places we visit. . . . The smaller the world gets, the more we seem to want it to be as much like home as possible (but with cleaner sheets and towels and without the washing up). (p.2)

According to surveys administered by Halifax Travel Insurance, British tourists on international vacations spent less than 8 hours a week outside of the hotel; three quarters of the 2,000 surveyed made no effort to learn the local language, and 70% never visited a local attraction (P. Thomas, 2009). Like tourists to New Mexico in the early 1900s, package tours to Spain for the British and to Jamaica or Mexico for U.S. tourists offer exotic yet often limited and sanitized experiences of the cultural Other. In addition to questioning the goal of looking for "home" when one travels, which often precludes intercultural exchange, it is important to note finding "home" when traveling (in the sense of finding what is familiar from your culture around the world) is not even an option for much of the world. Today, the cultural and economic hegemony of the West is experienced in contradictory ways by Western tourists. On the one hand, Western tourists desire and often demand the familiarity of "home," yet simultaneously, complaints abound that other cultures are too "Americanized," too "Westernized," or too much like home.

Tourism is one of the world's largest industries employing more than 258 million people worldwide (World Travel & Tourism Council, 2011). TV, magazine, and Internet ads; billboards; and travelogues present tourism as good for local economies. The travel industry purports that tourism brings in foreign capital, provides jobs, and preserves local cultures. Undoubtedly, international tourism is a source of foreign capital for many economies around the world; in cases like Mexico, tourism is a significant economic resource. Yet slick advertisements that display cultural and natural resources in alluring and desirable ways gloss over the economic, environmental, and social conditions just below the surface. Vying for the attention of consumers, city, state, and national governments collaborate with the tourist industry to offer ever-growing enticements, which frequently draw on natural and cultural resources as exotic, titillating, and romantic. In his book *The Society of the Spectacle*, Guy Debord (1973) introduced the concept of the **spectacle** to refer to the domination of media images and consumer society over the individual, which obscures the conditions and effects of capitalism. Seduced through leisure, entertainment, and consumption, the spectacle serves to pacify and depoliticize society. Happiness and fulfillment are found through consumption of commodities and spectacles.

In his analysis of the Mardi Gras celebration in New Orleans, urban studies scholar Kevin Gotham (2002) illustrated the impact of transforming cultural practices and urban spaces into spectacles. Mardi Gras—wild parties, exotic costumes, masked marauders, spectacular floats, lots of skin, nudity, and much more—is marketed as a once-in-a-lifetime "cultural" experience not to be missed. While Mardi Gras celebrations have taken place in New Orleans since 1857, the reasons for the celebration and the meanings associated with it have changed tremendously. Originally, Mardi Gras was a celebration of Lent created for and by locals, existing outside the logic of market exchange and capital circulation. Today, Mardi Gras is extensively marketed and promoted as part of a broader strategy to increase tourism to the city of New Orleans. Year-round, local, and national companies produce and sell paraphernalia that promote the celebration as a site of desire and fantasy. Divorced from its religious roots and reconstituted as part of Sin City's advertising package, many locals feel the celebration has been devalued (Gotham, 2002).

Corporate and trade conventions are scheduled at the time of the celebration; international media including crews from the BBC, Japan, and Playboy package the celebration for a global audience. Corporations like Bacardi, Coors, and Kool use their Mardi Gras–themed advertisements not only to sell their products during the celebration but as a means to shape their brand image nationally. As noted by Debord (1973), the process of commodifying areas of social life such as culture, religion, and leisure trivializes and destroys them. Mardi Gras, originally a celebration of rich and deeply rooted religious and cultural symbolism, is now leveraged to expand capitalism, remake desires, boost demand, and cultivate new needs (Gotham, 2002). When themes, motifs, and cultural symbols are created and circulated in ways that are easily identifiable by consumers, the commodity—in this case the cultural experience of Mardi Gras—has sign value, in addition to exchange and use value. **Sign value** (Gottdiener, 2000) is the symbolic value of commodities conveying social meaning and social positioning within the political economy of late capitalism.

Over 100 years ago, Karl Marx argued that when commodities are endowed with powers such as status, success, fame, and identity in a process of **fetishization,** the underlying social relations that govern the production and exchange of commodities are hidden or masked (Gottdiener, 2000). In this case, the marketing and consumption of Mardi Gras serves both to accumulate profits for commercial interests and at the same time constructs demands for and attempts to satisfy the tourists' desires for experiences—experiences that satisfy needs for self-expression and identity. Yet the fetishization of commodities and the spectacle society hide the exploitation of labor, damage to the environment, and the impact on culture that make them possible. In the case of New Orleans, tremendous social problems including population flight, loss of jobs, increased racial segregation, and poverty have accompanied the city's move from an industrial site to a tourist destination (Gotham, 2002). Mardi Gras—now celebrated in many cities in the United States and around the world—illustrates the global market for cultural experiences made possible through the exploitation of labor, culture, and the environment within inequitable relations of power.

Economic Responsibility and Intercultural Communication

U.S. Americans, 4.6% of the world's population, accounted for 33% of the global consumption. The 1 billion residents of high income countries consumed more than 80% of the global total. The 2.3 billion residents of low income countries consumed less than 3% (Cassara, 2007). Today, more than one fifth of the world's population lives on the brink of hunger and death. Spread of disease, degradation of the environment, exploitation of workers, global conflicts, and militarization impact the lives of billions of people daily. Robbins (2002) argued the following:

> Our analysis suggests that the root of these problems is the central and unarguable tenet of the culture of capitalism—the need and desire for perpetual economic growth. Each of the major elements of this culture—the consumer, the laborer, the capitalist and the nation-state—has a vested interest in the production and consumption of ever more goods and services. (p. 365)

Global problems are most often framed as economic ones, and solutions are proposed through financial means. Yet overlooked in the analysis is the central role of culture—the shared and contested beliefs, values, norms, and practices of the culture of late capitalism. As noted earlier, the values and practices of conspicuous consumption and perpetual growth are actually quite new to much of the world and only about seven decades old in the United States—the country most identified with consumer culture (Nandy, 2004). Given that the culture of capitalism has been constructed by people through historical processes, it can also be challenged and changed. Resistance to the culture of capitalism has been an important factor in history and continues today throughout the world in local sites and in national and international movements (George, 2004). Discussion of alter-globalization movements and resistance to global capitalism are addressed in the following two chapters. However, at this point, it is useful to think about our role in the culture of capitalism and consider what steps, small as they may seem, we can take toward changing a culture that promotes economic, political, social, and cultural injustice as well as threatens the sustainability of our home—planet Earth. Here are four steps you can take to get started:

1. Observe your consumption patterns.
   - Keep a journal of the things you purchase.
   - Note where you shop.
   - Note where the goods—things, entertainment, and experiences—are produced.

2. Educate yourself about the circumstances and impact.
   - As a consumer: Find out about the working conditions of the people who make the goods you consume; engage in dialogue with the people who provide services for you while on vacation or when consuming a cultural experience.
   - As a laborer/worker: Learn about the relationship between owners and workers in your organization/corporation; educate yourself about the norms, behaviors, and attitudes that have enabled the success (or lack of it) of your company/organization.
   - As a capitalist: If you have a savings account, investments, stocks, or other means of making money from money, learn about how this works.

3. Act responsibly based on your knowledge.
   - Make conscious and responsible consumer choices: For example, when you find out that the megastore where you prefer to shop is only able to provide such low prices because of exploitative labor and unsustainable environmental practices, seek out alternatives.
   - Transform sites of consumption into sites for intercultural praxis: Along with purchasing an object or experience, actively engage in intercultural dialogue.
   - Act to challenge inequities in the workplace.

4. Join others in challenging inequity and injustice.
   - Consider your spheres of influence: Make a point of talking with others about your decisions, and find others who support your values of social and economic responsibility.
   - Join consumer groups or activist organizations: One of the greatest losses of advanced capitalist societies is human connection, engagement with others, and civic contributions. Join or start your own group that creates alternatives and challenges the dehumanizing conditions of the culture of capitalism.

SUMMARY

In the context of globalization, everything, including culture, has been commodified. This chapter focused on the pivotal yet often unacknowledged linkages between intercultural communication and capitalism in the global context. The purpose of the overview of the culture of capitalism was threefold: The first goal was to situate the culture of capitalism historically to understand how we find ourselves where we are today; the second aim was to unmask what is seen as "normal" and "just the way things are" by revealing the values, assumptions, and ideologies that underlie and constitute the culture of capitalism; the third purpose was to understand how the culture of capitalism impacts intercultural interactions. Cultural dimensions in the workplace as well as trends in managing "diversity," multicultural teams, and virtual teams were reviewed to understand the challenges and benefits of an increasingly diverse workforce. Additionally, we explored the commodification of culture, tourism, and the production and consumption of cultural Others. The final section offered steps to move toward increased economic and social responsibility as intercultural actors in the global context.

KEY TERMS

capitalism	Confucian dynamism
use value	GLOBE dimensions
exchange value	assertiveness
mercantilism	performance orientation
neoliberalism	humane orientation
surplus value	multicultural teams
Hofstede's cultural dimensions	virtual teams
individualism–collectivism	commodification of culture
power distance	spectacle
uncertainty avoidance	sign value
masculinity–femininity	fetishization

DISCUSSION QUESTIONS AND ACTIVITIES

Discussion Questions

1. What are the trends in "managing" diversity at the workplace today? How do you think the cultural diversity you (and your coworkers) add to your workplace is "managed"?

2. How is diversity approached in the culture of capitalism? Is diversity profitable, or is it a barrier to capitalist development?

3. In the culture of capitalism, how are identities commodified? What does it mean when identity is commodified, and how does it influence intercultural communication?

4. What are the differences among use value, exchange value, and sign value? Think about a relatively expensive purchase you made recently; which type of value does the product most have?

5. What does it mean when cultural experiences are commodified? Discuss examples of how we produce, sell, and/or purchase our experiences.

6. What is fetishization? Discuss examples of how people give symbolic power to commodities.

Activities

1. Watch the documentary *The Corporation* (Achbar & Abbott, 2005), and discuss the following questions:

   a. What is the relationship between the corporation and commodification of culture?

   b. What is the relationship between the corporation and globalization?

   c. How does neoliberalism shape the corporate business practices across the world?

   d. Do you think the goal of corporations to accumulate wealth can coexist with economic responsibility and sustainable economy?

2. Watch the documentary *Wal-Mart: The High Cost of Low Price* (Greenwald, 2005), and discuss the following questions:

   a. What did you find most problematic about Walmart's business practices?

   b. How do Walmart's business practices impact local cultures?

   c. How do you think Walmart deals with issues of diversity? How does "culture" matter in their business goals?

   d. What can you do to become a more economically responsible consumer?

3. Exploring Economic Responsibility:

   a. Keep a list of things you purchased for a week, including the price, store, manufacturer, and the location of production.

   b. Based on your list, discuss the following questions:

      i. What did you learn about yourself as a consumer?

      ii. What can you learn about the culture of capitalism from your list?

      iii. How does the culture of capitalism affect intercultural communication?

      iv. How is your identity connected to or expressed by what you consume?

      v. What would you change in your consumer activity in order for you to become a more economically responsible consumer?

REFERENCES

Achbar, M., & Abbott, J. (Directors). (2005). *The corporation* [Motion picture]. New York: Zeitgeist Films.

Ackerman, P., & Duvall, J. (2000). *A force more powerful: A century of nonviolent conflict.* New York: Palgrave.

Beaud, M. (2001). *A history of capitalism: 1500-2000* (5th ed.). New York: Monthly Review.

Cassara, A. (2007). How much of the world's resource consumption occurs in rich countries? *EarthTrends.* Retrieved from http://www.globalpolicy.org/component/content/article/212-environment/45393-how-much-of-the-worlds-resource-consumption-occurs-in-rich-countries.html

Cruickshank, P. (2007). Immigrant diversity and communication practices in the New Zealand business sector. *Business Communication Quarterly,* 87–92.

Debord, G. (1973). *The society of the spectacle.* New York: Zone Books.

George, S. (2004). *Another world is possible if . . .* London: Verso.

Gibson, C. B., & Cohen, S. G. (Eds.). (2003). *Virtual teams that work: Creating conditions for virtual team effectiveness.* San Francisco: Jossey-Bass.

Gibson, C. B., & Manuel, J. A. (2003). Building trust: Effective multicultural communication processes in virtual teams. In C. B. Gibson & S. G. Cohen (Eds.), *Virtual teams that work: Creating conditions for virtual team effectiveness* (pp. 59–86). San Francisco: Jossey-Bass.

Gibson, C. B., & Zellmer-Bruhn, M. E. (2001). Metaphors and meaning: An intercultural analysis of the concept of teamwork. *Administrative Science Quarterly, 46,* 274–303.

Gotham, K. (2002). Marketing Mardi Gras: Commodification, spectacle and the political economy of tourism in New Orleans. *Urban Studies, 29*(10), 1735–1756.

Gottdiener, M. (2000). Approaches to consumption: Classical and contemporary perspectives. In M. Gottdiener (Ed.), *New forms of consumption* (pp. 3–31). Lanham, MD: Rowman & Littlefield.

Grachev, M. V., & Bobina, M. A. (2007a). Culture-sensitive global strategies. In C. Wankel (Ed.), *21st century management: A reference handbook* (pp. 376–385). Thousand Oaks, CA: Sage.

Grachev, M. V., & Bobina, M. A. (2007b). Intercultural collaboration: Instrumentality of the GLOBE study. In T. Ishida, S. Fussel, & P. Vossen (Eds.), *Intercutlural collaboration* (pp. 382–393). Berlin: Springer.

Greenwald, R. (Producer/Director). (2005). *Wal-Mart: The high cost of low price* [Motion picture]. Culver City, CA: Brave New Films.

Hall, S. (1997). Introduction. In S. Hall (Ed.), *Representation: Cultural representations and signifying practices* (pp. 1–45). Thousand Oaks, CA: Sage.

Harvey, D. (2005). *A brief history of neoliberalism.* New York: Oxford University.

Hatcher, E. P. (1967). *Visual metaphors: A methodological study in visual communication.* Albuquerque: University of New Mexico.

Hofstede, G. (1980). *Culture's consequences: International differences in work-related values.* Beverly Hills, CA: Sage.

Hofstede, G. (2001). *Culture's consequences: Comparing values, behaviors, institutions, and organizations across nations* (2nd ed.). Thousand Oaks, CA: Sage.

Holvino, E. (2008). *Multicultural organizational development model.* Retrieved from http://www.chaosmanagement .com/images/stories/pdfs/MCODmodel.pdf

hooks, b. (1992). *Black looks: Race and representation.* Boston: South End.

House, R. J., Hanges, P. J., Javidan, M., Dorfman, P. W., & Gupta, V. (2004). *Culture, leadership and organizations: The GLOBE study of 62 societies.* Thousand Oaks, CA: Sage.

Howard, K. H., & Pardue, D. F. (1996). *Inventing the Southwest: The Fred Harvey Company and Native American art.* Flagstaff, AZ: Northland.

International Labour Office. (2011). *Global employment trends 2011: The challenge of a jobs recovery.* Geneva: International Labour Organization. Retrieved from http://www.ilo.org/wcmsp5/groups/public/@dgreports/@ dcomm/@publ/documents/publication/wcms_150440.pdf

International Monetary Fund. (2009). *The implications of the global financial crisis for low-income countries.* Retrieved from http://imf.org/external/pubs/ft/books/2009/globalfin/globalfin.pdf

Jackson, B. W. (2006). Theory and practice of multicultural organizational development. In B. B. Jones & M. Brazzel (Eds.), *The NTL handbook of organization development and change* (pp. 139–154). San Francisco: Pfeiffer.

Leach, W. (1993). *Land of desire: Merchants, power, and the rise of a new American culture.* New York: Pantheon.

Lui, M., Robles, B., Leondar-Wright, B., Brewer, R., & Adamson, R. (2006). *The color of wealth: The story behind the U.S. racial wealth divide.* New York: New Press.

Matveen, A. V., & Nelson, P. E. (2004). Cross cultural communication competence and multicultural team performance. *International Journal of Cross Cultural Management, 4*(2), 253–270.

McCannell, D. (1976). *A new theory of the leisure class*. New York: Shocken Books.

Metha, A. (2009, February). Consumerism in India. *Nazar: A South Asian perspective*. Retrieved from http://nazaronline.net/travel-living/2009/02/consumerism-in-india/

Nandy, A. (2004). Consumerism: Its hidden beauties and politics. In F. Jandt (Ed.), *Intercultural communication: A global reader* (pp. 400–403). Thousand Oaks, CA: Sage.

Naples, N. A., & Desai, M. (2002). *Women's activism and globalization*. New York: Routledge.

Neil, D. (2009, June 1). When cars were America's idols. *Los Angeles Times*, p. A1.

Osland, J. S., & Bird, A. (2000). Beyond sophisticated stereotypes: Cultural sense-making in context. *Academy of Management Executive, 14*, 65–79.

Powell, G. (1993). Promoting equal opportunity and valuing cultural diversity. In G. Powell (Ed.), *Women and men in management* (pp. 225–252). Thousand Oaks, CA: Sage.

Ridgeway, J. (2004). *It's all for sale: The control of global resources*. Durham, NC: Duke University Press.

Rifkin, J. (2000, January, 17). The new capitalism is about turning culture into commerce. *Los Angeles Times*. Retrieved from http://www.uni-muenster.de/PeaCon/dgs-mills/mills-texte/Rifkin-Hypercapitalism.htm

Robbins, R. H. (2002). *Global problems and the culture of capitalism*. Boston, MA: Allyn & Bacon.

Rogovsky, N., & Schuler, R. (1997). Managing human resources across cultures. *Business and Contemporary World, IX*(1), 63–75.

Sorrells, K. (2002). Embodied negotiation: Commodification and cultural representation in the U.S. Southwest. In M. J. Collier (Ed.), *Intercultural alliances: International and intercultural communication annual, 25,* (pp. 17–47). Thousand Oaks, CA: Sage.

Stiglitz, J. (2002). *Globalization and its discontents*. New York: W.W. Norton.

Stone, O. (Director). (1987). *Wall street* [Motion picture]. United States: 20th Century Fox.

Snyder, B. (2003). Teams that span time zones face new work rules. *Stanford Business*. Retrieved from http://www.gsb.stanford.edu/news/bmag/sbsm0305/feature_virtual_teams.shtml

Thomas, D. (2008). *Cross-cultural management: Essential concepts*. Thousand Oaks, CA: Sage.

Thomas, P. (2009, February). The trouble with travel. *Geographic*. Retrieved from www.geographical.co.uk

Thomas, R. R. (1990). From affirmative action to affirming diversity. *Harvard Business Review, 68,* 107–117.

Tomlinson, J. (1999). *Globalization and culture*. Cambridge, UK: Blackwell.

UNICEF. (2009). *The state of the world's children*. Retrieved from http://www.childinfo.org/files/The_State_of_the_Worlds_Children_2009.pdf

United Nations World Tourism Organization. (2008). *Youth travel matters*. Retrieved from http://pub.unwto.org/WebRoot/Store/Shops/Infoshop/482C/09E7/89D4/2506/AA82/C0A8/0164/F5B4/080514_youth_travel_matters_excerpt.pdf

United Nations World Tourism Organization. (2010). *Facts and figures*. Retrieved from http://unwto.org/en/about/tourism

U.S. Department of Labor. (2011, February). Labor force statistics for the current population survey. *Bureau of Labor Statistics*. Retrieved from http://www.bls.gov/cps/prev_yrs.htm

Wallerstein, I. (2000). *The essential Wallerstein*. New York: New Press.

Winant, H. (2001). *The world is a ghetto: Race and democracy since WWII*. New York: Basic Books.

Wolf, E. R. (1982). *Europe and the people without history*. Berkeley: University of California Press.

World Travel & Tourism Council. (2011). *Travel and tourism economic impact*. Retrieved from http://www.wttc.org/bin/pdf/original_pdf_file/2011_world_economic_impact_rep.pdf

Xu, F., Morgan, M., & Song, P. (2008). Students' travel behavior: A cross-cultural comparison of UK and China. *International Journal of Tourism Research, 10*. Retrieved from Wiley InterScience.

Yúdice, G. (2003). *The expediency of culture: Uses of culture in the global era*. Durham, NC: Duke University Press.

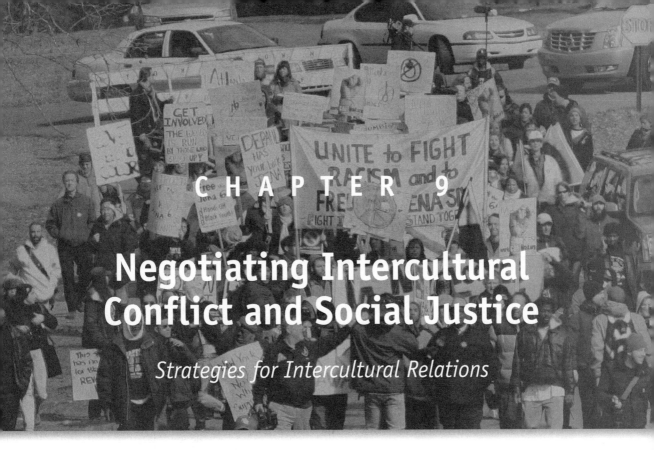

CHAPTER 9

Negotiating Intercultural Conflict and Social Justice

Strategies for Intercultural Relations

Interracial conflict in Jena, Louisiana, related to the Jena Six case sparked protests and calls for racial justice.

Scenario One: *They met through friends in southern California spending long days together getting to know each other. When Josh visited Patrice in Florida at her parents' house where she lives, he had a hard time feeling the closeness he had experienced in California. While her parents were gracious to him, her Haitian immigrant family seemed formal and structured compared to the close-knit, laid-back environment of his Jewish family in California. Josh's displays of affection in public made Patrice uncomfortable. And then, Josh wanted to talk about everything—whether there was a slight disagreement between them or a moment of closeness, he always wanted to express it.*

Scenario Two: *One hot day in early September during the crowded lunch period at a high school in Los Angeles, Tina bumped into Marta causing Marta's lunch tray to spill all over her blouse. Marta, embarrassed, looks up at Tina and yells, "What are you doing? I can't believe you did that. You did that on purpose." Tina laughs and shouts, "It was an accident . . . but if you don't stop yelling at me, I'm going to get my friends over*

(Continued)

Source: Chapter-opening photo © Alex Brandon/Associated Press.

(Continued)

here to prove it." A crowd surrounds the two girls, Armenian students backing up Tina and Latina/o students behind Marta each side hurling ethnic insults and yelling that the other is disrespecting their group.

Scenario Three: *Around the turn of the previous century Jews began to immigrate to Palestine with the goal of establishing a national homeland. There were many arguments about the appropriateness and availability of this land, but early Zionists sought to establish a Jewish State on what they claimed was their ancient holy land. On the same land, however, lived Arabs with historic and family claims to the land. This resulted in a clash over ownership and issues of self-determination, statehood, and identity. These two adversaries pose increasing obstacles and impediments to peace including settlement expansion, terrorism, assassination, religious fanaticism, and general recalcitrance. (Ellis, 2005, p. 49)*

The scenarios point to the likelihood of intercultural conflict as our lives, resources, and everyday experiences become increasingly interconnected with people from diverse cultures. Greater proximity, increased competition, diminishing resources, colonial histories, and exploitative conditions as well as exacerbated social and economic inequity fuel conflicts among individuals and groups from different cultural, ethnic, racial, religious, and national backgrounds. In the context of globalization, migration increases the presence of "foreigners" in locations all around the world escalating intercultural tensions. According to the Southern Poverty Law Center (Potok, 2006), extremist groups, which have grown exponentially in the United States since 2000, use immigration debates to incite violence toward immigrants, particularly Latinos/Latinas. While violent conflict between nation-states has declined worldwide in the past decades, open conflict between ethnic groups and the use of force by governments against nonstate groups has increased "in frequency and ferocity" (Eller, 1999, p. 1). Yet, today, people are also joining together around the globe in unprecedented ways to confront inequity and challenge injustice by building intercultural alliances. For example, the Center for Intercultural Organizing in Portland, Oregon, brings thousands of people together from diverse ethnic, racial, national, religious, and cultural backgrounds to build a multicultural movement for immigrant and refugee rights (Center for Intercultural Organizing, n.d.).

Intercultural conflict is defined here as the real or perceived incompatibility of values, norms, expectations, goals, processes, or outcomes between two or more *interdependent* individuals or groups from different cultures (Hocker & Wilmot, 1998). In the context of globalization, increased interdependence—economically, culturally, socially, and politically—has created unprecedented opportunities for and threats of intercultural conflict. While conflict is often characterized negatively, it's likely most everyone has experienced conflicts that were resolved in ways leading to positive outcomes or creative solutions—even if the paths to these outcomes were challenging. In interpersonal contexts, conflicts, if handled effectively, can clear the air and result in stronger bonds between two people. Workplace conflicts, if managed successfully, can result in better programs, products, or presentations. Movements for independence from colonial rule and social movements for human rights such as the civil rights movement, women's rights, and gay rights movements and the antiapartheid movement in South Africa have used conflict to move toward more equitable and just ends. Conflicts, while inevitably messy and infused with emotions, can lead to personal growth, creative and alternative solutions, as well as social change.

This chapter focuses on conflict, which is a central feature of human interaction and intercultural relations. Our goal is to understand how and why people from diverse groups engage in conflict, the conditions that lead to conflict, and the communication strategies that can increase effectiveness in addressing intercultural conflicts. In doing so, the relationship among intercultural conflict, communication, and social justice is highlighted. Histories of interaction between groups and the increasingly asymmetrical relationships of power today are critical dimensions to take into account. We begin by outlining a multidimensional framework for analyzing intercultural conflicts to grasp the complexities in the context of globalization. Following this, the multidimensional analysis is applied to three case studies. The chapter concludes with a discussion of strategies for addressing and negotiating intercultural conflicts using intercultural praxis.

INTERCULTURAL CONFLICT: A MULTIDIMENSIONAL FRAMEWORK OF ANALYSIS

Utilizing the intercultural praxis entry point of framing, we explore intercultural conflict from three interrelated frames: (1) the micro-frame that examines cultural orientations to conflict and communication styles; (2) the meso- or intermediate frame that broadens our view to address cultural group prejudices, cultural histories, and cultural identities; and (3) the macro- or geopolitical frame that expands our viewpoint to include the impact of media and discourse as well as political and economic factors on intercultural conflict.

Micro-Frame Analysis of Intercultural Conflict

The micro-frame analysis focuses on the individual-based interactional dimension of intercultural conflict. All intercultural conflicts, whether in the interpersonal context where neighbors argue over what is perceived as loud music, the intergroup context where two ethnic groups fight over entitlement to government resources, or the international/ global context where two nation-states engage in combat, have micro-frame components. Cultural orientations to conflict, communication, and facework impact the management of intercultural conflict. Differences across cultures in these areas can be sources of conflict themselves.

Cultural Orientations

Across cultures and historic times, tremendous variation exists in orientations to conflict as well as the styles and strategies for dealing with conflicts. For example, Taoism, a philosophical–religious tradition rooted in ancient China, views conflict as arising from an imbalance of opposites. Conflicts, from a Taoist perspective, are natural responses to disharmony in the flow of life and can be resolved by rebalancing what is out of proportion. Confucianism, Buddhism, and Taoism, which have influenced many

Asian cultures, all emphasize harmony, selflessness and an interdependent worldview. Broadly speaking, collectivistic cultures tend to cultivate an **interdependent orientation,** where the self is understood as relational and conflict is seen as a part of life that is managed in relationship with others. Ting-Toomey & Oetzel (2001) noted that in conflict situations people from collectivistic cultures tend to present opinions or ideas of the group, refrain from expressing personal emotions, and protect in-group members from accountability. Interdependent worldviews such as in China, Japan, and Korea tend to take indirect approaches to conflict, where maintaining harmony and accord in relationships is critical.

From an **independent orientation,** the individual is seen as an autonomous agent pursuing personal goals based on his or her beliefs. Individualistic cultures that promote an independent worldview such as the dominant U.S. culture tend to emphasize individual initiative and self-directed action, socializing people to assert personal opinions and hold individuals accountable for problems or mistakes. An individualistic, independent orientation often translates into approaches to conflict that use direct communication and generate multiple solutions to a problem. In cultures with an independent worldview, such as the European–American culture, conflict is seen as resulting from competition between personal interests of two or more people and as an incidental intrusion or infringement on individuals' autonomy or rights. Conflict is often viewed as a problem that must be overcome quickly, rationally, unemotionally, and directly. In contrast to interdependent-oriented cultures that stress relationship maintenance, the goal of mediation and conflict resolution in independent-oriented cultures is often to remove obstacles to the pursuit of individual goals (Markus & Lin, 1999).

The two approaches sketched out are generalizations that alert us to ways cultural assumptions, beliefs, practices, and institutions orient people to make sense of and manage conflict differently. Yet diversity of approaches and preferred orientations exist within groups as well. Today, rapid and circular migration; the depth and penetration of international media; and increases in intercultural relationships in homes, workplaces, and international settings blur distinct lines that categorize national and ethnic cultural orientations to conflict.

Communication and Conflict Styles

Varying styles of communication shaped by culture can be sources of misunderstanding and conflict in intercultural communication. Edward T. Hall (1976) introduced the concept of low and high context communication. **Context,** in this case, refers to the information that surrounds a communication event, which is closely tied to the meaning of the event. **High context communication** is "one where most of the information is already in the person, while very little is in the coded, explicit, transmitted part of the message" (Hall, 1976, p. 79). In other words, people rely on shared knowledge, the situation, and nonverbal cues to give meaning to communication. High context communication tends to be indirect. **Low context communication** is communication where the "mass of the information is vested in the explicit code" (Hall, 1976, p. 70). Low context communication is more direct, specific, and literal with less attention placed on gathering meaning from unstated contextual cues. Collectivistic cultures that have more interdependent worldviews and share close networks of relationships over long periods of time tend to display high context communication; on the other hand, individualistic cultures that are more independent in terms of worldview separate and compartmentalize personal and work relationships often require more explicit detailing of information to communicate and therefore tend to display low context communication.

Facework

The notion of "face" has roots in both Eastern and Western traditions and is used across cultures, yet the meanings associated with face differ in different historical and cultural contexts. In research in intercultural communication studies today, **face** can be defined as favorable social self-worth in relation to the assessment of other-worth in interpersonal relationships (Ting-Toomey & Kurogi, 1998). Face, which can be threatened, lost, protected, maintained, and saved, is a critical resource that is negotiated through communication in social interactions. **Facework** refers to the communication strategies used to negotiate face between the self and other. Ting-Toomey and Oetzel (2002) argued that people from individualistic or independent cultural orientations tend to be more concerned with protecting or saving their own face and, therefore, often use conflict styles that are more confrontational, controlling, and aimed at finding solutions. On the other hand, people from more collectivistic and interdependent orientations are more likely to be concerned with accommodating the other person's face or finding ways for mutual face-saving. Facework in more interdependent-oriented cultures leads to conflict styles that are more avoiding, obliging, or integrating.

Situational Factors

A wide range of situational and relational factors also contribute to decisions individuals make in conflict situations. Brew and Cairns (2004) found that cultural orientation alone did not explain or predict communication choices in conflict situations with East Asian and Australian employees at five Western organizations in Bangkok and Singapore. Situational constraints modified the expected communication strategies based on cultural norms. Australians are generally described as individualistic, low context communicators who are independent-oriented and egalitarian, valuing transparency, honesty, and direct communication. These characteristics may be experienced as blunt by those from more collectivistic cultures. Thais and Singaporeans are generally described as collectivistic, high context communicators who tend to avoid conflict, open displays of criticism, or dissent, which are seen as rude or damaging. Saving "face" is seen as a particularly important concern, which results in skirting challenging issues to avoid embarrassment to self and others (Chi-Ching, 1998).

Brew and Cairns (2004) argued that these broad generalizations may be useful as a guide to understand cultural orientations to communication and conflict, but in interpersonal communication in workplace settings individuals make decisions about how to act and respond that are also highly contingent upon situational factors. The situational constraint of time urgency, which is an increasing pressure in the context of globalization, may explain why Thai and Singaporean employees used more direct communication than expected based on their cultural orientation. Additionally, Australians used more indirect communication when interacting with Thai and Singaporean workers who were both superiors and subordinates, suggesting that Australians modified their communication strategies based on the cultural identity of the person with whom they interacted. The situational factor of the status of the other was significant for East Asians as they chose to communicate indirectly with superiors and more directly with subordinates.

The micro-frame draws our attention to cultural orientations to conflict, communication, and conflict styles, as well as different facework strategies. Additionally, we note how situational factors may play an important role along with cultural norms in determining individuals' choices and actions in conflict management. From the micro-frame of analysis of intercultural conflict, we now broaden our viewpoint to the meso- or intermediate frame of reference.

Meso-Frame Analysis of Intercultural Conflict

The meso-frame allows us to address the influence of group-based prejudices and ethnocentrism as well as cultural histories and identities on intercultural conflict. Attitudes, beliefs, perceptions, and attributions held by groups are often grounded in cultural group histories and are integral to cultural group identities. The perceived and real access to power or the group's positionality within hierarchies of power also plays a role in how conflicts unfold, entrench, and transform.

Prejudice, Ethnocentrism, and Racism

All intercultural conflict involves some degree of biased in-group perceptions and attributions as individuals or groups make sense of conflict situations. **In-groups** are groups of individuals for whom we feel concern, with whom we are willing to cooperate and from whom separation creates anxiety (Triandis, 1995). **Out-groups** are groups of individuals who are seen as separate and different from us, are often perceived as unequal to our group, as well as potentially threatening. Stereotypes, ethnocentric attitudes, or long-held prejudices from in-groups inform interpretations and experiences as well as the degree to which meaningful relationships can be formed with out-group members.

The degree to which distinctions between in-groups and out-groups are apparent and how these distinctions inform actions varies across cultures, contexts, and situations. However, conflict situations tend to tap into and bring out latent in-group/out-group distinctions, prejudices, and ethnocentric attitudes. As conflict situations escalate, "us vs. them" dichotomies often become entrenched (Ting-Toomey & Oetzel, 2001). For example, in the 1980s before the fall of the former Yugoslavian nation-state, Serbia and Croatian immigrants in Seattle, Washington, frequently engaged in social activities together and paid little attention to the ethnic distinctions between them. However, with the collapse of Yugoslavia in 1991 and the ensuing violence and ethnic cleansing, the immigrant communities in Seattle drew distinct lines between themselves, severing communication, and in a few cases, even sending death threats to members of the other group.

CULTURAL IDENTITY
INTERCULTURAL CONFLICT

In some situations, the initial source of conflict may appear to have little to do with cultural differences. However, once the conflict is triggered, hidden stereotypes and prejudices surface. Consider the following example.

A multicultural group of university students is assigned to work together to research a topic area and present their findings in class. The project requires students to meet outside of class on numerous occasions, and initially all members attend. Yet, over time, one member, Marissa, stops coming. She tries to contact her group members to let them know she is ill but gets no response. As the group makes final preparations, a heated argument develops. Some students think Marissa should be excluded from presenting and others argue that she should be allowed to share her part. A few students worry that her lack of participation will hurt their group grade. In the midst of the conflict, one group member says, "She's Hispanic. That's why she didn't do her work." Another Latino/Hispanic group member objects to the comment saying he won't present with a bigot. Clearly, our cultural identities, cultural histories, and the way cultural groups have been targeted historically combine to impact interpersonal and intergroup conflict.

Racism, sexism, classism, and heterosexism are sources of intercultural conflict as well as ubiquitous backdrops that play into differing interpretations of conflict in intercultural situations. In historical and contemporary contexts where everyday interactions and institutions provide systemic advantages to some and disadvantages to others, relatively small instances of exclusion based on race, gender, class, or sexual orientation can provoke conflict.

Cultural Histories and Cultural Identities

Cultural histories are shared stories and interpretations of cultural groups that are often passed along in written or oral form from generation to generation. While cultural histories often intersect with national histories, cultural histories explain events and experiences from the perspectives of the cultural group. Cultural histories of nondominant groups may complement or contradict the received national history and are viewpoints on history that are often hidden or silenced from the mainstream culture. Cultural histories provide cohesiveness for cultural groups and a foundation for sustaining unified group-based identities. People from nondominant groups generally know more about the cultural histories of dominant groups than the reverse (Kivel, 1996). Lack of knowledge of others' cultural histories or a refusal to validate the importance of cultural histories can limit intercultural understanding, increase the likelihood for misunderstanding, and exacerbate conflicts.

Shared cultural histories, experiences of exclusion, and struggles for recognition by nondominant cultural groups are often inextricably intertwined with defined and protected cultural group identities. Disrespect or rejection directed at individuals or groups based on their cultural identity can be a source of intercultural conflict as well as exacerbate conflicts that are not primarily focused on identity. Lack of respect and validation for a group's cultural identity often provokes efforts to regain face and respect for the group's identity. Ting-Toomey and Oetzel (2002) noted that validation–rejection, respect–disrespect, approval–disapproval, and valuing–disconfirming are identity-based issues that are linked to cultural values, beliefs, and assumption and can play a critical role in conflict situations. For example, once the perpetrator of the tragic massacre at Virginia Tech in April 2007 had been identified as a Korean alien resident in the United States, the president of Korea, representing the collective shame and loss of face of all people of Korea, expressed his sorrow and apologized to the families who had lost loved ones (Shim, Kim, & Martin, 2008).

Passage of legislation like Proposition 8 in California in 2008 that denied same-sex couples the right to marriage harnessed and perpetuated a climate of disrespect and rejection of lesbian, gay, bisexual, and transgender (LGBT) communities across the United States. While questions of access to rights and privileges equal to those afforded heterosexuals were the fundamental source of conflict, disapproval and rejection of the collective identities of LGBT people were necessarily interwoven with the passage of this legislation. As evidenced during the civil rights and the feminist movements, threats and attacks on cultural group identities also serve to define, unify, and mobilize group-based identities. The LGBT movement, punctuated by conflicts over civil rights across the United States in the past 40 years, has been instrumental in constituting a collective "queer" identity (Archer, 2004).

In intractable ethnopolitical conflicts such as the historically entrenched clashes between the Sinhalese and Tamils in Sri Lanka or between Israeli Jews and Palestinians, communication scholar Donald Ellis (2005) noted the following:

> Identities are strong, rigid and stable. They do not change easily. In fact, identities are so strong the conflict threatens the individual's sense of self. This threat evokes a powerful response. Typically, this response is aggressive and can escalate. Ethnopolitical conflicts usually involve polarized negative identities where one's sense of self is dependent upon being in opposition to another. (p. 47)

To varying degrees, intercultural conflicts involve issues of cultural identity, cultural histories, racism, ethnocentrism, and prejudice, which are linked to inequitable relations of power.

Power Imbalance

Imbalances in power are often pivotal features in conflicts in interpersonal, intergroup, and international/global contexts. Through the meso- or intermediate frame, we focus attention on group-based power. Power is always relational and can take multiple forms. Group-based power can be gained in a variety of ways including force and domination; majority representation; and control of economic, political, and social institutions, as well as control of resources considered valuable. In the United States, White European Americans represent a numeric majority (approximately 70% of the population) and have historically controlled access to institutions and resources. Nondominant or cocultural groups are expected to adapt and assimilate to European American values, communication styles, norms, practices, and standards due to this power imbalance. Increased numbers may augment group-based power, for example, the gains in political power made by Latinos/ Hispanics in the United States as this group's population increases. Yet numbers of people do not necessarily translate into power as was evident in apartheid in South Africa.

Inequitable relations of power and lack of access to power within society often lead cocultural or nondominant groups to make clear distinctions between those in the dominant group who hold power and those in nondominant groups who do not have access to power (Orbe, 1998). In the context of these power differentials, cocultural or nondominant groups tend to enact strong group-based cultural identities to preserve their languages, customs, practices, and identities. Dominant group members often find it hard to understand the need to preserve cultural identities, are bothered by cocultural groups' enactments of cultural difference, and are sometimes affronted by the lack of willingness to assimilate into the dominant culture. Real and perceived imbalances in power are sources of resentment and misinterpretation for both nondominant and dominant groups, which can lead to conflict. Hierarchies of power within societies also lead cocultural groups to fight with each other over access to limited resources.

The meso-frame highlights the role that group-based prejudices, cultural histories, and identities, as well as imbalances in power, have on intercultural conflict. Influences on conflict revealed through the meso-frame are undoubtedly interconnected to and impacted by issues made evident through the macro-frame.

COMMUNICATIVE DIMENSIONS
MEDIATING INTERCULTURAL CONFLICT

For 25 years, Mexican and Central American laborers gathered to look for work in the parking lot of a paint store on the corner of Beverly and La Jolla in Los Angeles. When the store ownership changed, the laborers were forced to stand on the corners. Some of the neighborhood residents, who were mostly elderly and Jewish, complained to the police. While the laborers had committed no crime and were on public property, the police harassed and arrested them. The laborers enlisted the help of a local organization, Day Laborer Leadership Program of the Coalition for Humane Immigrant Rights of Los Angeles (CHIRLA), who went door to door to talk with residents. While a small group of residents were upset about the laborers, others had hired workers in the past. Some of the older residents were also threatened by new Russian and Asian residents. CHIRLA used a wide range of communication strategies to negotiate the intercultural conflict. They talked and listened to residents, laborers, and the police; they worked to address the stereotypes each group held about the other. Through dialogue at a community forum, residents and laborers were able to come to an agreement about the use of neighborhood space.

Source: Cho, Puete, Louie, & Khokha (2004).

Macro-Frame Analysis of Intercultural Conflict

From the meso-frame of analysis of intercultural conflict, we broaden our view further to encompass the macro-frame, which allows us to consider the impact media, economic factors, and geopolitical power asymmetries have on intercultural conflicts.

Media

Events, decisions, and discourse at the macro-level may seem distant from our everyday life experiences. Yet discourses and media representations about controversial issues such as U.S. immigration, terrorism, U.S. troops in Iraq or Afghanistan, the global economic crisis, and the genocide in Darfur, to take only a few examples, have direct and indirect impact on our intercultural interactions. As discussed in Chapter 6, media representations are primary sources of information about groups of people, nations, and conflicts with which we have little or no contact or knowledge. Stereotypical or biased portrayals of non-dominant groups in the media perpetuate prejudices and ethnocentrism.

In conflict situations, ethnic minority groups are often depicted as criminals and as threats to national security. The case study of the uprising of Algerian immigrants in the suburbs of France presented in Chapter 5 illustrates this point well. The media often play a significant role in interethnic and international conflicts furthering divisiveness between groups by using **oppositional metaphors,** or metaphors that use rigid and polarized dichotomies, such "us vs. them," "good vs. evil," and "civil vs. barbarian." Media representation of interethnic conflicts in the former Yugoslavia, Rwanda, and Zaire in the 1990s relied heavily on shocking scenes that reduced the complexities of the conflicts to fighting between different "tribes" and often presented ethnic groups as "wild," "mad," and "volatile." Allen & Seaton (1999) argued that such representation "enables the governments of rich industrialized nations to absolve themselves of responsibility for what was happening, and helped them to adapt increasingly oppressive measures against immigrants and refugees" (p. 2).

While media often exacerbate conflicts and are frequently monopolized to advance the interests of powerful ethnic/racial and national groups, Melone, Terzis, and Beleli (2002) suggested that media can also be a vehicle for conflict transformation. The nonprofit organization The European Centre for Common Ground has worked in collaboration with local media owners, journalists, and reporters in Angola, Burundi, Greece, Iran, the United States, and the Middle East using a wide variety of media forms to create a common base among adversarial groups to cultivate conditions for conflict transformation. Common Ground has produced TV and radio programs, used street theater and comics, recorded peace songs from rival political groups, as well as facilitated intercultural dialogues to address interethnic and international conflicts.

Economic and Political Factors

As noted and discussed throughout the book, neoliberal policies implemented in the context of globalization have magnified economic disparity within nation-states and across nation-states, which often translates into a greater likelihood of intercultural conflict.

Struggles over limited resources such as money, jobs, or land are primarily economic and political in nature. Yet animosity and conflict are often framed in terms of ethnic, racial, religious, and cultural differences. In the context of the global economic crisis in the United States, fear and hostility toward immigrants has escalated and immigrants have become easy targets to blame for the nation's problems resulting in legislation such as Arizona's SB 1070, the most far-reaching and severe anti-immigrant measure in decades. Racial slurs and verbal attacks hurled on radio talk shows and violent crimes against Latinos/Hispanics have increased impacting individuals and cultural groups as well as educational, health care, and criminal justice institutions.

Deepa Fernandes (2007) brought to our attention the deeply troubling ways that economic and political factors have aligned since 9/11 in regard to national security, immigration, and intercultural conflict:

> Today, enforcing immigration policy has become the latest way to make a buck. . . . I call it the immigration-industrial complex. There is big money to be made as the government dramatically increases its reliance on the private sector to carry out its war on terror. On the home front, the prime targets of this war are immigrants. (pp. 169–170)

The **immigration industrial complex** refers to the "confluence of public and private sector interests in the criminalization of undocumented migration, immigration law enforcement and the promotion of 'anti-illegal' rhetoric" (Golash-Boza, 2009, p. 295). The immigration industrial complex uses the following: (1) rhetoric of fear, (2) the confluence of power interests, and (3) otherization discourse. A culture of fear targeting "illegals" as undesirable Others, racialized as Mexicans in the current context, justifies massive government expenditures. In an industrial complex, the marginalized group pays the biggest price while the powerful and well-connected are enriched (Golash-Boza, 2009).

Geopolitical Power Inequities

As noted throughout the book, the configuration of geopolitical influence and the asymmetrical relations of power that characterize the current context of globalization are rooted in histories of colonization, Western imperialism, and U.S. hegemony. In the first decade of the new millennium, over 45 significant armed conflicts were ongoing around the world. Many of these conflicts, lasting two, three, and even four decades, are in non-Western postcolonial states in Africa, Asia, and the Middle East (Eller, 1999). U.S. military intervention in countries from China, Korea, Iran, Guatemala, Vietnam, Cambodia, Laos, Haiti, Chile, Grenada, Nicaragua, Panama, Afghanistan, and Iraq, to name only a few, over the past 70 years have caused the deaths of millions and disrupted the lives and livelihoods of millions more (Blum, 1995). Criminology and public policy scholars Mullard and Cole (2007) noted the following:

> The wars in Iraq and Afghanistan are replays of colonial "civilizing missions" in Africa, clouded by deceit, corruption and corporate invasion of pacified homelands. Like the concessionaire and charted companies in nineteenth-century

Africa, the International Monetary Fund (IMF), the Word Bank, the Development Fund for Iraq (DFI), and other international financial institutions (IFIs) are, as a consequence of the war on terror, actively involved in the corporate takeover and economic occupation of Iraq. (p. 1)

Intervention, war, armed conflict, and occupation—whether justified by rhetoric attacking the barbaric actions of the enemy, defended by claims of political and moral inferiority of the Other, or warranted by assertions of human rights violations—foster deep and long-standing resentment and animosity. Since the global war on terror, initiated by former U.S. president George W. Bush following 9/11, U.S. citizens traveling abroad have experienced firsthand the role geopolitics plays in the reception and treatment of individuals and national cultural groups. One's real or perceived membership in a national cultural group or in an ethnic, religious, or racial group positions each us of differently in the complex web of global geopolitical relationships of power. Moustafa Bayoumi (2008) captured the struggles and challenges of seven young Arab Americans in the United States since 9/11 in his book entitled *How Does It Feel to Be a Problem?* Bayoumi told the stories of Arab Americans, the newest minority in the United States identified as communities of suspicion and targeted as the latest "problem." Yet, Bayoumi argued, "What you will find are seven Arab American narratives that are in the end very American stories about race, religion, and civil rights and about how the pressures of domestic life and foreign policy push on individual lives" (p. 11).

The macro-frame draws our attention to how intercultural conflicts are shaped by media representation, economic factors, and asymmetries in geopolitical power. Intercultural conflicts in the context of globalization are complex, often deeply rooted in history and situated within inequitable relationships of power. The multiframe model allows us to highlight the linkages and interplay between the micro-, meso-, and macro-frames. Three case studies of intercultural conflict from interpersonal, intergroup, and international contexts are presented next to illustrate the utility of a multidimensional framework of analysis (see Figure 9.1).

Figure 9.1   Multidimensional Framework of Analysis for Intercultural Conflict

Frames	Micro-Frame (Individual-Based)	Meso-Frame (Group-Based)	Macro-Frame (Discourse and Representation)
	Cultural orientation	Prejudice	Media
	Communication style	Ethnocentrism	Economic factors
	Language	Racism, sexism, homophobia, etc.	Political factors
	Conflict style	Cultural histories	Geopolitical power inequities
	Facework	Cultural identities	
	Situational factors	Power imbalance	

Source: Kathryn Sorrells.

Frames	Micro-Frame (Individual-Based)	Meso-Frame (Group-Based)	Macro-Frame (Discourse and Representation)
Context of conflict: Interpersonal conflict	Independent/ interdependent orientation Low/high context Indirect/direct Protecting own/other's face	Strong in-group/out-group orientation History of exclusion Lack of knowledge of others	Stereotypical/ misrepresentation in media Discriminatory discourse/ actions Perceived/real inequity in resource distribution
Context of conflict: Intergroup conflict	Defense of group-based face Communication style differences Conflict style differences Historically based mistrust/enmity	Group-based stereotypes Racism, religious discrimination History of conflict Defense of cultural identities Resistance to assimilation	Systemic inequities Lack of/misrepresentation in media Historic genocide Perceived/real inequity in resource distribution
Context of conflict: International/ global conflict	Language and communication style differences Value differences Facework	Ethnocentrism/prejudice In-group bias/pressure Negative identity Trauma of violence/long-standing conflict	Differing historical accounts Geopolitical pressure/ power asymmetry Oppositional metaphors/ discourse

CASE STUDY 1: INTERPERSONAL CONTEXT

Patrice, a Haitian Christian immigrant, lives in south Florida and is in a long-term, intimate relationship with Josh, a Jewish multigenerational resident of Southern California. Conflict is not unusual in their long-distance, interracial, and interreligious relationship affording both opportunities for growth and potential threats to their relationship. They met through friends in Southern California spending long days together getting to know each other. When Josh visited Patrice in Florida at her parents' house where she lives, he had a hard time feeling the closeness he had experienced in California. While her parents were gracious to him, her family seemed formal and structured compared to the close-knit, laid-back environment at his home. Josh's displays of affection in public made Patrice uncomfortable. And then, Josh wanted to talk about everything—whether there was a slight disagreement between them or a moment of closeness, he always wanted to express it. He wanted to deal with the issue right then and there and later say "I love you."

One day Josh met Patrice after she got off work. She was furious. In separate incidents, a customer and a coworker had treated her in demeaning ways. "It's because I'm a young,

Black women. I can't believe these people. They're so racist." Josh listened to her explanation of what had happened and offered several reasons other than race that could explain what had happened. Frustrated, Patrice sat there quiet and fuming.

Four years into the relationship, as Patrice and Josh manage the conflicts that arise from their differences, two issues remain central: (1) religion and (2) children. Josh wonders how it will be for his children if their mother is not Jewish and if he will be able to sustain a Jewish home environment. Will he be able to relate to the experiences of his children as biracial kids in a racialized U.S. society? Patrice worships at a fundamentalist Christian church in the Haitian community. While the preacher claims non-Christians are doomed to hell, Patrice doesn't think it's a big deal that Josh is Jewish.

Using the multiframe analysis introduced in the previous section, let's explore the range of intercultural communication issues confronting Patrice and Josh. Through the micro-frame, we see that the two have differing orientations to conflict and communication. While Patrice prefers a high context form of communication, Josh is more comfortable with low context communication. In conflict situations, Josh, operating from an individualistic, independent worldview, wants to "get it all out on the table," have each of them share their opinions and come up with solutions. Patrice, enculturated into a more interdependent worldview, would rather let some things go instead of making every issue a conflict by talking about it. Her approach to conflict is more indirect, where she assumes building a strong relationship between them will safeguard against threatening conflicts.

From the meso-frame, questions of race, prejudice, cultural histories, and group-based power differences come into play. According to Patrice and Josh, neither racism nor ethnocentrism play central roles in the relationship between the two of them, yet how their relationship is perceived by others in society as well as their differing experiences of race in the world are sources of conflict. When Josh finds other explanations for what Patrice experiences as discrimination and racism, Patrice feels invalidated and dismissed. Josh is certainly aware of the history of discrimination against Blacks in the United States, yet, from the perspective of a White man shielded by White privilege, he resists Patrice's interpretation of the events. Their different interpretations, informed by their standpoints and positionalities, are sometimes hard to bridge.

Religion plays an important role in both Patrice and Josh's lives offering each a set of beliefs that guide their daily lives as well as communities of belonging with long-held cultural traditions, histories of suffering, and survival. Understanding the purpose of religion in the life of their partner has been an important step toward reconciling their religious differences. As an immigrant, church connects Patrice on a weekly basis with her Haitian heritage, sustains and deepens her cultural ties, and offers her support from her cultural community. Josh sees his Jewish faith as a way to connect on a spiritual level with all people regardless of race, religion, or creed. Separating institutional religious beliefs from their individual interpretations of their respective religions was a significant step in building tentative bridges across their differing religious orientations.

The macro-frame brings into view the role of media, discourse, economic, and political factors in intercultural conflict. Josh's concern about raising biracial children stems primarily from depictions of non-Whites in the U.S. media and popular discourse. The realities of racial prejudice and injustice in U.S. society add an extra level of care and tension to their decision-making process about marriage and children. Additionally, Patrice has to deal on a regular basis with stereotypes perpetuated in the media about Haiti. While the realities of poverty in her country of origin are disturbing, what troubles Patrice the most is the lack of information provided to U.S. audiences about the history of struggle of her country, the role the United States has played in undermining economic growth and democratic processes in Haiti, and the portrayal of Haiti as corrupt, poor, and unable to manage itself.

Macro-, meso-, and micro-frame issues intertwine in Patrice and Josh's relationship shaping a context for communication, which often leads to misunderstanding, tension, and conflict. Yet sorting through their differences and staying in the difficult dialogues that emerge also provide opportunities to learn from each other and enrich their understanding of their cultures and the globalized world they inhabit.

CASE STUDY 2: INTERGROUP CONTEXT

Grant High School is a large, multicultural public school in the heart of the San Fernando Valley in California. Like many high schools in the United States, students from different ethnic and racial groups tend to segregate themselves from each other. In the past years, the quad in the center of the school has been divided spatially—the Armenian students congregate around the tree at the north end and Latinos/Latinas gather near the open-air lunch area. While the school has students from a wide range of different cultural backgrounds, the tensions and conflicts revolve primarily around the two groups with the largest representation: Latinos/Latinas and Armenians.

One hot day in early September during the crowded lunch period, Tina bumped into Marta causing Marta's lunch tray to spill all over her blouse. Marta, embarrassed, looked up at Tina and yelled, "What are you doing? I can't believe you did that. You did that on purpose." Tina laughed and exclaimed, "It was an accident . . . but if you don't stop yelling at me, I'm going to get my friends over here to prove it." A crowd surrounded the two girls, Armenian students backing up Tina and Latino/Latina students behind Marta each side yelling that the other was disrespecting their group. Ethnically derogatory names were hurled, food trays were used as weapons, and fists started punching whoever was in sight.

The most salient feature in the analysis of the conflict from the micro-frame is the question of face and facework, which is inseparable in this case from the meso-frame issues of cultural histories, cultural identities, and power. The two groups at the high school have drawn clear lines between in-group and out-group based on cultural identities and histories. In the conflict that was previously described, Armenian and Latino/Latina students defend their cultural group's face. When their collective face is threatened, each group's facework strategies are limited to dominating and denigrating the other. Each group's stereotypes and long-held prejudices toward the other feed ethnocentric attitudes of superiority of their in-group and inform their interpretations of experiences.

The two cultural groups share much in common including their experiences as relatively recent immigrant groups in the United States, yet the uniqueness of their cultural histories is also significant. The Armenian Genocide, which began in 1915, was a systematic and organized destruction of approximately 1.5 million Armenians by the Ottoman Empire. Acknowledged as the first modern genocide, the Armenian Holocaust spurred the Armenian diaspora, where Armenians fled to destinations in Eastern Europe, the Middle East, and South America (Bournoutian, 2002). Since the 1970s, Armenian communities have grown in the United States and Canada as later generations of Armenians left the Middle East. The Armenian students at Grant High School are part of the most recent wave of Armenian immigration prompted by the fall of the former Soviet Union in the early 1990s and the economic conditions in the Republic of Armenia.

The horrific genocide defines and marks the cultural history of Armenian communities worldwide. At Grant High School, this manifests as expressions by students of intense pride in their culture and history as they learn from their community to vigilantly protect their Armenian cultural identity from external threats and from mainstream forces of assimilation. Perceived as "old world," "traditional," and "resistant to assimilation" by administrators and teachers at the school, Armenian students are taught by their families to maintain close-knit Armenian cultural bonds and friendship ties.

On the other hand, generally, most often the Latino/Latina students at Grant High School were born in the United States into migrant families from Mexico and Central America. While these students are grouped together, officially and informally referred to as "Hispanic" at the school, most prefer to identify as Mexican, Honduran, or Salvadoran often espousing bicultural, hybrid identities that acknowledge both their family's country of origin and their U.S. cultural backgrounds. Their collective identity as "Hispanic" is less salient due to their national culture differences and the varied political and economic circumstances that propelled their family's migration to the United States. Yet the students are targets of stereotypes and misperceptions held by some administrators and teachers that claim Hispanic students are "lazy" and "not interested in education."

Meso-frame issues are intertwined with the broader historical, political, economic, and media issues revealed through the macro-frame of analysis. Lack of official recognition of the Armenian Genocide by both the U.S. and Turkish governments for political and economic reasons dismisses and devalues the cultural history and struggles of Armenian communities worldwide (Payaslian, 2005). Commemorative events, scheduled each year on April 24th in Los Angeles and around the world, serve to educate the broader public about the genocide and also galvanize Armenian solidarity. The pride and protection Armenian youth at Grant High School take toward their culture today is impacted by these geopolitical dynamics. Administrators, teachers, and students are also influenced by stereotypical representations of Latinas/Latinos in movies, TV programs, and news as well as anti-immigrant rhetoric. Additionally, the historic segregation and current hostilities and violence in U.S. schools provide a backdrop that normalizes intergroup conflict.

Addressing the conflict at Grant High School requires an understanding of how different in-group/out-group perceptions and prejudices, cultural group histories, and inequitable geopolitical power relations intertwine in complicated and layered ways to shape, provoke, and sustain the intercultural conflict. The multiframe analysis draws attention to the linkages between issues highlighted by each frame that are critical for addressing the intergroup conflict.

CASE STUDY 3: INTERNATIONAL AND GLOBAL CONTEXT

Around the turn of the previous century, Jews began to immigrate to Palestine with the goal of establishing a national homeland. There were many arguments about the appropriateness and availability of this land, but early Zionists sought to establish a Jewish state on what they claimed was their ancient holy land. On the same land, however, lived Arabs with historic and family claims to the land. This resulted in a clash over ownership and issues of self-determination, statehood, and identity. There was violence between these two groups from the early 1920s with various degrees of intensity. The United Nations partitioned the land in 1947 and established two states—one Arab and one Jewish Israeli. The Palestinians rejected this partition and war broke out in 1948. Israeli Jews refer to this war as the War of Independence and claim the Arabs started it. Palestinians refer to the same war as "the disaster" and accuse the Jews of predatory territorial acquisition arguing that the United Nations had no right to partition the land in the first place. Israeli Jews and Palestinians have fought numerous wars since 1948 with Israel on one side and Arab nations on the other. The 1967 war led to additional land under Israeli control and created the conditions for Israeli occupation of territories and violent opposition to this occupation. The Oslo peace accords of 1993 was hailed as a breakthrough, but ended in failure. These two adversaries pose increasing obstacles and impediments to peace including settlement expansion, terrorism, assassination, religious fanaticism, and general recalcitrance (Ellis, 2005, p. 49).

The magnitude, the long-term intractable nature, and the geopolitical dimensions of this conflict suggest a macro-frame analysis as a starting point for making sense of the conflict. One of the pivotal aspects of the Israeli–Palestinian conflict is the vastly different perceptions and interpretations held and promoted by each group regarding the historic and ongoing episodes of the conflict. Each group marks the origins, causes, and experiences of successive conflicts in vastly different ways and holds firmly to their group's perceptions often to the exclusion of the other's. Thus, questions of representation—how the events are represented—in interpersonal interactions; in popular discourse; and in local, national, and international media are central in maintaining the oppositional metaphors, fueling the intractable nature of the conflict and inhibiting movement toward solutions.

The previous description is a representation of the conflict. Both sides of the conflict would undoubtedly argue this representation leaves out information critical for understanding the conflict. For example, the scenario does not mention that Judea, home of the Jews in ancient times, was captured and renamed Palestine by the Romans. The scenario does not address the role of Britain, following the Balfour Declaration in 1917, in establishing Palestine as a national home for the Jews as a League of Nations mandate. Additionally, the scenario does not detail the 700,000 or more Palestinians who were displaced in the 1948 War (United Nations Relief and Works Agency, 2007); nor does it mention that the number of Palestinian refugees has grown to 4.9 million with refugee camps in Gaza, the West Bank, Jordon, Lebanon, and Syria (United Nations Relief and Works Agency for Palestine Refugees, 2011). The scenario also neglects to address the role of the United States in providing military support and funding for Israel. Clearly, a

Figure 9.2 Deeply rooted in historical, political, economic and cultural differences, and inequities, intercultural conflict among Israelis and Palestinians persists.

No:572462.02 Date:02.01.2009 Credit:HALEY/SIPA
Headline: Jerusalem: "Day of Wrath"
Caption: On the seventh day of Israeli air attacks on Gaza, Hamas has called for a "Day of Wrath" throughout Palestine. On Friday, Muslims under 50 were prevented from going to prayer on the Al Aqsa esplanade in Jerusalem. Israeli forces were omni-present in and around the Old City of Jerusalem to thwart any Palestinian protest. Many muslims prayed in the city streets near Lion's Gate. Jerusalem, Israel. Jan. 2, 2009.

Source: © HALEY/SIPA/Associated Press.

critical aspect of all conflicts and particularly ones with international and global implications is the role of representation—whether in interpersonal interactions or media—in framing the conflict, in interpreting and constructing meaning about the conflict, as well as in choices made about what information is disseminated and to whom. Additionally, the macro-frame analysis draws our attention to how the geopolitical power inequities between Palestinians, who are seen as nonstate actors and Israel, which is officially recognized as a nation-state, entails both political and economic ramifications. As nonstate perpetrators of violence, Palestinians are labeled "terrorists," while Israel's violent use of force is framed as "national defense" or "national security."

The meso-frame analysis reveals how differences in Jewish Israeli and Palestinian cultural histories and identities not only fuel the deeply entrenched conflict but have become deeply intertwined with and dependent upon the conflict. In-group biases support ethnocentric attitudes and perceptions as well as perpetuate stereotypes and lack of trust. Ellis (2005) argued that both groups hold "harmful stereotypes, mutual delegitimization, and negative identity. Their identities are rooted in a conception of the land as sacred, and supported by religion, historical narratives of persecution, and myths" (p. 49). **Negative**

identity refers to group identity that is "based on being the opposite of the other, or 'not' being the other" (p. 51). The identities of Israeli Jews and Palestinians are structured in opposition to each other such that the positive identity of one entails the negative image of the other.

Intractable conflicts take place in the context of power imbalances (Coleman, 2003). The dominant group, Israeli Jews, in this case, competes with the less powerful group, Palestinians, over what constitutes violence, morality, criminal behavior, legal rights, and self-definition. As Ellis (2005) noted, these contestations are institutionalized by the dominant group in ways that further disenfranchise and victimize the nondominant group. Intractable conflicts are also characterized by groups who are interrelated geographically, politically, and economically yet have very little contact with each other, which exacerbates misinformation and stereotypes. In addition, protracted ethnopolitical conflicts engender extreme emotions including humiliation, indignation, self-righteousness, and defensiveness. The trauma of violence and the concomitant emotions are long-standing and are often passed along from one generation to the next making them highly resistant to change (Coleman, 2003; Ellis, 2005).

Issues highlighted through the macro- and meso-frames are intertwined with and exacerbated by differences in cultural norms of communication and interaction between Israeli Jews and Palestinians that are made evident through a micro-frame. Greifat and Katriel (1989) identified the Arab linguistic term **musayara**, which refers to the act of accompanying one's conversational partner in dialogue. This cultural communication style, broadly shared by Arab cultures, is aimed at maintaining and promoting harmony and is often accomplished through flourishing language, use of repetition, and metaphors. The style is generally characterized as high context, indirect, rhetorically complex, and aimed at the preservation of the listener's face. Interruptions in many situations are interpreted as a lack of respect for the speaker (Greifat & Katriel, 1989). In contrast, Jewish Israeli communication style, characterized by the term **dugri,** or straight talk, is described as direct, simple, forceful, and concerned with the preservation of the speaker's face. Jewish interactional styles are described as polyvocal and fast-paced, where turn-taking is rapid and where participation by multiple speakers and interruptions are experienced as forms of bonding not as disruptions.

Yet, in mediated dialogue sessions between Israeli Jews and Palestinians, situational factors such as the political context of the event as well as the erosion of culturally held patterns of communication modify and mitigate cultural communication styles. Research (Zupnik, 2000) conducted during political dialogue groups suggested that Israelis modified their communication style to allow for and listen to the perspectives of Palestinians while Palestinians tended to adopt a style that included interruptions to a degree similar to Israeli Jews, suggesting the contextual nature of communication styles (Zupnik, 2000).

As illustrated through the case studies, intercultural conflicts are compelling, contentious, and complex. The multiframe analysis enables us to see how intercultural conflicts operate on multiple levels and how each level informs the other. To navigate intercultural conflicts in the context of globalization, we need to be aware of how communication styles, orientations to conflict, and facework strategies differ across cultures. The meso-frame brings into view the role of group-based prejudices, stereotypes, cultural histories, and cultural identities that impact intercultural conflict. Intercultural conflicts are also influ- ence by macro-frame factors such as media, discourse, and economic forces that are situ- ated in the context of asymmetrical geopolitical power. The multiframe analysis brings to our attention the potential short- and long-term causes of intercultural conflicts and the conditions that escalate and entrench conflict among cultural groups. We turn now to a discussion of strategies to address intercultural conflicts in our everyday lives.

STRATEGIES FOR ADDRESSING INTERCULTURAL CONFLICT

Intercultural praxis discussed throughout the book is used here to provide strategies for addressing intercultural conflicts on interpersonal, intergroup, and international levels. Engaging in intercultural praxis in intercultural conflict situations raises our awareness, increases our critical analysis, and develops our socially responsible action.

Inquiry

One of the greatest challenges in intercultural misunderstandings and conflicts is cultivat- ing an interest in and empathy for seeing the situation from the other person's point of view. Our tendency is to hold firm to our own position and defend it from alternative perspectives. The entry point of inquiry requires that we suspend our judgments about others, loosen our posture of defensiveness, and have a willingness to know the experiences of the other. There are risks involved as our way of viewing the situation may be challenged by hearing and acknowledging the views of others. Further, through inquiry, we may actually change our position, which if long-held and deeply intertwined with our identities can be scary.

In some conflict situations, asking questions with a sincere desire to know can be enough to shift the contentious nature of the conflict toward one of mutual understand- ing. In other situations, inquiry may be accomplished more effectively through careful observation of those who are culturally different from us. Through observation, we can begin to see the patterns of engagement that make sense from the other's perspective; the ways our approach, attitudes, or beliefs may cause friction; and how we can make adjust- ments to ease the misunderstanding or conflict. For example, in Josh and Patrice's situa- tion, their differing communication and conflict styles exacerbate the tension between them. However, over time, they have both learned to balance direct inquiry and explicit expression of feelings with more implicit forms of inquiry. In the case of interethnic con- flict at the high school, classroom activities and structured learning exercises provided an opening for all students including Latino/Latina and Armenian students to gain knowledge about each others' backgrounds and recognize commonalities as well as differences (Sorrells, 2003).

Framing

As demonstrated in the case studies, it is critical to have the capacity to intentionally ana- lyze intercultural misunderstanding and conflicts from micro-, meso-, and macro-frames as well as appreciate how issues on different levels impact each other. Conflicts between Israeli Jews and Palestinians can and do occur on a daily basis. It is important to look at the micro-level differences in communication and conflict styles. As we broaden the frame, we see how the history of conflict, cultural identities, patterns of inequities, as well as broader relations of power affect the particular and situated intercultural conflict. As we focus in and foreground the micro-frame of intercultural communication, we need to keep the wider background frame in mind as it provides the context in which meaning about the particular is made. Also our perspectives, our views on ourselves, others, and the world around us are always and inevitably limited by frames. Our goal in engaging in intercultural praxis is to recognize the frames of reference that allow for and limit our view and experience of the world.

Positioning

In intercultural conflict situations, awareness of how and where we are positioned in relation to others in terms of socially constructed hierarchies of power is critical. Our gender, ethnicity, race, class, religion, nationality, and sexual orientation all inform the locations from which we speak, listen, act, think, and make sense of the world. Our positionality within these categories also offers and limits our access to privilege and power. Recognizing how Josh's positionality impacts his perceptions and interpretations may allow him to reevaluate his responses to Patrice and listen with greater empathy to her interpretation instead of minimizing her experiences. Awareness of his positionality enables Josh to use his position of privilege as a White male to intervene in situations where discrimination and systemic inequity occur.

Positioning as a strategy in conflict situations also directs us to attend to who can speak and who is silenced; whose actions have the power to shape and impact others; and whose actions are dismissed, unreported, and marginalized. As illustrated in the Israeli–Palestinian conflict, it is critical to investigate whose version of the story is privileged and agreed upon as true and whose knowledge is deemed unworthy, insignificant, or unnecessary.

Dialogue

Dialogue, informed by inquiry, framing, and positioning, is a central strategy for managing and negotiating intercultural conflicts. Dialogue provides the opportunity to reach across differences and creatively engage with points of view, ways of thinking, and beliefs different from our own. Yet dialogue with people who hold perspectives, beliefs, and worldviews that are different from our own is often quite difficult. Communication scholars Sonja Foss and Cindy Griffin (1995) proposed **invitational rhetoric** as a form of communication committed to equality, recognition, and self-determination. Instead of entering or engaging in conflict situations with the intention of changing, persuading, or conquering the other, the goal of invitational rhetoric is to shift the frame of the engagement to one of invitation, cooperation, and coordination. In the initiative to address the ongoing conflict between Latino/Latina and Armenian students at Grant

High School, university students were trained to facilitate dialogue sessions with students at the school, which included conversations, group activities, and role plays to reframe their differences as opportunities for learning and building upon their commonalities (Sorrells, 2003).

Additionally, the notion of cooperative argument can be a useful strategy in intercultural conflict situations. **Cooperative argument** refers to a model of argument that manages the resolutions of disagreement within a set of rules that are responsive to intercultural differences (Ellis, 2005). Shifting from an adversarial and competitive model of argument, cooperative argument seeks understanding and the formulation of solutions for groups whose livelihoods and existences are interdependent.

> The participants see themselves as members of a deliberative community; that is, the process is one of ethical dialogue with a concern for relational integrity, empathy, and using the arguments and information of the other culture to make decisions built on a common framework of understanding. (Ellis, 2005, p. 60)

Reflection

Reflection is central to learning, growth, and change in all situations, yet the ability to be self-reflexive and to see oneself as a creative, flexible subject with the capacity to change is essential to effectively manage intercultural conflict. The ability to employ the strategies of framing and positioning requires that we consciously observe ourselves and critically analyze our interrelationships with others. Reflection is necessary to initiate, maintain, and sustain dialogue across bumpy, unknown, and difficult terrain of intercultural conflicts. Sometimes reflection takes place on our own. We think back over a conversation, a misunderstanding, or a conflict we had and consider how we can act and engage differently to encourage understanding and meaningful exchanges. Sometimes reflection occurs in dialogue with the person with whom we are in conflict or with a third party. At other times, we need structured environments such as dialogue groups, conflict resolution, or formal negotiations to access, express feelings, develop empathy, and reframe conflicts in constructive ways. Reflection informs our actions. Reflection that incorporates critical analyses of micro-, meso-, and macro-frames of intercultural conflicts, that recognizes our own and others' positioning, and that engages us in genuine dialogue enables us to act in the world in meaningful, effective, and responsible ways.

Action

Intercultural praxis is not only about deepening our understanding; rather, intercultural praxis means we join our increased understanding with responsible action to make a difference in the world—to create a more socially just, equitable, and peaceful world. In conflicts, the intercultural praxis entry point of action can take the form of doing research to learn more about the background and history of the individuals or groups in conflict. It can involve speaking up and using your access to power or privilege to challenge discrimination or prejudice among friends and coworkers. It could also entail joining with others to move initiatives, policies, or practices forward that create equitable access and benefits for all in your organization, community, or state.

Action can also entail joining an intercultural coalition or activist group aimed at creating systemic change toward greater equity and justice. In the early 2000s, students on campuses across the country used sit-ins, rallies, and marches in campaigns to end the use of sweatshop labor in the $2.5 billion collegiate clothing industry. Students from over 70 universities across the country formed the Campus Antiwar Network (CAN) organizing actions such as national demonstrations, direct aid to victims of Hurricane Katrina, referendums such as the "College Not Combat" ballot measure in San Francisco, as well as collaborations with international peace organizations (CAN, n.d.). Intercultural praxis offers us points of entry for critical, reflective thinking and acting that enable us to navigate the complex and conflictive intercultural spaces we inhabit interpersonally, communally, and globally.

SUMMARY

Conflicts among individuals and groups from different cultural, ethical, racial, religious, and national backgrounds are propelled today by greater proximity, increasing competition, and diminishing resources. Colonial histories, exploitative conditions, and magnified social and economic inequity also shape the causes and consequences of intercultural conflict. A multiframe model was presented in this chapter to analyze the complexities of intercultural conflict, to inform our understanding of how and why diverse groups engage in conflict, and to guide our awareness of the situational factors that lead to and exacerbate conflict in the global context. The model highlighted the interplay between the micro-, meso-, and macro-frames that impact intercultural conflicts. Case studies of intercultural conflict from interpersonal, intergroup, and international contexts were used to illustrate the multiframe analysis. Intercultural praxis provided an approach for effective communication strategies to address and negotiate intercultural conflicts.

KEY TERMS

intercultural conflict
interdependent orientation
independent orientation
context
high context communication
low context communication
face
facework
in-groups

out-groups
cultural histories
oppositional metaphors
immigration industrial complex
negative identity
musayara
dugri
invitational rhetoric
cooperative argument

DISCUSSION QUESTIONS AND ACTIVITIES

Discussion Questions

1. What is your orientation to conflict? Using the key concepts from the chapter (i.e., independent/interdependent orientation, facework, low/high context, invitational rhetoric), discuss how you are inclined to act in conflict.

2. As the world becomes more globalized and each nation more multicultural, why do we continue to witness intercultural conflicts across the world? Is conflict innate to human nature? Is conflict inherent in the process of globalization? Is conflict profitable? If so, who benefits from conflict and how?

3. What is the relationship between intercultural conflict and social justice? Why is social justice important when we address intercultural conflict?

4. Think about the most recent or difficult conflict you had with others. How did culture or cultural differences shape the conflict? How do you think intercultural praxis might help you and others address the conflict effectively?

Activities

1. Applying the Multidimensional Framework of Analysis

   a. In groups of 3 to 4 people, select an incident of intercultural conflict (interpersonal, intergroup, or international).

   b. Apply the multidimensional framework used in this chapter to analyze the micro-, meso-, and macro-levels of the conflict.

   c. Discuss how the micro-, meso-, and macro-frames interrelate with and influence each other.

2. Utilizing Intercultural Praxis

   a. Using the intercultural conflict analyzed in Activity 1, discuss how you can use intercultural praxis to manage the conflict.

   b. Discuss specific ways in which you can engage both individually and collectively in the process of addressing intercultural conflict.

3. Different Definitions of Culture in Conflict Negotiation

   a. In groups of 2 to 3 people, create a list of how intercultural conflict can be understood and addressed differently through various definitions of "culture" discussed in Chapter 1.

   b. In your list, discuss how culture as (1) shared meaning, (2) contested meaning, and (3) a resource shape the ways we approach and manage intercultural conflict.

   c. Finally, discuss in your group the role of culture in producing and/or resolving conflict.

REFERENCES

Allen, T., & Seaton, J. (Eds.) (1999). *The media of conflict*. New York: Zed Books.

Archer, B. (2004). *The end of gay: And the death of heterosexuality*. New York: Thunder's Mouth.

Bayoumi, M. (2008). *How does it feel to be a problem? Being young and Arab in America*. New York: Penguin.

Blum, W. (1995). *Killing hope: U.S. military and CIA interventions since World War II*. Monroe, ME: Common Courage.

Bournoutian, G. (2002). *A concise history of Armenian people*. Costa Mesa, CA: Mazda.

Brew, F. P., & Cairns, D. R. (2004). Do culture or situational constraints determine choice of direct or indirect styles in intercultural workplace conflicts? *International Journal of Intercultural Relations, 28*(5), 331–352.

Campus Antiwar Network. (n.d.). *Formation and growth of the U.S. independent, democratic and grassroots antiwar student movement*. Retrieved from http://www.grassrootspeace.org/campus_antiwar.html

Center for Intercultural Organizing. (n.d.). *Our history*. Retrieved from http://www.interculturalorganizing.org/who-we-are/our-history/

Chi-Ching, E. Y. (1998). Social-cultural context of perceptions and approaches to conflict: The case for Singapore. In K. Leung & D. Tjosvold (Eds.), *Conflict management in the Asia Pacific: Assumptions and approaches in diverse cultures* (pp. 123–145). Singapore: Wiley.

Cho, E. H., Puete, F. A., Louie, M. C. Y., & Khokha, S. (2004). *BRIDGE: A popular education resource for immigrant & regugee community organizers*. Oakland, CA: National Network for Immigrant and Refugee Rights.

Coleman, P. T. (2003). Characteristics of protracted, intractable conflicts: Toward a development of a metaframework—I. *Peace and Conflict: Journal of Peace Psychology, 9*, 1–37.

Eller, J. D. (1999). *From culture to ethnicity to conflict: An anthropological perspective on international ethnic conflict*. Ann Arbor: University of Michigan Press.

Ellis, D. G. (2005). Intercultural communication in intractable ethnopolitical conflicts. In W. J. Starosta & G. Chen (Eds.), *Taking stock in intercultural communication: Where to now?* (pp. 45–69). Washington, DC: International and Intercultural Communication Annual XXVIII.

Fernandes, D. (2007). *Homeland security and the business of immigration*. St. Paul, MN: Seven Stories.

Foss, S. K., & Griffin, C. L. (1995). Beyond persuasion: A proposal for invitation rhetoric. *Communication Monograph, 62*, 15–28.

Greifat, Y., & Katriel, T. (1989). Life demands musayara: Communication and culture among Arabs in Israel. In S. Ting-Toomey & F. Korzenny (Eds.), *Language, communication and culture: Current directions*. London: Sage.

Golash-Boza, T. (2009). The immigration industrial complex: Why we enforce immigration policy destined to fail. *Sociology Compass, 3/2*, 295–309.

Hall, E. T. (1976). *Beyond culture*. New York: Anchor.

Hocker, J. L., & Wilmot, W. W. (1998). *Interpersonal conflict* (5th ed.). New York: McGraw-Hill.

Kivel, P. (1996). *Uprooting racism: How white people can work for racial justice*. Philadelphia: New Society.

Markus, H. R., & Lin, L. R. (1999). Conflictways: Cultural diversity in the meanings and practices of conflict. In D. A. Prentice & D.T. Miller (Eds.), *Cultural divides: Understanding and overcoming group conflict* (pp. 302–333). New York: Russell Sage Foundation.

Melone, S. D., Terzis, G., & Beleli, O. (2002). Using the media for conflict transformation: The Common Ground experience. *Berghof handbook for conflict transformation*. Berlin, Germany: Berghof Research Center for Constructive Conflict Transformation. Retrieved from http://www.berghof-handbook.net/articles/melone_hb.pdf

Mullard, M., & Cole, B. A. (2007). *Globalisation, citizenship and the war on terror*. Cheltenham, UK: Edward Elgar.

Orbe, M. (1998). *Constructing co-cultural theory: An explication of culture, power and communication.* Thousand Oaks, CA: Sage.

Payaslian, S. (2005). *United States policy toward the Armenian questions and the Armenian genocide.* New York: Palgrave McMillan.

Potok, M. (2006). Hate group number top 800. *Southern Poverty Law Center Report.* Retrieve from http://www.splcenter.org/center/splcreport/article.jsp?aid = 187

Shim, T. Y., Kim, M., & Martin, J. N. (2008). *Changing Korea: Understanding culture and communication.* New York: Peter Lang.

Sorrells, K. (2003). Communicating common ground: Integrating community service learning into the intercultural classroom. *Communication Teacher, 17*(4), 1–14.

Ting-Toomey, S., & Kurogi, A. (1998). Facework competence in intercultural conflict: An updated face-negotiation theory. *International Journal of Intercultural Relations, 22,* 187–296.

Ting-Toomey, S., & Oetzel, J. G. (2001). *Managing intercultural conflict effectively.* Thousand Oaks, CA: Sage.

Ting-Toomey, S., & Oetzel, J. G. (2002). Cross-cultural face concern and conflict styles: Current status and future directions. In W.B. Gudykunst & B. Mody (Eds.), *Handbook of international and intercultural communication* (2nd ed, pp. 143–206). Thousand Oaks, CA: Sage.

Triandis, H. C. (1995). *Individualism & collectivism.* Boulder, CO: Westview.

United Nations Relief and Works Agency. (2007). *The United Nations and Palestinian refugees.* Retrieved from http://www.unrwa.org/userfiles/2010011791015.pdf

United Nations Relief and Works Agency for Palestine Refugees. (2011, July). *UNRW: In figures.* Retrieved from http://www.unrwa.org/userfiles/2011092751539.pdf

Zupnik, Y. (2000). Conversational interruptions in Israel-Palestinian "Dialogue" events. *Discourse Studies, 2*(1), 85–110.

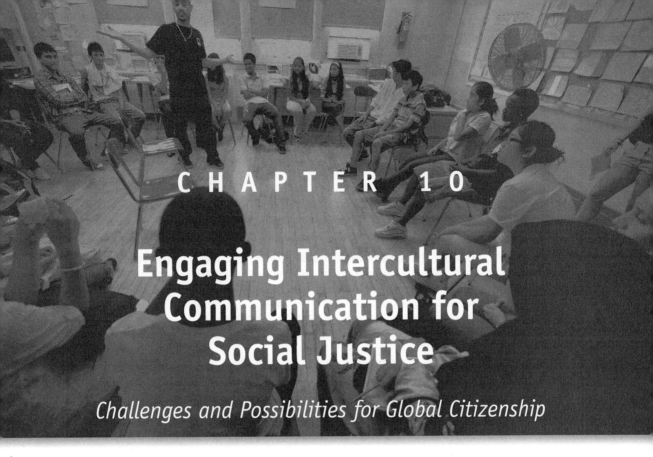

CHAPTER 10

Engaging Intercultural Communication for Social Justice

Challenges and Possibilities for Global Citizenship

Social Justice class for refugees in Brooklyn, New York

We began our conversation about intercultural communication in this book by acknowledging the increasing interconnectedness and interdependence of the nearly 7 billion people who call planet Earth "home." The emphasis, from the start of our dialogue through this concluding chapter, has been on "we," the 7 billion people of the world. As noted throughout, the accelerated interrelationship among people from diverse cultures, fueled by advances in communication and transportation technologies and forged through neoliberal economic and political policies, has dramatically impacted intercultural communication in the context of globalization offering both challenges and possibilities.

The challenges are many. Neoliberal economic and political polices have reconstituted colonial and imperial relations of power. Inequities in and across countries and cultures have magnified. Interethnic and interracial tensions and conflicts have escalated. Poverty and hunger have increased with devastating impact on human health. The environmental health of our planet is in peril (Robbins, 2002). These are real challenges affecting each of us to varying degrees in observable and hidden ways.

Source: Chapter-opening photo © Bebeto Matthews/Associated Press.

Possibilities, in the context of globalization, also abound. Potential for democratization and the spread of human rights is at hand (Ackerman & DuVall, 2001). We need only look to the "people-powered" revolutions occurring across the Middle East for evidence of this. Knowledge to address and ensure the basic human needs of food, shelter, health, education, and cultural maintenance for all 7 billion people is obtainable. Consciousness of a world where benefits are shared broadly rather than funneled for the advantage of an elite few is rising. Networks to build coalitions that resist injustice and establish new terms of engagement are available (George, 2004). Many opportunities to take action not only for ourselves but socially responsible action in collaboration with others are available (Boggs, 2011). The knowledge, attitudes, and skills learned by studying intercultural communication and engaging in intercultural praxis prepare us to build connections, alliances, and coalitions. Thus, we must join our knowledge, capacities, and skills with intention and commitment to manifest a more equitable and socially just world.

In a world saturated by media spectacles, where scenes of violence, corruption, and human and natural devastation replay 24/7, it is easy to become apathetic and think of social justice as unrealistic and idealistic. It is tempting to let indifference or despair overcome us when we are inundated by daily demands and struggle in a climate of reduced resources and limited access. We may think, What can one person do? or There've always been the "haves" and the "have-nots." I just have to look out for myself. Things are never going to change. It's not my problem. Yet the people, throughout history and today, who are the most actively involved in organizing for change, challenging injustice, and seeking alternatives for a more equitable world are the ones who are most hopeful.

As we culminate our exploration together, this chapter focuses on applying our intercultural knowledge, skills, and attitudes to create a more equitable, just, and peaceful world. Education scholars Maurianne Adams, Lee Anne Bell, and Pat Griffin (2007) defined **social justice** as both a goal and process in their book *Teaching for Diversity and Social Justice*: "The goal of social justice is full and equal participation of all groups in a society that is mutually shaped to meet their needs" (p. 1). Social justice includes a vision of the equitable distribution of resources where social actors experience agency with and responsibility for others. The process of reaching the goal of social justice should be "democratic and participatory, inclusive and affirming of human agency and human capacities for working collaboratively to create change" (Adams et al., p. 3).

We begin this chapter by identifying the capacities necessary for global citizenship in the 21st century. The model of intercultural praxis introduced and developed throughout the book is used here as the basis for our discussion of intercultural competence. Following this, personal testimonies from people who are active in community-based advocacy and international activism illustrate how we can move from apathy to empowerment as we engage in intercultural praxis. We then turn our attention to a case study to learn how intercultural alliances in the context of globalization are sites where injustice is challenged and responsible action creates possibilities for a more equitable, just, and peaceful world. The chapter concludes with a review of four principles that have provided the foundation for engaging in intercultural communication for social justice throughout the book.

BECOMING GLOBAL CITIZENS IN THE 21ST CENTURY

Daisaku Ikeda, Buddhist leader, educator, peace activist, and founder of the Boston Research Center for the 21st Century, has identified three **qualities of global citizens**. First, he proposed that wisdom is necessary. Specifically, Ikeda (2005) referred to the wisdom to perceive the interconnectedness of all life. As shown throughout this book, the economic situation in China and India, political upheaval in the Middle East, the fallout from a natural disaster in Japan do indeed impact our lives in the United States. At the macro-level, our foreign policies and economic strategies are affected. Yet events and actions on the global stage also influence the micro-level. The triple tragedy of the earthquake, tsunami, and nuclear crisis in Japan in 2011 had global consequences as costs for consumer goods such as cars, electronics, and food as well as interest rates rose. Shortages translated into $500 to $2,000 increases for U.S. car buyers and auto facilities closed in the U.S. causing job loss as a result of disrupted supply chains (Peterson, 2011).

The second quality of a global citizen is courage—"the courage to respect one another's differences and use them as impetus to creative living, rather than rejecting or excluding others on the basis of culture, nationality and race" (Ikeda, 2005, p. x). The third quality is compassion, which "means being a true friend who hears the anguished cries of others, striving with them to overcome and surmount suffering" (Ikeda, 2005 p. x). Compassion is often associated with empathy. **Empathy** refers to the ability to share the pain of others and the capacity to know the emotional experience of others from within their frame of reference.

Commonly, the notion of citizenship has been used to refer to membership in and identity associated with a nation-state. For example, you may identify yourself as a U.S. citizen or a citizen of Sweden, Brazil, or Turkey. People recognized as citizens are seen as having specific rights, duties, responsibilities, and privileges that go along with citizenship. Citizenship in certain nations, namely, wealthy First World nations, confers benefits and privileges of international mobility that are denied many in the global context. The notion of national "citizenship" is problematic given the racialized, classist, and heteronormative policies that prescribe inclusion and exclusion in nation-states.

Today, we live in a world where interactions, commerce, communication networks, media representations, and conflicts are increasingly global. Yet no one global government exits to which we can swear allegiance, call on for protection, or access for defense of rights (Noddings, 2005). Given this, Peggy McIntosh (2005) argued for a redefinition of the notion of "citizenship" in the context of globalization. She suggested that conceiving of and enacting global citizenship requires a sense of belonging in the world that goes beyond loyalty, responsibility, and protection based on one's city, region, or nation. "Within this vast world, the marks of a global citizenship would need to include affection, respect, care, curiosity and concern for the well-being of all living beings" (McIntosh, 2005, p. 23).

Capacities for Global Citizenship

McIntosh (2005) proposed a set of capacities of mind, heart, body, and soul that reimagine citizenship based on "needs" rather than "rights." **Capacities for global citizenship** are capacities that reimagine citizenship based on human needs rather than rights. The capacities of mind she outlined for global citizenship provide a foundation for intercultural competence for the 21st century:

1. The ability to observe one's self and the world around one

2. The ability to make comparisons and contrasts between these worlds

3. The ability to see "plurally" as a result

4. The ability to understand that both "reality" and language come in versions

5. The ability to see power relations and understand them systemically

6. The ability to balance awareness of one's own realities with the realities of others (p. 23)

Understanding the world as complex, multifaceted, and plural is critical for global citizenship in the 21st century. Having the capacity to see the interrelationship between various perspectives; to validate multiple perspectives, realities, and experiences; and to see how these perspectives are shaped by relations of power are all necessary capacities for effective global citizenship.

McIntosh (2005) identified the following capacities of the heart that are essential for global citizenship:

1. The ability to respect and delve into one's own feelings

2. The awareness of others' feelings and the ability to validate others' feelings

3. The ability to experience a mixture of conflicting feelings without a loss of integrity

4. The ability to experience affective worlds plurally while keeping one's core orientation

5. The capacity to wish competing parties well

6. The ability to understand how the "politics of location" affects one's own and others' positions and power in the world

7. The ability to balance being heartfelt with the knowledge of how culture is embedded in ourselves and others (p. 23)

In intercultural interactions, misunderstandings, and conflicts, we have a tendency to allow our own feelings and perceptions to eclipse the emotional experiences of others. Awareness of the feelings of others as well as our own is critical. Having the capacities to hold and validate both—a plurality of affective worlds—is essential. Poet and essayist Terry Tempest Williams (2005) noted the following:

> The human heart is the first home of democracy. It is where we embrace our questions. Can we be equitable? Can we be generous? Can we listen with our whole being, not just our mind, and offer our attention rather than our opinion? And do we have enough resolve in our heart to act courageously, relentlessly, without giving up, ever—trusting our fellow citizens to join us in a determined pursuit of a living democracy? The heart is the house of empathy, whose door opens when we receive the pain of others. This is where bravery lives, where we'll find our mettle to give and receive, to love and be loved, to stand in the center of uncertainty with strength, not fear, understanding this is all there is. The heart is the path to wisdom because it dares to be vulnerable in the presence of power. (p. 39)

Additionally, "the politics of location," as used by McIntosh and discussed throughout the book as "positionality" and "positioning," refers to our awareness of how we are positioned or "located" differently in relation to others within systems of power. Our positionality as individuals and members of socially constructed groups affords and limits our access to power, privilege, and resources. Awareness of the "politics of location" provides insight into who is advantaged and privileged within interlocking systems and who is disadvantaged or targeted systemically.

Interestingly, McIntosh (2005) noted that people who have a great deal of formal education often manifest weaker capacities of the heart than those who have less education. In strengthening the abilities to compete successfully in the competitive world of capitalism, have we lost our capacities for emotional connection, empathy, and compassion? McIntosh (2005) coupled the capacities of the mind and heart with those of the soul and body. The capacities of the body and soul include respect for our own and others' physical needs and the pursuit of nondestructive ways to preserve and enhance all people physically and spiritually. Finally, the capacities of the global citizenship include engaging rather than withdrawing from tensions, conflicts, and contestations. Global citizens serve the greater good by acting to alleviate both danger and suffering.

The capacities previously outlined are often gendered as "feminine" and thus are devalued, diminished, and seen as "weak" and insignificant in societies infused with "masculine" values. McIntosh (2005) advocated a shift in paradigm from "human rights," invented by 18th-century European thinkers, to "human needs," which are empirically verifiable and universal.

> Water, food, clothing, shelter, and meaningful connection with other human beings are basic needs without whose fulfillment we die. The ethos of global citizenship, I believe, must start with providing, and caring about providing, these basic human necessities and the protections for sustaining ecosystems that humans depend upon. (McIntosh, 2005, p. 26)

Intercultural Competence

Intercultural competency refers to the knowledge, attitudes, and skills needed to engage effectively in intercultural situations. The model of intercultural praxis presented throughout the book provides a blueprint for developing intercultural competencies for global citizenship in the 21st century. As described along our journey, intercultural praxis is a way of being in the world that joins critical, reflective, and engaged analysis with informed action for socially responsible action and global justice. All moments in our day provide opportunities to practice and develop our communication competence by engaging in intercultural praxis. The competencies discussed here elaborate on the points of entry for intercultural praxis.

Inquiry, as an intercultural competency for global citizenship, is characterized by an "interrogative" mode of being in the world (Gadamer, 1989; Heidegger, 1962). The interrogative mode both challenges and complements the received Western tradition of advancing statements or assertions as truth claims. Curious inquiry about those who are different from ourselves leads us to engage with others, learn about how they are both different from and similar to ourselves, and recognize, as McIntosh (2005) proposed, the plurality of perceptions, experiences, and feelings among ourselves and others.

As an intercultural competency, inquiry requires motivation to know about others and ourselves. Often, it is easier to stay with what is comfortable and familiar instead of taking risks to learn about others. Seemingly, it takes much less effort to hold on to our judgments about others and take refuge in old stereotypes rather than suspend judgments and question our preconceived ideas of those who are different from us. On the surface, it seems much less painful and disruptive just to stick with our received assumptions and perceptions about the world than being receptive to challenging and changing the way we think, feel, see, and act in the world. Frequently, people who are in dominant groups—for example, Whites, men, heterosexuals, people in middle and upper classes, and Christians in the United States—do not feel the need or incentive to step outside their comfort zones. Today, the rapid and increasing movement of people; demographic shifts in neighborhoods, schools, and workplaces; as well as local and international events can and do prod people from their comfort zones. However, inquiry, as an intercultural competence for the 21st century, is not only a reactive capacity; inquiry means that individuals and groups are *motivated* and take the initiative to engage with people who are different from themselves recognizing both the challenges and benefits of intercultural interactions, relationships, and alliances.

Framing as an intercultural competence entails an awareness that our perspectives, our views on ourselves, others, and the world around us are always and inevitably enabled and constrained by frames. We see things through multiple frames or lenses—individual, cultural, regional, and national—that necessarily include some things and exclude others. Not only does this process of "highlighting" and "hiding" impact our everyday perceptions of the world but our frames also represent and advance certain dominant or oppositional interests. Thus, frames serve political ends as well as sense-making functions.

As demonstrated in previous chapters, framing also means we have the competency to shift among micro-, meso-, and macro-frames of perception and analysis. Shifting frames, we are able to map out the ways particular and situated intercultural interactions, misunderstandings, or conflicts are positioned and contextualized within interpersonal, local, and national as well as broader geopolitical and global relations of power. The flexibility to shift perspectives between the particular, situated dimensions of intercultural communication and the broader, global dimensions while maintaining awareness of multiple frames is an important intercultural competence for global citizenship.

Positioning, as an intercultural competence for the 21st century, entails understanding how we are positioned in relation to others. As noted throughout the book, the world in which we live is stratified by socially constructed categories based on culture, race, class, gender, nationality, religion, age, and physical abilities, among others. These categories not only serve to divide and group us; categories of difference also position us socially, politically, and materially in relation to each other and to hierarchal configurations of power. Awareness of positioning as an intercultural competence not only draws attention to the material and symbolic consequences of our differing positionalities but also requires us to use our access to power, privilege, and resources to challenge inequitable systems that disproportionately advantage some and disadvantage others.

Additionally, positioning, as an intercultural competence, reminds us to investigate who can speak and who is silenced in any given situation. It is critical to be cognizant of whose communication styles, both verbal and nonverbal communication, and whose behaviors are seen as "normal" as well as how communication is used to marginalize and exclude.

We need to examine whose actions are dismissed or criminalized and who is in positions of power to make decisions. Attending to positioning as a competency for intercultural communication reveals the relationship among positionality, power, and what we regard as "knowledge." Instead of accepting what is presented to us as "true" in the media, by government leaders, teachers, parents, or friends, positioning requires that we ask what interests are served by a particular version of a situation, event, or crisis. We also ask who benefits if we believe and act in accordance with a particular version of "truth."

Dialogue, as an intercultural competence, may seem easy. However, as conceptualized here, dialogue entails bringing the competencies of inquiry, framing, and positioning to bear on our conversations, interactions, and engagements with others. Dialogue in intercultural interactions inevitably requires the ability to stretch ourselves; to extend into unknown territory; and to stay in conversation even when it is difficult, painful, and challenging. This is no easy task. Cultural differences as well as differences in power and positionality in intercultural interactions require us to imagine, experience, and engage creatively with points of view; ways of thinking, being, and doing; and beliefs different from our own while accepting that we may not fully understand or come to common agreement. Intercultural dialogue—from initial encounters to the development of intercultural friendships to resolving intercultural conflicts—requires an ability to deal with ambiguity. **Managing ambiguity** refers to an individual's or group's ability to handle the uncertainty, anxiety, and tension that arises from the unknown in intercultural situations.

Communication scholar Sara DeTurk (2006) argued that structured dialogue among individuals from diverse cultures and positionalities can facilitate intercultural alliances as perspective-taking personal agency and responsibility develop among people. Additionally, when individuals are exposed to muted and silenced voices, dialogue can diminish intercultural conflict.

Reflection, as an aspect of intercultural competence, is central to each of the intercultural competencies already addressed. To engage in curious inquiry, one must be able to reflect on oneself as a subject—a thinking, learning, and acting subject. Self-reflection allows for awareness and knowledge of self to develop. **Self-awareness** in intercultural communication refers to an awareness or consciousness of oneself as a cultural being, whose beliefs, assumptions, attitudes, values, and behaviors are contoured by culture. Self-awareness gained through reflection allows one to critically analyze one's positionality and interrelationship with others, which are essential for the competencies of positioning, framing, and dialogue. Critical self-awareness gained through reflection is important as we initiate, maintain, and sustain dialogue across the new and often difficult intercultural terrain of the 21st century.

As Paulo Freire (1998) observed, reflection can itself serve political functions. Through reflection, we can intervene in uninformed actions that may otherwise be normalized as "the way things are" and "the way things must be." By disengaging from the taken-for-granted and the nonreflexive flow of everyday actions, knowledge systems, and value commitments, the act of reflection allows us to reposition and reframe what may well be oppressive conditions or relations of power (Sorrells & Nakagawa, 2008).

Action, as an intercultural competence, joins analysis and reflection. Having the competence to deepen our understanding of ourselves, others, and the world in which we live is critical; however, as we strive toward global citizenship in the 21st century, we must actualize and manifest our increased understanding through responsible and liberatory action that makes a difference in the world. Each of us takes actions every day both individually and collectively that can bring about change toward a more just and equitable world. Our actions and decisions in educational, work, and relational contexts provide opportunities for informed engagement and critical intervention. In a capitalist society, our consumer choices about what media we view, how we entertain ourselves, and what we purchase and consume are all actions that can and do impact the world we live in. When we recognize our complicity in furthering inequities, we have the opportunity to confront ourselves and others about the choices we make through our consumer actions. We can also join others to organize and take collective action. Everyday actions informed by the intercultural competencies of inquiry, framing, positioning, dialogue, and reflection can be catalysts for actions that engage and produce social justice and global transformation.

Developing the intercultural competencies outlined here enable us to use our multifaceted identity positions and shifting access to privilege and power to identify allies, build solidarity, imagine alternatives, and intervene in struggles for social responsibility and social justice.

> As a critical practice, pedagogy's role lies not only in changing how people think about themselves and their relationship to others and the world, but in energizing students and others to engage in those struggles that further possibilities for living in a more just society. (Giroux, 2004, pp. 63–64)

In her book *Another World Is Possible If . . .* , scholar and activist Susan George (2004) asserted the following:

> My answer is that another world is indeed possible—but only when the greatest possible number of people with many backgrounds, viewpoints and skills join together to make it happen. Things change when enough people insist on it and work for it. No one should be left out and feel they can not contribute. No one who wants to help build another world should, for lack of knowledge or connections, remain on the sideline. (pp. xii-xiii)

Too often, people in positions of greater social, economic, and political power develop visions and actions with the intent of "helping" disenfranchised groups. Yet if the voices, perspectives, needs, and experiences of marginalized groups are not at the table, the process and outcome of the effort repeat and reinforce rather than rectify injustices. The involvement of multiple and diverse points of view and social actors with different positionalities is critical to envision and enact another world, a more socially just world.

"HOPE IN THE DARK": FROM APATHY TO EMPOWERMENT

News of current events and forecasts of the future often depict dark realities and project dire prospects. In her book entitled *Hope in the Dark: Untold Histories, Wild Possibilities*, activist and cultural historian Rebecca Solnit (2004) noted that few people recognize the radically transformed world in which we live. Undoubtedly, the world has been changed by the devastating consequences of global capital and global warming. Yet what often goes unnoticed is the ways in which our world has also been altered "by dreams of freedom and justice—and transformed by things we could not have dreamed of" (Solnit, 2004, p. 2). Mainstream media frequently focus on violence, crises, and disasters creating spectacles that serve to distract or entertain rather than inform. In an effort to ferret out the untold side of the stories of conventional outlets, alternative media often focus on misrepresentations and distortions in the mainstream media revealing even deeper realities and consequences of devastation. Both sets of stories are incomplete. What stories are missing? What accounts of the current realities and everyday experiences of the 7 billion people on planet Earth are left out?

The stories of students, teachers, and workers who decide to take action in ways that work toward collective social and economic good are often missing. The reports of consumers who change their patterns of consumption to challenge their complicity with practices that exploit and dehumanize others are passed over. The accounts of soldiers, corporate managers, and citizens who refuse the use of violence to force others' submission, who challenge systems that benefit a few and abuse the less powerful, and who take stands against social injustice are rarely told.

INTERCULTURAL PRAXIS FOR SOCIAL JUSTICE
COMMUNICATION FOR SOCIAL JUSTICE

Reverend James Lawson, a close associate of Dr. Martin Luther King Jr. and leading architect of the civil rights movement, worked closely with the California State University, Northridge, campus community on the *Civil Discourse and Social Change Initiative* from 2010 to 2011. Now in his 80s, Reverend Lawson has devoted his life to nonviolent social change working to dismantle racism and sexism and gain living wages for workers and equal rights for lesbian, gay, bisexual, and transgender (LGBT) communities. Informed by the philosophy of nonviolence practiced by Mahatma Gandhi, Reverend Lawson has trained students and activists in the United States and around the world on strategies for nonviolent direct action. Nonviolence does not mean passivism. Rather, the 20th century concept of nonviolence refers to the use of people power for political action. Nonviolent direct action means engendering another view of power—an alternative to violent, destructive power—where people power is used to create equity and justice. History books often focus on wars and bloody revolutions, yet the 20th century provides ample evidence of the extraordinary power of nonviolence to overcome colonial rule, the suppression of human rights, and dictatorial control. In the book *A Force More Powerful*, Ackerman and DuVall (2001) documented history-altering reforms created through nonviolent struggle in Russia, Denmark, India, the United States, Poland, and Chile to name only a few. The revolution in Egypt in 2011 is a recent example of the power of nonviolent direct action.

In the context of globalization, our narratives of intercultural alliances for social change—small and big—need to be told. We need to hear the stories of how our world has been transformed by dreams, hopes, and actions for social justice and peace. Solnit (2004) commented on the role of hope on the path to empowerment and social change:

> Causes and effects assume history marches forward, but history is not an army. It is a crab scuttling sideways, a drip of soft water wearing away stone, an earthquake breaking centuries of tension. Sometimes one person inspires a movement, or her words do decades later; sometimes a few passionate people change the world; sometimes those millions are stirred by the same outrage or the same ideal and change comes upon us like a change of weather. All that these transformations have in common is that they begin in the imagination, in hope. To hope is to gamble. It's to bet on the future, on your desires, on the possibility that an open heart and uncertainty is better than gloom and safety. To hope is dangerous and yet, it is the opposite of fear, for to live is to risk. (p. 4)

"Hope"—as envisioned by Solnit—is not blind hope. Rather, hope is a belief in a way forward, a belief in finding a door to walk through. If no door exists, then hope is the possibility of creating a new one. Despair is easier, safer, more predictable, and less demanding. Hope requires risk in uncertain times and the courage to act against unpredictable odds.

Drawing from various sources, **intercultural activism** is defined here as engagement in actions that create a democratic world where power is shared; diversity is protected and valued as a resource; and where discrimination, domination, and oppression based on race, ethnicity, class, sexual orientation, religion, and nationality are challenged (Broome, Carey, De La Garza, Martin, & Morris, 2005; Solnit, 2004). Intercultural activism can take many forms including protests, boycotts, canvassing, sit-ins, teach-ins, and street theater. Intercultural activism can also take the form of intervening through consciousness-raising in classrooms, churches, and at family gatherings as well as in emergent opportunities in informal settings—where pressure is exercised "on the fault lines of a network of power" (Yep, 2008, p. 196).

In the following pages, the narratives of individuals who have the wisdom to see their interconnectedness with others, the courage to respect and use cultural differences as resources, and the compassion to feel the pain and suffering of others are told. Through engagement in intercultural activism, people move from apathy and fear to empowerment and hope.

Another World Is Possible: Student to Student Empowerment for Change

In Chapter 9, we analyzed the intergroup conflict at Grant High School in Los Angeles, California, in a case study. Narratives and reflections from Communicating Common Ground, a nationally sponsored project initiated to address the conflicts at Grant High School, are drawn on here to illustrate how university students developed and used their intercultural competencies to intervene in intercultural conflict (Sorrells, 2003). By the late 1990s, relations between Latino/Latina and Armenian students had worsened at Grant High School to the point where annual riots were a tradition at the school (Sauerwein, 2000). In an effort to break the cycle of violence, students in intercultural communication courses were brought

Figure 10.1 Protest for Immigrant Rights in Los Angeles, May 2006

Source: Kathryn Sorrells.

into the high school over a period of 5 years to work with 9th and 10th graders to address the escalating tensions. Many university students reported that facilitating dialogue groups, community building activities, and conflict resolution sessions across ethnic and racial groups at Grant High School was the most powerful learning experience of their educational careers. By creating a cycle of empowerment—student to student—the tradition of violence was challenged and changed. Here are a few student accounts of the experience:

Teresa Ramos: What I learned at Grant High School will stay with me throughout my life. Not only have my experiences helped me to grow as an individual, I think we helped the high school students grow. Despite the negativity from the racial tension, I think the time we spent with the students has opened their eyes to exactly how powerful they really are. At the end of the sessions, I felt as if we had made a difference. I did not expect to make an impact on these students. I truly believe that [Grant students] do realize there are alternatives to racial tension . . . they acknowledge that another way—a way without violence—is possible.

(Continued)

(Continued)

Sachi Sekimoto: The visit to Grant High School started with excitement, nervousness, and surprise since it was my first time to visit a high school in the United States. From the beginning, the oppressive atmosphere of the school intimidated me; the school buildings surrounded by ugly fences, security guards at the entrance and the schoolyard where invisible lines separated [Latino/Latina] and Armenian students. As we walked around campus, the students stared at us with skeptical eyes that were by no means eyes of curiosity. Their eyes reminded me of my race as Asian—not a source of pride or privilege but as a source of fear and racial hatred. . . . As the weeks passed, it became such an enjoyable and rewarding experience to visit Grant High School and work with the students. When I look at each student, they are not racist. It is the system of racism in the school and the communication produced by fear and power struggles that make them stereotype and hate people of other races. The only way to break the system is through interaction and communication with others. It is so rewarding to see students engaging in the sessions and learning new things. Being about to assist their learning and learn myself was an empowering experience.

Justin Weiss: During one of the group sessions, one of the high school students, Charlotte, stated that the teachers are against the students and "we can't do anything to change it." I learned that these students may not be getting the tools at home or school that they need so maybe that's why their initial thought is that they can't change anything. But by helping the students understand that they are meaningful and by reinforcing their sense of agency through encouragement and positive examples, they were able to see that they could make a change. I noticed that the high school students really do want to make a change. I also realized and understand that there is power in numbers and by sending a clear message that change starts with "You," it can spread to others like a ripple and multiply. One person who believes in their abilities will turn into two people who believe change is possible, which will become four people, then ten and then one hundred people. And before you know it, there will be a large and significant representation of people who believe in their abilities to create positive change.

The narratives point to the powerful experiences of both university and high school students who were involved in the Communicating Common Ground project. While initially skeptical and hesitant, their willingness to engage in intercultural praxis and use the competencies of curious inquiry, framing, positioning, dialogue, reflection, and action enabled them to serve as role models, teaching the benefits and challenges of intercultural communication and intercultural activism to the high school students. The narratives illustrate how the university students used their knowledge, skills, and attitudes—their intercultural competencies—to empower the high school students and in the process were empowered themselves.

Figure 10.2   Multicultural identity collage created by students at Grant High School, Los Angeles

Source: Kathryn Sorrells.

Another World Is Possible: Individual and Collective Action for Change

The brief stories included next reveal how individual actions and collective alliances can make a difference in creating a more equitable and just world. Acting in alignment with beliefs in social justice and struggling to overcome historically embedded divisions, the narrative provides examples of hope in the dark and the realization that another world is possible, as George (2004) claimed, if people from diverse backgrounds join together and insist upon change.

Mary Ann Wright served her country for 35 years as a member of the U.S. military and diplomat. In March 2003, she resigned from her position as a foreign service officer and senior diplomat protesting the policies of the Bush administration. Wright believed that the Bush administration's international policies in Iraq, Israel, and North Korea as well as the restrictions imposed on civil liberties in the United States made the world a more dangerous rather than a safer place to live (Wright, 2005). Here are her words to the U.S. public:

I encourage all Americans to look critically at what our government is doing in our name. If we do not agree with an administration's policies, it is our responsibility as citizens to let our voices be heard. But you don't have to give up your job to try to influence U.S. policies—letters and emails to

(Continued)

> (Continued)
>
> the administration and to our congresspeople are also important, as are actions by social justice, peace, and religious groups. Attend public demonstrations, marches, and rallies in large numbers, which will force the media to cover them. In particular, we cannot stand by and let our Congress be hoodwinked into giving the president wide-ranging powers, including the power of waging war. We have the responsibility to make our concerns known, especially when an administration does not want to listen to alternative viewpoints. Above all, when our own government takes actions that put us all in jeopardy, we can not sit back. (Wright, 2005, p. 22)

Rose Kabute was raised in a Ugandan refugee camp after her parents fled the conflict between Hutus and Tutsis in Rwanda. She joined an opposition movement and army, the Rwandan Patriotic Front; served as mayor of a city in Rwanda; and is now a member of the Rwandan army. In an effort to bridge the conflict between Hutus and Tutsis after the massive genocide that occurred in the mid-1990s, the Rwandan government set up a Unity and Reconciliation Commission so that members of both groups could learn about each other as well and the perspectives and experiences of the other group. With this model in mind and the goal of addressing the ongoing conflict between Rwanda and the Congo, a group of women from both countries attended conflict resolution training in the United States in 2000. Here are Kabute's (2005) words about the process:

> In the beginning we listened to each other with a mediator. Later, we learned how to listen on our own. We also learned that each one of us had a point. We were already in a better place. And we tried to figure out a solution together: they couldn't arrest the militia members in the Congo, but they could lobby the Congolese government to stop supporting them. And we could lobby the Rwandan government to pull out of their territory. When we went back home, I was able to talk to my leaders about what Congolese and Rwandan women, together, thought might work. Some people think it is strange that I work for peace, because I am in the army. But others are glad. They say to me, "You waged war and now you are waging peace!" I know how terrible wars can be. That's why I want to leave behind a safer world for our children. (p. 40)

In June 2009, the democratically elected president of Honduras, Mel Zaleya, was ousted in a coup supported by the Honduran military and ruling elites. While coverage in the United States was limited and the Honduran population was divided by the regime change, the coup prompted the emergence of a broad-based multicultural coalition of resistance in Honduras. In October 2009, at a forum titled Repression and Resistance in Honduras at the California State University, Los Angeles, feminist political theorist and activist Breny Mendoza (2009) described the coalition movement to reinstate democratic rule in Honduras:

Like never before in the last 500 years, the coup has brought forth new actors who threaten to dismantle the structures of the coloniality of power and its interwoven systems of gender, class, race and sexual oppression. The *National Resistance Front* against the Coup is a coalition of peasants, labor unions, schoolteachers, housewives, youth, the elderly, students, lawyers, artists, environmentalists, *Garifunas* (people of African and indigenous descent in Central America), indigenous, gays and lesbians, and feminists. This rainbow coalition is catalyzing Hondurans in unprecedented ways. It is prefiguring the new Honduras that will come out of this horrible experience.

The creative energy that derives from the collective uprising is expressed daily in the streets as protestors come together dancing to the music of the *Garifunas*; when *mestizo* Christians participate in the religious rituals of the *Garifuna* and the indigenous peoples in the streets and begin a conversation about racism as a social pathology of Honduras. It is reflected when different street protests converge to defend the cause of feminists when women's rights are violated, when the queer community becomes politicized and is welcomed to join forces with those that once excluded them; when the young and old protect each other from police brutality; when teachers and students alike march hand in hand; when all of these groups walk together behind an old woman that was an activist of the General Strike of 1954 singing the hymn of the Resistance: "They are afraid of us, because we are fearless." (Mendoza, 2009)

Each of these stories illustrate the potential of intercultural activism—collaborative actions taken by individuals and groups across cultural, racial, and national lines—to challenge and dismantle systems of domination and discrimination, to build relationships that respect and use diversity, and to create a more democratic and equitable world.

INTERCULTURAL ALLIANCES FOR SOCIAL JUSTICE

Intercultural alliances are increasingly necessary and frequent in the context of globalization. As discussed in Chapter 7, intercultural alliances are sites where cultural differences, positionalities, and issues of power and privilege are negotiated, translated, and potentially transformed. Intercultural alliances in interpersonal relationships and political organizing play critical roles in improving intercultural communication and challenging prejudices and stereotypes. Importantly, alliances that form and sustain among groups across ethnic, racial, cultural, and religious differences threaten social, economic, and political systems that have historically divided and isolated groups pitting each against the other. Intercultural alliances offer alternatives to the status quo "divide and conquer" paradigm applying pressure in public and private arenas, advocating for policy changes, accessing and channeling resources, and empowering communities to create a more equitable and socially just world.

As noted in other chapters, intercultural alliance building requires a sense of mutual interdependence among allies, processes to develop trust and dialogue, where people can speak openly and authentically as well as hear and empathize with the pain and difficulties of others. Having the motivation and skill to identify and work through misunderstandings, tensions, and conflicts is crucial to developing and sustaining intercultural alliances (Allen, Broome, Jones, Chen, & Collier, 2002). While inevitably challenging and uncomfortable, cultural differences are viewed as necessary, vital, and productive resources in intercultural alliances. Intercultural alliances require that we engage in intercultural bridgework, as discussed in Chapter 7, where we traverse multiple positions, identify points of intersection, and negotiate pathways of connection. When our intercultural competencies—inquiry, framing, positioning, dialogue, and reflection—inform collaborative action, intercultural alliances have the potential to create more humane, equitable, and just communities and societies. A case study is provided here to illustrate what can be accomplished through intercultural alliances.

CASE STUDY: COMMUNITY COALITION OF SOUTH LOS ANGELES

The Community Coalition of South Los Angeles was founded in 1990 by a group of dedicated community leaders to address the devastation wrought on South LA from the crack cocaine epidemic in the 1980s. The initial goal was to provide preventative community-based solutions to the drug problems. Karen Bass, elected speaker of the California Assembly in 2008, and U.S. representative for California's 33rd District in 2010, was one of the original founders. The Community Coalition has distinguished itself as an intercultural alliance of African Americans and Latinos/Latinas working together to build a prosperous, safe, and healthy South LA community where educational, social, and economic opportunities are available to all. The Community Coalition serves all ethnic/racial groups in South LA with a wide representation of cultural groups functioning in leadership roles in the Community Coalition.

The Community Coalition accomplishes their goals through a variety of programs including the Land Use Committee, the Prevention Network, Kinship in Action, the Civic Engagement Committee, Parents in Action, and the Academy for Architecture, Construction and Engineering (ACE). The Prevention Network works to remove the disproportionate number of liquor stores, motels, and recycling centers in South LA that lead to a concentration of criminal activities. In 2008, they won support from the city of LA to pass the Nuisance Abatement Ordinance giving residents more power to challenge negligent businesses. The Prevention Network is an alliance of social service providers who advocate for proactive policies that increase and improve services to the most vulnerable residents such as ex-offenders transitioning from prison and those precluded from welfare.

The Kinship in Action program supports family members who take in children who have lost their parents to drug addiction, prison, or mental illness. While children often do much better in the care of extended family members, relatives do not receive the same resources and support that is offered through traditional foster care. The Community Coalition trains family and community members how to advocate on their behalf for increased and equitable resources to provide care for children of the community. In 2006, the Community Coalition won $82 million in state money for foster care reform, which included $36 million for relative caregivers to keep families together.

The Community Coalition recognizes that political power is central to developing public policy and leadership that serves the community. The goal of the Civic Engagement Committee is to build political power to serve the community of South LA by strengthening residents' civic engagement and developing strong leadership. The Committee's activities include voter registration initiatives, town hall meetings, and leadership training. The leadership training addresses issues of race and racism, perspectives and challenges of unifying Blacks and Latinos/Latinas, as well as strategies for community organizing. Parents in Action trains parents and caregivers to advocate for policies that improve the education for students in schools in South LA. Approximately 60% of the youth who attend schools in South LA "disappear" from school before graduation. To address this startling reality that leaves young people of color with few options, the ACE Academy was formed with the goal of providing a pathway to employment in high-skilled jobs such as architecture, construction, and engineering.

The Community Coalition's South Central Youth Empowerment Through Action (SCYEA) recognizes the critical role youth can play in organizing for change and how the knowledge and skills gained through organizing for community change can enhance the academic and life goals of youth. SCYEA is a group of African American and Latino/Latina youth working together to create the next generation of leadership for positive change in the schools and community of South LA. SCYEA provides academic mentoring for youth, college preparation, and an annual road trip to colleges and universities, as well as training in community organizing and opportunities to work collaboratively to make positive change in the community. Youth organizing with SCYEA in conjunction with the Community Coalition has led to the allocation of $153 million to repair dilapidated schools in South LA, the passing of the A-G resolution that brought courses required for college to South LA schools, and $350 million to reduce overcrowding in schools and provide counselors (Community Coalition, 2009).

Here are the words of two youth participants in the SCYEA:

Tylo White: I know what it's like to struggle, to be poor. I know what it's like to be abused and neglected. I've experienced racism, but I refuse to become a statistic. I want far too much out of life to let anything hold me back. Everyone has a story. Everyone wants something. It's just a matter of how bad and what they're willing to do for it. Me? I'm going to a university, I'm going to study abroad, come back and help my community. I'm going to enlighten and empower myself, because with God there is nothing I can't do! (Community Coalition, 2009)

Shenekah Cayatano: The Community Coalition has inspired me throughout the two months I've been attending to be a positive leader in life. Even though I have not been here long enough to talk about a big step I have overcome, like participating in a strike, etc., I feel that I have taken a big step in joining a program that is not required for me to do so and making an attempt to come to every meeting. I've learned to be more responsible and think like a community organizer. I have a chance to go to college and become something. I am preparing for this Bay Area trip and hope to help someone understand that they can succeed too. (Community Coalition, 2009)

The Community Coalition has had tremendous success. These successes have been attained through the long-term commitment of key members, the strength in organizing the powerful voices of large numbers of people, and the sustained vision that a better world is possible if people work collectively across racial and ethnic lines. The challenge to move residents from apathy to empowerment is ongoing. The struggle to build bridges across diverse identities, cultural differences, and cultural histories is continuous. The effort to create networks across vastly different positionalities using the influence of individuals and the collective power of groups is constant. The Community Coalition uses many forms of intervention—protests, training on race and racism, advocacy and organizing, educational and support programs, and public policy initiatives—to create change in South LA.

As noted by Collier (2002), there are many more institutions, practices, and ideological forces operating in society to maintain hierarchies of difference than ones that encourage and support intercultural alliances. The Community Coalition is an example of an organization that recognizes the importance of analyzing, reflecting, and dialoguing on power, privilege, and dominance as a necessary first step toward change. Given the complex and dynamic nature of intercultural alliances such as the Community Coalition, attending to the multifaceted nature of individual and group identities and histories is critical. Building and sustaining intercultural alliances is hard work, yet intercultural alliances have the potential to map out new possibilities, dismantle inequitable relations of power, and move toward social justice on interpersonal, community, and global levels.

SUMMARY

Closing the Conversation

As discussed throughout the book, our current context—the context of globalization—has dramatically altered the conditions that shape, enable, and constrain intercultural communication. The context of globalization is characterized by an intensification of intercultural interaction and exchange in an increasingly dynamic, mobile world. Changes in economic and political policies, governance, and institutions have escalated global intercultural interdependence ushering in an era of shared interests, needs, and resources as well as tensions and conflicts. The financial crisis in the United States in the fall of 2008 launched shock waves throughout the entire global financial system illustrating clearly the intricate web of interdependence and the ubiquitous yet asymmetrical impact of globalization.

Global interdependence has also intensified intercultural, interethnic, interracial, and international tensions and conflicts. Yet, as described in this chapter, intercultural alliances occur more frequently than ever before and collective calls for justice echo around the globe. The popular uprisings to end authoritarian rule and demand democracy in 2011 reverberated far beyond the Middle East. The forces of globalization have magnified inequities within and across nation-states exacerbating already-existing injustices that limit and exclude access to education, jobs, services, and opportunities. Increased disparities structure and bind intercultural relationships in terms of power, privilege, and positionality. Importantly, injustice forged through colonization, Western domination, and U.S. hegemony, while reconfigured today, continues to define and shape intercultural relations.

Our global interdependences coupled with the inequitable distribution and access to resources present current and future generations an imperative to envision new relationships of engagement and innovative strategies for sustainability in the 21st century. Taking up our responsibilities as global citizens, developing our intercultural competencies, and engaging in intercultural activism offer opportunities to challenge systems of domination, question hierarchies of power, and create a more equitable world.

Perspectives and approaches for imagining and enacting a more equitable and socially just world have provided the foundation for understanding and engaging in intercultural communication in this book. Let's review the principles that have guided our journey together in our exploration of intercultural communication in the context of globalization. First, throughout, we have defined *culture* as a site of contestation where meaning-making is a struggle and not a static entity that remains fixed and stable. Understanding culture from a critical perspective as "contested meanings," along with more traditional notions of culture as "shared meanings," we are able to question the ways that dominant perspectives, values, and practices are privileged. Viewing culture as a site of contested meaning allows alternative, nondominant, and competing standpoints and voices to be valued and heard. Numerous examples and case studies throughout the book exemplify this definition of culture. The historical construction of "race," how race has signified differently over time and location, and the way race is rearticulated today illustrate the dynamic and negotiated nature of cultural meaning-making processes. Contested and hybrid cultural spaces, migrants' actions that challenge dominant assumptions about the superiority of the United States, as well as readings of popular culture texts that negotiate and resist hegemonic cultural ideologies also demonstrate how culture is a contested site.

Additionally, the concept of culture as a "resource" that is exploited for economic development and harnessed for empowerment was introduced and elaborated throughout the book. Hip hop culture with its origins in the Bronx, its deterritorialization and reterritorialization globally, and the commodification of hip hop culture all illustrate how culture is a resource in the global context. In the world today, as our discussion of Pueblo pottery, Mardi Gras festivals, and tourism typify, culture is packaged, bought, and sold in the global intercultural marketplace. The notion of culture as a resource draws attention to the production and consumption of cultural "Others"; it also highlights the cultural agency and empowerment used in intercultural activism and movements for social justice. Defining culture as a resource reveals the symbolic and material realities of cultural inequality, difference, marginalization, and empowerment in the context of globalization.

The second principle that informs this book is the role history and relations of power play in intercultural communication. The broad historical context of the past 500 years of colonization, Western imperialism, and U.S. hegemony, which include the anticolonial and independence struggles, the civil rights movements, and the alterglobalization movements, are critical for understanding intercultural communication today. Yet the conditions of globalization also require simultaneous attention to new and reconfigured sites of economic, political, and cultural power. The multifocal vision employed in the book, for example, in our discussions of globalization, world migration, and capitalism, connects the present with the past while recognizing the ways current conditions may also depart from and transform the past. While the legacy of colonization and

U.S. hegemony are key to understanding intercultural communication today, non-Western centers of capital and cultural production are well established and positioned today to challenge Western domination in future decades (Shome & Hegde, 2002).

We have noted the impact on intercultural relations of "free" trade policies in the global context and observed how neoliberal policies and practices rearticulate a 21st-century version of labor exploitation that built and consolidated the economic wealth and political power of Europe and the United States during the colonial period. Many of the intercultural challenges facing societies around the world today—racial and ethnic discrimination, tension and conflict, intensified economic inequity, as well as disputes over immigrant rights and immigration policies—are embedded in and structured by racist, classist, heteronormative, and ethnocentric ideologies forged and institutionalized through the past 500 years of colonization and Western imperialism. Underscoring the connections between the past and the present not only makes us aware of the deeply embedded inequities and highlights how asymmetrical relationships of power are reproduced over time but it also reveals the pressure points for effective intervention for social justice as illustrated in the case study about the Community Coalition of South LA.

The third foundational principle is that intercultural communication today is always and inevitably situated within specific, local contexts as well as broader global contexts with interwoven cultural, social, economic, and political dimensions. Today, people, identities, cultural forms, practices, and ideas are located in particular places and simultaneously connected through phone, e-mail, text messaging, advanced modes of transportation, social networks, and media with places around the globe. Case studies and examples presented throughout the book of cultural spaces, media circuits, interpersonal relationships, and multicultural teams demonstrate the importance of understanding intercultural communication within interrelated contexts. Emphasizing linkages among various contexts—from the local to the global—makes visible the continuity and ties of cultural communities across geographic space as well as the disruptions and changes in cultural norms, values, and practices as people and cultural forms collide and coalesce in the global context.

The multilevel analysis used in the case studies on postcolonial migration and intercultural conflict highlights relationships of power, positionality, and privilege that inform intercultural communication in the global context. Attending to the local/global linkages and utilizing a micro-/meso-/macro-analysis bring inequities and injustices on systemic and interpersonal levels into focus and illustrate how individuals and groups use their agency to create a more socially just world.

The fourth principle threaded throughout the book grounds the study and practice of intercultural communication in critical engagement, democratic participation, and social justice. The model of intercultural praxis introduced and developed along our journey joins the conceptual perspectives, affective capacities, and skill-based strategies needed to engage in intercultural communication for social justice. As we couple our theories and critical analysis with our individual engagement and collective action, we can create a more equitable, socially just world. As George (2004) noted, diversity of backgrounds, viewpoints, and skills are needed to address the challenges facing us—the 7 billion people who call this planet home. As a student and practitioner of intercultural communication, you are now positioned well to engage in critical, reflective action that includes multiple and diverse voices, builds alliances, and develops solidarity across various and shifting positionalities.

Consider these questions: Why are you learning about intercultural communication? How will you use what you have learned? We assume you are not learning about the topic so you can become more effective in taking advantage of others. We also assume you are not gaining skills and strategies so you can be more efficient in exploiting those who are positioned with less power than you. Having gained knowledge, capacities, and skills for intercultural communication, you have the potential to use your intercultural competence to join others as allies; connect across racial, gender, ethnic, cultural, and national boundaries in intercultural alliances; and engage in intercultural activism to create and struggle for a more equitable and just world. Imagine a world where equity and justice are the norm and not the exception. Using intercultural communication as a site of interventions, democratic participation, and transformation, you, in alliance with others, can create this world.

KEY TERMS

social justice
qualities of global citizens
empathy
capacities for global citizenship

intercultural competency
managing ambiguity
self-awareness
intercultural activism

DISCUSSION QUESTIONS AND ACTIVITIES

Discussion Questions

1. Based on the issues addressed in this chapter, how do you define "social justice"? What does it look like? How can we practice it?

2. What communication skills are needed to engage in intercultural praxis for social justice?

3. Have you engaged in intercultural activism? What are your experiences and insights? What kind of beliefs and values guided your activism?

4. Why do you think social justice is the exception rather than the norm in society?

5. What are the four principles that guided our journey throughout the book?

6. What do you take away from this course, and how will you use it in future intercultural interactions?

Activities

1. Researching Local Community Organizations
   a. Research local community organizations that engage in social justice work. Study their websites and/or interview those who work at the organizations.

   b. Address the following questions:

      i. How does "culture" matter in their social justice work? Do they approach culture as resource, a system of shared meaning, and/or a site of power struggle?

      ii. How is intercultural praxis relevant in their activism? Do they exercise any of the elements of intercultural praxis?

      iii. Do the processes of globalization influence their activism? If so, how?

2. Qualities and Capacities of Global Citizenship

   a. Review qualities and capacities of global citizenship discussed in this chapter.

   b. In groups of 3 to 4 people, develop a concrete plan for developing global citizenship in your school, neighborhood, and/or community. Consider the following:

      i. Educational curriculum

      ii. Events and forums

      iii. Community organizing, intercultural activism

      iv. Creative expressions and activities

REFERENCES

Ackerman, P., & DuVall, J. (2001). *A force more powerful: A century of nonviolent conflict.* New York: Palgrave.

Adams, M., Bell, L. A., & Griffin, P. (2007). *Teaching for diversity and social justice.* New York: Routledge.

Allen, B. J., Broome, B. J., Jones, T. S., Chen, V., & Collier, M. J. (2002). Intercultural alliances: A cyberdialogue among scholar-practitioners. In M. J. Collier (Ed.), *Intercultural alliances (International and intercultural communication annual)* (Vol. 25, pp. 279–319). Thousand Oaks, CA: Sage.

Boggs, G. L. (2011). The next American revolution. *Sustainable activism for the 21st century* (pp. 1–51). Berkeley: University of California Press.

Broome, B., Carey, C., De La Garza, S. A., Martin, J., & Morris, R. (2005). "In the thick of things": A dialogue about the activist turn in intercultural communication. In W. J. Starosta & G. M. Chen (Eds.), *Taking stock in intercultural communication: Where to now? (International and intercultural communication annual)* (Vol. 26, pp. 145–175). Thousand Oaks, CA: Sage.

Collier, M. J. (2002). Transforming communication about culture: An introduction. In M. J. Collier (Ed.), *Transforming communication about culture: Critical new directions (International and intercultural communication annual)* (Vol. 24, pp. ix–xix). Thousand Oaks, CA: Sage.

Community Coalition. (2009). *SCYEA Youth.* Retrieved from http://www.cocosouthla.org/

DeTurk, S. (2006). The power of dialogue: Consequences of inter-group dialogue and their implications for agency and alliance. *Communication Quarterly, 54*(1), 31–51.

Freire, P. (1998). *Pedagogy of freedom: Ethics, democracy, and civic courage.* Lanham, MD: Rowman & Littlefield.

Gadamer, H. G. (1989). *Truth and method* (Rev. ed.) (J. Weinsheimer & D. G. Marshall, Trans.). New York: Crossroad.

George, S. (2004). *Another world is possible if . . .* London: Verso.

Giroux, H. A. (2004). Cultural studies, public pedagogy, and the responsibility of intellectuals. *Communication and Critical/Cultural Studies, 1*(1), 59–79.

Heidegger, M. (1962). *Being and time* (J. MacQuarrie & E. Robinson, Trans.). London: SCM.

Ikeda, D. (2005). Forward. In N. Nodding (Ed.), *Educating citizens for global awareness* (pp. ix–xi). New York: Columbia Teachers College.

Kabute, R. (2005). Warriors for peace. In B. Medea & J. Evans (Eds.), *Stop the next war now* (pp. 39–40). Maui, HI: Inner Ocean.

McIntosh, P. (2005). Gender perspectives on educating for global citizenship. In N. Nodding (Ed.), *Educating citizens for global awareness* (pp. 22–39). New York: Columbia Teachers College.

Mendoza, B. (2009, October 28). Hondurans in resistance. *Forum: Repression and resistance in Honduras.* California State University, Los Angeles.

Noddings, N. (Ed.) (2005). *Educating citizens for global awareness.* New York: Columbia Teachers College.

Peterson, K. (2011, March 15). Japan's crisis has worldwide impact. *MSN Money.* Retrieved from http://money.msn.com/top-stocks/post.aspx?post = 37b24afd-df57-4e91-818c-4c0cefcf9c7a

Robbins, R. H. (2002). *Global problems and the culture of capitalism.* Boston, MA: Allyn & Bacon.

Sauerwein, K. (2000, January 13). Peer Pressure: Grant High students cross ethnic lines to foster peace on campus. *Los Angeles Times, Valley Edition.*

Shome, R., & Hegde, R. S. (2002). Culture, communication and the challenge of globalization. *Critical Studies in Media Communication, 19*(2), 172–189.

Solnit, R. (2004). *Hope in the dark: Untold histories, wild possibilities.* New York: Nation Books.

Sorrells, K. (2003). Communicating common ground: Integrating community service learning into the intercultural classroom. *Communication Teacher, 17,* 1–4.

Sorrells, K., & Nakagawa, G. (2008). Intercultural communication praxis and the struggle for social responsibility and social justice. In O. Swartz (Ed.), *Transformative communication studies: Culture, hierarchy, and the human condition* (pp. 23–61). Leicester, UK: Troubador.

Williams, T. T. (2005). The open space of democracy. In B. Medea & J. Evans (Eds.), *Stop the next war now* (pp. 36–39). Maui, HI: Inner Ocean.

Wright, M. A. (2005). Essential dissent. In B. Medea & J. Evans (Eds.), *Stop the next war now* (pp. 21–22). Maui, HI: Inner Ocean.

Yep, G. A. (2008). The dialectics of intervention: Toward a reconceptualization of the theory/activism divide in communication scholarship and beyond. In O. Swartz (Ed.), *Transformative communication studies: Culture, hierarchy and the human condition* (pp. 191–207). Leicester, UK: Troubador.

Glossary

CHAPTER 1

A system of shared meanings: Anthropologic definition of culture that meanings are shared through symbols from generation to generation and allow us to make sense of, express, and give meaning to our lives

Action: Port of entry into intercultural praxis where you take actions based on critical reflection to create a more socially just, equitable, and peaceful world

Culture as a site of contestation: Cultural studies definition of culture that views culture as an apparatus of power within a larger system of domination where meanings are constantly negotiated

Cultural identity: Situated sense of self that is shaped by our cultural experiences and social locations

Dialogue: Port of entry into intercultural praxis in which you engage in exchange of ideas, thoughts, and experiences that have both oppositional and transformative dimensions

Ethnocentrism: Idea that one's own group's way of thinking, being, and acting in the world is superior to others

Framing: Port of entry into intercultural praxis in which you are aware of the frame of reference you use and are able to examine the situation both from micro- and macro-level perspectives

Hegemony: Domination through consent where the goals, ideas, and interests of the ruling group or class are so thoroughly normalized, institutionalized, and accepted that people consent to their own domination, subordination, and exploitation

High culture: Culture of the elite class, or ruling class, who have power, including those who are educated at prestigious schools and are patrons of the arts such as literature, opera, and ballet; associated with European culture

Inquiry: Port of entry into intercultural praxis in which you have a desire and willingness to know, ask, find out, and learn without judgments and with willingness to take risks and be challenged/changed

Intercultural praxis: Process of critical analysis, reflection, and action for effective intercultural communication in the context of globalization; six ports of entry: inquiry, framing, positioning, dialogue, reflection, and action

Low culture: Culture of the working class, who enjoy activities such as popular theater, folk art, "street" activities, movies, and TV

Popular culture: Culture that belongs to the "masses," much of which was previously considered low culture; artifacts the general populous or broad masses within a society share or have some understanding

Positionality: One's social location or position within an intersecting web of socially constructed hierarchical categories such as race, class, gender, sexual orientation, religion, nationality, and physical abilities

Positioning: Port of entry into intercultural praxis where you consider how you are positioned within the geographical, sociopolitical, and historical relations of power and knowledge

Reflection: Port of entry into intercultural praxis where you use the capacity to learn from introspection, to observe yourself in relation to others, and to alter your perspectives and actions based on reflection

Resource: Definition of culture as resource for political development, economic growth, and

exploitation, as well as collective and individual empowerment, agency, and resistance

Standpoint theory: Feminist theory that claims that the social groups to which we belong shape what we know and how we communicate; one's position within social relations of power produces different standpoints from which to view, experience, act, and construct knowledge about the world

Symbols: Words, images, people, ideas, actions, and so on, that stand for or represent other things

CHAPTER 2

Americanization: Global cultural homogenization with U.S. culture, such as McDonald's and Disney

Cultural globalization: Globalization characterized by migration, the formation of transnational cultural connectivities, cultural flows in the context of unequal power relations, and the emergence of hybrid cultural forms and identities

Cultural imperialism: Domination of one culture over others through cultural forms such as pop culture, media, and cultural products; a dimension of cultural globalization in which unequal and uneven flow of culture and cultural forms negatively impact local industry and culture

Democratization: The transition toward a more democratic political system

Deterritorialized: Culture in the context of globalization where cultural subjects and cultural objects are uprooted from their situatedness in a particular physical, geographic location

Developing country/Developed country: Terms commonly used today based on a nation's wealth (gross national product [GNP]), political and economic stability, and other factors

Diasporic communities: Groups of people who have been forced to leave their homeland

and who maintain a longing for—even if only in their imagination—a return to "home"

Economic globalization: Globalization characterized by a growth in multinational corporations; an intensification of international trade and international flows of capital; and internationally interconnected webs of production, distribution, and consumption

Economic liberalization: Economic policies that increase the global movement of goods, labor, services, and capital with less restrictive tariffs (taxes) and trade barriers

First World: During Cold War, First World nations were countries friendly to United States and identified as capitalist and democratic; developed nations, more commonly used today, refer to former colonial powers with advanced capitalist economy, such as United States, Europe, Australia, Canada, and Japan

Free trade agreements: Trade agreements that liberalize trade by reducing trade tariffs and barriers transnationally while maintaining protection for some industries

Globalization: Complex web of forces and factors that bring people, cultures, cultural products, and markets, as well as beliefs and practices into increasingly greater proximity to and interrelationship with one another

Global South/Global North: Terms in use today that highlight the socioeconomic and political division between wealthy, developed nations (former centers of colonial power) in the Northern Hemisphere and poorer, developing nations (formerly colonized countries) in the Southern Hemisphere

Historical legacy of colonization: Processes of globalization shaped by historical legacy of colonialism and unequal power relations among nation-states politically, economically, and culturally

Hybrid cultural forms: New and distinct cultural form created by a mix of different cultures and appropriation of other cultural forms based on local knowledge and practice

Ideology: Set of ideas and beliefs reflecting the needs and aspirations of individuals, groups, classes, or cultures that form the basis for political, economic, and other systems

International Monetary Fund (IMF): International organization established immediately following WWII to maintain global economic stability

Maquiladoras: Foreign-owned assembly plants originally located in Mexico that allow companies to import materials duty free and export products around the world

North American Free Trade Agreement (NAFTA): Trade agreement established in 1994 among Mexico, the United States, and Canada that eliminates trade barriers and tariffs

Political globalization: Globalization characterized by the interconnectedness of nation-state politics, the formation of bodies of global governance (i.e., WTO, IMF, WB), and global movements of resistance responding to inequities in political power

Remittances: Financial support sent to a distant location

Reterritorialized: Culture in the context of globalization where cultural subjects and cultural objects are relocated in new, multiple, and varied geographic spaces

Second World: During Cold War, Second World nations were countries perceived as hostile and ideologically incompatible with the United States, such as the former Soviet bloc countries and China and their allies; identified as communist

Third World: During Cold War, Third World nations were countries seen as neutral or nonaligned with either the First World (capitalism) or the Second World (communism); developing nations, more commonly used today, are formerly colonized countries and are economically less developed than First World nations

World Bank (WB): International organization established after WWII to address poverty through development and education

World Trade Organization (WTO): International organization established in 1995 as a successor to the post–WWII General Agreement on Tariffs and Trade (GATT); deals with the global rules of trade between nations

CHAPTER 3

Body politics: Practices and policies through which power is marked, regulated, and negotiated on and through the body

Both/and approach: Approach to simultaneously hold contradictory, oppositional realities

to guard us against essentializing, stereotyping, and closure

Constructing the "Other": Process by which differences marked on or represented through the body are constructed as significant and are infused with meaning through a hierarchical racial system that justify and promote domination and exploitation

Hierarchy of difference: Hierarchical racial categorization developed in the late 18th century with the Caucasians on the top, followed by the Malay, the Americans, the Mongolian, and the Ethiopian or Black race

Intersectionality: An approach to understanding how socially constructed categories of difference, such as race, gender, class, and sexuality operate in relationship to each other

Racial hierarchy: Socially constructed hierarchy of different racial groups in which Whites are placed at the top, and non-Whites are placed as inferior to Whites; legitimates conquest, colonization, and exploitation of labor in the rise of capitalism

Racial historicism: Belief that non-White people lack in cultural development but through education are capable of developing civilizing behaviors, democratic values, and self-determination

Racial naturalism: Belief that White people of European descent are naturally or biologically superior to non-White people

Semiotics: Study of the use of signs in cultures

Silenced histories: Histories hidden, unrecognized, and/or excluded from the historical record and awareness

Social construct: Idea or phenomenon that has been "created," "invented," or "constructed" by people in a particular society or culture through communication

Social construction: Based on a sociological theory of knowledge, concepts, identities, social relations, practices, and so on, that are created and maintained through collectively agreed-upon conventions, norms, and rules rather than inherent in the external world

Signifiers: Body, things, actions, images, or words

Signified: Idea or mental concept

Signs: Consists of signifiers and signified; system of meaning (i.e., culture, language) produced through the process of assigning a signified to a signifier

Social construction of gender: The use of physical differences in human bodies to construct two mutually exclusive gender categories: women/men, femininity/masculinity

Social construction of race: Process of separating people into hierarchical categories using the physical characteristics of our bodies such as skin color, facial features, hair texture, and body type

The power of texts: Texts construct, maintain, and legitimize systems of inequity and domination by creating authorized and preferred versions of history and leaving out other perspectives, experiences, and stories

Third gender: People who live across, between, or outside of the socially constructed two-gender system of categorization

Transgender: People whose gender identities differ from the social norms and expectations associate with their biological sex

Whiteness: Location of structural advantage; a standpoint; and a set of core values, practices, and norms in which White ways of thinking, knowing, being, and doing are normalized as the standard

White supremacy: Historically based, institutionally perpetuated system of exploitation and oppression of continents, nations, and people of color by people and nations of European

descent for the purpose of establishing and maintaining wealth, privilege, and power

CHAPTER 4

Appropriation: Borrowing, mishandling, and/or stealing other people's culture to make it your own; raises questions about authenticity, ownership, and relations of power

Ascribed identity: The way others may view, name, and describe us and our group

Avowed identity: The way we see, label, and make meaning about ourselves

Contested cultural space: Geographic locations where conflicts engage people with unequal control and access to resources in oppositional and confrontational strategies of resistance

Cultural space: Communicative practices that construct meanings in, through, and about particular places

Deindustrialization: Process of economic globalization in which manufacturing jobs are lost to cheaper and less regulated labor conditions outside of the United States

(Dis)placing culture and cultural space: Cultural space that emerges due to global circulation of people and products, constructed by displaced, intersecting, and colliding cultures that are geographically removed from the places of origin

Hybrid cultural space: The intersection of intercultural communication practices that construct meanings in, through, and about particular places within a context of relations of power

Hybrid cultural spaces as sites of intercultural negotiation: Hybrid cultural spaces as innovative and creative spaces where people constantly adapt to, negotiate with, and improvise between multiple cultural frameworks

Hybrid cultural spaces as sites of resistance: Hybrid cultural spaces where people

challenge stable, territorial, and static definitions of culture, cultural spaces, and cultural identities

Hybrid cultural spaces as sites of transformation: Hybrid cultural spaces where hegemonic structures are negotiated and reconfigured through hybridization of culture, cultural space, and identity

"In-hereness": Characteristic of globalization where a particular location or "here" is linked to other places around the world and how this linkage of places reveals colonial histories and postcolonial realities

Glocalization: Dual and simultaneous forces of globalization and localization where globalizing forces always intersect with and operate in relationship to localizing forces

Locations of enunciation: Literal and figurative sites or positions from which to speak

"Out-thereness": Characteristic of globalization where places around the world, out "there," are linked to particular locations "here" and how this linkage of places reveals colonial histories and postcolonial realities

Polysemic cultural space: Condition in which multiple meanings are constructed about certain places, people, and phenomena

Segregated cultural spaces: Segregated spaces based on socioeconomic, racial, ethnic, sexual, political, and religious differences, both voluntary and imposed

Time–space compression: Characteristic of globalization that brings seemingly disparate cultures into closer proximity, intersection, and juxtaposition with each other

CHAPTER 5

Acculturation: Process by which migrants gain new information and insight about the norms and values of the culture and adapt their behaviors to the host culture

Adjustment: Adjustment to a new environment as the sojourner learns to negotiate the verbal and nonverbal codes, values, norms, behaviors, and assumptions of the new culture

Anticipation: Excitement about the new culture characterizes the sojourner's experience

Assimilation: Migrant values the host's culture more than his or her own culture

Bracero Program: Guest worker program started in the 1940s that allowed Mexican migrants to work legally in the United States

Brain drain: An aspect of high-skilled migration in which high-skilled workers migrate to another country, resulting in a huge loss in terms of knowledge, skills, investment, and capital for sending countries

Contract workers: Contracted to work through labor agreements established between the governments of sending and receiving countries

Chain migration: Linkages that connect migrants from points of origin to destinations, leading to the segmentation of ethnic groups in the United States

Culture shock: Disorientation and discomfort sojourners experience from being in an unfamiliar environment

Deculturation: Process by which migrants unlearn some aspects of their culture of origin

Feminization of the workforce: An increased demand for female migrant workers as domestic caretaker and low-skilled factory workers; women are often preferred for low-skilled work—can be paid less and are more easily exploited

First wave of world migration: Traced to the European colonial era from the 16th century through the 19th century; included thousands of migrants who sailed out of ports of Europe for colonies in the Americas, Africa, and Asia

Guest workers programs: Workers from the periphery of Europe, Mexico, and so on, to fill the labor shortages in industrialized Western Europe and the United States due to the war and declining population after WWII through labor agreements established between the governments of the sending and receiving countries

High- and low-skilled laborers: Educated, high-skilled workers—migrate to developed countries to work in high-tech and medical professions; low-skilled laborers—migrate to wealth-concentrated countries driven by poverty and seek work in places such as factory, agriculture, food processing, sex industry, and domestic labor

Human trafficking: A form of involuntary migration in which people are transported for sex work and other types of labor against their will

Immigrants: Voluntary migrants who leave one country and settle permanently in another country

Integration: Migrant values both her or his own culture and the host culture

Integrative theory of cultural adaptation: Theory of cultural adaptation that the individual and the environment codefine adaptation process, including the attitudes and receptivity of the host environment, the ethnic communities within the majority culture, and the psychological characteristics of the individual

Intercultural transformation: Occurs as a result of the stress–adaptation–growth process and includes three outcomes for migrants: (1) increased functional fitness, (2) improved psychological health, and (3) a shift toward an intercultural identity

Internally displaced persons: Refugees within one's own country of origin

Involuntary migrants: Migrants who are forced to leave due to famine, war, and political or religious persecution

Marginalization: Migrant places little value on either his or her own culture or the host culture

Melting pot: Metaphor of U.S. society that the migrants' adaptation to a new culture inevitably requires and allows newcomers to "melt" or "blend" into the mainstream to form a cohesive whole

Migrant–host modes of relationship: The attitudes of migrants toward their host and own cultures

Migrants: People who move from their primary cultural context, changing their place of residence for an extended period of time

Migrant networks: Interpersonal connections among current and former migrants, as well as nonmigrants in origin and destination areas through ties of kinship, friendship, and shared origin

Nativist movements: Movements that call for the exclusion of foreign-born people

Pluralism: An ideology that emphasizes the maintenance of ethnic and cultural values, norms, and practices within a multicultural society

Postcolonial migrants: Migrants who leave former colonies and relocate in colonizing countries

Push-pull theory: A theory of migration that circumstances in the country of origin "push" people toward migratory paths and conditions

in the country of destination "pull" people toward particular locations

Refugees: People who are forced to flee for safety from their country of origin due to war, fear of persecution, or famine

Relative deprivation: A perceived sense of deprivation caused by the increased disparity in income levels and heightened exposure to images of material wealth that make people in the lower economic ranks desire to find ways to make money and accumulate wealth

Second wave of migration: Took place from the mid-1800s to the early 1900s during the Industrial Revolution, when peasants from the rural parts of Europe, fleeing poverty and famine, migrated to urban areas in Europe and North and South America

Social capital: Sense of commitment and obligation people within a group or network have to look after the well-being and interests of one another

Separation: Migrant values her or his own or home culture more than the host culture

Sojourners: Voluntary migrants who leave home for limited periods of time and for specific purposes, such as international students, business travelers, tourists, missionaries, and military personnel

The third wave: Often labeled the postindustrial wave; more diverse and multidirectional than previous migrations and encompasses patterns of movement since WWII

Transmigrants: Migrants who move across national boundaries to new locations for work and family reunification and also maintain cultural, social, economic, and political ties with their country, region, or city of origin

Transnational communities: Communities constructed by transmigrants, characterized by intertwining familial relationships across locations, identification with "home" or sending locations, and the ability to mobilize collective resources

U-curve model: Model of cultural adaptation, consisting of three stages: (1) anticipation, (2) culture shock, and (3) adjustment

Voluntary migrants: Migrants who voluntarily choose to leave home to travel or relocate

W-curve model: Extension of the U-curve model addressing the challenges of reentry or return to one's home culture

World-systems theory: A theory of migration that international migration today is a result of the structure of the global capitalism

Xenophobia: Fear of outsiders

CHAPTER 6

Alternative media or independent media: Media practices that fall outside of or are independent from the mainstream corporate-owned and controlled mass media

Citizen media or participatory media: Media texts created by average citizens who are not affiliated with mainstream, corporate media outlets

Cultural corruption: The perceived and experienced alteration of a culture in negative or detrimental ways through the influence of other cultures

Cultural forms: The products' format, structures, languages, and narrative styles that are produced when media technologies and institutions come together

Cultural homogenization: Convergence toward common cultural values and practices as a result of global integration

Culture industry: Industries that mass produce standardized cultural goods that normalize dominant capitalist ideologies and create social practices that are uniform and homogeneous among people

Cultural imperialism: Domination of one culture over others through cultural forms such as pop culture, media, and cultural products; a dimension of cultural globalization in which

unequal and uneven flow of culture and cultural forms negatively impact local industry and culture

Culture jamming: The act of altering or transforming mass media and popular culture forms into messages or commentary about itself; a form of public activism that challenges, subverts, and redefines dominant, hegemonic meanings produced by multinational culture industries

Decoding: Construction of mass mediated meaning by culture industries

Dominant reading: A way of reading/decoding in which the viewer or reader shares the meanings that are encoded in the text and accepts the preferred reading, which naturalizes and reinforces dominant ideologies

Encoding: Active interpretative and sense-making processes of audiences

Folk culture: Localized cultural practices enacted for the sole purpose of people within a particular place

Fragmegration: Dual and simultaneous dynamic of integration and fragmentation that has emerged in the context of globalization

Media: The modes, means, or channels through which messages are communicated

Negotiated reading: A way of reading/decoding in which the reader or viewer generally shares the codes and preferred meanings of the texts, but may also resist and modify the encoded meaning based on her or his positionality, interests, and experiences

Network media: Media such as the World Wide Web, which connects multiple points to multiple points, and serves interpersonal and mass media functions

Oppositional reading: A way of reading/decoding in which the social position of the viewer or reader of the text places them in opposition to the dominant code and preferred reading; reader understands the dominant code yet brings an alternative frame of reference, which leads him or her to resist the encoded meaning

Popular culture: Culture that belongs to the "masses," much of which was previously considered low culture; artifacts the general populous or broad masses within a society share or have some understanding

Telenovelas: TV soap operas made and popularized in Latin America

CHAPTER 7

Antimiscegenation: Laws prohibiting marriage between people of different "racial" groups existed in over 40 states until 1967 when the laws were overturned in the landmark *Loving v. Virginia Supreme Court* case

Coping stage: The second stage—couples develop proactive and reactive strategies to manage challenges

Class prejudice: Personal attitudes individuals of any class culture may hold about members of other classes

Classism: The systemic subordination of class groups by the dominant, privileged class

Ethnicity: Shared heritage, place of origin, identity, and patterns of communication among a group

Exploratory interaction phase: A phase in intercultural friendship development process in which relationships move toward greater sharing of information, increased levels of support, and connection and growing intimacy

Fetish: A spectacle that is represented as a commodity that is sought after, purchased, and consumed

Flaming: Abrasive, impulsive, or abusive behavior online

Heteronormativity: The institutionalization of heterosexuality in society and the assumption that heterosexuality is the only normal, natural, and universal form of sexuality

Heterosexism: An ideological system that denies and denigrates any nonheterosexual behavior, identity, or community

Identity emergence: The third stage—couples take charge of the images of themselves, challenge negative societal forces, and reframe their relationship

Initial encounter phase: A phase in intercultural friendship development process characterized by light conversation about general topics, beginning awareness of cultural differences and misunderstandings, and a process of questioning preconceived notions and stereotypes

Intercultural alliance: Relationships in which parties are interdependent, recognize their cultural differences, and work toward similar goals

Intercultural ally: A person, group, or community who works across borders of nationality, culture, ethnicity, race, gender, class, religion, or sexual orientation in support of and partnership with others

Intercultural bridgework: Developing sensitivity, understanding, and empathy and extending vulnerability to traverse multiple positions, creating points of contact, negotiation, and pathways of connection

Intercultural relationships: Relationships between people from different racial, ethnic, linguistic, national, religious, class, and sexual orientation groups

Interethnic relationships: Relationships between people who identify differently in terms of ethnicity or ethnic background

International relationships: Relationships that develop across national cultures and citizenship lines

Interracial relationships: Relationships that cross socially constructed racial groups

Interreligious or interfaith relationships: Relationships between people from different religious orientations or faiths

Miscegenation: Comes from Latin roots meaning "mixed" and "kind" and is used to refer to "mixed-race" relationships, specifically intermarriage, cohabitation, and sexual relationships between people of different races

Ongoing involvement phase: A phase in intercultural friendship development process marked by greater connection, intimacy, involvement, shared rules of engagement, and norms that guide interaction with each other

Racial/cultural awareness: The first stage of intercultural romantic relationship in which partners develop awareness of similarities and differences as well as how they are viewed by others

Relational identity/culture: The system of understanding between relational partners as they coordinate attitudes, actions, and identities within the relationship and with the world outside the relationship

Relational maintenance: The fourth stage—couples negotiate racial, cultural, ethnic, class, and religious differences between themselves and with the society at large

CHAPTER 8

Assertiveness: One of the dimensions of GLOBE on the extent to which individuals in organization or societies are assertive and confrontational

Capitalism: A complex social logic that produces a set of relationships among capitalists, laborers, and consumers

Commodification of culture: The practice in which cultural experiences are produced and consumed for the market

Confucian dynamism: Hofstede's cultural dimension that highlights the characteristics of East Asian countries such as long-term orientation to time, hard work, frugality, and respect for hierarchy

Exchange value: The value of commodity determined by the profit it generates through exchange

Fetishization: The process of endowing commodities with symbolic and social power

GLOBE dimensions: Nine cultural dimensions of Global Leadership and Organizational Behavior Effectiveness (GLOBE), including institutional and group collectivism, gender egalitarianism, power distance, uncertainty avoidance, future orientation, assertiveness, performance orientation, and humane orientation

Hofstede's cultural dimensions: Five dimensions of culture identified by Geert Hofstede, including individualism–collectivism, power distance, uncertainty avoidance, masculinity–femininity, and Confucian dynamism

Humane orientation: One of the dimensions of GLOBE on the degree to which organizations/society reward people for being fair, friendly, generous, and kind to others

Individualism–collectivism: Hofstede's cultural dimension that highlights the differences between individualistic cultures and collectivistic cultures

Masculinity–femininity: Hofstede's cultural dimension that distinguishes the societies with distinct gender roles and achievements (masculinity) and societies with flexible gender norms and balanced lifestyle (femininity)

Mercantilism: The implementation of protectionist policies that exclude foreign goods and subsidize cheap labor in certain industries

Multicultural teams: Task-oriented groups composed of members from different national and ethnic groups

Neoliberalism: The reassertion of liberal ideologies for reduced state intervention, deregulation, privatization, decreased social protection, and elimination of labor unions

Performance orientation: One of the dimensions of GLOBE on the extent to which an organization/society rewards members for their quality of performance and level of involvement

Power distance: Hofstede's cultural dimension that highlights how the less powerful members accept unequal distribution of power within organizations

Sign value: The symbolic value of a commodity that conveys social meaning and social positioning

Spectacle: The domination of media images and consumer society over individuals and their relationships with others

Surplus value: The profit made by reducing labor costs

Uncertainty avoidance: Hofstede's cultural dimension that highlights the tendency to feel threatened by unknown and uncertain situations

Use value: The value of commodity determined by its utility

Virtual teams: Work groups with members who are geographically dispersed and who rely on technology-mediated communication.

CHAPTER 9

Context: The information that surrounds a communication event and shapes the meaning of the event

Cooperative argument: A model of argument that manages the resolutions of disagreement within a set of rules that are responsive to intercultural differences

Cultural histories: Shared stories and interpretations of cultural groups that are passed along in written or oral form from generation to generation

Face: Favorable social self-worth in relation to the assessment of other-worth in interpersonal relationships

Facework: The communication strategies used to negotiate face between the self and other

Dugri: A Jewish Israeli communication style characterized by direct, simple, aggressive, and fast-paced communication that values the preservation of the speaker's face and simultaneous participation by multiple speakers

High context communication: Communication where most of the information is implicitly communicated through indirect, nonverbal, and mutually shared knowledge

Immigration industrial complex: A systematic criminalization and exploitation of undocumented migrants from which public interests and private sectors mutually benefit

Independent orientation: A cultural orientation that views the self as an autonomous agent pursuing personal goals based on his or her individual beliefs

In-groups: Groups of individuals that one belongs to culturally, socially, and emotionally

Intercultural conflict: The real or perceived incompatibility of values, norms, expectations, goals, processes, or outcomes between two or more interdependent individuals or groups from different cultures

Interdependent orientation: A cultural orientation that views the self as relational and values harmony and selflessness

Invitational rhetoric: A form of communication committed to equality, recognition, and self-determination through invitation, cooperation, and coordination

Low context communication: Communication where a large amount of information is explicitly communicated through direct, specific, and literal expressions

Musayara: A communication style broadly shared by Arab cultures that promotes harmony and dialogue through the use of rhetorically complex language, repetition, careful listening, and high context communication

Negative identity: Group identity that is based on being the opposite of the Other or portraying a negative image of the Other

Oppositional metaphors: Metaphors that use rigid and polarized dichotomies

Out-groups: Groups of individuals that one sees as separate and different from him or her and as unequal to or potentially threatening to him or her

CHAPTER 10

Capacities for global citizenship: Capacities of mind, heart, body, and soul that reimagine citizenship based on human needs rather than rights

Empathy: The ability to share the pain of others and the capacity to know the emotional experience of others from within their frame of reference

Intercultural activism: Engagement in actions that create a democratic world where power is shared; diversity is valued; and discrimination, domination, and oppression are challenged

Intercultural competency: The knowledge, attitudes, and skills needed to engage effectively in intercultural situations

Managing ambiguity: The ability to handle the uncertainty, anxiety, and tension that arises from the unknown in intercultural situations

Qualities of global citizens: Three qualities defined by wisdom, courage, and compassion

Self-awareness: An awareness or consciousness of oneself as a cultural being, whose beliefs, assumptions, attitudes, values, and behaviors are contoured by culture

Social justice: A goal and process of enabling the equal participation of all groups and the equitable distribution of resources in society

Index

Note: In page references, f indicates figures.

intercultural conflicts and, 221
intercultural friendships and, 157
intercultural relationships and, 151, 155,
   160, 164, 167, 168
romantic intercultural relationships and, 163
sexuality in intercultural relationships
   and, 154
Proposition 8, 208
Protectionist polices, 178
Protests:
   community coalition and, 244
   for immigrant rights, 237f
   intercultural activism and, 236
Pueblo, J., 190
Puete, F. A., 103
Push-pull theory, 107, 115

Qualities of global citizens, 228–229, 262
Queers See Lesbian, Gay, Bisexual, Transgender,
   and Queer (LGBTQ)

Race issues:
   action and, 20
   community coalition and, 244
   contested cultural spaces and, 92
   cultural notions of friendships and, 157
   cultural spaces and, 78–79
   culture and, 65
   culture as a system of shared meanings and, 8
   economic crisis and, 176
   economic disparities and, 37
   globalization and, 61–66
   hip hop culture and, 68
   individual/collective action for change
      and, 241
   intercultural activism and, 236
   intercultural competency and, 232
   intercultural conflicts and, 212, 214, 221
   intercultural relationships and, 150, 151–152,
      156, 157, 158, 160, 164, 167
   interethnic relationships and, 152
   international relationships and, 152–153
   media/popular culture and, 139, 140, 145
   migration and, 103, 108
   nonverbal communication and, 52
   popular culture and, 128–129, 130
   positionality and, 12
   positioning and, 18

producing/consuming popular culture
   and, 137
racial difference and, 54–55
recoded as class, 88
romantic intercultural relationships and,
   161, 162
segregation and, 90
signification systems for, 56
social construction of, 56–60, 70
standpoint theory and, 13
working class and, 179
Racial/cultural awareness, 162, 260
Racial hierarchy, 58, 178, 254
Racial historicism, 62, 254
   See also Histories
Racial naturalism, 62, 70, 254
Racial profiling, xiv, 103, 141
Racism:
   capitalism and, 181
   community coalition and, 244
   culture of capitalism and, 182
   cyberspace/intercultural relationships
      and, 166
   end of, 62
   individual/collective action for change
      and, 241
   intercultural conflicts and, 214
   intercultural relationships and, 155, 159
   media/popular culture and, 140
   meso-frame/intercultural conflicts and,
      206–207
   migration and, 103, 104, 109
   migration/intercultural adaptation and,
      114, 117, 118
   nonviolent resistance and, 235
   resignifying race in the context of globalization
      and, 64
   resisting/re-creating media/popular culture
      and, 143
   romantic intercultural relationships and, 161
   sexuality in intercultural relationships
      and, 155
   struggles against, 66
   student empowerment for change and, 238
Ram, A., 134
Refugees, 105, 256
   history and, 28
   media and, 210

About the Author

Kathryn Sorrells is professor of communication studies at California State University, Northridge (CSUN), where she teaches undergraduate and graduate courses in intercultural communication, critical pedagogy, performance, cultural studies, and feminist theory. She combines critical/cultural studies and postcolonial perspectives to explore issues of culture, race, gender, class, and sexuality. Kathryn grew up in Georgia; has lived in different regions of the United States; has studied and worked in Brazil, Japan, and Turkey; and has traveled extensively in Asia, Europe, and parts of Latin America. The critical, social justice approach she uses to study and practice intercultural communication is informed by her experiences growing up in the South during the tumultuous and transformative civil rights movement and her subsequent participation in the antiwar; women's; lesbian, gay, bisexual, and transgender (LGBT); and labor and immigrant rights movements. Kathryn has published a variety of articles related to intercultural communication, globalization, and social justice. She has been instrumental in organizing a campus-wide initiative on Civil Discourse and Social Change at CSUN aimed at developing students' capacities for civic engagement and social justice. Kathryn is a recipient of numerous national, state, and local community service awards for founding and directing Communicating Common Ground, an innovative service learning project that provided students opportunities to develop creative alternatives to intercultural conflict. Additionally, Kathryn has experience as a consultant and trainer for businesses and educational organizations in the areas of intercultural communication and multicultural learning.